Power on the Left

Books by Lawrence Lader

1955
Margaret Sanger and the Fight for Birth Control

1961
The Bold Brahmins: New England's War against Slavery (1831–1863)

1966
Abortion

1969
Margaret Sanger: Pioneer of Birth Control (Juvenile)
(With Milton Meltzer)

1971
Breeding Ourselves to Death

1972
Foolproof Birth Control: Male and Female Sterilization

1973
Abortion II: Making the Revolution

1979
Power on the Left: American Radical Movements since 1946

Lawrence Lader

Power on the Left

American Radical Movements Since 1946

W·W·NORTON & COMPANY
New York · London

Lader, Lawrence.
  Power on the left.

  Bibliography: p.
  Includes index.,
  1. Radicalism—United States—History. 2. Right and left (Political science) 3. Social move-
ments—United States. I. Title.
HN90.R3L33   1979   301.24′2′0973   79–19153
ISBN 0–393–01258–1

1 2 3 4 5 6 7 8 9 0

For

My Mother
Myrtle Powell Levison

My Wife
Joan Summers Lader

My Daughter
Wendy Summers Lader

Contents

Prologue

A book about the American Left since 1946 must deal not only with forces that changed the country deeply but with stereotypes and prejudices that obscured their effect. Many of us have been too influenced by European models to look more closely at the significance of our own movements, too traumatized by the cold war demonology of a worldwide Communist conspiracy originating in Moscow to see that the Soviet experience, particularly after 1956, may have had little bearing on our own revolts. It has too often been assumed that every Left movement in America must be a Communist movement. Thus, we have ignored the possibility that the Left may take many shapes and originate from diverse ideologies, rather than being dominated by the Soviet brand of Marxism-Leninism.

It is the intention of this book to show that the Left in recent decades has been essentially pragmatic, nurtured by American needs and not by a closed system imposed from abroad. The Left has generally aimed at limited goals, not cataclysmic revolution. And it has been highly fragmented.

This fragmentation obviously raises the problem of what organizations and movements should qualify for inclusion on the Left. The problem was simple in 1946, when the Communist party and its closed system—with bases in organized labor and occasional allies in the American Labor party and other organizations—represented the Left. But from 1960 on, the problem becomes increasingly complex. This book deals with a few movements that might belong in the "civil liberties" or "reformist" categories. But it does so because these seeds of rebellion often led to far more radical organizing. The black students, for example, who sat down at white lunch counters and invaded the white restaurants of bus terminals throughout the South between 1960 and 1962 had no ideological system or structure. They were simply struggling for rights long denied them. Their acts were hardly radical in themselves. But the massive resistance the students triggered eventually produced a new concept called "Black Power," and a decisive confrontation with the Southern oligarchy and 300 years of economic and racial exploitation, that revolutionized the South.

For the orthodox Marxist, of course, class organizing and class struggle are essential ingredients of the process that ostensibly produces a communist society. This book has interpreted the meaning of the process quite broadly. Since the tightly structured Marxist-Leninist model of a "vanguard" party, the Communist party, rarely applies to the American experience after 1956, I have included on the Left many movements that deal more with "human organizing" than class organizing.

Human organizing—the process that seeks personal liberation—becomes fundamental to the American Left in the 1960s. Its concern as a whole is meeting human needs rather than economic needs. Yet the two can rarely be separated, as this book will try to show.

No struggle, for example, was more basic to the women's movement than the human needs of abortion. The right to legal abortion, combined with safe and efficient contraception, has produced such far-reaching changes in our society that the full effects may not be felt for years. By controlling their childbearing, women have not only altered the makeup of the family and the relations between men and women; they have immeasurably expanded their own horizons. Beyond human needs in education and careers, the impact of abortion rights extends to economic needs, giving women the chance for financial independence both inside and outside the "nuclear" family.

The orthodox Marxist will claim that the women's movement, even in the abortion-rights struggle, has simply eliminated one set of evils, and that women cannot be totally liberated until the whole system is overthrown. Most radical feminists reject this claim, insisting that Marx ignored half the human race.

This book, consequently, differs from orthodox Marxism-Leninism by including on the Left many movements with limited objectives, so long as these objectives produce far-reaching changes in our society. I have interpreted "the Left" to mean the organizing of power on a local as well as national basis, the organizing of power by diffuse and often unconnected groups. The Left, therefore, is a movement that seeks decisive, lasting, social, political, and economic change for large numbers of oppressed and disadvantaged people. Ultimately, the Left should be directed toward socialist planning and programs and collective ownership.

This book will attempt to show that the New Left and the black and women's movements of the 1960s grew out of a special set of circumstances that required different approaches from the closed Stalinist system of the Old Left. What are the differences between these approaches?

The Communists concentrated on their base in the Congress of Industrial Organizations (CIO),* which became the classic expression of organizing the proletariat for the class struggle. By helping to organize millions of workers in steel, auto, and other industries after 1935, Communist cadres succeeded brilliantly in putting the Leninist vanguard concept into practice. John L. Lewis, the first CIO president, purged Communists from his own Miners but recognized that Communists were essential in mass organizing and that the CIO depended on a coalition of Left and center unions.

By 1945, the Communists controlled or influenced CIO unions with about 900,000 members (at least 20 percent of the CIO's total membership) and held one-third of the votes on the federation's executive board. By giving form and purpose to the demands of the working class during the Depression, the Communists attained a commanding position among the proletariat.

Yet within a few years, the CIO Left was shattered. Its downfall stemmed from the general pressures of the cold war, as we shall discuss later. But its real failure lay in Communist control and strategy. As a disciplined vanguard party, with unwavering allegiance to the Kremlin, the CP forced the unions to follow a misconceived Stalinist "line." Instead of continuing to expand the Left through intensive organization of the unorganized and wresting greater worker control of profits and production from the logical enemy, the CIO Left became the American representative of Soviet foreign policy. Once isolated from the rest of the labor movement, it became an early victim of the cold war and was quickly destroyed.

By contrast, the American Left since 1960 has generally rejected Soviet-type entanglements. Our second example, the Black Panther party of Oakland, California, represents a unique form of local base-building. It recruits and organizes in the whole community—not just among blacks, but among Mexican-Americans, union labor, the "lumpen" poor. The Panthers have built city-wide alliances through free food and clothing programs and a quality school aimed at mi-

---

*A list of acronyms will be found on page 347.

nority interests. With Oakland the second largest port in the country, the party has also formed close ties with the dock unions, and the AFL-CIO Council supported Panther candidates in recent elections. The Panthers even allied themselves with California's Governor Jerry Brown in 1976.

Such broad strategies may seem opportunistic, particularly for a party that claims to be Marxist. But the Panthers want immediate results; their Marxism remains largely rhetoric. Having polled more than 35 percent of the vote at a recent Oakland election, they want more control of the city council and the police, the first handle on power. They want more control of city housing and new jobs. They often develop "alternate structures" that knit people together in semisocialist projects. As a Panther leader noted, "You can't eat revolution."[1]

By comparison with the closed system that Stalin imposed on the Communist party here and elsewhere, the American Left since 1960 appears disturbingly complex, even incoherent. There is rarely a consistent "line." In the black movement, for example, the Muslims looked on whites as total evil until recently and demanded their own, separate world. The Panthers, however, joined with the white Left in the Peace and Freedom party of 1968. The blacks of the Student Nonviolent Coordinating Committee (SNCC) welcomed whites in the early southern struggle, and then ousted them under the imperative of "Black Power."

Still, the recent Left developed its own character by emphasizing immediate results and direct action, usually in a heroic mold of individual intervention. Black students, organizing their own political units in southern communities, were beaten and jailed by the thousands—and occasionally killed—in order to build local power bases. White students in California threw themselves in front of trains carrying troops to embarkation ports for Vietnam. Despite the lack of unified ideology and vanguard leadership, the pragmatism and spontaneity of the Left, and its very lack of structure, made it particularly effective in challenging American neoimperialism in Vietnam.

If we find any unifying framework on the recent Left, it is the constant experimentation and struggle for new tactics and methods of organizing. The Left constantly goes beyond accepted avenues of political and social change—sometimes to nonviolent sit-ins, demonstrations, and draft-card burnings; sometimes to violent confrontations and bombings.

The Left attempts to break down old forms of society and to replace them with new ones. The Panther "survival" services, for example, make the party a surrogate for the state, in effect replacing the state. Similarly, the rape counseling centers of the women's movement provide an emergency haven for victims that local government has neglected. Workers in thousands of urban and rural communes—4 to 5 million people were living in "drop-out" style in 1976, according to a Stanford Research Institute study—have cut themselves off from the capitalist factory system and produce their goods for pleasure and subsistence rather than profit.[2]

All this represents the Left's attempt to build on the humanist ideals of Marx. For the guiding vision of the recent Left has not been to downgrade Marxism but to reinvigorate it in new forms. But is this enough? Can we assume that the Left has never been revolutionary, but only "hyped-up reformism"? This book will attempt to define where the Left has succeeded and where it has failed. It will examine the black movement at its most violent stages—armed Panthers, for example, engaged in constant shootouts with the police. It will try to determine whether this stage was more or less productive for the ghettos than the later stage of human organizing.

It may be that the distinction between revolution and reformism has become meaningless. Robert C. Tucker, the Princeton University professor of political science, has suggested that even the Soviet ruling group has departed from the "spirit and practice of revolutionary Marxism-Leninism" and that "deradicalization must be the eventual fate of all radical movements whether or not they achieve political power. . . ." The American Left may be a significant example of this tendency.[3]

The research for this study has taken more than five years, and the personal experience that led to it a good many more. I have had the small advantage—some may consider it a disadvantage—of participating in one phase of the American Left. From 1946 through 1950, I was district leader and at most times public relations adviser to Congressman Vito Marcantonio of New York City, perhaps the most effective and controversial practitioner of radical politics ever to sit in the House. I also ran unsuccessfully on his American Labor party ticket in 1948 and later helped to organize a Reform Democratic club in part of his old district, which tried for many years to carry on his work.

This involvement may have dimmed what some like to call "objectivity." My history of the legal, medical, and social aspects of abortion in 1966—when that subject had been banned by social stigma for 100 years—was often considered an emotional misinterpretation of reality until those of us advocating abortion rights were vindicated by the United States Supreme Court decision of 1973.

It would seem that personal involvement can often be used to advantage. I should like to think that I have done so in this book—taking the case of Marcantonio again, by drawing parallels between his speeches against the cold war from 1946 to 1950 and our relations with the Soviets today. The Left, including Marcantonio, often misjudged history. But the bulk of his words appears amazingly prescient today; the tragedy is that a government that stumbled from the cold war into the Vietnam debacle learned nothing from radical protest.

If the government's anti-Communist containment policy ignored Marcantonio's warnings, the New Left overlooked him equally. The core of his pragmatism was to build a coalition of diverse ethnic and political viewpoints. Perhaps the main weakness of the New Left was its failure to build more workable and lasting coalitions beyond the campuses to shape the movements of the 1970s. I have used my own experience with Marcantonio to show that the New Left's demise stemmed in part from its inability to grasp the lessons of the past.

In my approach to research, I have consulted a considerable portion of the archives and documents about the recent Left at the New York Public Library, New York University's Tamiment collection, Columbia University's Oral History Collection, and the CIO files in Washington, D.C., among other depositories. These are listed in my bibliography and notes.

But I have tried to balance public records with personal interviews and with diaries, letters, and reporters' notes that have been made available by individuals involved in key events. I have interviewed Black Panthers in California and SNCC veterans at a reunion in Atlanta. Many of those who contributed to Left history are still alive. I have tried to fulfill my responsibility by reaching them before memories erode.

Justice Oliver Wendell Holmes has said, "Life is action and passion. I think it is required of a man that he should share the action and passion of his time at the peril of being judged not to have lived."[4] I hope this work has achieved a synthesis between the recollected action and passion of black students in a Mississippi jail and the less subjective record in archives and files.

Power on the Left

· 1 ·

The Campaign against Labor
and the Left
1946

In the turbulent months of May and June 1946, a nation that should have been celebrating the homecoming of its victorious overseas forces confronted a crisis that President Harry S. Truman believed could "ultimately destroy our country." What triggered the President's fears was a strike on May 23 by 250,000 members of two railroad unions. Across the country, trains sat idly in their yards; not a passenger's footstep broke the silence of cavernous terminals.[1]

The administration, which many critics like *Time* magazine considered "bogged down in ludicrous futility," suddenly moved into action. Truman had already ordered seizure of the railroads. Now he went on radio on the evening of May 24 to announce he would address a special joint session of Congress the next day to request emergency powers to break the strike. If the strikers were not back at work at that time, he added ominously, "I shall call upon the Army. . . ."[2]

The President had faced a growing wave of strikes. When John L. Lewis pulled his soft-coal miners out of the pits the previous May, Truman had seized the mines under the wartime powers of the Smith-Connally Act, still in force until the official end of the war. Now the miners went out again, forcing a dimout in 22 eastern states to conserve coal, and the President ordered a second seizure. He had always insisted his relation with labor had been based on "sympathy and support." But he was rushing into increasingly dictatorial solutions that Philip Murray, president of the Congress of Industrial Organizations (CIO), believed would lead to "the destruction of the labor movement." With a nationwide maritime strike threatened for June 15, 1946, Truman authorized Secretary of the Navy James V. Forrestal to recruit reservists and former navy personnel to man the ships "to break the maritime strike."[3]

Since the end of the Japanese war, in fact, almost 5 million workers

1

had closed down the nation's largest plants. On November 21, 1945, 225,000 United Auto Workers walked out of General Motors; on January 15, 1946, 174,000 United Electrical Workers struck; on January 21, almost 800,000 steelworkers. It was the greatest single confrontation between labor and industry, the most sweeping tie-up of industrial production in U.S. history.

This confrontation with labor was closely linked with the mounting confrontation with the Soviet Union. Truman's fear of Russian intrusion in Eastern Europe had already produced the administration's "get tough" policy, which would be even more bluntly enunciated by former British Prime Minister Winston Churchill in his "Iron Curtain" speech at Fulton, Missouri, on March 5, 1946.

The speech had been delivered at Westminster College, the alma mater of General Harry Vaughan, a White House aide and Truman crony. To give it his imprimatur, the President introduced Churchill and even went over the text of the speech, although he denied doing so at a press conference.

In stentorian language, Churchill's speech shattered the surface amity between East and West, labeling Stalin "a firebrand of war," proclaiming that, "from Stettin in the Baltic to Trieste in the Adriatic, an iron curtain has descended across the Continent." Indicting the "growing challenge and peril to Christian civilization," Churchill called for a "fraternal association of the English-speaking peoples"—in effect, a military alliance between Great Britain and the United States to stem Russian expansion.

Months before the end of the war, Frederick C. Crawford, chairman of the executive board of the National Association of Manufacturers, stood before the war memorial at Verdun, France, and told an army news correspondent in the presence of another correspondent, "We must prepare now for the war against Russia." This preventive-war thesis had caused Rep. A. J. Sabath (Dem., Ill.), the patriarchal chairman of the House Rules Committee, to call for "an informal 'Congressional group to win the peace' in order to offset the activities of the fascist groups who are extremely busy in America trying to involve us in a war with Russia." General Dwight D. Eisenhower, U.S. army chief of staff, was so disturbed by military gossip about impending war that he tried to quell it in a speech the New York *Times* headlined, "Eisenhower Calls War Talk 'Vicious.' "[4]

The fear of Communist expansion in Europe served to strengthen anti-labor antagonisms at home. The public, with its pent-up demand for cars and other consumer items unavailable during the war, took out its anger on the most convenient target, the radical CIO unions. Many business leaders and newspapers exploited this anger, some even charging that the strikes were a Communist "plot." They had never lost their hatred of the CIO, which had organized millions of workers in the bloody sit-down strikes and picket lines of the 1930s. The present strikes, conveniently enough, involved maritime and electrical workers and a few other unions influenced by the Communists.

On the other hand, John L. Lewis, first president of the CIO until his resignation in 1940, was virulently anti-Communist, as were most CIO unions. The railroad unions belonged to neither the CIO or American Federation of Labor (AFL), and A. F. Whitney, the well-tailored, pudgy, 73-year-old president of the Railway Trainmen, seemed the prototype of the small-town Rotarian. Such facts, however, were ignored in a surge of anti-Communist rhetoric—Rep. John Rankin (Dem., Miss.) charged Whitney with a long list of "Communist-front" affiliations.[5]

The link between Communist expansion and the radical unions was pushed by David Lawrence, editor of *U.S. News* and a prominent conservative spokesman, who charged that the strike wave sprang from the "germs of collectivism," and that union leadership "has been pressed from within by direct activists and radicals who are not and will not be dismayed either by violence or bloodshed."

Few corporation executives openly supported the thesis of a Communist plot behind the strikes. But they were hardheaded enough to recognize the opportunity to increase their own profits while rolling back the sizable union gains made under the New Deal. This required the passage of punitive anti-labor legislation, and the destruction of the Office of Price Administration (OPA), which would undoubtedly bring a spurt of new profits. The National Association of Manufacturers "wants price controls abolished and labor placed in a straitjacket," insisted Rep. Frank Hook (Dem., Mich.) after the NAM had spent almost $1 million on fullpage ads attacking the OPA.[6]

Anti-labor legislation had the fervent support of the Chamber of Commerce and the NAM, whose president had already met secretly in New York with leaders of steel, automotive, and other industries to organize a united front against the strikes. It also had almost unanimous backing from the nation's newspaper publishers—the Providence *Journal,* for example, demanded "a permanent gag on all labor unions." Extremists in the Committee for Constitutional Government, mainly financed by Frank Gannett, head of the Gannett newspapers, damned unions as a "monopoly power" and raged against the right to strike as "a barbarian, savage, outlaw weapon." Calling for abolition of the Wagner Act, which was responsible for most of labor's gains after 1935, as a step toward a union-free paradise, the committee concluded: "Those workers who do not like the methods of a given employer are free to quit and work elsewhere."[7]

The drastic increase of wartime profits had put industry in a favorable position for this anti-union drive. Corporate profits had amounted to $26 billion in the lean years of 1936 to 1939; they rose to $117 billion between 1940 and 1945 and would soar 30 percent again in 1946 over 1945. Two-thirds of all wartime contracts had been given to the 100 dominant manufacturing firms. Many war plants had been built with public taxes. And at the end of the war, the 250 largest corporations managed to buy up almost three-fourths of the publicly built plants—at about 60 percent of the original cost.[8]

By contrast, labor had suffered severely from postwar inflation. Even in Whitney's traditionally elite Brotherhood, engineers on passenger trains were only making $8.96 a day, switchmen $7.14. The supposedly well-paid GM auto workers averaged $1.12 an hour, a deceptive figure since the industry imposed long layoffs for retooling. Among the lower-paid electrical workers, Joseph Stevenson, employed by Westinghouse for 26 years, pointed out, "I'm now trying to support my wife and mother-in-law on 89 cents an hour." Doris Duvall, also of Westinghouse, demanded, "How can I support my four dependent children on $24.80 a week?"[9]

Even worse, these marginal salaries had been eroded by a 45 percent rise in living costs between 1940 and 1945; wages had been restricted by federal guidelines to a 15 percent rise in the same period. Except for Lewis's mineworkers, who refused to accept government controls, the AFL and CIO had dutifully agreed to Roosevelt's demand for a no-strike pledge during the war years. Shorn of their one weapon, the workers were in a bitter and explosive mood by the end of 1945. Rank-and-file rebellion erupted constantly—a trainmen's meeting in New York, for example, furiously booed its leadership when its strike was called off for five days.[10]

The disparity between management and labor positions was sharply etched in negotiating sessions between GM's crusty, silver-haired president, Charles E. Wilson, whose salary was $459,000, and Walter Reuther, the newly elected president of the United Auto

Workers with a salary of $7,000. GM's wartime profits came to $882 million, its reserves to $749 million; UAW membership had dropped from about 1,243,000 to 540,000 as a result of reconversion layoffs. GM, like most corporations, had resources that gave it the staying power for a long strike. As a consequence, the snowbound picket lines around GM were forced to march for 113 days during that bitter winter of 1945–46.

To settle the strikes, President Truman shunted aside the normal process of collective bargaining and established a three-man fact-finding committee. His policy of seizing one industry after another—coal, oil, packinghouse, railroads—under his wartime powers pressured unions into accepting his fact-finding formula. In effect, the government had taken over collective bargaining. Almost all the dominant unions fell into line behind the Truman formula of approximately an 18 1/2 cent-an-hour raise. But the corporations usually got far more out of price increases than they gave up in wages. U.S. Steel, for example, shrewdly traded a wage increase costing $185 million for a price rise that produced $435 million.[11]

The new circle around the President abetted this labor policy. By February 1946, Truman had replaced all of Roosevelt's cabinet except Secretary of Commerce Henry A. Wallace with conservative appointments. He would eventually appoint Attorney General Tom Clark, a conservative Texan, to the Supreme Court. Secretary of the Treasury John Snyder, nicknamed "Donald Duck" by reporters because of his waddling gait, was a Saint Louis banker "continually representing the point of view of steel," Murray of the CIO insisted. Forrestal, former president of Dillon Read & Co., and Under Secretary of State Robert A. Lovett, former partner in Brown Brothers Harriman & Co., represented Wall Street and financial interests,[12] like many of the inner circle.

Truman knew his labor negotiator was close to settlement when he ascended the Speaker's rostrum of the House before a joint session of Congress at 4 P.M. on Sunday, May 25, 1946. His jaw tight-set, wearing a dark-blue summer suit and white shirt, he was greeted by a boisterous ovation from Republicans as well as Democrats.

The legislation Truman presented—he was interrupted repeatedly by clapping, cheers, whistling, and even rebel yells—was probably the most unprecedented demand for power made by any President. First, he wanted authority to draft strikers into the armed forces for a period of six months after the official declaration of the end of the war. This involved two deceits—that the "war" still continued and that strikers would be defying the government when, in reality, the government was simply imposing a settlement by armed force and eventually returning the mines or railroads to their private owners. Then, the President wanted the power of injunction against a union leader who incited members to leave work or to refuse a return to work—crippling the Norris-La Guardia Act on which the New Deal had built its labor program.

All during the presidential address, as everyone knew, negotiators had been working frantically at a nearby hotel to finish the details of the railroad settlement, signed at 3:57 P.M. on the 18 1/2 cents-an-hour formula the two unions had previously rejected. The news reached the President at Congress halfway through his speech, and he announced it to wild applause. Still, he never modified his demands, possibly figuring that Congress couldn't be sated at this point, or that the military draft could be turned on the troublesome mineworkers.

So eager was the House, in fact, to pass any anti-labor program that even before the President spoke, it voted to suspend its time-honored rules in order to allow Rep. John McCormack, (Dem., Mass.), the majority leader, to call up Truman's bill immediately. "Spearheading the opposition," the *Times* reported, was Vito Marcantonio, the frail, swarthy, raspy-voiced representative from New York's East Harlem-Yorkville district, first elected as a Republican protégé of Mayor Fiorello La Guardia, now seated for the American Labor party and regarded as the symbol of radicalism in Congress.

Marcantonio insisted the House was considering a bill "not even in existence. . . . No member of Congress knows what it will contain." Attacking "monopolists" who "sought to smash the equality that labor has obtained in collective bargaining," he was on his feet constantly, demanding that a rules change required a two-thirds vote, calling for a quorum, using every parliamentary maneuver to stall debate. "I know I am a voice crying in the wilderness," he admitted. Indeed he was. The rules change was passed, and the debate on the President's bill began.[13]

Again Marcantonio led the attack, branding the bill "the most drastic anti-labor legislation that has ever been presented to the Congress of the United States." Excoriating the draft of labor into the armed forces, which Truman himself as a senator had opposed in wartime, Marcantonio hammered at the injunction process, which would make the federal government the agent for private monopolies. "We are marching here towards a fascizing of America," he concluded.

With the Democratic leadership behind the bill, it was rammed through by a startling majority of 306 to 13. Only a few diehard liberals joined Marcantonio; dozens of once-noted liberals withheld their vote under pressure from the Democratic whip.[14]

The outcry from labor was furious. Murray of the CIO branded the bill "wild hysteria"; Reuther of the Auto Workers called it "a return to slavery." Whitney of the Trainmen, one of the prime targets, swore he would spend $47 million in the union treasury to defeat Truman at the next election, and $2.5 million to defeat every House member supporting the bill—a sum so vast he had to reduce his figures sharply the next day. Even William Green, the prim, conservative president of the AFL, whose old-fashioned, craft-based unions had hardly participated in the recent strike wave, described the bill as "slave labor under fascism."[15]

Most newspaper editorials greeted the vote jubilantly, although, rather ironically, the *Wall Street Journal* editorial warned of "the President's erratic and probably unconscious plunge in the direction of dictatorship." There was a demand for a third party to oppose Truman in 1948 by A. Philip Randolph, president of the Brotherhood of Sleeping Car Porters, who would soon swing back into the Truman camp. Simultaneously, Secretary Wallace, ousted as Roosevelt's running mate in 1944 by Truman, was attacking third-party talk at a New York dinner of the American Labor party, which would become the keystone of Wallace's third-party bid in 1948. To complete the irony, *The Nation* announced that almost all labor and liberal leaders were positive the Truman bill "has killed any chance of his being elected President in 1948. . . . American Labor will never forget it."[16]

Since the President's "draft labor" bill was stalled in the Senate, anti-labor forces, led by Rep. Francis Case (Rep., S.D.) now pushed their own punitive legislation. The Case bill, passed by the House in February, had undergone so many Senate changes that Republican conservatives forced it to the floor again on May 29.

The Case bill was a drastic curtailment of the Wagner Act. It gave the President the right to seize any industry where a strike involved "public health, safety or security," thus turning the sweeping powers of the wartime Smith-Connally Act into a permanent weapon.

Marcantonio led off the debate, insisting, "If you destroy the right to strike, you make collective bargaining a mockery." His allies were both more numerous and more influential than four days before. Rep. Emanuel Celler (Dem., N.Y.) charged that the bill "sets up a penal colony." Rep. Andrew Biemiller (Dem.,Wisc.), a frequent labor spokesman, labeled it a "monstrosity." Majority Leader McCormack claimed it would revive "all the evils against which the Norris-La Guardia Act was directed. . . ."[17]

Ironically, McCormack was now harnessing the President's forces against the bill. Since Truman had made his bid for conservative support with his anti-labor tirade of May 25, he could now try to woo labor back.

Even the Democratic leadership, however, failed to stem the tide. The Case bill swept through by 230 to 106 (with 94 not voting), falling short of the one-third vote needed to sustain a presidential veto. With William Green pledging 7 1/2 million AFL members would turn "rebels" if Case passed, Marcantonio was again put in charge of the House opposition. Adopting the rare device of a veto petition, he rushed through House offices and cloakrooms in the next few days to collect enough signatures to uphold a veto. Obviously, if the President was convinced he had the support, the chance of his veto would be considerably strengthened.

On June 7, Marcantonio announced he had 110 signatures on his petition, with another 25 committed votes. The bill was placed on the President's desk on June 11, and he vetoed it immediately. The House voted the same day, with 135 members successfully sustaining the veto, the exact number of votes Marcantonio had pledged.[18]

This victory momentarily stalled the anti-labor drive. But the old radical–New Deal coalition would soon be decimated. Out of a bloc of 135 votes Marcantonio had just put together, 55 would be defeated in the Republican landslide at the next election. Marcantonio himself would become one of the most maligned politicians in the country. He would survive until 1950, but most radicals—most of labor's staunchest defenders—would be wiped out in the 1946 or 1948 elections.

The Case bill and Truman's draft-labor bill were only surface portents. The conservatives sought a bigger target—the destruction of CIO militants, particularly the Left unions that made up about a quarter of its membership. The leverage would be provided by the threat of Russian expansion, a threat that would soon provoke national cold-war hysteria. The destruction of labor's gains under the New Deal, and the destruction of the CIO Left, were the immediate targets. The long-range aim was to bend the CIO to the needs of

United States foreign policy—to force the unions into a cold war partnership with government and business that would produce both an economic boom in military spending at home and the dominance of American business abroad. Thus, foreign and domestic interests would be united in the containment of the Soviets, a policy that was to shape the fate of the American Left for at least a decade.

·2·

Vito Marcantonio and the Congressional Battleground

No elected politician has ever symbolized the Left in Congress more consistently than Vito Marcantonio, an untiring spokesman for unions, blacks, and the poor since 1934.

First elected as a Republican—he won the Republican nomination as late as 1944—his strength was his ability to fuse the interests of all parties in his district, including Tammany Democrats, liberal Democrats, and the radical American Labor party (ALP). His enemies, unable to understand this strange coalition, labeled him a Communist. "The Moscow-loving, rabble-rousing Congressman," the New York *World-Telegram* called him.[1]

Since he became between 1946 and 1950 the very essence of the left-wing threat as pictured in the conservative press, it is important to understand Marcantonio's skill as a vote-getter through the American Labor party. Communists had never done well at the polls; their influence was primarily in the unions and other "front" groups. The Socialists had failed dismally in elections since Roosevelt had siphoned off their votes. The Socialist Workers (Trotskyists) were a Marxist splinter group. But the ALP, although confined to New York State, regularly amassed a half-million votes at elections, more than any Left party in the country. Further, Marcantonio's position in Congress gave the ALP nationwide impact and made it the model for radical organizing in California, Illinois, and other industrial areas.

A master of coalition politics, Marcantonio united behind him a polyglot constituency following Populist, socialist, and sometimes Communist line programs. His constituency cared little for labels as long as he fought for the district's needs.

As the inheritor of La Guardia's East Harlem district when the "Little Flower" became mayor of New York, Marcantonio built his base on a sprawl of tenements and cubby-holed brownstones inhab-

10

ited by Italians, blacks, Puerto Ricans, and Jews at the northern end; by Hungarians, Czechs, Irish, and Germans at the south. The district was virtually an extension of himself—the coal yards on the East River, the mammoth Ruppert brewery, the clothes flapping from tenement fire escapes, grandmothers in widow's black gossiping on the stoops, sweating card players in their undershirts at their Italian social clubs on the steaming summer nights. In his boyhood, some of these blocks housed 5,000 people, the densest concentration in the city. By 1930, 150,000 Italian-Americans jammed the district. They were the core of Marcantonio's political strength. He had molded thousands of these children of immigrants into political clubs, into the Vito Marcantonio Political Association. The *World-Telegram* branded them his "hoodlum followers." They called themselves "Gibbones"—a slang word implying a tight-knit ethnic clan bound by race, religion, immigrant status, and poverty.[2]

Marcantonio never felt at home anywhere but on the House floor or in the slums of East Harlem. If he made an occasional speech elsewhere, he returned immediately. He never went outside the continental United States or Puerto Rico, never even visiting the Italian village 150 miles southeast of Naples where his mother's family lived, and which considered him its most illustrious citizen. His ethnic links were also expressed in his religion. Despite the Communist epithets hurled at him, he always listed himself as a Roman Catholic in *Who's Who.* Although he attended services infrequently, he prided himself on fund raising for local churches and invariably kept a madonna figure or religious medal in his pocket.

Marcantonio used the ALP to bolster his coalition strategy. By throwing 435,374 ALP votes to La Guardia in 1941, he provided the mayor with his slim margin of victory over William O'Dwyer and naturally enhanced his own influence at City Hall. In 1942, ALP votes were primarily responsible for the election of six New York City Democratic congressmen. Since Roosevelt's majority in the House, continually diminished since 1936, had now been cut to 11, the administration showed its appreciation by naming Marcantonio to the crucial House Judiciary Committee. But when southern Democrats, detesting him for his leadership of Negro rights, threatened to bolt the party, he withdrew his name.

Radical parties have been notably unsuccessful in translating their votes into political influence on Capitol Hill. Eugene Debs polled about 915,000 votes as Socialist candidate for President in 1920; Norman Thomas about 885,000 in 1932. Yet only a single Socialist congressman was elected in 1920, none in 1932. And Senator Robert M. La Follette, Sr., failed to elect more than a handful of followers to Congress despite winning 4,822,319 votes as Progressive candidate for President in 1924.

By contrast, Marcantonio was the acknowledged leader during the early New Deal of a radical bloc that ranged from twenty-five to thirty members, including such flamboyant figures as Rep. Maury Maverick (Dem., Tex.) and Rep. (later Senator) Ernest Lundeen (Farmer-Labor, Minn.). This group consistently radicalized New Deal objectives, supporting public ownership of electric power that resulted in the Tennessee Valley Authority, attacking the administration's Social Security bill for its excessive tax on workers, forcing more generous allotments of unemployment funds.

Even when Marcantonio's radical support dwindled by 1940 and almost vanished by 1946, he forced the House to debate issues that most members shunned. His attack on the poll tax became a landmark years before the civil rights movement. The tax—Marcantonio called it "the most shameful blot on our democracy"—had been used since Reconstruction in southern states to keep blacks and poor whites from the polls. It disenfranchised nearly 10 million people and restricted the right to vote to less than 12 percent of the eligible constituency.[3]

Marcantonio's first bill to abolish the poll tax was buried in the southern-dominated Judiciary Committee in 1942. But in 1943 and 1944, he forced his bill to the floor and got it passed by the resounding votes of 265 to 110 and 251 to 105. Both times a Senate filibuster blocked it.

Marcantonio opposed all discrimination, introducing a resolution to investigate racial prejudice in baseball, forcing the American Red Cross in World War II to reverse its policy against blood donations from blacks. In 1942, he concentrated on the Fair Employment Practices Committee (FEPC) and convinced President Roosevelt to put antidiscriminatory clauses into all government war contracts. Marcantonio had already introduced the first bill in U.S. history to ban employment discrimination on a permanent basis. In his last House term, he was still struggling to force his bill for a permanent FEPC out of committee.

His championship of the Puerto Rican people was attacked as motivated solely by their voting strength in his district. Yet he introduced his first bill for Puerto Rican independence in 1936, long before the massive immigration into East Harlem after World War

II. In 1939, when the island boasted a 25-cent-an-hour minimum wage law, he presented the House with evidence that thousands of workers received from 2 to 12 1/2 cents an hour.[4]

Without a microphone, Marcantonio's voice—high-pitched, slightly nasal, rising in intensity—could reach the length of a block. He had a sharp, jutting jaw; a Neapolitan face, sensuous yet ascetic. He invariably wore a broad-brimmed gray hat, jammed back on his head, that gave a rakish look to his conservative clothes. As he spoke, his clenched right fist pounded the air. He banged his heel on the platform for punctuation. The tempo grew faster and louder, the words pounding out a rhythm that gradually caught his audience and drew it along with him.

From 10:00 in the morning till late evening over weekends, people streamed up the rickety wooden stairs at Marcantonio's club on First Avenue into a cavernous, dingy hall. They sat, often 50 and 100 at a time, on camp chairs—mothers nursing infants, children scampering up and down the aisles, old men on crutches, veterans back from the war still wearing remnants of army clothing. Marcantonio's records show he saw at least 30,000 a year. He sat in a small office at the front of the hall, his secretary, lawyers, and other aides nearby. He would talk with each visitor personally before referring him to an aide.

Marcantonio and his staff constantly rushed for court orders to stop an eviction before the city marshal threw a tenant's furniture on the street. If they got there late, they would help move the furniture back upstairs. If they couldn't stop eviction, they would house the family at the club, which was equipped with folding cots and electric heaters, until new quarters could be found.

Marcantonio was particularly persuasive at squeezing funds for public housing, playgrounds, and schools out of federal and city officials. His lifelong friendship with Mayor La Guardia obviously gave him special leverage. Even Robert Moses, who held down a string of state and city jobs and usually needed no help in accumulating funds for his projects, came to Marcantonio for aid in 1945 to expedite back pay owed City Park Department employees. The congressman, who had no political love for Moses, wrote slyly to the mayor, "Bob Moses and I are in complete accord on this issue, and when he and I see eye to eye, how can you or anybody else be right?" The back pay was quickly restored.[5]

The crucial ingredient in Marcantonio's success was organization. He attracted and trained skilled captains. A captain, and a few aides, handled each election district, an area of two or three square blocks, including about 1,000 votes.

One captain, Robert Rusch, recalled:

You have to know everything about your neighbors—a family that's having trouble with Social Security, newlyweds that need a public-housing apartment, a retired city worker who's having a fight over his pension. You keep a card on each person. You record each visit. You discuss his problems, and the legislation and work that Marc's done to solve them. Sometimes you pay two or three visits before you pin him down to voting for Marc.[6]

All captains were expected to report back to their clubs every night at 10:00, where Marcantonio checked the canvassing reports. Day by day, Marcantonio compiled a chart of his support, based on the registration lists and the past records of each district, a chart so accurate he could often predict his election total within a few hundred votes.

Marcantonio's father, a carpenter and son of an Italian immigrant, was killed by a streetcar when his son was young. Marcantonio became the main family support. At 17, he organized rent strikes and gave a speech at school in favor of old-age pensions and social security. The guest speaker that day, Congressman Fiorello La Guardia, was impressed enough to put the student on his organizing staff. The widowed and childless La Guardia virtually adopted Marcantonio, calling him "Sonny" all their lives and housing him in his apartment. Marcantonio got his law degree from New York University Law School in 1925 and was appointed assistant U.S. district attorney in 1930.

When La Guardia lost his congressional seat in the Roosevelt-Democratic landslide of 1932, Marcantonio helped organize the fusion campaign (a combination of anti-Tammany Democrats and liberal Republicans) that made his mentor mayor of New York City in 1933. Taking over the La Guardia club, Marcantonio ran for Congress and won in 1934.

Marcantonio ran again as a Republican in 1936, facing a two-pronged attack. Worried that the Tammany scandals, which plagued New York during the early 1930s, might keep the unions from voting on the Democratic line, Roosevelt induced Sidney Hillman, head of the Amalgamated Clothing Workers, to organize the American Labor party. Marcantonio's support was thus diffused by two parties, and in the outpouring of Roosevelt votes he lost to a strong Roosevelt man.

Marcantonio's labor record convinced 49 New York unions to

back him in 1938. La Guardia added his influence with banners proclaiming, "Mayor La Guardia says, 'East Harlem needs Vito Marcantonio in Congress.' " As a result, Marcantonio won the ALP as well as Republican primaries and went on to beat the Democrat resoundingly.[7]

By 1940, Marcantonio was being attacked as a "stooge of the Communist Party." However, his vote for the Neutrality Act of November 4, 1939—which allowed France and Britain, now at war with Germany, to buy "cash and carry" arms at U.S. ports—was hardly in accordance with the Kremlin line. The Soviets had made their pact with Germany in 1939, and the U.S. Communist party therefore opposed his vote.[8]

Marcantonio, who recognized the Spanish civil war as the last clear-cut opportunity to stop Hitler and Mussolini, attacked congressional restrictions on aid to Spanish Republicans. If this stance conflicted with his former opposition to military entanglements, he insisted, as did a broad spectrum of liberals like Norman Thomas, that the crisis demanded collective action.

The Munich agreement of September 29, 1938, where Britain and France sacrificed Czechoslovakia to the Nazis, made Marcantonio attack the imperialistic policy of the western democracies. Only Russia had been willing to go to war against Germany to save Czechoslovakia. But despite the Russian-French defense pact, France and Britain, without even consulting Russia whose security was at stake, allowed the dismemberment of the Czechs at Munich.

With the Russo-German pact of August 23, 1939, the Nazi conquest of Poland and France, and the domination by Hitler of Pétain's Vichy French government, Marcantonio insisted, "It is an imperialistic war." The Russo-German pact horrified the West. It seemed like a Machiavellian armageddon. However, Stalin's brutal realism must be judged in historical perspective. Deserted by the West at Munich, certain he would be the prime target of Hitler's juggernaut, and struggling to bring his army into combat readiness, he was buying both time and defensive positions in Poland and on the Finnish front.[9]

Again Marcantonio was branded for following the Soviet line on June 22, 1941. When the Nazi armies swept into Russia, the U.S. Communist party switched overnight into unqualified support of the war. Marcantonio withheld his support for almost four months. Finally, on October 16, he announced to the House that the invasion of Russia "transformed that war which was predominantly imperialistic into a war which is essentially one of national defense. . . . We were not in military danger as long as Hitler had on his eastern boundary a powerful, well-armed Soviet Union," he claimed. But "a conquered Soviet Union would place a Nazi military bridgehead within a rowboat distance of our own northwestern shores, Alaska."[10]

As often as he agreed with the Communists on foreign and domestic issues, Marcantonio continued to insist on rigorous independence. He backed the $3 billion loan to Britain after the war (which the Communists opposed), stating on July 13, 1946, "I support it because I believe that world peace is dependent upon the strengthening of unity among the Big Three." In fact, he had the ALP endorse many candidates whom the Communists opposed. In the 1945 City Council race, he insisted that the ALP vote first for its own candidate under proportional representation, and other candidates later. The Communist party wanted a single "bullet vote" for its candidate.

Marcantonio spoke for the Indian position of an immediate ceasefire in the Korean war in 1950, which the Communist party bitterly attacked. By 1951, he was refusing campaign donations from Communist fur union officials, reprimanding them for "all the doubletalk and broken promises that your check represents." He quarreled with the Communists when they refused to back the ALP candidates for mayor in 1953 and severed all political ties with them.[11] "Despite our common stand on many issues," reported George Charney, the ranking Communist official in Manhattan for many years, "he maintained a detached, if not distant, attitude to the party."[12]

Marcantonio denied from the start that he was a Communist. "I'm a member of the ALP, I'm not a Communist, and anyone who calls me a Communist lies," he told a questioning House member in 1939. During a later campaign, he affirmed his belief in capitalism. "I believe in a strictly regulated form of capitalism in the United States, so I can't be an advocate of that kind of capitalism and be a Communist."[13]

Yet he never flinched from defending the rights of Communists and all minority parties. "I disagree with the Communists . . . but they have a perfect right to speak out and to advocate communism," he declared.[14]

The Communist label at first hardly affected Marcantonio's voting strength. Although Tammany opposed him in 1944, and the Liberals supported the Tammany candidate, Marcantonio won the Democratic primary and the Republican and ALP ones as well. Not a single vote was cast against him in the general election.

By 1946, Marcantonio seemed at the peak of his power. His coalition had given dignity and ethnic identity not only to Italian-Americans and Puerto Ricans but also to many blacks, who saw in him the prototype of their own racial struggle. His enemies never grasped how fully he embodied the aspirations of the working class. His votes came from German-American artisans and Irish-American civil servants—groups that might not register ALP but always supported him at the polling booth.

Outside his district, the ALP's 450,000 or so votes had a more complex source. About 40,000 undoubtedly consisted of Communist party members; perhaps an equal number came from Communist allies. But the great bulk came from disparate groups—union members; teachers, professionals, and intellectuals; socialists frustrated by the vagaries of their own parties; liberals and New Dealers. Some had Marxist leanings, but the great majority were drawn to Marcantonio and the ALP for courage in confronting issues that the Democratic and Liberal parties avoided.

For the half million who pulled down the ALP lever on election day, the Communist issue had little relevance. Most everyone recognized that the Communist party and Communist-led unions contributed money to ALP campaigns, that Communists held offices in many ALP clubs, and that hundreds of Communist canvassers poured into Marcantonio's district in the last week or two of a campaign. At the same time, Communist help was greatly exaggerated by the press. Most of Marcantonio's money came from a small circle of wealthy liberals; last-minute Communist canvassers were mainly a glamorous topping to months and years of campaigning by regular captains.[15]

Marcantonio was a political pragmatist who borrowed from Marxism to solve a specific issue but was never dominated by it. He read omnivorously in American history, but there is no evidence he had ever made a serious study of Marx, Engels, or Lenin. If anything, he was a product of Christian ethics and socialist evolution.

In a period when the American Communist party and its inflexible line dominated the Left, Marcantonio represented a unique phenomenon: a successful politician who knew that socialism could only be built in his district in slow, careful stages. He moved his constituents into semisocialist structures—workers' alliances, tenant groups, ethnic groups. He avoided the rhetoric and tactics of revolution, being willing to stay within the system as long as he could push it constantly to the left. By changing the lives of his constituents slowly but inexorably, he understood that semisocialist structures often had to be the first step to revolution, a conclusion that some Communist parties in Europe only reached three decades later.

What made Marcantonio so dangerous to the established parties was his success: his ability not only to be reelected constantly in his district but to provide swing votes in other New York City districts. His coalition politics proved that a popular front including the Communist party could succeed at the polls. By offering a model for other urban ghettos, it threatened the two-party system with the specter of similar American labor parties elsewhere. Coalition politics broke down eventually, both in New York and in the CIO, because liberals needed an alliance with the Democratic party more than they needed a progressive front, and because the convolutions of Soviet-American conflict after 1945 isolated the Left. Only Marcantonio's toughness enabled him to survive a few more years.

· 3 ·

The Left's Challenge to Truman
1946-47

New York's Madison Square Garden was packed with 19,000 people the night of September 12, 1946, when Secretary of Commerce Henry A. Wallace challenged President Truman's get-tough policy with Russia. Wallace had begged the President for months to repair the unity badly eroded since Roosevelt's death. On March 14, he had proposed a trade project with the Soviets, but Truman had ignored his letter. On July 23, he had pleaded with the President to consider the impact of air bases around the globe, the world-circling mass flight of B-29 bombers, the atom bomb tests at Bikini. Would the United States not be "horrified and angered" if Russia demanded internationalization of the Panama Canal as we were demanding it for the Danube?[1]

" 'Getting tough' never brought anything real or lasting—whether for schoolyard bullies or businessmen or world powers," Wallace told the crowd. Referring to Churchill's Fulton speech and to mounting talk of preventive war, he insisted, "We must not let our Russian policy be guided or influenced by those inside or outside of the United States who want war with Russia." The core of his speech was a sharp denunciation of Truman's policy of blocking Communist influence in Poland and Eastern Europe, and an insistence on balanced Soviet and American spheres. "We should recognize that we have no more business in the *political* affairs of eastern Europe than Russia has in the *political* affairs of Latin America, western Europe, or the United States," Wallace exhorted.

Concluding that "the Russians will try to socialize their sphere of influence just as we try to democratize our sphere of influence," Wallace challenged the administration's demonology of a Russia bent on world conquest. His vision for the two superpowers was a "friendly peaceful competition" that would make them "gradually become more alike."

At first, the President did not seem to realize that the speech—he later called it "an all-out attack on our foreign policy"—had brought the two men to a showdown. In a meeting at the White House two days before, Wallace claimed Truman went over the speech "page by page" and "didn't have a single change to suggest." When a reporter asked whether Truman considered the speech in conflict with State Department policy, the President interjected, "I do not." Afterward, he insisted he had never read the speech, had simply "approved the right" of Wallace to make it, and "did not wish to indicate that I approved the speech as an instrument of the foreign policy of the country."[2]

Truman's acerbic and conservative secretary of state, James F. Byrnes, who would shortly break with Truman and support the States' Rights Party in 1948, refused to be satisfied with such evasions. Attending a meeting of the Council of Foreign Ministers in Paris, he demanded that unless Wallace was muzzled, ". . . it would be a grave mistake from every point of view for me to continue in office, even temporarily." Senator Arthur Vandenberg, the Republican mainstay of the administration's bipartisan policy, objected equally strenuously. "The President can have me on his team for foreign affairs, or he can have Henry, but he can't have both of us," he told two cabinet members.

On the morning of September 20, the President, as he recalled, telephoned Wallace and asked for his resignation. Wallace's version is that Truman first sent over a letter—"not abusive, but it was on a low level"—and that the President had retrieved it at Wallace's suggestion. The President then announced the resignation in a press statement, citing "a fundamental conflict" between the administration and its secretary of commerce. That same day, Truman wrote to his mother and sister, "Well, now he's out, and the crackpots are having conniption fits. I'm glad they are. It convinces me I'm right. . . ."[3]

Truman's folksy aphorisms were sharper than his view of history. The fundamental conflict over foreign policy would increasingly ravage the nation for the next 25 years. And the get-tough policy with Russia was already splitting the CIO and inciting a frenzy of domestic anti-Communism that would last more than a decade. In California, a former navy officer, Richard M. Nixon, was waging the first of his obliteration campaigns, based on the issue that his opponent, Rep. Jerry Voorhis, was a puppet of the CIO and its "Communist line." In Wisconsin, a minor judge named Joe McCarthy, who had defeated the veteran Robert La Follette, Jr., in the Republican primary for the U.S. Senate, was preparing the anti-Communist tactics that would stamp his name on the era.

"A kind of hysteria on the subject," Phil Murray described reports of the CIO split at its convention in November. "Do not let this issue divide you," A. F. Whitney, the Trainmen's president, begged the convention. Murray assured the assemblage: "The CIO is not going to be divided by anyone."[4]

But Murray, one of the few men in the country with the power to stand up against the hysteria, was wrong. In a few years, the CIO would be split irrevocably. Murray too would be riding with the pack. The tides of the cold war would engulf not only the CIO and the American Left but most liberals as well.

Perhaps we can date the beginning of the cold war on April 23, 1945, when President Truman called Soviet Foreign Minister Vyacheslav Molotov to the White House over the Polish issue and tongue-lashed him like a servant. "I have never been talked to like that in my life," Molotov protested afterward.

Admiral William D. Leahy, a leading hardliner among White House advisers, called Truman's language "more than pleasing to me." Navy Secretary Forrestal wanted "a showdown with them now rather than later." Wallace blamed Averell Harriman, ambassador to the Soviet Union, for "the tough doctrine." When Elmer Benson, former governor of Minnesota, and C. B. Baldwin, later manager of Wallace's campaign, visited Truman at this time, the President insisted, "We have got to get tough with the Russians. I'm going to be tough with them."[5]

What Truman had conceived as a counterforce to Soviet policy in Poland was a world in which American power could bring Russia to its terms. It was a world in which the United States could force its policy of "open door," democratic capitalism to the borders of Russia in Eastern Europe. Yet the Soviets could never be allowed to intrude in Latin America, Western Europe, or our new spheres of influence in the Pacific. It was a world remarkably close to "the American Century" envisioned in 1941 by the publisher of *Time* and *Life* magazines, Henry Luce, who proclaimed America "the dynamic center of ever-widening spheres of influence . . . principal guarantor of the freedom of the seas . . . dynamic leader of world trade."

The fundamental assumptions of this world were that Soviet Communism demanded unlimited expansion, and that the United States, as the proponent of good against evil, must maintain its military and economic structure at peak levels to wage the impending struggle. The immediate strategy was soon labeled "containment."[6]

The Soviet Union's concern in this early period, before Stalin heightened tensions with his own confrontation policy, was geographic security. Devastated by war, the Russians had suffered at least 13 million dead—the Russians had more killed at Stalingrad alone than the United States lost in the entire war.

The nightmare that haunted the Politburo was "capitalist encirclement." The Soviet leaders could never forget that after the 1917 revolution, British, French, Japanese, and even United States troops (under the guise of protecting supplies at Murmansk and Archangel) invaded Russia and fought with the White and Czarist armies to destroy the Bolsheviks. When that failed, the Allies tried to seal off the Soviets by creating a *cordon sanitaire* of Lithuania and other Baltic states. From 1933 on, Soviet leaders were convinced that many British and American industrialists and other influential groups wanted to buy off Hitler and turn the Nazi juggernaut toward Russia. Two days after the German invasion in June 1941, Senator Harry S. Truman, in a frank expression of this policy, suggested, "If we see that Germany is winning, we ought to help Russia, and if Russia is winning, we ought to help Germany, and that way let them kill as many as possible."[7]

All these nightmares had been calmed by Big Three unity during the war, and the Soviets were now taking a surprisingly conservative position. They sided with the United States and Britain against separation of the Ruhr from Germany, overruling the French Communist as well as Socialist and DeGaullist parties, which demanded separation for national security. Stalin insisted that the Italian Communists join the Soviets in recognizing Marshal Badoglio's government, warning them against a revolutionary takeover.

In Yugoslavia, Stalin urged Tito to keep King Peter on the throne. Stalin not only withheld aid from the Yugoslav Communist move to establish their own régime but ordered Tito in 1948 to cut his alliance with the Greek leftists. In Greece, Stalin stuck to his wartime agreement with Churchill and gave Britain dominant status.[8]

When he made Poland the test case of Soviet-American unity, Truman ignored its critical role in Russian security. For centuries Poland had been the corridor through which enemy hordes invaded

Russia. Stalin could yield in Iran and many areas, but friendly governments in Poland and the whole eastern bloc were fundamental to Soviet policy.

Although Truman advocated eastern intervention, he would never have allowed similar Soviet moves toward our new bases in Iceland, Greenland, the Aleutians, and Okinawa, or toward Latin America. In fact, Truman brushed aside Stalin's protests by insisting on seating Perón's pro-facist Argentina at the United Nations. And the President, swayed by the Vatican campaign for "Christian Spain" and the possibility of military bases and commercial investment, joined Britain in blocking the Spanish issue before the UN Security Council.

As a result of Truman's Polish policy, "the Russians concluded that the West was resuming its old course of capitalist encirclement, that it was purposefully laying the foundation for anti-Soviet regimes in the area defined by the blood of centuries as crucial to Russian survival," Arthur W. Schlesinger, Jr. observed.[9]

A major irritant in the get-tough policy was the use of economic pressure for political ends. On May 11, 1945, three days after the end of the German war, Truman ordered a drastic cutback of Lend-Lease, on which Russia's crippled economy depended. When all Lend-Lease terminated in August, Stalin complained that Truman was trying to hammer him into political docility.

No factor intensified Truman's get-tough policy more than the success of the first atom bomb on Hiroshima on August 5, 1945 (Washington time). It was final proof that the United States held sole and unprecedented power to back up its demands. Before, we had desperately needed Russia's help in the war against Japan. Now the success of the bomb made Russian aid superfluous.

On August 8, fulfilling their commitment, the Russians declared war on Japan and pushed into Manchuria. On August 9, the second bomb was dropped on Nagasaki.

The Japanese command had been given almost no time to assess the impact of the bomb or the Russian offensive. Very likely, the second bomb had more political than military motivation. Truman could well have wanted to crush Japan before the Russian offensive had made enough headway to give the Soviets a role in the Japanese occupation or Far East policy. Ironically, at the same time that Truman was seeking to thwart Soviet security demands in Eastern Europe, he forced Stalin to accept American dominance in the Pacific.

Although the President claimed that the bomb "saved the lives of untold thousands of American and Allied soldiers," Japan was already prostrate, suing for peace, and could probably have been starved into submission with Soviet assistance. General Marshall and most armed forces heads saw no military need for the bomb. General Eisenhower himself concluded, "It wasn't necessary to hit them with that awful thing." The U.S. Strategic Bombing Survey stated: "Japan would have surrendered even if the atomic bombs had not been dropped, even if Russia had not entered the war, even if no invasion had been planned or contemplated."[10]

The administration's mounting confrontation with Russia released a pent-up hatred in the United States against Communists and the whole American Left. This antipathy had been largely bottled up during the wartime alliance, when Earl Browder, the Communist chieftain, remolded his party into fervent support of the war; and even the conservative president of the Curtis Publishing Company could place his imprimatur on the popular front. "To make America a better place to live," Walter D. Fuller announced in 1944, "we must all work together, and that includes the Communists." The almost unstinting admiration of the American public for the Soviet war effort further allayed anti-Left feelings.

By 1946, however, each step in the confrontation—Churchill's Fulton speech in March, the atom bomb tests at Bikini in July, Byrnes's negotiations for an Iceland air base as part of our chain encircling Russia—made it easier to promote anti-Communism at home. The attack ranged from the dismissal of Dr. Homer Rainey as president of the University of Texas for his supposedly radical views to subpoenas by the House Un-American Activities Committee (HUAC) against the Joint Anti-Fascist Refugee Committee, which aided Republican victims of the Spanish civil war.

By December 1946, the National Association of Manufacturers, meeting in New York City, would vote $6 million for anti-Communist advertisements. And within the year, a speaker at the CIO convention would be denouncing former Governor George H. Earle of Pennsylvania for proposing that "we ought to drop atomic bombs on the Soviet Union."[11]

The anti-Communist wave would greatly affect the CIO itself. While the 15 or so unions, classified as Left, formed the strongest radical base in the country, their strength had always been exaggerated. Numerically, there were only 600 or 700 Communist party members in the National Maritime Union, for example, out of a membership of 90,000. Further, anti-Communism had always been rife in such influential unions as steel and textile. Above all, the early CIO had been ruled by a triumvirate with Lewis at the top and Murray and Sidney Hillman of Amalgamated Clothing as its bases. Now Lewis and Hillman, both masters at maintaining the Left coalition, were gone—Lewis had resigned as president in 1940 and Hillman died in July 1946.

Truman's tough policy further strained CIO unity. "You wouldn't like what's developing with us," a Steelworkers officer told Len DeCaux of the CIO before its convention in May 1946. Murray's own union—he remained president and drew his salary from Steel while heading the CIO without salary—quickly pushed through a resolution against "Communists, Socialists or any other group" attempting "to infiltrate, dictate or meddle in our affairs."

The pressure against the Left before the CIO convention in November 1946—the mood was set when someone stole the Soviet flag from the Atlantic City convention hall—forced Murray to concoct one of his typical compromises. Appointing a committee of six, three each from the Right and Left, he made them hammer out a resolution committing the CIO to "resent and reject efforts of the Communist Party or other political parties and their adherents to interfere in the affairs of the CIO." The Left voted almost unanimous approval, closing ranks behind Murray, who in turn assured the convention the measure was not repressive.[12]

Yet the resolution paved the way for further restrictions against the Left. The CIO Executive Board, its radical members compliant again, quickly voted Murray the power to take over the funds and property of state and local industrial councils, which were Left strongholds in most urban areas; and then forbade the same councils any statements or actions contrary to CIO policy.

Walter Reuther, a coldly intellectual politician with a flair for blending personal ambition and social vision, exploited anti-Communism in seizing control of the Auto Workers. Murray feared Reuther eventually wanted the CIO presidency. Calling him "that little red-headed bastard" in private, Murray tried to block Reuther at first.[13]

Reuther, the head of the UAW at General Motors, drew his support from a strange mix of southern conservatives, socialists, and the Association of Catholic Trade Unions (ACTU), with a strong base among Detroit Catholics. George Addes, Richard Leonard, and

Richard Frankensteen, heading other factions, joined together in 1939 to make R. J. Thomas president. None of them was Communist, or even close to it. Yet their coalition was often labeled Left, although Communists controlled only a few locals.

Ironically, Reuther had started on the Left himself. Born in West Virginia in 1907, the son of a militant German socialist, he had campaigned on streetcorners for Norman Thomas in 1932 and consequently lost his job as a Ford foreman. Walter and his brother Victor —with a third brother, Roy, they made an irrepressible team in the UAW, often dubbed the "Rover Boys"—set off around the world, working in Russia for 16 months in an auto factory.

Reuther, in fact, was an original member of the R. J. Thomas "unity" coalition, and in those tumultuous days when every union official was a red to the manufacturers, wrote, "So let's all be careful that we don't play the bosses' game by falling for their red scare." This quotation would haunt him in 1946 when he was using the same red scare against the Thomas coalition.[14]

By 1936, Reuther had left the Socialist party. By 1940, with his highly publicized blueprint for converting auto assembly lines to plane production, he had become the darling of the New Deal. Then he was ready to take on Thomas, whose hard drinking and tobacco chewing contrasted sharply with Reuther's ascetic life-style. Reuther built his machine carefully. A relentless schemer who kept his own counsel but was a passionate orator before an audience, he based his whole campaign in 1946 on the Communist issue. Murray dreaded the hysteria that Reuther was exploiting and came to the convention to give tacit support to Thomas. Still, Reuther won the presidency by a slim margin of 4,444 to 4,320 votes. It was a crushing blow to coalition in the CIO. By 1947, Reuther virtually erased the Left from the UAW board.

The anti-Communist hysteria exploded at the same time in the 650,000-member United Electrical Workers. The attack, led by James Carey, first president of the UE, started in 1940. A year later, a coalition headed by Julius Emspak and James Matles defeated Carey for the presidency and replaced him with Albert Fitzgerald. But the new leadership still supported Carey for secretary-treasurer of the CIO.

Carey's personal ambitions dovetailed with ACTU's concentration on the UE and its large Catholic membership. ACTU's influence had grown steadily since 1940, when Lee Pressman noted that "representatives of the church" at the CIO convention "initiated the practice of sitting on the platform in a solid mass. . . ." In Pittsburgh, a center of UE strength, ACTU was directed by a driving and inventive labor priest, Father Charles O. Rice, who was determined to put "Jim Carey back there as President. . . ." Rice was close to Phil Murray—he was his confessor—and helped shape his later policy against the Left. The steel union backed Rice solidly. Its district director became president of Pittsburgh ACTU in August, 1947, and Murray himself approved payments of $1,000 a month to ACTU from 1948 on.[15]

To drive Fitzgerald out of the presidency, Carey, Rice, and their allies formed UE Members for Democratic Action and put up their own candidates at the Milwaukee convention in September 1946. Their voting strength was still meager, and Fitzgerald won reelection by 3,029 to 525.

Murray made a special point of attending the convention. While aiding ACTU behind the scenes he showered praise in his speech on the UE and its officers, who he said had "sustained and maintained and fought for all national policies and supported the President of this organization [CIO] in the furtherance of these policies." In a warning to the new faction, he stressed, "Let no enemy of the CIO get by glibly with the argument that they are going to destroy an organization like yours." Yet Murray would soon join the destroyers.[16]

There was one last attempt to keep a united front coalition together. In September, a conference of progressives met in Chicago, representing such liberal and Left organizations as the National Farmers Union, the National Association for the Advancement of Colored People, the CIO, and the UE, and including prominent New Dealers like Harold Ickes and Henry Morgenthau, Jr. The meeting concluded with a rousing call for unity by Phil Murray, "the most important in progressive history," C. B. Baldwin of National Citizens Political Action Committee called it. A smaller committee met in Washington in November but broke up prematurely. The liberals had started to follow the CIO into aggressive anti-Communism. "The conference was torpedoed by Murray, Carey and ACTU," Baldwin insisted.[17]

The united front ended irrevocably with the founding of Americans for Democratic Action in January 1947. An amalgam of New Dealers like Leon Henderson of the OPA, Hubert Humphrey, and Eleanor Roosevelt with CIO anti-Communists like Reuther and Carey, ADA supported virtually all of Truman's get-tough policies with Russia.

By the November 1946 elections, Republicans had pinned the

red label on most liberals. Truman had replaced Roosevelt's officials with reactionaries like Byrnes and had tried to reach a consensus with Republicans on both foreign and domestic issues, producing instead a chaotic program that satisfied no one. OPA was crippled; inflation was destroying the country's buying power. The unions were still furious at the President for his draft-labor bill.

Measured by previous off-year elections, the country should have cast 43 million votes in 1946. But only 35 million bothered going to the polls. Liberals and New Dealers were swamped. Of 318 candidates supported by the CIO Political Action Committee, only 73 were elected. Of the House Democrats elected, almost half were southern conservatives. Of 77 Republicans who had scored 80 percent on the *New Republic* magazine's scorecard of liberal issues, only 36 survived. The Republicans controlled both Houses of Congress.[18]

The Left would be isolated even more by Truman's first bold intervention in the Mediterranean—"America's answer to the surge of Communist tyranny," he called it. When Britain informed the White House that its shaky economy precluded aid to Greece and Turkey after March 31, 1947, the President went before a special joint session of Congress on March 12 to proclaim a new policy "to support free peoples who are resisting attempted subjugation by armed minorities or by outside pressures." Specifically, he requested $400 million for military and economic aid to Greece and Turkey, running to June 30, 1948.[19]

The "Truman Doctrine," as it was immediately called, staked out a drastic concept. The Monroe Doctrine of 1823 had simply warned other nations to keep out of the western hemisphere. Now the United States, bypassing the United Nations, appointed itself policeman of the world, asserting the right to intervene anywhere.

The President's inflammatory language suggested that the United States was offering a blank check to all anti-Communist governments, no matter how reactionary. His roseate reference to "free peoples" hardly applied to the corrupt Constantin Tsaldaris government in Greece, shunned by most liberal and moderate parties. Ironically, not Stalin but Tito abetted the Greek opposition. And Turkey had only befriended the allies in the waning moments of World War II and was unthreatened by Communism.

Truman envisioned both containment and a new sphere of economic expansion in the Mediterranean. Forrestal concluded that "our support of Greece and Turkey might be the forerunner of many other and very much larger economic and political actions in other parts of the world. . . ."[20] In historical perspective, the Truman Doctrine produced some shaky assets. In return for naval bases, air fields, and eventually missile sites that kept atomic warheads on the fringe of the Soviet Union, as well as limited economic advantages including Turkey's opium traffic, we gained decades of repressive governments in Turkey, and an unsavory monarchy and a military dictatorship in Greece.

The American Institute of Public Opinion in late 1946 polled Democrats on their choice for the next President. Forty-eight percent favored Truman, 24 percent Wallace, and 10 percent Byrnes. Wallace was becoming a serious contender. He insisted through the summer of 1947 that "progressive forces" must stay within the Democratic party "as an instrument of National progress."

The Progressive Citizens of America (PCA), however, pushed increasingly for a third party. Founded on December 28, 1946, incorporating National Citizens Political Action Committee and the Independent Citizens Committee of Arts, Sciences and Professions, including luminaries like Bette Davis and Albert Einstein, it sought to become a vehicle for the old united front. The Communist party opposed the merger; it hardly wanted a third party at this point. Phil Murray, too, forbade CIO officers affiliation with either PCA or ADA, but he removed the ban on ADA in 1948.[21]

Wallace's speaking tour in May 1947 drew unprecedented crowds. In Chicago, at the first political rally to charge for tickets, 22,000 jammed the stadium; thousands more listened to loudspeakers on the streets. There was another sellout crowd in Detroit. In Los Angeles, Wallace drew 30,000 at Gilmore Stadium. From coast to coast, more than 200,000 people paid admission to Wallace rallies, a new phenomenon in politics.

Truman's policy of building Germany as a bulwark against Russia was now being implemented by a team of bankers and brokers that typified the administration's conservatism. Charles Saltzman, assistant secretary of state, was a former vice president of the New York Stock Exchange. Brigadier General William H. Draper, deputy commander in Germany, had been vice-president of Dillon Read & Co., largest underwriter of loans for Hitler's principal steel trust in 1933. This team rushed over $1 billion in economic aid to West Germany in 1947 alone, with another $2 billion planned for the next few years.

Obviously frightened by the German buildup and the prospect of atomic bombs at their doorstep in Greece and Turkey, the Soviets again bolstered their eastern defenses. In Hungary, where Admiral Nicholas Horthy had been a devoted ally of Hitler, Russia insisted that the ruling Smallholders party had become an asylum for reactionary politicians. A new leftist government was forced on the country in June. Whether the Soviet analysis was justified or not, its coup represented another extension of its defensive perimeter. Clearly jittery Kremlin leaders were reacting to the Truman Doctrine.

At almost the same moment, speaking at the Harvard commencement on June 5, 1947, Secretary of State George C. Marshall announced another plan—henceforth known as the Marshall Plan—to pour huge sums of money into the economic development of Europe. Combining both humanitarian and political objectives, obviously aimed at supporting centrist governments in Italy and France against their powerful Communist parties, the plan "helped to save Europe from economic disaster and lifted it from the shadow of enslavement by Russian Communism," Truman later claimed.[22]

The President asked Congress for $17 billion over four years, most of which was eventually granted. On July 12, 1947, 16 nations met in Paris to found the European Recovery Program (later changed to the Mutual Security Administration, to fit the inclusion of military assistance).

The Soviets now made a serious strategic blunder. They not only refused to join the Marshall Plan but pressured Czechoslovakia, which had already accepted, into reversing its decision. Although Congress would undoubtedly have attached endless impediments to funds for Russia or the eastern bloc, or might have refused funds altogether, Russian opposition eliminated an excellent tactical opportunity. By joining the Marshall Plan, the Soviets could have demonstrated their desire to cooperate in Europe.

As it was, Russia and its allies joined together in a similar pact known as the Cominform, and eventually in a military combine under the Warsaw Pact. When the Marshall Plan members developed their military arm through the North Atlantic Treaty Organization (NATO), these rival organizations became locked in the cold war.

Soviet opposition to the Marshall Plan had critical impact on the Left unions of the CIO. The issue came to the floor at the CIO's annual convention on October 13, 1947, in Boston. Murray had a resolution introduced that cautiously never mentioned the Marshall Plan by name but simply supported "food and other economic aid for the rehabilitation of other countries."

What the Left hadn't expected was Murray's last-minute invitation to Secretary of State Marshall to be the main speaker at the convention. The floor was taken over by rabid demonstrations against the Left. When Marshall arrived, he was escorted to the platform accompanied by the blare of a navy band and the shouts of another prolonged demonstration. It was obvious that Murray had committed the CIO to the Marshall Plan, and a dangerous split was in the offing.[23]

An even more immediate crisis would confront labor. The strike waves of 1945 and 1946, and the conservative Congress elected in November 1946, had prepared the way for drastic anti-labor legislation. When John L. Lewis announced another strike in November 1946, the President secured an antistrike injunction from federal district court. When the miners struck anyway, Judge T. Alan Goldsborough fined the union $3.5 million and Lewis $10,000 personally. The U.S. Supreme Court upheld the conviction on March 6, 1947, but eventually lowered the fines.

This struggle between Lewis and the President intensified anti-labor bitterness throughout the country. Truman's attempt to break the railroad strike by military draft, and his use of a federal injunction against Lewis, spurred the Republican Congress to pass the Taft-Hartley Act, the ultimate vengeance.

Reversing numerous provisions of the Wagner Act of 1935, Taft-Hartley virtually wiped out the "closed shop" (union membership as a condition of employment) and other traditional protective contracts. The court injunction, long contained by the Norris-La Guardia Act, would once again become a potent weapon against unions. If a presidential fact-finding board found any strike damaging national health and safety, the President could use a court injunction to halt a strike during a cooling-off period.

Section 9-H required all union officers to sign annual affidavits disavowing Communist party membership or belief in "the overthrow of the United States government by force or by any illegal or unconstitutional methods." If officers did not swear under 9-H, their union would be denied facilities at the National Labor Relations

Board. The union could not appear on the ballot in board elections, could not be certified as the bargaining agent in an organized shop.

Although Murray labeled Taft-Hartley "a direct step towards fascism," and Truman came out against the bill, the CIO was surprisingly tepid in its opposition. Almost one-half million workers quit the plants on April 24, 1947. But when the Electrical Workers proposed a nationwide strike to the CIO executive board, Murray vetoed it as "too political."[24]

This failure of the AFL and CIO to mount a massive stand against Taft-Hartley—a week's strike tying up the country, even a one-day general strike—proved a turning point in labor's waning influence. The attack on the Left unions had already sapped the militancy of the CIO. Many conservative leaders almost welcomed section 9-H as an opportunity to raid and divide the Left.

Truman vetoed Taft-Hartley on June 20, but the veto was overridden 331 to 83 in the House and 68 to 25 in the Senate. Still, Truman's veto became the pivot of the 1948 campaign. Even A. F. Whitney of the Trainmen, a sworn enemy since the draft-labor bill, returned to the Democratic fold.

At first, all CIO affiliates pledged the executive board not to sign the anti-Communist affidavits. At the CIO convention on October 13, 1947, Murray defied 9-H as "a matter of principle," demanding why Congress had not also required a union officer to swear he was not a Ku Klux Klan member. But then Murray made one of his dangerous compromises. Stressing that affiliated unions have "the greatest possible degree of autonomy," he admitted that some unions might sign the affidavits and go along with Taft-Hartley. He had unplugged the dam. Section 9-H was the first major offensive in the anti-Communist war, and the CIO, probably the only force in the country that could have stopped it, had abrogated its responsibility.

One source of Murray's spinelessness was his fear of a clash with Reuther. He knew that Reuther would sign 9-H—the auto leader announced it publicly on October 31. Reuther had also cemented his control of the UAW, and at his November convention won 18 of 22 seats on the executive board. Having crushed the Left, he now launched his raids on the Electrical Workers, which made the CIO split inevitable. Rubber, textile, shipbuilding, and other conservative unions quickly joined the 9-H bandwagon. The anti-Communist hysteria and the McCarthy era were guaranteed by those who should have stood strongest against them.

Only Lewis of all dominant labor leaders opposed Taft-Hartley to the end. After convincing the AFL executive council to boycott 9-H, and learning at the AFL convention in October that the council had betrayed its pledge, Lewis flayed them mercilessly. "I represent an organization whose members believe they pay their officers to fight for them, not to deliver them into slavery . . ." he told the assemblage. ". . . I don't think the Federation has a head. I think its neck has just grown up and haired over." He walked out of the convention alone. On December 12, the Miners left the AFL for good. Lewis wrote to Green with a blue crayon on a half-torn, rumpled sheet of paper: "Green. We disaffiliate. Lewis."[25]

The Truman Doctrine, the Marshall Plan, the President's hard line with Russia solidified opposition to the administration's foreign policy that fall of 1947. As the focus of the opposition, Henry Wallace addressed a Labor Day rally of 50,000 in Detroit and packed stadiums in New York, Boston, Providence, Philadelphia, and Baltimore. In a message to the New York rally, former Mayor La Guardia, who would be dead 10 days later, stated that the crisis "does not mean there must necessarily be a third party. It does mean a third party must be ever ready in reserve."

Third-party talk was rampant, and a Progressive slate in the Chicago judicial elections on November 4, 1947, provided the first test of strength. One Progressive candidate polled 313,000 votes or 16 percent of the total; others were not far behind. In California, by contrast, former Attorney General Robert W. Kenny insisted that the liberal bloc could win the state for Wallace in the Democratic primaries and opposed third-party fever.

The House Un-American Activities Committee added to the hysteria with its investigation of Communist influence in Hollywood, sparking lurid headlines from the press when prominent producers, writers, and directors, labeled the "Hollywood Ten," refused to testify and were cited for contempt. Such hysteria also deprived the Communist and American Labor parties of 2 seats each out of 23 on the New York City Council. The "proportional representation" system of voting—giving each party seats equal to its share of the total vote—was revoked by referendum at the fall elections.

In late November, C. B. Baldwin, now executive director of Progressive Citizens of America, called a meeting of state executives. Baldwin had been pushing a third party for two years, and PCA was almost unanimously behind it. Wallace, long insistent on working within the Democratic party, was gradually yielding to the necessity of a new party.

Later it became popular to call the Communist party the driving force behind third-party organization. The evidence, however, is scanty. Eugene Dennis, a high Communist official, had written in 1946, "Steps towards forming a third party should be taken early in 1947." But similar trial balloons had been launched all through 1946 by A. F. Whitney and other labor leaders revolting against Truman. By August 1947, Dennis had pulled back, warning against "abortive or ill-timed actions."

The Communist-influence thesis stemmed primarily from the testimony of Michael Quill, head of the Transport Workers and formerly a pillar of the CIO Left. In 1950, Quill would claim that Dennis brought him, Matles, and Emspak of the UE and other Left officers to a meeting on October 18, 1947, and ordered them to support a third party. Robert Thompson, another Communist leader, supposedly demanded they back Wallace "even if it splits the CIO right down the middle."[26]

There were many flaws in Quill's story. Even Baldwin had no firm commitment from Wallace on October 18. The Electrical Workers never supported Wallace officially, although its three top officers backed him. Quill, on the other hand, spoke out vigorously for Wallace at the CIO executive board on January 2, 1948, and did not resign from the American Labor party until April 20, 1948.

PCA provided almost all the impetus for the Wallace campaign. In fact, Communist party support, whatever its impact, arrived extremely late, probably not until early December, and was probably triggered by a frantic attempt to counter CIO approval of the Marshall Plan at its October 1947 convention. At a December 2 meeting of PCA executives, Wallace finally gave his commitment to run. On December 29, he announced his decision from Chicago over a radio network, insisting that the dominant issue was peace: "The larger the peace vote in 1948, the more definitely the world will know that the United States is not behind the bipartisan reactionary war policy which is dividing the world into two armed camps and making inevitable the day when American soldiers will be lying in their arctic suits in the Russian snow."[27]

Wallace called his new party "Gideon's Army" after the Old Testament warrior who had defeated hordes of desert marauders with his small band. For Wallace faced crushing odds. With no organized political base except New York and California, with no organized farm support, and only a scattering of prominent New Dealers and CIO Left unions behind him, he was struggling to reverse the momentum of Truman's policy and a headlong rush toward open conflict with the Soviets.

At best, he might poll 5 million votes—an optimistic assessment, since most of the old Roosevelt coalition, particularly the labor and liberal vote, was so fearful of putting Governor Thomas Dewey in the White House that they would stick to the Democrats. For the Left, the risks were even worse—isolation from the labor and liberal mainstream, even destruction. There was an element of fanaticism in the third-party movement, an element of what even Left critics would call sheer adventurism. Yet, convinced that a platform of protest had to be offered the nation, Wallace plunged into his campaign.

· 4 ·

The Wrath of the Prophets: Henry Wallace and the Progressive Party 1948

It was a one-man campaign from the start. Without Henry Wallace, there would have been no Progressive party. He made it almost a religious revival. With his Calvinist devotion to duty, his determination to bring the Lord's work into politics, he gave his platform of planned economy the fervor of a camp-town meeting. He laced his speeches with biblical quotations, calling the wrath of the prophet Isaiah upon Truman's get-tough policy: "Woe to those that trust in chariots." His Gideon's Army had to save the nation from its plunge toward war. It had to restore the dreams of the New Deal. To succeed, Wallace was convinced he had to rebuild the wartime popular front, even though Communist support would become the heaviest cross he would bear.

There was a messianic tone to his language. "In Hyde Park they buried our President—and in Washington they buried our dreams," he told one audience. There was a sense of destiny and showmanship in each appearance—the organized chants booming his name over the loudspeakers, the folksingers crying, "Be a real smarty, join the New party," the crescendos of applause that often lasted 10 minutes before the crowd allowed him to speak.

But beneath all the surface revivalism, a Chicago *Daily News* reporter concluded, "Wallace is an incurably simple soul. His belief in God and Christian doctrine is as real as his devotion to simple fare." In 1944, after his rejection for a second term as Vice-President, he campaigned for Roosevelt 16 hours a day through the summer and fall. Once he had to catch a crowded day-coach to make his next speech and stood in the aisles from 6 P.M. to 2 A.M. No one offered him a seat or even seemed to recognize him. Associates often tried to argue him out of carrying his heavy suitcase from the station to his distant hotel. Was he trying to save a cab fare? Wallace admitted he liked to save money. But it wasn't really

36

that. "I need the exercise," he insisted.[1]

Above all, there was an energetic martyrdom about the 1948 campaign, particularly in his southern tours, where Wallace refused to speak to segregated audiences or stop at hotels or restaurants that turned away black members of his group. After daily barrages of rotten fruit and smashed windshields, a mob in Gadsden, Alabama, rocked his crowded car for five minutes and almost overturned it. His distraught associates begged him to call off the rest of the tour, but Wallace refused.

The campaign was driven by the desperation of apparently impending war. At a Chicago dinner in January 1948, Marshall Field, publisher of the Chicago *Sun-Times* and New York's *PM,* reported to the Progressive leadership that Pentagon officials expected war within six months. "We were convinced that if we got 5 million votes, we could stop the rush to war. We could have headed off the Korean war and perhaps the Vietnam debacle," Albert Fitzgerald of the UE, chairman of the new party's labor committee, concluded afterward. James A. Farley, who had guided Roosevelt to his first two victories, predicted that Wallace would get those 5 million votes.[2]

If the campaign seems flawed, with hindsight, by political ineptness—Wallace let Truman pin the Communist label on his party and convince the country that a Wallace vote would guarantee a Republican President—Wallace gave it an integrity and prophetic accuracy that was uncanny. Almost every speech rings startlingly true 30 years later. His assault on each provocation in the cold war pointed unerringly toward a constant line of confrontations from Greece to the Bay of Pigs, Vietnam, and Cyprus. Yet his words swayed few, and his own political flaws, and his party's, restricted the efficacy of the campaign.

His awkwardness in 1948 simply magnified the errors of his 1944 renomination campaign for the vice-presidency. Hating the crudities of politics and refusing to deal with the power brokers, Wallace did not even name an official campaign manager in 1944. "Why, hell, he'd been there presiding over the Senate for almost four years," Truman noted caustically years later, "and I'll bet there wasn't half a dozen Senators who'd call him by his first name." The Gallup poll in 1944 showed Wallace was favored by 65 percent of enrolled Democrats, but Roosevelt was irritated by Wallace's refusal to cultivate the big-city bosses who had joined Robert E. Hannegan, chairman of the Democratic National Committee, in an alliance to block renomination.[3]

Wallace left his campaign in the hands of Sidney Hillman and the CIO Political Action Committee. But Hillman—despite the canard that everyone was to "clear it with Sidney"—was also playing Roosevelt's evasive game. The Hannegan alliance, concerned about Roosevelt's health and determined that Wallace's extreme New Dealism would never control the White House, pushed hard for Truman, a border-state Democrat. Roosevelt may simply have been forcing Wallace to fight it out with the big-city bosses. More likely, his total concentration on the war effort made him hesitant to alienate any power bloc by pushing Wallace too vigorously.

On the first ballot at the convention, Wallace received 429 1/2 votes to Truman's 319 1/2. On the next ballot, Wallace reached 472 1/2 before most southern delegates swung to Truman, and Hannegan's carefully engineered stampede took over the floor. Hannegan supposedly remarked later that the only epitaph he wanted on his gravestone was the credit for keeping Wallace out of the White House.

All through Wallace's career, his complex and introverted personality made him an alien in the smoke-filled room. Secretary of Labor Frances Perkins praised his "nobility of character." Secretary of Interior Harold Ickes disliked his consuming ambition. "No one could make deals with Henry," an associate recalled. When politicians closed in on him, he would slump in his chair, a rumpled, baggy figure, his blue-gray eyes half-closed as if bored, almost as if he were dropping off to sleep. He was aloof, morally austere, uncomfortable among backslappers. In his shyness, probably the result of a rigid Calvinist upbringing, he rejected small talk, liquor, and dirty jokes. "He liked the common man in mass, but couldn't relate on a one-to-one basis," recalled another associate.[4]

Yet the visions that made Wallace the boogieman of industrialists turned out to be surprisingly realistic. His doctrines of national economic planning and welfare-state financing became the core of scores of government programs from farm price-supports to the "ever-normal granary," which controlled agricultural gluts and shortages through government storage, purchases, and sales. Wallace was often treated by the anti-New Deal press as a crackpot. His 1945 book, *Sixty Million Jobs,* advocating government social services and budgetary controls for full employment, was damned as "woolly-minded." But his target was reached in the astonishingly short span of six years.

Even in his personal life, his visionary experiments in hybrid corn, and the founding of the Pioneer Hi-Bred Corn Co. in 1926, paid off munificently. His stock in the company (some sold to the public in 1974) then had a value of about $125 million.

The attacks on Wallace's "woolly-mindedness" reached their peak in March 1948, when Westbrook Pegler, Hearst's vitriolic right-wing columnist, published the so-called guru letters. Born a Presbyterian and converted to Episcopalianism, Wallace was a lifelong student of Buddhism, Mohammedanism, and all Oriental cults, mysticism, and numerology. Through his studies, he met and corresponded with Nicholas Roerich, a Russian-born painter and mystic whose followers supposedly considered him a god.

At a press conference at the Progressive convention in July, Pegler demanded that Wallace affirm or deny the letters' authenticity. Wallace handled himself clumsily, refusing to discuss the affair. As a result, he emerged for millions of readers in a vindictive press as a bumbling eccentric whose occult gropings could damage his mastery of national politics.

Wallace's personality was full of paradoxes; this mystical bent, for example, contrasted sharply with his concentration on athletics. A robust man with unruly gray hair and shaggy eyebrows whose slightly stooped shoulders made him seem shorter than 5 feet 11 inches, Wallace exuded enormous energy. After an exhausting day, he liked to impress associates by performing 25 push-ups. He played relentless tennis—his form was poor, but he always seemed to get the ball back—as well as squash and volleyball. He became an expert boomerang thrower, to the delight of press photographers, and at the age of 56 learned to fly his own plane. Wallace's mania for physical fitness, in fact, paralleled that of his boyhood idol, President Theodore Roosevelt, whose insurgent Progressive party in 1912 was backed by Wallace's father. Wallace borrowed the name in 1948.

Wallace was born on October 7, 1888, into a distinguished agricultural family. His grandfather, known as "Uncle Henry," was a Presbyterian minister who gave up the pulpit because of illness to become a prosperous Iowa farmer. Wallace's father, Henry Cantwell Wallace, held a professorship at Iowa State Agricultural College and founded *Wallace's Farmer,* the most influential farm journal in the Midwest. He used the paper to rally farmers behind Teddy Roosevelt, fight the railroads and monopolies, and advance himself to become secretary of agriculture under Presidents Warren G. Harding and Calvin Coolidge.

Henry Agard Wallace grew up shy and reticent. Dedicated to his studies, making few friends, he inherited his Old Testament passion from his father and grandfather, and even during campaigns held family hymn singings after Sunday supper. He was also influenced by George Washington Carver, the black chemurgist and botanist then working at Iowa State, who spurred his interest in civil rights and his experiments in plant genetics. In 1914, Wallace married a classmate at Iowa State, Ilo Browne. They had three children. His wife, who wanted the trappings of the presidency but not the hurlyburly of politics, never approved of his 1948 campaign; she confided to friends that Marcantonio and other associates were just not "her husband's kind."[5]

Like his father, Wallace made the family newspaper a powerful political weapon. Although a Republican, he supported a Progressive candidate, Senator Robert M. La Follette, in 1924. Determined to unite farmers and eastern labor with the liberal middle class, he switched to Governor Alfred E. Smith and the Democratic party in 1928. Campaigning tirelessly for Roosevelt in 1932 (but still donating $25 to Norman Thomas), he was appointed secretary of agriculture.

He became the cutting edge of the New Deal, a folk hero for labor and liberals, but the target of endless scorn from the Republican press. He plowed under 10 million acres of cotton and slaughtered 6 million small pigs to bolster farm prices. His "ever-normal granary" and crop insurance made the Agricultural Department a model for production planning. His aid to poor farmers, both black and white, through the Farm Security Administration, constantly angered southern legislators, who tried to withhold funds from his agencies.

Roosevelt, devoting himself almost exclusively to foreign affairs and the impending war, demanded the convention nominate Wallace as his running mate in 1940. The new Vice-President began to preach his vision of a postwar world that would eradicate imperialism and colonialism and replace it with global New Dealism. Instead of Henry Luce's imperialist American Century, Wallace called for "the Century of the Common Man," the title of his 1943 book. "The people's revolution is on the march," he cried, "and the devil and all his angels cannot prevail against it."[6]

After his appointment as head of the Board of Economic Warfare in 1941, Wallace's theories of global economic planning soon clashed with those of Jesse Jones, the secretary of commerce. Roosevelt alleviated the conflict by establishing a new superagency over the contenders. In 1945, when Wallace was appointed secretary of commerce, a tide of reactionary opposition in the Senate stripped his office of the lending power Jesse Jones had controlled.

Thus, the battle lines had hardened long before 1948. The Wallace presidential campaign was the climax of a domestic as well as foreign-policy struggle. All the simmering issues—poll tax, civil rights, anti-Communist hysteria, a planned economy—would dominate debates in that critical year. Wallace's antagonism to Truman sprang partly from his conviction that the new President failed to fight seriously for the New Deal's social goals. Then too, he was bitter that except for the machinations of Democratic politics, he would be occupying the White House himself. He always called Truman "that little fellow" or "the salesman." Their paths crossed once in the 1948 campaign at the Dallas air field. "Wallace got out of his rented DC-3, and saw the giant presidential plane taxiing for a takeoff," an associate recalled. "He looked away quickly. You could see the pain on his face."[7]

At first Wallace held his own against the big-city bosses who had defeated him at the 1944 convention. A special House election was called for February 17, 1948, in New York's Bronx County, long the preserve of Ed Flynn, a kingpin of the Democratic machine. Wallace toured the district in support of Leo Isacson, the American Labor party candidate. The district had a large Jewish vote, and Wallace was idolized for his early support of a Jewish state. He hammered away at Truman's indecisive mishandling of the UN's partition plan for Israel.

Isacson scored a startling upset, taking almost double the votes of the Democratic candidate. Even *Life* magazine, admitting Wallace's chances were sharply improved, concluded that the Isacson victory "threw a real scare into the Democratic high command." The new chairman of the Democratic National Committee, J. Howard McGrath, appealed on a radio broadcast for Wallace to return to the Democratic camp.

There was a further note of optimism. Wallace's speaking tours, which had drawn unprecedented crowds and $267,000 in contributions in 1947, maintained their record pace in the winter of 1948. Fund-raising spectaculars produced almost $90,000 in January and February alone. The real money, however, came from a few wealthy individuals—Frederick Vanderbilt Field; Elinor S. Gimbel, head of

Wallace's women's division; the businessmen's committee; and above all, Anita McCormick Blaine of Chicago, heiress of the Cyrus H. McCormick reaper fortune, who was said to have donated $800,-000.[8]

But by spring, the flood began to dry up. Progressive headquarters nationally reported only $1.5 million in total contributions (with at least another million raised in the states). The miniscule union contributions were particularly disappointing, since the AFL and CIO gave at least $1.5 million to Truman.

The worst aspect of the campaign was organization at state and local levels. Wallace's headquarters staff had few experienced professionals. Only Marcantonio in New York controlled a functioning state machine. California, with almost half a million Progressive petition signatures collected for the spring primary, failed to build a local club system. In Illinois, a potential anchor state with 300,000 votes for Progressive judicial candidates the year before, the courts ruled Wallace off the ballot for insufficient valid petition signatures in each county—a restrictive system later overturned by the U.S. Supreme Court.

Above all, the Wallace campaign failed to build a union base. Big labor was not only petrified of a Republican victory but was placated by the booming production, full employment, and rising wages of the cold war.

Further, Truman shrewdly undercut Wallace's labor support by moving sharply to the Left in his domestic program while exploiting the anti-Communist hysteria by pinning the red label on Wallace. In his message to Congress in February 1948, the President advocated an anti-lynching bill, outlawing segregation in interstate commerce, and other measures even more advanced than Roosevelt's civil rights platform.

But Truman's rhetoric failed to ignite political enthusiasm. Marcantonio's amendment to block government funds in states with discrimination in jobs and education lost in the House by 119 to 40. Senator William Langer's amendment to ban discrimination in the armed forces was beaten 67 to 7, although Truman would soon sign an executive order with the same ban.

Even the CIO Left unions failed to build a block-by-block organization for Wallace. Although Fitzgerald chaired the Progressive labor committee, and national UE officers supported the campaign, the giant UE never voted an official position on Wallace. "It would have split the union," Jim Matles explained. "We had to avoid reckless militancy, the 'let's go down fighting' recklessness that eventually crippled the Left."[9]

The Progressive party had to depend on small unions like Harry Bridges's Longshoremen and Hugh Bryson's Marine Cooks and Stewards in the West, the Fur Workers and Furniture Workers in the East, and Mine, Mill and Smelter in the Midwest. None of them produced enough doorbell ringers to make a political dent outside New York.

The Progressives were no more successful in the farm bloc. The National Farmers Union, headed by Wallace's longtime friend James Patton, backed the campaign only in scattered regions. Similarly, the "Townsend Plan" clubs, an organization of elderly citizens whose program was part of the Progressive platform, proved surprisingly ineffective even in California, their main political base.

Meanwhile, Truman struggled to unify the Democratic party while its liberal and labor leadership searched for an alternative to the floundering Truman candidacy. Determined to find a winner, the ADA went after General Dwight D. Eisenhower, who had never expressed Democratic leanings and whose support of both universal military training and the draft countered the ADA's own position. Giving up principles for an acclaimed military hero, the ADA national board came out for Ike in April, and ADA delegates surrounded Ike's house at New York's Columbia University, pleading with him to run. Many CIO officials joined this draft movement. But Eisenhower issued an irrevocable "No" on July 9, leaving liberal Democrats forlorn when the convention opened in Philadelphia three days later.

If they couldn't have a winner, the ADA at least wanted a vigorous civil rights stand. Truman, desperate to hold the South, fought for moderation. Fortunately for him, as it turned out, the liberals won, and Truman was handed a platform that strengthened his campaign considerably. The President later claimed in his memoirs he had demanded a tough civil rights stance from the start.[10]

After Truman took the nomination on the first ballot, the hardcore segregationists walked out of the convention, forming the States Rights Party at Birmingham, Alabama, a few days later. The President thus had the South besieging him on his right, the Progressives on his left.

Truman, however, soon turned the Wallace campaign to his advantage. He had already exploited anti-Communist hysteria against government employees by establishing a Loyalty Review Board by executive order in March 1947. With no trial by jury, no hearings before a regularly constituted court, and no review or appeal to higher courts, the board pursued the same totalitarian philosophy it was supposed to be rooting out.

Now Truman could use the Communist label that the Republican Right had long tried to pin on him by going after the Progressives. In effect, the President stole the Republican's most flamboyant technique.

"I do not want and I will not accept the political support of Henry Wallace and his Communists," Truman announced on March 17. "He [Wallace] ought to go to the country he loves so well and help them against his own country if that's the way he feels," Truman added 12 days later.

He reserved the master stroke for July 20, three days before the opening of the Progressive party convention, so that no one could miss the point. A federal grand jury created the year before by Attorney General Tom Clark handed down an indictment against twelve Communist officials, six of whom were arrested that evening. The indictment, under the Smith Act of 1940, charged that the defendants "did conspire" as the Communist party of the United States "to teach and advocate the overthrow and destruction of the Government of the United States by force and violence." The American Civil Liberties Union (ACLU) immediately branded the Smith Act unconstitutional, and Mike Quill condemned the arrests as "the first step in a reign of terror similar only to Hitler's Reichstag fire scare."[11]

Truman also interpreted the Smith Act to make ex-Communists deportable and launched a wave of deportation cases against Communist party members or people who had been members decades before, no matter how brief or casual their allegiance. To emphasize the Wallace connection, Ferdinand C. Smith, a black National Maritime Union officer, was arrested on March 1, the day after he had spoken from the same platform as the Progressive candidate. The 16-year drive to deport Harry Bridges, another dedicated Wallace backer, had started in 1934, but Truman pursued it with special vengeance until the courts overruled him in 1950.

The pattern set by the White House focused anti-Communist hysteria on the Progressive party. Columnist Dorothy Thompson called the Wallace campaign "a mask for communism." *Collier's* magazine labeled Wallace "the voice of Russia." The Scripps-Howard chain and other newspapers printed long lists of Wallace petition-signers, subjecting them to threatening community pressure and even loss of jobs. This barrage achieved the expected result—a Gallup poll showed that 51 percent of the public thought the Progressive party "communist-dominated."

Firings increased on college campuses—assistant professor James Barfoot of the University of Georgia and professor Clyde Miller of Teachers College, Columbia, among others, lost their jobs as a result of Progressive candidacies or affiliations. When Wallace spoke at Evansville, Indiana, on April 6, 150 pickets crashed the coliseum, roughing up Baldwin and a number of ushers. After a cross was burned on his lawn, a black editor running for the U.S. Senate in Macon, Georgia—the first black candidate there since Reconstruction—had to employ a permanent bodyguard. Professor Curtis D. MacDougall, a candidate for the Senate, was struck by 10 stones, and others in his party were stoned or slugged, while being run out of West Frankfort, Illinois. "I told the mob that I now know what it was like in Hitler's Germany," MacDougall concluded. "The fever of hate and hysteria over their faces was appalling."[12]

Anti-Communism was transformed into legislation through the Mundt-Nixon bill, introduced by freshman Congressman Richard M. Nixon (Rep., Cal.), who branded Wallace "a fellow traveller." The bill not only required the registration of Communist party members but of "Communist-front" organizations—the only criterion for this listing being the attorney general's edict, with no appeal to the courts on his decision possible. "Its objective," Wallace insisted, "is to frighten all the American people into conformity and silence." It passed the House in May 319 to 58, but died in the Senate, only to be incorporated two years later into the McCarran Act.

The Communist issue would decimate the Progressive campaign. Exploited by Truman, the press, and even the CIO and ADA, it imprisoned Wallace and kept him increasingly on the defensive. He insisted again and again, "The Progressive Party is not controlled by Communists nor was its convention or program directed by them." His opposition to political violence was clear—"I do not accept the support of any person or group advocating the violent overthrow of the government of the United States." Contrary to claims he never criticized Russia, he condemned many aspects of Russian policy—thought control, slave labor, the Cominform's opposition to the Marshall Plan, which he thought "probably a propaganda mistake."

He constantly expressed his hatred of totalitarianism—"I detest the whole idea of dictatorships. . . ." At the same time, he asked more objective analysis of the concept of a monolithic world Communist conspiracy run from Moscow, which obsessed White House strategists for the next two decades. Insisting in prophetic words that "the Chinese Communists are pro-Chinese rather than pro-Russian," he concluded, "It by no means follows that a victory for the Chinese Communists would place Russia in control of the country."[13]

Although denying Communists controlled the Progressive party, Wallace refused to join the red-baiting pack. "If I fail to cry out that I am anti-communist," he announced in Los Angeles, "it is not because I am friendly to communism, but because at this time of growing intolerance, I refuse to join even the outer circle of that band of men who stir the steaming cauldron of hatred and fear." He would obviously have profited by excluding the Communists from the Progressive coalition: he once suggested it might lose him 100,000 votes but gain him 3 million. Still, he insisted that Communists had the right to vote for him or anyone else: to force them out of the coalition would destroy his democratic principles.

The red label was ironic because Wallace was a devout, often conservative defender of the American system. He supported a strong military force—"greater than any aggressor could possibly match." He spoke up constantly for "free enterprise," once in a speech as secretary of commerce using the words six times in two paragraphs. He insisted that the Progressives were the best hope for "independent business enterprise, free trade unions, and a productive capitalist economy."[14]

Yet Wallace could never escape from the devouring pressures of the cold war, which forced him into defensive and often naïve positions. Nothing hurt him more than the Czechoslovak crisis.

The Eduard Beneš coalition government in Czechoslovakia was admired in America as the symbol of independent, democratic traditions living under the Soviet shadow and still cooperating with the West. In a free election, the Czech Communists won 38 percent of the vote. After three anti-Communist parties tried to bring down the coalition, the Communists accused the National Socialists of provoking armed revolt. On February 25, Premier Klement Gottwald formed a Communist government. On March 10, Foreign Minister Jan-Masaryk either jumped, fell, or was pushed to his death from a window at his office. Benes resigned two months later.

Czechoslovakia was certainly geographically critical to Soviet defense, and even Senator Robert Taft, leader of conservative Republicans, called the takeover a "consolidation step," but the Communist

coup was an indefensible provocation in the cold war. It forced
Congress to rush through appropriations under the Marshall Plan
and gave the extremists a long-sought opening. Former Secretary
Byrnes, for one, called for "action" in case of threats to Greece or
other western bases, explaining that action meant the use of arms.[15]

Soviet security undoubtedly required a Communist Czechoslovakia eventually. But with effective power at Prague already in
Communist hands, the coup was precipitate.

Wallace reacted by defending Russia's security needs. But he went
further, excusing the coup as a reaction to a rightist plot, which he
claimed had been fostered by U.S. Ambassador Laurence A. Steinhardt. Actually Steinhardt had been away from Prague from November 24, 1947, to February 19, 1948. This was hardly an airtight
defense in the light of later revelations of CIA intervention in Chile
and elsewhere. But lacking facts to link Steinhardt to the coup, and
suggesting Masaryk's death might have been a cancer-motivated
suicide, Wallace seemed like a clumsy apologist.

Except for such occasional lapses, Wallace's foreign-policy statements were constructive and imaginative. Seeking a formula that
would break through East-West confrontations, he appealed directly
to Stalin in an "open letter" on May 11 that contained a blueprint
for both superpowers, including arms reduction, outlawing methods
of mass destruction and export of weapons to any country, and
international relief through the United Nations. Surprisingly, Stalin
answered the appeal on May 17, calling Wallace's suggestions "a
good and fruitful basis for such an agreement and for the development of international cooperation. . . ." In a decidedly conciliatory
tone, Stalin concluded, "The coexistence of these systems and a
peaceful settlement of the differences between the USSR and the
United States are not only possible but also doubtlessly necessary in
the interests of general peace."[16]

The Wallace-Stalin letters seemed like a remarkable breakthrough. They sent a thrill of expectancy through the country, offering Truman a firm basis for negotiation. Yet the President ignored
the letters and refused the chance for a summit meeting, just as he
had done the week before when Foreign Minister V. M. Molotov
suggested "a discussion and settlement of the differences between
us."

Wallace also hammered at international relief. Warning that the
Marshall Plan would be used as a political weapon, he proposed
instead that $5 billion a year for 10 years be administered through

a UN reconstruction fund on the basis of need, not politics. He opposed the draft and universal military training as further escalation of the cold war. He urged the government to give military aid to the Jews in Palestine, constantly demanding that Truman recognize the Jewish state (he finally did on May 14). He called for repeal of Taft-Hartley, criticizing organized labor as "more interested in fighting Russia and Communism than it is in getting social justice for the working man. . . ." He branded the Truman Doctrine a "long, slow, painful, national suicide."

Wallace's vision, unfortunately, was constantly thwarted. In late June, climaxing a jurisdictional squabble over four-power control of Berlin, the Soviets blocked all freight and barge traffic into the city, cutting off its food. Stalin undoubtedly considered the blockade a counterstroke to the Truman Doctrine. The President thought Russia "might deliberately choose to make Berlin the pretext for war." He ordered an armada of planes to shuttle food and supplies into the city, an emergency airlift that continued until Russia lifted the blockade a year later.[17]

The crisis focused national sympathy on beleaguered Berlin, the enemy only a few years before but now the center of resistance, and further dampened Wallace's call for peace. By the time the Progressive party convention opened on July 23, Wallace's standing in public-opinion polls had dropped to its lowest point.

The more than 3,000 delegates and alternates rode special trains to Philadelphia. The Pennsylvania Railroad usually designated its specials by color, but to avoid a "Red Special," the line renamed its trains the "Common Man" or "World Peace" specials. The same sensitivity induced Marcantonio to change a meeting of his rules committee at the Bellevue-Stratford from the Pink Room to the Green Room.

It was a boisterous, youthful convention—the average delegate was no older than 30—a convention more reminiscent of a country hayride than a smoke-filled room. They were mainly housewives, teachers, students, veterans, union officers, black business and professional people. They chanted endlessly, "One, two, three, four, We don't want another war." They waved exotic signs: "Armenia to the Armenians." They mocked other candidates in song. On Governor Dewey: "One thing I just cannot take—A mustache bigger than a candidate."

At Shibe Park on July 24, 32,000 packed the climactic rally, paying $30,000 in admission and contributing an added $50,000. Paul Robeson sang Loyalist songs from the Spanish civil war and "Old Man River," which he had immortalized. Wallace, driven around the ballpark in an open car while the crowd "shouted until it could scream no more," as one reporter noted, exhorted his followers to fulfill "the dream of the prophets and the founders of the American system."[18]

One unique product of the system was the Progressive vice-presidential candidate, Senator Glen Taylor of Idaho, who had made his living as a cowboy singer. He brought his troupe to Shibe Park—his wife, three small sons, and his brother. The son of an itinerant evangelist preacher, Taylor had no formal education after age 15. He had worked as a welder in a California plane factory, but mainly he roamed Idaho with his troupe, sleeping in his car at night among the sagebrush and rabbits. "In fact, had it not been for those jack rabbits, we might well have starved to death," he admitted.

He had twice won the Democratic nomination for senator but lost to Republicans before being elected in 1944. He played his guitar at political rallies and dramatized his rural background by riding his horse up the Capitol steps in Washington. "I am not leaving the Democratic Party," he announced on joining Wallace. "It left me. Wall Street and the military have taken over."[19]

Considering the accusations of Communist dominance hurled at the platform committee, the Progressive platform was amazingly moderate. The committee was chaired by Rexford Guy Tugwell, a prominent New Dealer and former under secretary of agriculture, with Lee Pressman as secretary. Three different drafts of the platform had been prepared ahead, one in New York, one in Chicago, one by Leo Huberman and Paul Sweezy, editors of the Marxist *Monthly Review.*

Their combined efforts on foreign policy included a disarmament agreement to ban the atomic bomb; internationalization of the Dardanelles, Suez, Panama, and other trouble spots; the control of the Ruhr by the Big Four; a unified homeland for the Irish; indemnities for Japanese-Americans detained during the war; and the "right to independence" for Puerto Rico.

On domestic policy, the platform supported the Townsend Plan's $100 a month for persons 60 years and older; the vote starting at age 18; national health insurance; federal aid to public schools; rigorous price controls; more Tennessee Valley authorities, particularly in the

South; federal legislation to wipe out the poll tax, lynching, and racial discrimination in employment, the armed forces, and inter-state travel; the closing of tax loopholes; public ownership of tideland oil; and "raising women to first class citizenship."

Almost all these planks were adopted years later, or came close to adoption. Those that failed, like internationalization of the Suez Canal and public ownership of tideland oil, might have spared the nation considerable anguish if they had gained more support. The only plank that could be tabbed "radical" was public ownership of major banks, railroads, and electric power and gas systems. Even this plank seems less controversial today, with the development of feder-ally sponsored railroads like Amtrak, and the increasing appeals for government aid by manufacturers like Lockheed. The irony is that Wallace's bitterly criticized "mixed economy" has become essential to industry itself.

Liberals were vehement against Wallace. Professor Adolf A. Berle, Jr., New York State Liberal party chairman, accused Wallace of being "a front for an international intrigue." Tugwell, who had resigned from ADA in February, attacked ADA's "resort to un-scrupulous and demagogic denunciation worthy only of the cheapest of politicians—insincere, hypocritical and immaterial."[20]

The liberals seemed driven to outdo conservatives in their fury. Often Communist party members or leftist allies in the past, they seemed consumed by guilt and a disillusionment with the Stalin régime that could only be expiated by the intensity of their hatred. Their tactical objective, they claimed, was to destroy Wallace in order to keep Dewey out of the White House. But their emphasis on anti-Communism and the Wallace campaign as the presumed men-ace generally blinded them to loyalty purges, FBI assaults on civil liberties, and support of dictatorships in Greece and elsewhere.

Liberals often cited as prime evidence of Communist domination at the Progressive convention the rejection of the "Vermont resolu-tion." Presented on the floor by three Vermont delegates, it stated: "Although we are critical of the present foreign policy of the United States, it is not our intention to give blanket endorsement to the foreign policy of any nation." It was an intelligent demurral, but the point had been reasonably covered in a plank already accepted: "Responsibility for ending the tragic prospects of war is a joint responsibility of the Soviet Union and the United States."

Tugwell, therefore, called it "redundant." Baldwin and Marcan-tonio, who were off the floor at meetings, later stated they would have supported it if present. But even if the resolution had passed, which it probably should have, it would have had no practical effect in diluting the pro-Communist charges hurled at the new party.[21]

Progressive party policy was made by Wallace; Baldwin; Ralph Shikes, the director of publicity; Lew Frank, the main speechwriter, and to some extent by former Governor Elmer Benson, Fitzgerald of the UE, Elinor Gimbel, and Jess Gitt, a Pennsylvania publisher. None was a Communist.

The real controversy centers on John Abt and Lee Pressman. Abt, a soft-spoken lawyer and son of a wealthy manufacturer, became Sidney Hillman's legal expert at Amalgamated Clothing after holding government jobs in Agriculture, the Works Progress Administration and NLRB. Before joining the Progressives, he made it clear his wife was editor of *Soviet Russia Today* and his sister public relations director of the Communist party. Wallace still wanted him. When Abt and Pressman were grilled before HUAC and refused under the Fifth Amendment to answer questions about Communist ties, Wallace again refused to accept their resignation.

Pressman had secured enormous power at CIO headquarters—the last link to the Left unions—before Murray fired him in February 1948. Murray's respect for him had been so great that he never called Pressman to his office but walked down the hall to see him. Murray wept at the firing. At the CIO, Pressman adopted the trappings of a business tycoon—expensive clothes, an immaculate, almost empty desk top, and an imperiousness that disturbed friends, particularly when he ordered around servants at their homes. He would later admit to brief Communist party membership during government service in the 1930s—ironically, Wallace had fired him from Agriculture. In the same testimony before HUAC, he named three Communists, including John Abt.[22]

Abt and Pressman had considerable influence on Wallace, but there is little evidence they pushed Progressive policy to the left. The strongest push came from Marxists like Sweezy and Huberman, and both soon dropped out of active campaigning. No other dominant figure ever tried to radicalize the Progressives, including Marcantonio. Intent on rolling up a large vote for the ALP, he took little interest in Progressive strategy. The Communists certainly had real power, but on a local, not a policy level, in areas of New York, California, Pennsylvania, Massachusetts, and Colorado. They were organizers and local functionaries, not master planners.

While anti-Communist hysteria increased that summer with charges that Alger Hiss, a former State Department official, had belonged to a prewar Communist cell in Washington, Wallace invaded the South. He became the first presidential candidate to insist on black voting rights. No other party since Reconstruction had placed so many blacks on its slate. If it accomplished nothing else, the Progressive party gave an urgency and dignity to the civil rights struggle that prepared the way for later advances.

The Progressive campaign was actually a continuation of the registration and voting drives of the 1930s. In North Carolina alone, Wallace needed petitions signed by 35,000 registered voters just to get on the ballot. A million leaflets against segregation were distributed in Georgia, resulting in hundreds of arrests. Ten Progressives were abducted from a house in Augusta and might have been beaten critically if state police cars had not arrived in time. Black unionists from the Tobacco Workers in North Carolina, International Longshoremen in New Orleans, and Oil Workers in Texas formed the core of the Progressive drive.

Senator Glen Taylor first tasted violence on May 1 in Birmingham, Alabama. When Eugene ("Bull") Connor, the public safety commissioner, ordered segregation for a black youth conference, Taylor entered through a door marked "colored" and was seized by police. He identified himself as a United States senator but was still dragged to a police car, found guilty by a police court judge, and fined $50 with a 180-day jail sentence eventually suspended.

Wallace toured seven southern states from August 29 to September 3, speaking to 30 unsegregated meetings in 28 cities and making 12 radio broadcasts.

In North Carolina, where the governor opposed violence, a National Guard sergeant with drawn revolver and four plainclothes police escorted Wallace to a Durham meeting. Afterward, it took almost an hour for the escort to get Wallace through a howling mob and fistfights to his car. At Burlington, he was pelted with eggs and tomatoes on Main Street and could never give his speech. At Charlotte, there were three arrests, and a Progressive worker was badly stabbed. "Am I in America?" Wallace asked.

Although the municipal auditorium had been hired at Savannah, Georgia, for an unsegregated audience, the police cut the microphone cord, lowered the curtain, and dragged the chairman from the platform. The next day in unsegregated black halls, Wallace addressed two audiences of 1,000 each.

Forbidden to use any unsegregated halls in Memphis by E. H. ("Boss") Crump, Wallace drew 2,000 people outdoors at Bellevue Park. His car was rocked, his windshield smashed as he left. He was allowed no unsegregated meetings anywhere in Mississippi but Vicksburg, where 125 people heard him on the courthouse lawn. Later, he flew to Houston and El Paso, where his audience of 4,000 made up the largest unsegregated political gathering since Reconstruction.

Wallace returned to a triumphant rally at New York's Yankee Stadium on September 10. "Fascism has become an ugly reality— a reality which I have tested," he announced. There had already been 20,000 in the stands the night before when a drenching rain caused postponement. The second night, 48,000 people paid $70,000 admission and donated $60,000 more—undoubtedly the largest paid mass meeting in New York political history. Summing up the southern campaign, Paul Robeson concluded, "Wallace has marched into the Southland and given hope to Negroes all over the land."[23]

In Los Angeles on October 2, Wallace addressed a paid audience of 22,000; only 16,000 had come to hear Truman for free at the same stadium the week before. Such figures, however, were illusory, since they reflected hardcore support in strongholds like New York and California. All polls showed that Wallace had slipped badly.

The President had succeeded in exploiting Wallace's most vulnerable point—that a Wallace vote would ensure a Republican victory. "Don't waste your vote," Truman urged at Los Angeles. Insisting that Communists had "lined up solidly to put a Republican President in the White House," he concluded at Oklahoma City: "The Communists want a Republican administration because they think that its reactionary policies will lead to confusion and strife, on which communism thrives." Later surveys showed this approach had cut deeply into the Progressive vote, that even devoted Progressive workers at the moment of reckoning in the voting booth had pulled the Truman lever.

Truman achieved another brilliant stroke—he virtually stole the peace issue from Wallace. Although rejecting a summit meeting after the Wallace-Stalin letters in May, the President asked Chief Justice of the Supreme Court Fred Vinson on October 3 to head a peace mission to Moscow. At the same time, the White House booked all networks for a half-hour of radio time for a major statement. Truman later claimed that Secretary of State Marshall had opposed the mission, and that a press leak and consequent cries of "appeasement" from the Republicans had forced him to cancel the trip. The cancellation supposedly embarrassed the President. But whether by design or not, a seeming blunder actually "made the Democratic Party the peace party to assuage the anxieties of the voters," Thomas L. Stokes, the columnist, concluded.[24]

Meanwhile, the Progressive command, desperate to eradicate the image that its congressional candidates were "spoilers" intent on defeating liberal opponents of the Marshall Plan, announced a wholesale pullout in local races. Actually, the Progressives already supported Democratic candidates in many areas—six in New York, for example, including Paul O'Dwyer, the mayor's brother. And in California, they had invited liberals like Chet Holifield and Helen Gahagan Douglas to cross-file on the Progressive line but had been turned down.

Now the Progressives announced that in 26 out of 35 marginal districts they would pull out their candidates and either endorse or not oppose the Democrats. This was particularly important for Holifield and Douglas, and in Connecticut, for Chester Bowles in his race for governor. In Minnesota, where Progressives under Governor Benson had lost control of the Democratic–Farmer-Labor Party in what many claimed was a stacked decision, the Progressives pulled out of the Senate race against Hubert Humphrey. To approve this move, Left Progressives outvoted the Right, "another bit of evidence to confound those who insist that the Wallace movement was a communist plot to elect Republicans," MacDougall claimed.

Nothing seemed to help at this point. The returns on election day were a devastating blow; Wallace received only 1,157,140 votes nationwide, or 2.38 percent. Truman was reelected in a startling upset, winning 49.51 percent of the votes to Dewey's 45.13 percent. Senator Strom Thurmond on the States Rights line even outpolled Wallace with 2.40 percent.

No important Progressive candidate survived except Marcantonio. With a three-party coalition against him in the Bronx, Rep. Leo Isacson went down to defeat. Although Marcantonio was prohibited by a new state law from running in another party's primary without approval of its county committee, he managed to block the opposition from uniting on one candidate and won with 36,000 votes in a three-cornered race. Further, the ALP accounted for over half a million votes in New York State, about half of Wallace's national total.

Legal and technical obstructions denied Wallace a considerable number of votes. In Illinois, the courts had ruled him off the ballot completely, wiping out a reasonable share of 300,000 votes Progressive judicial candidates had won the year before. In Ohio, the courts allowed only an "independent electors" list with no Wallace identification; the resulting confusion probably invalidated about 150,000 votes.[25]

In Missouri, with 53,000 petition signatures and a Progressive vote of about 4,000, Progressive officials had documented evidence of locked lines on voting machines and fake counts that stole thousands of votes. The worst thefts probably occurred in the South—Georgia, for example, with 80,000 petition signatures recording 1,600 votes.

Was the Wallace campaign and all its agony worthwhile? On the prime issue of peace, Baldwin contended, "We won for the world that precious gift of time." His estimate may be exaggerated, just as the threat of a Russian war was probably exaggerated. Yet Wallace undoubtedly forced Truman in the last months to reshape his image into that of the peace candidate, to soften his get-tough policy through numerous compromises like the settlement of the Berlin blockade.[26]

If the Progressive party had polled 4 to 5 million votes, it might have not only slowed down the cold war but established a new Left force, independent of the Communist party. The incessant problem of the Left in this period was how to develop a base that concentrated on American needs and was not dominated by Soviet policy. This had been Marcantonio's aim in New York, and Wallace and the Progressive leadership were certainly trying to work toward it. But anything close to radicalism had little chance of keeping a non-Soviet identity. The anti-Communist hysteria, exploited by Truman as well as the Right, would overwhelm all dissent.

Still, the principles Wallace forced the public to confront have gained new stature since 1948. He was a poor politician, but with his humanity, vision, and identification with global suffering, he grasped what other politicians ignored. His conception of United States foreign policy foresaw almost every problem that has arisen since. On the night of his defeat, he scribbled a penciled message to President Truman: "The destiny and salvation of the United States is to serve the world—not to dominate it."[27]

· 5 ·

The Purge of the CIO Left
1948-50

The CIO convention that opened on November 22, 1948, in Portland, Oregon, began the purge that decimated the Left unions, the main base of radical power in the country. The convention turned into a celebration of Truman's election and a bitter assault on the unions that had opposed him. "We have saved the day, and we have helped save our nation," Phil Murray announced. "Who more than the CIO brought out the vote?" Jacob Potofsky of Amalgamated Clothing asked jubilantly.

Murray, who had proceeded cautiously against the Left until now, himself, flailed those delegates who had supported Henry Wallace. Whenever a Left delegate tried to speak, the floor erupted in a torrent of boos and catcalls. Reuther bore down on the minority delegates, demanding: "Are you going to be loyal to the CIO or loyal to the Communist party?"

This, of course, was a rhetorical perversion of the real issue. What had brought the confrontation with about 900,000 members of the Left unions was their failure to back Truman and the cold war program. The real issue was union conformity. Harry Bridges of the Longshoremen reminded the convention that he had offered to support Truman if the President won a referendum of the CIO membership earlier that year—but not if the CIO board forced a Truman endorsement on every union. When the Longshoremen had joined the CIO a decade ago, Bridges had asked, "Must we go down the line on CIO political decisions on political matters?" CIO headquarters had replied, "The answer, of course, is No."[1]

But after the CIO board had rejected the third party at its January 1948 meeting, Murray had insisted that every affiliated union get behind Truman. All the Left asked was no endorsement of any candidate—the right of each union to make its own choice. Murray rebuffed them. At the CIO board's summer meeting, the pro-Truman policy became official.

In vain Fitzgerald of the Electrical Workers tried to appease the convention by stressing that only the UE's top officers, not the membership itself, had supported Wallace—a stand also adopted by some of the smaller Left unions. "If President Truman makes a sincere effort to carry out the promises he made in his platform," Fitzgerald announced in a final attempt at conciliation, "I will tell the Progressive party to go to hell, and I will be on President Truman's bandwagon."[2]

It was too late. The 1948 elections had wedded the CIO irrevocably to the Democratic administration, and Murray had decided to crush the center-Left coalition that had built the CIO in the 1930s.

The inexorable pressures of the cold war, as well as defense-production prosperity that punctured the militancy of the CIO, intensified the confrontation. The big CIO unions had too much at stake in contracts and favors from the Democratic administration to tolerate any anti-Truman harassment. Samuel Lubell, the political analyst, reported this change in two studies of Chrysler Local 7 of the UAW. In 1940, the local's headquarters exuded the spirit of street barricades and sit-down strikes. The education director lectured on "class consciousness." Strike pictures cluttered the walls. In 1948, almost half the local's members, enjoying the fruits of soaring auto sales, owned their own homes. Headquarters looked almost like a lodge hall, with pictures of union picnics and sporting events covering the walls, and cups and trophies on the shelves. The education director had been purged.[3]

This affluence particularly affected the CIO leadership. Jim Matles of the UE, at his first convention after wartime army service, was startled to find union officials ensconsed in sumptuous hotel suites enjoying steaks and champagne. Most CIO officials would soon sport robust salaries, chauffeured cars, and other trappings of the management class. Two early militants, Joe Curran of Maritime and Mike Quill of Transport, who would break with the Left, purchased a stable of racehorses and a Florida hideaway respectively.

If the economic advantage of the Truman partnership had won over the Murray régime, most of the Left unions had changed too, mainly under the influence of the Communist party. Since Earl Browder had been deposed as Communist chieftain in the spring of 1945 and replaced by William Z. Foster with his hard line against the cold war, the Left had generally adopted a rigid, almost intractable stance, bound to widen the CIO rift. This rigidity was characterized on a local level by the Communists' insistence that all unions fight a subway and bus fare rise in New York City from five to ten cents, a stance partially responsible for Quill's break with the Left. It was characterized on a national level by the Communist demand for fanatical opposition to the Marshall Plan and down-the-line support by every union member for Henry Wallace.

The Communists would not tolerate the minutest deviation in the unions they influenced. "It was in the spirit of Stalin," observed George Charney, a former Communist official. Ranking French Communists, in fact, told Charney they were amazed that the Left had allowed the Marshall Plan confrontation to be blown up to such disastrous proportions.

"The importance of the Left-center coalition was highly overrated," Matles observed. "Murray used it as long as he needed it. The Left rode along on the myth from 1939 on, enshrining it as an immutable historic development, failing to keep organizing vigorously and enlarging its base. The Left pretty much wasted those 10 years."

The Communists winnowed out dissidents endlessly. Foster after 1945 insisted on devoted party-line cadres no matter what the damage to broad coalitions—"Better less, but better," he ruled.

The principal avoiders of this strategic bungling were the Electrical Workers and Maritime Union, the only leftist unions to survive the next three decades. They always maintained a strong radical coalition of Trotskyists, anarchists, Social Democrats, Communists, and veteran Wobblies (International Workers of the World), as well as conservatives (particularly the UE locals in New England). Both leaderships were often overruled by their memberships. Bridges's opposition to the Marshall Plan, for example, never made much headway among his locals.[4]

The UE infuriated the Communist party by refusing to force a membership vote on Wallace. UE leadership, always aware that its Irish-Catholic membership in many areas was anti-Wallace, refused to risk a split. The UE also stood behind its membership no matter what their political affiliations. When two Trotskyists (ironically, the Communists' most bitter enemy) were fired as "security risks" in 1948 under Truman's loyalty program, their whole Philadelphia local went out on strike. Local 107 thus became the only union to shut down a plant on the spot by membership consensus, to take on Westinghouse and the government together, and to force reinstatement of both workers.

Still, the UE was handicapped from the start of the purge by its refusal to sign the 9-H affidavits. This made it vulnerable to raids by steel and auto. Since such affidavits were required for certification in a Labor Board election, opposing factions could easily sign up enough members at a plant to call a special election and often take away part or all of the UE's local.

Murray had always branded 9-H "a dangerous witchhunt." Yet he played a duplicitous game, seemingly deploring Reuther's raids but too intimidated to make any effort to stop him. Murray even failed to block his own Steel workers from signing the affidavits. In the end, the raids became the crucial factor that split the UE from the CIO. "If Murray had banned the raids," Matles observed, "we would have stayed in the CIO."

Although the UE claimed to have beaten off most of 456 raids in the year after April 1948, the Carey faction alone controlled 114,000 former UE members by early 1949.[5]

The Truman administration and Congress cooperated enthusiastically in these takeovers. Before the Westinghouse election in 1949, Carey and Monsignor (formerly Father) Charles O. Rice arranged with Rep. Francis Walter (Dem., Pa.) to bring the whole UE slate before the House Un-American Activities Committee, smearing the union with lurid anti-Communist headlines in the papers. "Many UE members I attacked as Communists turned out to be FBI plants," Rice admitted later. Catholic priests throughout Pittsburgh were ordered to preach against the UE. "They announced it would be a mortal sin to vote UE—the nuts took over," Rice concluded.

The administration gave further support to raids at plants with sensitive military contracts—Knolls Atomic Power in Schenectady, for example—by using the loyalty program to ban the UE as bargaining agent. On many occasions, Truman intruded openly in union elections by sending his secretary of labor to make anti-UE speeches at plant gates. The President even wrote a letter to the 1949 CIO convention backing the Carey faction—"an action rare in the history of the Presidency," Louis Koenig commented.[6]

Hypersensitive and insecure, Murray needed the White House as a crutch. His policy completely reversed the fervent independence of John L. Lewis, who had kept the CIO removed from government influence, even Roosevelt's. Murray had started as little more than a secretary to Lewis. He never sought power and often seemed to fear it. Yet his hunger for status required that he address Lewis as "Jack" while other CIO officials were restricted to "John." Murray's break

with Lewis became the most traumatic experience of his life; for
months afterward, he was physically and psychically ill. Lewis remained a phantom always haunting Murray.[7]

Deeply patriotic and staunchly Catholic (with friends in the hierarchy like Edward Cardinal Mooney of Detroit and Richard Cardinal Cushing of Boston), Murray was convinced by 1948 that Soviet
policy made war inevitable. He was equally convinced that the Marshall Plan was America's first line of defense.

Torn by the conflict between political reality and his own kindly
impulses, "Murray's wounds were always close to the surface," a
former aide observed. He depreciated himself constantly, admitting
that as a young official he thought a briefcase was something to carry
his rubbers in, often quoting his older sister, Mary, who liked to say:
"We are humble people." His main relaxation over weekends was to
visit neighboring miners, to sit on their porches and gossip.

Murray was born in Scotland in 1886, the son of an Irish coal
miner who emigrated to Westmoreland County, Pennsylvania, in
1902. Murray helped his father load three coal cars a day at one
dollar each; at night he studied correspondence school courses in
mathematics and economics. By the age of 30, he became a district
vice-president of the Mine Workers; by 34, a national vice-president.
He was a shrewd negotiator, always backing up his arguments with
statistics delivered in a rolling Scottish burr.

With miners still working twelve hours a day, seven days a week,
after the 1920 coal strike failed, Murray helped Lewis rebuild the
union. When Lewis made him head of the steel organizing campaign
in 1936, he forced U.S. Steel to sign a union contract that other "big
steel" companies quickly followed. But "little steel" ringed itself
with armies of company police and held out for five more years in
a bloody struggle that took 15 lives.

There was a tough grain to Murray beneath the Irish charm. As
a young man in Pennsylvania, he had struck a "weigh boss" whom
the miners accused of cheating on their accounts. Dispossessed from
his company-owned house, he was ordered out of town. When some
of his pickets were arrested during a Pittsburgh strike, Murray invaded the sheriff's office, cursed him heatedly, and told his men to
go home without interference from the startled sheriff. Although
deeply attached to Fitzgerald, Murray treated him ruthlessly once he
had committed himself to the Truman alliance.[8]

The three top officers of the UE were close to Murray in background. All shared early desperate poverty and immigrant origins;

two were Catholics. Fitzgerald, an Irish-Catholic like Murray, was born in Newburyport, Massachusetts, in 1906. Hulking, ruddy-faced, and gracious, with the same Irish wit as Murray's, Fitzgerald helped build the union at GE, became head of the Lynn, Massachusetts, local, and was still working on the assembly line when elected president of the UE.

Julius Emspak, the UE secretary-treasurer, was born in Schenectady in 1904 of parents who had emigrated from Austria-Hungary. He was brought up as a Catholic until his mother took him from the church after his father's death. Julius, a brilliant student, attended Union College and Brown for graduate study, earning his way with night jobs, scholarships, and loans.

Emspak helped organize Schenectady GE and RCA at Camden, New Jersey. When these and other independent locals met in New York in 1935, they elected him secretary of the association that became the UE next year. After a turbulent four-week strike, RCA signed with the new union. Jim Matles brought in 21,000 members of the Machinists Union.

Matles, the UE director of organization, was born in Rumania in 1909 and passed his apprenticeship as a machinist while still at high school before emigrating to New York in 1929. Lean, hard-driving, perennially youthful (at 65, his black hair was hardly flecked with gray), Matles organized Metal Workers locals in Brooklyn in the Depression. When his independent machinists were rebuffed by the AFL for an industry-wide charter, he came to the UE, and built it to 600,000 members by 1943. The UE constitution restricted its top officers to a salary no higher than any worker on the line—about $14,500 in 1975, or a fraction of what most unions pay their chiefs.

While a few dozen UE officials were open Communists, and the UE generally aligned itself with the Left, Fitzgerald, Emspak, and Matles always denied party membership.

Similarly, Harry Bridges was hounded for almost 25 years by convictions for Communist membership that were invariably overturned by the courts. In 1945, Justice Frank Murphy commented: "Seldom if ever in the history of this nation has there been such a concentrated and relentless crusade to deport an individual [Bridges, an Australian, was accused of lying about party membership] because he dared to exercise the freedom that belongs to him as a human being and that is guaranteed to him by the Constitution. . . ."[9]

The Scripps-Howard newspapers in 1946 claimed to identify Emspak as "Comrade Juniper," a top-ranking trade unionist in the Communist party," and Matles as a "veteran Communist party member as long ago as November, 1933." With Fitzgerald, they were called before a Senate investigating committee in 1947. All denied the Communist charge. They were investigated by HUAC again that year, and three more times in the next four years by a variety of congressional committees.

Emspak and Matles were finally cited for contempt by a federal grand jury in 1951, but the charges were dismissed. Both were cited for contempt of Congress for refusing to answer questions, but the Matles case was set aside by federal district court, the Emspak case by the U.S. Supreme Court. Charged with falsely swearing he was not a Communist when naturalized in 1934, Matles had his citizenship revoked until the Supreme Court reversed all charges in 1958. The courts, of course, were ruling on whether the top UE officers were Communists at that time, not whether they had been members in the past.[10]

Rep. J. Parnell Thomas (Rep., N.J.), chairman of HUAC and the most persistent scourge of the UE, did not fare as well. Convicted of illegal salary kickbacks, he was fined $10,000 and sent to jail in 1949.

At the opening of the UE's Cleveland convention on September 19, 1949, Carey, backed by Murray and the Catholic Trade Unions, called for mass secession from the UE and the formation of a new electrical union that would follow the CIO line. The Truman administration cooperated in the harassment of the Left. Delegates from 26 Canadian locals of the UE were stopped by the Justice Department from crossing the border to attend the convention.

To save itself from total destruction, the UE now voted to withhold its dues from the CIO unless Murray banned the raids. In an even more drastic step, which had to be taken for the UE to participate in NLRB elections and fight off such takeovers, the convention approved the signing of 9-H affidavits. "A bitter pill to swallow," Matles noted.

Everyone knew that the primary objective of the CIO convention in Cleveland on November 1, 1949, was to expel the Left. The attack began almost from the opening gavel. "I have waited for this opportunity for a good many years," Emil Rieve of the Textile Workers rejoiced. Reuther condemned the leftists as "colonial agents" carrying out "the needs of the Soviet foreign office." Curran castigated them for "loyalty to the Communist party."

Murray tried to explain: "There is enough room within the CIO movement to differ about many subjects, many ideas, questions of reform within the CIO, economic, social and trade union policy . . . but there is no room within the CIO for communism."[11]

But who was to define where legitimate debate about economic and social issues left off and allegiance to Moscow began? When many Americans outside the Communist party opposed the Marshall Plan, or at least wanted foreign aid administered by the UN as Wallace had proposed, should unions be purged for debating such critical subjects? What about criticism of such Truman policies as pouring huge sums into Franco's Spanish dictatorship, or rebuilding former Nazi cartels? Or the rash of pardons suddenly granted convicted Nazi war criminals?

Could a purge be based on the premise that Left unions took their orders from the Communist party when, even before the convention opened, the UE announced it was resigning from the CIO in direct opposition to party policy?[12]

No attempt was made to thrash out such questions. The Murray forces rammed through the purge by passing a constitutional amendment (Article IV, Section 4), which ruled that no officer or board member of any CIO union could be a member of the Communist party or any fascist or totalitarian organization. The CIO board was further empowered to investigate the Left and to expel any union disobeying this provision.

But leaving aside a few obvious cases like Ben Gold of the Fur Workers, an open Communist, how could the CIO pass judgment on officers like Harry Bridges, when the U.S. government in 25 years had not been able to convince the courts of his Communist links?

Even more illogically, the convention voted to expel the UE immediately without investigation or trial—although the UE had already announced its resignation and no UE delegate attended the convention. A new charter was granted the Carey faction, which would now be called the International Union of Electrical, Radio and Machine Workers (IUE).

The CIO hastened the destruction of the UE, already reduced to 326,000 members, by sending telegrams to all companies with UE contracts urging that they be broken or new elections be called. Most companies were only too happy to oblige. In this struggle between competing unions, GE and others had a rare chance to emasculate the labor movement.

Two former radical strongholds, Maritime and Transport, had already deserted the Left. Curran's break involved a curious four-year struggle. He had never been a radical, never felt really comfortable with the Left. His four top officers were avowed Communists, and he increasingly resented being used as a front man. His rising salary and taste for luxury bolstered his need for closer ties with Murray and the White House. At the same time, he was able to enlarge his base in the union by exploiting the cold war policy of mandatory security clearances for those seamen who shipped with the merchant marine.

Weakened by a violent personality clash among its own leaders and by its purge of dissidents, the Communist faction made the mistake of challenging Curran for control. It was the kind of rashness and arrogance that characterized the party in this period, the result of Foster's demands to install his hard-line policy in many unions where the Left held only nominal power.

Curran took over the national council by 1948 and within two years established an absolute dictatorship, even forcing through a resolution excluding aliens from membership. By the time he retired in 1974, this craggy, bald-headed, ex-seaman, who had once marched in May Day parades and slept on park benches with newspapers inside his jacket for warmth, took with him pensions and benefits totaling almost $1 million.[13]

Mike Quill's clash with the Left was an even more startling reversal. Once nicknamed "Red Mike," almost certainly a Communist cardholder, he was "so extreme in his championship of Communist causes," one reporter noted, "that the party itself had to cool off his ardor."

This cherubic dervish, who flaunted his shillelagh, his brogue, and a limp he claimed came from a British bullet in the Black and Tan wars in Ireland, had damned ACTU for years—"no decent Catholic would belong to it." But by 1946, ACTU had made sizable inroads in his power base, the predominantly Irish-Catholic New York Local 100. Quill viewed the challenge nervously.

The critical moment came in 1948 when Quill's surveys showed that two-thirds of his members, as well as ACTU, supported a fare rise from five to ten cents in order to get the union a wage hike. Perhaps more important, Quill found that his membership was swinging overwhelmingly to Truman over Wallace.

Yet, with the same rigidity he showed in the Curran struggle,

Foster insisted that Quill give undeviating support to both Wallace and the five-cent fare. Some of the New York hierarchy tried to argue with Foster. When the Steel Workers and other unions were getting wage raises at the expense of higher prices, why should the Transport Workers be sacrificed? Foster was adamant. Convinced he would only hold his union by joining the Truman bandwagon, "Red Mike" split with the Left. Mixing chicanery with power politics (when the Left sent out 18 telegrams for a strategic meeting, Quill cancelled it through 18 telegrams under Left signatures), he ousted most of the left-wing officers in nine months.[14]

The CIO purge, therefore, had few targets—the Fur and Leather Workers also resigned before the trials began. The objective in each trial was to prove that the accused union had slavishly followed the Soviet line from supporting the Russian-German pact in 1939 to opposing the Truman Doctrine and Marshall Plan. The Left based its defense on the autonomy principle—that the CIO constitution controlled only federation policy, not union policy.

Such legalistic debate seemed meaningless, since the expulsion of the Left was a foregone conclusion. "The committee decision to recommend expulsion was so certain," reported Paul Jacobs, then on the CIO staff, "I began to work on the writing of it while the trial was still in progress." By 1950, 11 unions had been purged, costing the CIO about 900,000 members out of a total of 5 1/2 million (although Murray would claim that 70 percent eventually returned to the fold).[15]

The Left unions had been virtually eliminated as an independent force. Only Bridges's Longshoremen—so dominant on the West Coast that even the McCarthy frenzy hardly touched it—maintained and increased its strength. The UE, although battered for a decade by raids and even radical defections, gradually fought its way back to an influential position and a membership of 180,000. Mine, Mill and Smelter survived independently for a while but was eventually swallowed up by Steel and other unions. The Fur Workers eliminated their Communist leadership—Ben Gold was supposedly incensed that the Communist party pressured him to resign because of his overt Communism—and then merged with the Amalgamated Meat Cutters and Butchers in order to attain respectability within the AFL-CIO. The weaker Left unions joined with stronger allies or simply disintegrated.

Surveying this debacle years later after apologizing for his part in the purge and breakup of the UE, Monsignor Rice concluded: "The CIO became part of the McCarthy hysteria. It was tragic that the Left was crushed. The CIO needed opposition and criticism. An ideal union requires strong opposition."

But were opposition and criticism enough? The CIO Left before 1950 had, of course, built some highly effective unions that fought —often brilliantly—for wage gains and other standard objectives of the labor movement. Even the dissenting leadership of the Fur Workers—Richard B. O'Keefe was one of two members of the International Board who refused to support Wallace—could boast: "I think we have the best, fightingest, progressive, democratic union in the country."[16]

The Left also had its share of failures—the United Public Workers and the United Office and Professional Workers hardly made a dent in organizing legions of white-collar employees.

The CIO Left became the main base of radicalism in America after 1935 because of its manpower, money, discipline, cohesion, and above all, its revolutionary spirit. But with all its obvious assets, the Left never fulfilled its potential.

Why was the Left so vulnerable? It was, to begin with, a victim of its own obsessions. Instead of concentrating on working-class issues, it was consumed by international policy. Instead of meeting the needs of American workers, it worried about the strategic needs of Moscow. It overestimated the peril of war and the significance of controversies like the Marshall Plan. It involved itself endlessly in picket lines and demonstrations to block the European Recovery Program, accomplishing little more than infuriating the mass of the CIO.

Rather than a frontal assault on the Marshall Plan, which was extremely popular among most liberals and unionists, the radical unions might well have focused on its obvious flaws. By fighting for European aid through the UN, by attacking Truman's support of dictatorships like Franco, the Left would have reached a sympathetic audience in the CIO.

"Our troubles stemmed from a compulsion to turn Soviet diplomatic necessity into an American political virtue," observed Al Richmond, executive editor of the Communist *People's World* until his resignation from the party.

The two strongest unions on the Left, the UE and Longshoremen, shrewdly never became sidetracked by international obsessions.

They concentrated on organizing the unorganized. The UE signed up 150,000 new members in 1946, 180,000 in 1947, and had contracts covering 512,000 by 1948. Bridges accomplished an organizational breakthrough by recruiting 30,000 sugar and pineapple workers by mid-1946 to add to his 50,000 West Coast members. His successful 1949 strike in Hawaii gave his union a new dimension. He brought the wretched wages of the island up to modern standards. By using his union to mold the ethnic melting pot of Hawaii into an assertive political force, registering many of his members to vote for the first time, he broke the stranglehold of the planter aristocracy.[17]

In only rare cases was the Left able to focus its influence politically. After the disastrous elections of 1946, Marcantonio was really the only member of Congress on whom the Left could count. By squandering its energies squabbling on international policy, it failed to build lasting political bases. Even on the West Coast Congressman Hugh De Lacy and U.S. Senator Hugh Mitchell (both Dems., Washington) went down to defeat in 1946, foreshadowing the Wallace disaster two years later.

The CIO Left ignored new groups ripe for organization, like the migrant farm workers in the West. It offered no program for nationalization—not even for the railroads, long nationalized in Europe. It never made an issue of national medical insurance, still lacking in 1979.

The Left purge drained the CIO of its traditional force and made it almost a flaccid copy of the AFL. All meaningful debate, all minority opposition were stilled. CIO affiliates toed the line on every controversial issue and endorsed only those political positions that headquarters approved.

As a virtual partner of the administration, the CIO harnessed its unions to official government programs. Its leaders joined owners and managers in running the corporate system, contributing to "the formation of the national power elite," as C. Wright Mills pointed out. "They want in, 'just like the big shots,' to share the key decisions." They made trips to London and Paris on government assignments, lunched with the secretary of labor and the President. They took on "the hardened cynicism of political ward bosses," observed A. H. Raskin of the New York *Times.*[18]

The CIO became as much an extension of U.S. foreign policy as the AFL. Reuther received $50,000 from the CIA, Irving Brown of the AFL $2 million a year. Such funds were lavished on right-wing German, French, and Italian unions to build "an alliance with the pro-fascists in order to beat the Communists," Ronald Radosh observed.

The anti-Communist mania had so distorted the CIO that Jim Carey, its secretary-treasurer, would tell an NAM luncheon in New York in 1950: "In the last war, we joined with the Communists to fight the Fascists; in another war, we will join the Fascists to defeat the Communists."[19]

By 1951, the *New Republic* could detect "only a faint reminiscence of the CIO of yesteryear." Its southern drive collapsed. By 1953, total membership dropped below 5 million. After the merger of the AFL and CIO in 1955, the combined federations could hardly recruit 200,000 a year.

One example of the damage done by the purge was the declining union influence at General Electric. Before the purge, UE alone had represented 70 percent of the GE workforce. By 1962, UE, IUE, and other unions together represented only 40 percent.

The CIO's fading militancy produced weaker contracts. Wage increases in 1954 were at the lowest level since the 1930s. Reuther, under heavy membership pressure, had to renegotiate his unproductive five-year auto pacts two years before expiration. George Meany, the new president of the combined AFL-CIO, would boast that, "I never went on strike in my life. I never ran a strike in my life. I never ordered anyone to run a strike in my life, never had anything to do with a picket line."[20]

The munificent salaries paid union officers led Raskin to conclude: "American labor is suffering from an advanced case of hardening of the arteries." In his small union, Curran would draw $80,000 a year and a heavy expense account. Meany was driven to work each morning by a uniformed chauffeur in a union-owned Chrysler and had his own Cadillac for weekends. He wore tailor-made suits and waistcoats from London and belonged to a country club. Such costly ways of life induced union officials to build self-perpetuating bureaucracies. A federal court, in fact, had to nullify one NMU election because Curran had rigged the constitution to limit potential candidates to a fraction of the membership. By 1962, the swollen AFL-CIO bureaucracy had produced a ratio of one paid officer to 300 union members, compared with one to 2,000 in Britain. "Today unionism is big business, and its power structure resembles that of a corporation," concluded Kermit Eby, the former CIO education director.[21]

The labor movement's tragedy was that fanaticism on both sides produced a split that should never have occurred. The anti-Communist mania of the CIO and the supermilitant irresponsibility of the Left pushed the movement toward suicide. Had both sides showed restraint, the coalition might have survived until passions cooled with McCarthy's downfall, and Soviet-American relations improved. Instead the Left was decimated. The CIO became a satellite of the AFL. The labor movement never recovered from the shock.

· 6 ·

Destroying the Communist Party: The 1949 Trial

On August 27, 1949, at a bucolic picnic ground just north of the Westchester suburbs of New York City, Paul Robeson was scheduled to give a concert under Left-union auspices. Robeson and had just been a witness for the Communists at their trial. The local American Legion announced that it would stop the concert. By 8 P.M., a mob of Legionnaires and their supporters had swelled to 1,000, shouting "Lynch Robeson" and "Every Nigger bastard dies here tonight." About forty men and older boys in the audience were trying to protect scores of women and children huddled on the concert platform. It was the start of the "battles of Peekskill."

The mob attacked with fence posts and rocks, forcing the cluster of defenders back against a protective line of trucks. Although newsmen were all over the grounds, not one policeman answered an emergency call to Governor Thomas E. Dewey and local authorities. The mob piled up wooden chairs, set them on fire, and began to dance around them as if preparing for a blood-letting. Thirteen defenders were eventually injured and 14 cars overturned. Robeson's car had been stopped by a traffic jam miles away and never entered the grounds.

Not until three hours after Legionnaires barricaded the gate did state troopers arrive with ambulances. An ACLU investigation, finding no more than six policemen by 10 P.M., reported that "effective police protection" had been "deliberately withheld." The New York *Sun,* which had no sympathy for Robeson's politics, concluded: "The local and county police clearly let the demonstration against the concert degenerate into a riot."

The Left unions announced a second concert for September 4. Organized by battle-hardened Spanish civil war veterans of the Fur Workers, and particularly by Robert Thompson, a high Communist official and decorated veteran of World War II, the defense plan stationed 2,000 husky unionists in virtually shoulder-to-shoulder rings around the concert grounds. This time, the state and local police put about 1,000 officers on patrol.

Robeson, who had already been blacklisted professionally, gave his performance without incident. But the "second battle of Peekskill" erupted at the end. As streams of cars inched out through the exits, roving bands of Legionnaires and youths pelted the windshields with rocks, often unmolested by nearby police. One unionist struck in the face by a rock, was hospitalized for eight weeks and lost the sight of an eye.

At all three exits, and at overpasses for miles around, mobs bombarded the crawling cars. One car with five adults and a child, covered in blood, pulled up at a gas station to phone for help and was attacked again. Even the union defense perimeter was roughed up by police on the excuse of searching for weapons. None were found. At least 140 persons were injured, some seriously. The ACLU investigation called police security a "sham."[1]

With this sweeping denial of First Amendment rights, Peekskill became a symbol of the convulsions of that period: on the one hand, the reactions of a community programmed to mounting anti-Communism; on the other, the "let's go down fighting" desperation that often perverted the Communist party's judgment.

With the opening of the trial of its 11 top officers on January 17, 1949 (William Z. Foster, the chairman, had been separated because of his heart condition), the Communist party faced virtual annihilation. The government's case against the leadership—they had to be prosecuted as individuals, not as a party—was brought under the Smith Act of 1940, purportedly a defense against dangerous enemy aliens and long considered of dubious constitutionality by many legal scholars. It had only been applied once before, in 1941, against 18 members of the Socialist Workers party, followers of Leon Trotsky and the Communists' bitter antagonists. The Communists had pushed for conviction then; their failure to stand up for the civil rights of all Left factions now harmed their own case. Since the Supreme Court had refused to review the Trotskyists' case, the constitutionality of Smith had never been tested.

Not a single charge of violence, treason, espionage, subversion—or any act—was brought against the Communist leadership. Although the government had leaked stories of an espionage indictment since 1947, the grand jury could find no grounds. So the Communists were accused under Smith solely of *conspiracy*—a conspiracy to teach and advocate the violent overthrow of the government.

As the trial opened in the heavily guarded U.S. courthouse on Manhattan's Foley Square, Federal Judge Harold Medina repeatedly instructed the jury to pay special attention to evidence of conspiracy —the secret Communist schools, the false names Communists assumed, the false passports they occasionally traveled under. The press had already established a lurid mood of conspiracy in reporting the trials of Alger Hiss, among others, then going on in New York.

While Communist pickets circled the courthouse, Medina presided with consummate theatricality. An elegantly mustached, pink-faced man with lifted eyebrows and large, melancholy eyes, the judge traded sallies with the defense counsel at dazzling speed. He could lecture like a schoolmarm, his voice biting like a whip. Occasionally, when the defense counsel exhausted his patience, the judge would get up and walk out of the courtroom.

Medina contended that his life was in danger, citing the threatening letters he received at home. He trained for his ordeal like an athlete. Cutting himself off from all social life, he went to bed each night after dinner. He had lunch alone in his chambers (always a lamb chop and spinach) and napped at least half an hour afterward.[2]

Medina baited the Communist leadership and defense counsel frequently—one observer noted that his face turned beet-red at these moments. In fact, Medina's prejudices were so obvious that when the case reached the U.S. Supreme Court, Justice Felix Frankfurter observed, "The trial judge should not have combined in himself the functions of accuser and judge. No judge should sit in a case in which he is personally involved."

The defense counsel were hardly blameless themselves, generally acting more as an extension of the Communist party than as an independent legal defense. Justice William O. Douglas criticized "the spectacle of the bench and the bar using the courtroom for an unseemly discussion of ill will and hot tempers."

In addition, the jury-selection system was badly warped. Federal juries in the southern district of New York traditionally drew on such aristocratic sources as *Poor's* list of corporation directors, the *Social Register,* and *Who's Who in New York.* The Federal Grand Jury Association, which arranged for corporations to put executive personnel on jury duty at full pay, showed its slant in its publication, *The Federal Juror,* with editorials against unions and low-rent housing. Of 23 members of the grand jury that would indict the next group of Communist leaders, there was not a single manual worker or black.

One juror, a theatrical producer and author named Russell Janney who would subsequently vote to convict the Communist leaders, stated during the proceedings that anti-Communism required "a fight to the death." An actress who saw him frequently at this time and wrote 89 pages of notes quoted him as referring to "those goddam Communists." Despite Janney's prejudice, Medina refused to remove him for a substitute juror.[3]

Medina's crucial influence on the trial was his interpretation of the words "teach" and "advocate" under the Smith Act's conspiracy provision. He ruled the defendants could be guilty if they aimed at or taught the overthrow of the government "as speedily as circumstances permit," and that a "sufficient danger of substantive evil" called for conviction.

This ruling not only cut sharply into the boundaries of free speech; it virtually made the "clear and present danger" test—the doctrine accepted by the Supreme Court since 1919—a dead letter. In Medina's interpretation, "clear and present danger" was not meant to protect "professional revolutionaries" but only impulsive and hot-headed agitators for reform. Or, as the circuit court of appeals later suggested, this interpretation would allow a wild speech from an old-fashioned soapboxer, but not from a Communist official.[4]

The Supreme Court majority eventually watered down "clear and present danger" to the far looser yardstick of "the gravity of the 'evil,' discounted by its improbability." Yet Justice Black would insist: "No matter how it is worded, this is a virulent form of prior censorship of speech and press, which I believe the First Amendment forbids."[5]

Since there was no charge of violence or subversion, the government's case depended on a "battle of quotations." The prosecutors read to the jury innumerable books and pamphlets, many written before the 1917 Russian Revolution and employing such phrases as "smashing the state machinery." The prosecutors intended to prove that the language of conspiracy and revolution in other countries had been the program of American Communists since 1945, when the party had been reshaped following its wartime years of cooperation with the White House.

This interminable Marxist rhetoric was dumped on the jury day after day. It would have taken them years to read it—if they could ever have fathomed the dialectic. And from "this process of piling inference upon inference," as two legal scholars pointed out, the jury would be "convicting defendants who, so far as the record shows, never uttered a word while they were members of the Communist party, or if they did, said only what many citizens are saying every day in the week."[6]

To link the defendants in this and later trials with the Marxist language of revolution, the government produced a battery of paid informers. Herbert A. Philbrick, for example, a slight, curly-haired young man from Massachusetts who had been an FBI plant for nine years, would earn a fortune from movie, magazine, and newspaper sales of his story. Louis Budenz, an ex-*Daily Worker* editor, made $20,000 from magazine articles, $17,000 from book royalties, $24,-000 from lectures, and considerable witness fees.

Although the conspiratorial picture given by these witnesses buttressed the government's case, many former Communists like Manning Johnson and Paul Crouch damaged the Justice Department by perjury in subsequent cases. In fact, after Johnson identified Harry Bridges at a Communist meeting, the longshore leader was able to prove by newspaper clips and affidavits that he was addressing a union meeting far away at that moment. Harvey Matusow, who would implement his career as a witness with a brief marriage to one of Senator Joseph McCarthy's chief financial backers, later recanted most of his testimony. In sworn affidavits, he admitted he had lied when he called a Mine, Mill and Smelter official a Communist at his trial and in his statements about two defendants in the "second string" Communist trial. As a result, the two defendants, already jailed, had to be retried and reconvicted.[7]

The Communist presentation at the first trial was as long-winded and garbled as the government's. Foster, despite his heart condition, tried to direct every strategic detail from the ninth floor of party headquarters on Manhattan's East 12th Street. Instead of focusing the defense on First Amendment rights, which could have built a broad base of support among liberals, he insisted that the trial be used as a platform for Communist dogma. He damaged the defense further by including interminable expositions of Marxist theory that made the defendants seem like pawns in an international intrigue.

On October 14, 1949, the jury voted conviction. Medina handed down the strongest sentence allowed by law—five years imprisonment and $10,000 fine for all defendants except Thompson (given three years because of his combat record and Distinguished Service Cross in the war).

In addition, Medina punished the six defense attorneys, who had harangued him during the trial probably as much as he had baited them. Acting as accuser and judge, he gave them jail terms for contempt of court ranging from one to six months, seriously damaging their legal careers. Such punishment raised a larger issue after Attorney General Clark urged that state bar associations take any Communist defense counsel "to the legal woodshed." Would lawyers —even political conservatives—defending an unpopular cause now be subject to disbarment? Would defendants soon find it impossible to find counsel willing to face such risks? "For when men are so hated that they are limited in their choice of a lawyer to those willing to risk their livelihood to defend them," Professor Fowler Harper of Yale Law School pointed out, "their rights are seriously impaired."

The structure of justice was further imperiled when the attorney general asked the removal of Federal Judge Delbert E. Metzger after he lowered bail for seven accused Communists in Hawaii. President Truman abetted such pressures by refusing to reappoint Metzger at the end of his term.[8]

The Communist leaders in New York carried their case to the appeals court, where the conviction was upheld, and finally to the Supreme Court. On June 4, 1951, in its *Dennis* decision (named after Eugene Dennis, the prime defendant), the Court affirmed the conviction by a six to two vote (Justice Tom Clark not participating since he had brought the indictment as attorney general). The decision was bluntly political, weighing the potential threat of the Communist party against the resulting limitations on free speech. Chief Justice Fred Vinson, justifying the convictions, placed the "highly organized conspiracy" of the party in the context of the cold war: "the inflammatory nature of world conditions, similar uprisings in other countries, and the touch-and-go nature of our relations with countries with whom petitioners were in the very least ideologically attuned. . . ."

This meant that the government could now suppress liberties according to its own definition of a political threat. But how far could the fear of such a threat be extended? Justice Douglas in his minority opinion warned: "But never until today has anyone seriously thought that the ancient law of conspiracy could constitutionally be used to turn speech into seditious conduct. . . . Not a single seditious act is charged in the indictment." Justice Black concluded: "The [First] Amendment as so construed is not likely to protect any but those 'safe' or orthodox views which rarely need its protection. . . ."[9]

The Communist party reacted rashly. Convinced, with some reason, that the government intended to jail its leadership and that the country stood "on the edge of the precipice" of fascism, the party ordered four convicted defendants (Thompson, Gilbert Green, Gus Hall, and Henry Winston) to jump bail and go underground. Hundreds of other national and state officials, not yet arrested, were also ordered underground to take assumed names and sever all ties with their families and anyone else except the small party cell to which they were assigned. The bail jumping was a self-destructive decision, supporting the government's picture of a conspiratorial band. It hurt the chances of other Communists coming up for trial.

The party crisis intensified with the conviction of 13 "second string" leaders under the Smith Act on January 21, 1953. This time, however, Judge Edward J. Dimock, whose dignity on the bench contrasted with Medina's theatrics, limited the sentences to a range of one to three years.

The government's dragnet spread to city after city—fourteen convictions in Los Angeles, seven in Hawaii, six in Seattle, five in Pittsburgh. Almost 150 Communist officials were eventually arrested under the Smith Act—all under the vague conspiracy provision, with no allegation of espionage. About an equal number of alien Communists were deported. Over eight years, the government would succeed in exhausting the finances and energies of the party in legal battles. But the real havoc in this period went far beyond the Communist leadership. The government, which had made a legal party illegal, helped to stifle a broad range of radical thought. The country would have to wait for "calmer times, when present pressures, passions and fears subside," as Justice Black noted in his *Dennis* dissent, before First Amendment liberties could be restored "to the high preferred place where they belong in a free society."[10]

The Federal Employee Loyalty Program, which had been established by President Truman in 1947, probably gave one public official —the attorney general—the most unchecked power ever exercised in U.S. history. Dorothy Bailey, who had worked for the U.S. Employment Service and became the first person to be discharged from government service under the loyalty program, was denied trial by jury, the right to know the evidence against her, the right to confront her accusers or even to know their identity. Despite such broad destruction of constitutional rights, only 378 people were dismissed by mid-1952 after an FBI check on 4 million federal employees. The loyalty board chairman admitted that no case involved a hint of espionage.

But much as Truman tried to appease Republican reactionaries with his own brand of anti-Communism, he was assaulted by forces beyond his control. The collapse of Chiang Kai-shek's resistance in the spring of 1949 and the proclamation of Red Chinese sovereignty over the mainland that September produced a feeling of panic in many Americans—a conviction that our muddled policy had led to disaster, that "reds" and "pinks" in the State Department were somehow to blame. It was a thesis that the Republicans would use increasingly against the President and Democratic candidates after him.

Truman's position was eroded further by the announcement on September 23, 1949, that the Russians had developed their own atomic bomb. The public had long been saturated with propaganda on Soviet scientific incompetence, and America's exclusive possession of the bomb stood as a symbol of American dominance. Now the prospect of two superpowers with equal weaponry intensified the panic.

As a result, when Rep. Harold Velde (Rep., Ill.) announced that Soviet spies were "infesting the country," his hyperbole was generally believed. When Governor Val Peterson decided to use martial law against local Communists, numbering about 25, Nebraskans accepted the action as necessary. There was little protest about the denial of a visa to a Los Angeles minister who had been invited to speak at the hundredth anniversary of Unitarianism in Australia, since such suppression was State Department policy.[11]

The forces of suppression, whether they originated with Republican extremists or the government, built their own momentum, until fear itself congealed into public policy. The process was fueled by the case of Alger Hiss, indicted in December 1948. Here was the symbol of New Deal aristocracy, a graduate of Johns Hopkins and Harvard Law School, founding secretary of the UN Conference on International Organization, president of the Carnegie Endowment for International Peace, a confidant of Supreme Court justices, Governor Adlai Stevenson (Dem., Ill.), and Dean Acheson—now caught in a mystifying web spun by Congressman Nixon and Whittaker Chambers.

The Hiss trials—the first in 1949 ended in a hung jury, the second in early 1950 ended in a conviction and five-year jail sentence—actually resulted from a perjury indictment. Chambers, a self-confessed former Communist and a *Time* editor with a history of psychological conflict, had from 1939 to 1948 been accusing Hiss of belonging to a Communist cell in Washington. But Chambers never said he had been a Communist himself after 1937, nor claimed that either he or Hiss was involved in espionage. Chambers later changed his story after Hiss filed a libel suit against him. Chambers then claimed Hiss passed him classified documents in 1938—an obvious contradiction—as well as in 1937.

The charges against Hiss—chewed over by HUAC and Nixon, with splashy headlines in the press before the case reached the courts—were based on a nightmarish tangle of microfilms (the notorious "pumpkin papers") and a missing Woodstock typewriter (on which the incriminating documents were supposedly typed.)

This maze left many legal scholars unconvinced of Hiss's guilt. In 1978, in fact, Hiss would file a *coram nobis* petition, asking the federal district court in New York to overturn his perjury conviction, maintaining that his Fifth and Sixth Amendment rights had been violated on the basis of new evidence obtained under the Freedom of Information Act.

Among a mass of revelations from hitherto secret FBI-Justice Department files, there was considerable evidence that the government had employed informers who "infiltrated" Hiss's defense staff; and that the much-publicized Woodstock typewriter—which may have been planted on the defense, and which became a decisive factor in the conviction—could not have been the Hiss typewriter. All this evidence was concealed from Hiss and his attorneys, who introduced *a* Woodstock typewriter for the defense under the belief (later claimed to have been mistaken) that it was *the* Woodstock typewriter Hiss and his wife had once owned.

There was further evidence in 1978 that many of Chambers's statements to the FBI about his Communist past—he was the only witness to testify to any Communist or unlawful activities on Hiss's part—were totally inconsistent with Chambers's trial testimony. There was also further evidence that the government permitted perjurious testimony to be presented to the court and jury—some of it from Edith Murray, the only witness to place Hiss and Chambers together except for Chambers and his wife.[12]

In 1978, these revelations would throw serious doubt on Hiss's guilt. But in 1950, the general public considered the Hiss case the ultimate proof of Communist penetration into respectable Washington officialdom. The case gnawed at the country's sense of security and showed many Americans that the supposed cancer of subversion had gone deep indeed.

This wave of fear seemed confirmed by the case of the British scientist Dr. Klaus Fuchs, who pleaded guilty of violating the British Official Secrets Act in March 1950. Then came the arrests of Harry Gold, David Greenglass, Morton Sobell, and Ethel and Julius Rosenberg, whom the press inferred—largely through the FBI's misleading announcements—were Fuchs's American confederates. Yet no evidence of this charge was ever brought in court. The Rosenberg death sentences would make the issue of disloyalty a national mania.

Local witchhunts, given a mantle of legality by loyalty-oath ordinances in at least 33 states and innumerable communities, swept through colleges, schools, and civil service ranks. Often conducted by American Legion posts and PTA officers, these hunts provided no jury trials or due process of law and meant instant dismissal for anyone refusing the oath.

In New York City, 100 teachers were forced to resign although there was no proof they had tried to indoctrinate their students.* At the University of California, nearly 150 professors were dismissed, resigned in protest, or refused appointments. A faculty member at the University of Virginia, passed over for promotion, lashed back at three professors with charges of Communist affiliations.[13]

The most terrifying aspect of the loyalty hunt was that almost anyone could become a grand inquisitor, and almost no evidence was needed to set off an inquisition. The movie industry, whose backbone had already been crushed by the trials of the Hollywood Ten, shelved a picture on Hiawatha after six months of work because its theme of peace among warring Indian nations might be taken as Communist propaganda. When three ex-FBI agents established themselves as the watchdogs of radio and television, listing hundreds of actors, writers, and directors in their *Counterattack* bulletins, network executives were paralyzed with fear. A single accusation that a suspect had attended a left-wing dinner a decade before was enough to bring blacklisting by the networks and advertising agencies.

The hunt had many categories of victims. It went to absurd lengths —the leading actress on radio's "Aldrich Family" was fired not because of Communism (a charge quickly proved false), but because

---

*Many were reinstated in the 1970s after the laws sanctioning their dismissals were declared unconstitutional by the U.S. Supreme Court in 1967 and 1968.

she had become too "controversial." More tragic was the case of Philip Loeb, a star of "The Goldbergs." Unable to find work after being blacklisted, and with an institutionalized son to support, he committed suicide in a New York hotel.

As the hunt grew in anger and irrationality, "the forces that seek to whiplash the American people into a blind acceptance of the anti-Communist police state," as Carey McWilliams pointed out, went after all factions of the Left, all dissent, all "dangerous" thoughts. James Kutcher, an open member of the Socialist Workers party who had lost both legs in combat at the Italian front, was fired as a clerk in the Veterans Administration and not-cleared until 1956. Old-line socialists, liberals, even the ADA—which had made a fetish of its anti-Communism but opposed Medina's refusal to grant bail to the Communist leadership—all came under attack. A Los Angeles TV station owner fired a woman employee who refused to sign his loyalty oath, although she had long been an active Republican.

The overall objective was total thought control. "The miasma of thought control that is now spreading over the country is the greatest menace to the United States since Hitler," observed Robert W. Hutchins, chancellor of the University of Chicago.[14]

The Communist party's decline was almost as much the result of internal corrosion and strategic blundering as external assault. It had been triggered by an article by Jacques Duclos, a prominent French Communist, in the April 1945 issue of *Cahiers du Communisme.* Demanding a return to the traditional class struggle of orthodox Marxism, through which a radicalized proletariat wars against the bourgeois master-class, Duclos ridiculed the popular-front concept of Earl Browder which had dominated the party during World War II. In all probability, Foster had supplied the evidence and rationale for the article to Moscow through go-betweens.

No one in the U.S. Communist party before or since held so much power as Browder. He had been enshrined as a folk hero. The party extolled his American roots going back to the Colonial period and even adapted as its slogan, "Communism is 100 per cent Americanism." To dramatize his objective of peaceful coexistence between capitalism and socialism, Browder converted the party into the Communist Political Association and seemingly rejected the class struggle. He considered Roosevelt the symbol of a new leadership guaranteeing the popular front. Through long-term collaboration between the Soviets and the United States, Browder aimed at a slowly evolving socialism that would win over both labor and the liberal middle class.

Now the Duclos article, interpreted as a signal from Moscow, heralded Browder's downfall. Foster, the only prominent official who had quietly clung to the hard line of class struggle all these years, seized control. At the national committee meeting on June 18, 1945, the verdict was obvious. Browder sat in a corner of the room, isolated by a ring of empty chairs, greeted by no one. In February 1946, he was expelled from the party as a "social imperialist."

William Z. Foster, the new party chairman, was born in Taunton, Massachusetts, in 1881, the son of an immigrant Irish father and a mother of English-Scottish stock. Raised as a Catholic in the slums of Philadelphia, Foster quit school at the age of 10 and worked as a farmhand, lumberman, dockworker, and seaman. He joined the Socialist party at 20, drifted into the ranks of the Wobblies, and then organized the Chicago meatpackers for the AFL. His principal achievement was organizing the steelworkers' strike in 1919, which eventually failed but laid the groundwork for the successful CIO drive later. He helped found the U.S. Communist party, studied in Moscow in 1921, and was sent as an emissary to the fledgling party in China. By 1928, he had reached the top of the American hierarchy. He was chosen as its presidential candidate that year and again in 1932.

Tall, slender, and handsomely patrician, although an unimpressive speaker, Foster stayed aloof from most party officials. Perhaps his only close friend was Robert Thompson, his tough, abrasive, often sulky alter-ego, who carried out his unyielding policy. "Foster lived in a make-believe world of his own . . . strangely remote from his own land and people," one official commented. He dominated the party, brooking no opposition. Self-centered and consumed by a hunger for status, he turned out streams of books and pamphlets, determined to be recognized by Stalin as the leading Marxist in the western hemisphere.[15]

Foster seemed obsessed by the need for Kremlin approval. Once when an editor of the *Daily Worker,* often critical of Foster's policy, attacked his tactics, Foster snapped, "What's the matter with you guys? What will they think of me over there?" The editor retorted: "The important thing is what they'll think here."

This was the crux of the rift that tortured the party—whether it should adapt to American political needs or be a slavish echo of the

Kremlin. Eugene Dennis, the general secretary, struggled to find a unifying ground. A commanding figure, tall, robust, and ruddy-faced with a mop of gray hair, he was painfully shy, and his weak voice rendered him ineffective at party councils. Irresolute in standing up to Foster, his chief contribution was the formulation of position papers that tried to temper the chairman's hard line with the phraseology of compromise.

Cut off from the reality of American politics, Foster never understood that the party would have to find its own independent road to socialism if it were to survive. Addicted to Marxist rhetoric that had little application to the present crisis, he was constantly attacking "right opportunism," often a semantic abbreviation for the attempt by Left unions to hold their forces together under the cold war barrage. At the moment that the CIO Left was faced with expulsion, Foster launched his own hunt for heretics among union leaders. With his passion for dedicated cadres purged of nonconformist taint, he once eliminated 86 percent of the membership of a Communist club at a major steel plant. Max Gordon recalled that some New York unionists were so revolted by Foster that they paid their party dues directly to the *Daily Worker.*

Foster insisted on treating the Chinese and North Vietnamese as appendages of Moscow rather than as fervent nationalists building their own forms of socialism. This unshakable rigidity alienated liberals during the early Communist trials when the party needed them most. Some indicted Communists like George Charney, acting on his own behalf, contacted Norman Thomas, who turned out to be "keen and eager to help." The Socialist leader, as well as other liberals like Eleanor Roosevelt and the Reverend A. J. Muste of the Fellowship of Religious Reconciliation, who considered the Smith Act unconstitutional, eventually raised defense funds and enlisted ACLU support.[16]

Foster's drive against heresy could be shockingly petty. When screenwriter Albert Maltz, later imprisoned as one of the Hollywood Ten, insisted in a 1946 *New Masses* article that literary content need not be dominated by political tactics, the outrage at party headquarters was so violent that Maltz apologized in a second article for his critical apostasy.[17]

Foster's concept of party infallibility sealed his divorce from reality. At no time before or since had the American party been so inculcated with the belief that its program followed the "Dialectic of History," that the class struggle would inevitably lead to the supremacy of the proletariat, and that the party was the vanguard of the struggle. Persecuted beyond any precedent in the American past, convinced that his party alone knew the road to salvation, each member became the embodiment of the driving force of history. Reduced in numbers from about 80,000 to 54,000 by increasing defections, Foster's own purges, the terror of FBI infiltration, and the relentless spying of one Communist on another, the party developed steel-like discipline but lost contact with the masses.

After the first Smith trials, Foster regrouped the party in cells of three—each of the top three in each area in touch with three below, and so on down the line—and then tightened his structure further by abolishing clubs or "fractions" in the unions. This obviously increased discipline. But by purging many fringe members, it had the disastrous effect of cutting off the lower leadership from rank-and-file unionists.[18]

Just as the party was being terrorized from without by the Smith trials and McCarthyism, Foster initiated an almost hysterical witch-hunt of his own—the notorious "white chauvinism" purge. As always, Foster's aim was to purify the party further. But more important, he had to scourge the party for its failure to make any headway in the organization of blacks.

The purge, lasting from about 1948 to 1953, was bitter and often trivial. One New York State committee official, for example, with 20 years in the party, was removed from his post for telling an off-color story at an affair honoring a black woman union leader. Ironically, at a time when the party was ignoring the crackdown against Jewish institutions, journals, and writers in Russia, the purge harassed and often crippled the effectiveness of the predominantly Jewish, New York membership. The damage was intensified by the fact that "the mantle of spokesmanship on Negro affairs" had been assumed largely by white Communists, often Jewish, "thus burying the Negro radical potential deeper and deeper in the slough of white intellectual paternalism," Harold Cruse pointed out.

The basic problem, however, was the long-range failure of the party's black policies, which seesawed back and forth between unproductive positions. The Communists had for a while embraced the concept of an "oppressed nation" in the Black Belt of the South, a vague concept that approached black problems as if they were solvable by separatism and independent statehood. Still, the Communists always insisted that black liberation could only be won as part of the total working-class struggle for a Marxist order. Then Foster pushed the oppressed-nation approach again after World War II—*Political Affairs,* the party's academic journal, heralded it as "a great leap forward." Yet black recruitment lagged dismally. The party claimed 15,000 black members in 1946, although the figure was probably inflated.[19]

In the midst of the Communist struggle for survival after the Smith Act convictions, it seems inconceivable that Foster could have alienated Vito Marcantonio, the last important radical politician. Yet Foster increasingly called Lillian Landau, Marcantonio's chief aide, to party headquarters after 1948 and castigated her so sharply for tactical errors that she finally refused to see him. Foster also ordered Communists in the American Labor party to take as many key positions in local clubs as possible during Marcantonio's campaign for mayor in 1949.

Marcantonio himself misjudged his chances. Convinced that the two major parties were about to disintegrate as the Whigs and Democrats had done before the Civil War, and eager to follow his mentor, La Guardia, to City Hall, he expected to run up about 850,000 votes, or enough to win in a three-way race.

Marcantonio's campaign, however, failed to sway the city's large Jewish and Italian-American blocs. He underestimated the extent to which he had been smeared by the Communist label, and even the continuing impact of the murder of Joseph Scottoriggio. (A Republican worker in Marcantonio's district, Scottoriggio had been assaulted on election-day morning in 1946 and died a few days later. Although the assailants were never discovered, and no evidence linked Marcantonio to the attack, he was constantly branded by the press for his "flying goon squads" and "underworld machine.") As a result, he ran a poor third with only 356,423 votes, far behind both the winning Democratic candidate, William O'Dwyer, and the Republican-Liberal.

With the total fury of the cold war now concentrated on one congressman ("Marc is a world figure," the *Daily Mirror* had written), his political life hung precariously on the 1950 House campaign. All three opposing parties combined against him with a single candidate, a former Democratic state senator named James Donovan. The press hammered at Marcantonio savagely. One paper claimed he hung Karl Marx's picture behind his desk—it turned out to be Giuseppe Garibaldi. Kate Smith interrupted her nationwide radio broadcast to call for his defeat. When two Puerto Rican nationalists tried to assassinate President Truman, the press discovered that one had been an ALP registrant and linked his name to Marcantonio's by innuendo.

The statistical odds—Marcantonio had polled 38 percent of the vote previously—were too huge to overcome. Although he increased his share to 42 percent, he went down in defeat with 35,835 votes against 50,391.[20]

The tensions between Marcantonio and the Communist party had been aggravated even before the election by a drop of almost 100,000 in ALP registration, mainly in the Communist-led clubs. Marcantonio accused the Communists of secretly cutting the ALP candidate for mayor (a new race necessitated by O'Dwyer's resignation). When the 1952 draft resolution of the CP's national committee criticized "the rigid 3rd party line that had no sound foundation," it signaled the end of Communist support for the ALP. Foster now called for a "mass coalition policy" that would "unfold the struggle for peace within the Democratic party" and the Liberal party and ADA as well. For Foster, the ALP had ceased to be a "major vehicle." The Communists had come full circle, returning to the Browderite concept of influencing a major party rather than being isolated in a dwindling Left.

It became an open break with the 1953 mayorality elections. When a *Daily Worker* editorial urged union members and the Left to back the Democratic candidate, Robert F. Wagner, Jr. (who won easily, leaving the ALP candidate with a pitiful 54,372 votes), Marcantonio called a press conference to blast the "double-cross" of a "minority" in the ALP. He refused to name them but obviously meant the Communists. Then Marcantonio announced his resignation from the ALP.

It was a bizarre ending for a party that had been born at the behest of Franklin D. Roosevelt in 1936 and for almost two decades had been the most powerful, radical political force in the country. Once again Foster's irrational strategy had killed off an important coalition base.[21]

For all intents and purposes, the Communist party was impotent. Yet, to look ahead briefly, it gained some recompense at the conclusion of the Smith Act trials. The California Communist leaders went to court in 1952, convinced that they had to reverse the error of Foster's strategy and fight their case wholly on First Amendment rights. Foster opposed them as always. They had the further obstacle of a particularly vindicative judge, who kept them in jail 104 days without bail until the Supreme Court intervened. They lost in federal district court, getting the usual five-year sentence and $10,000 fine. Again the judge refused bail until the appellate court overruled him.

When the case reached the Supreme Court in 1955, the defendants decided that their total concentration on First Amendment rights required a lawyer unassociated with the Left and committed to a constitutional test. They secured Augustin Donovan, an impeccably conservative Republican, a former vice-president of the California Bar, and a prominent lay Catholic. Even Foster had switched his line now; his spokesman in *Political Affairs* admitted that the *'central'* issue was and is the Bill of Rights and the Constitution.[22]

It was also a different Supreme Court, presided over by Chief Justice Earl Warren. Strengthened by President Dwight D. Eisenhower's three other appointments, the Court had already proved itself sensitive to libertarian issues in its unanimous opinion outlawing school segregation.

On June 17, 1957, the Court voted six to one to acquit five defendants (two justices did not participate). While not explicitly overruling *Dennis,* the *Yates* decision (named for the prime defendant, Oletta O'Conner Yates) modified it so drastically that the sedition sections of the Smith Act became null and void.

Justice John Marshall Harlan for the majority drew a firm line between "the advocacy or teaching of abstract doctrine" and "concrete action," concluding: "The essential distinction is that those to whom the advocacy is addressed must be urged to *do* something, now or in the future, rather than merely to *believe* in something." The clear-and-present danger test had finally been restored to the high, preferred place given it by the Court almost 40 years before. While not going as far as to sanction "complete freedom of expression for all ideas," which Hugo Black supported, the Court established that the First Amendment was a shield broad enough to protect any views on the principles of government, no matter how radical.[23]

But the ruling was too late to stave off the disintegration of the Communist party, already the victim of its own internal blunderings as well as of the cold war.

·7·

"A Cowed and Frightened People"— The Agony of Radicalism 1950-55

The remnants of the Progressive party met in convention in Chicago's chilled and shabby Ashland Auditorium in February 1950— 1,000 delegates keeping up their spirits by singing "Glory, Glory Hallelujah" during every gap in the speechmaking. There was little glory left. By the end of the year, there would hardly be a Progressive party. Although many non-Communist radicals, socialists, and other proponents of dissent had still not recognized the signs, they would soon be warned by the advertisement of a leading aluminum company: "Socialism is dangerous; it leads to communism."

In an all-consuming drive against communism that would soon battle any form of dissent, an alliance of government, business, and, to an increasing extent, big labor had harnessed the nation in the cold war against the Soviet Union. By 1953, the Packinghouse Workers, a tough-minded union still conformist enough to escape the CIO purge, lamented: "We are rapidly becoming a nation of cowed and frightened people. . . ."

Henry Wallace came to the Progressive convention in 1950 determined to erase its Communist image. Insisting in his keynote address that "we are not apologists for Russia" and that both Russia and the United States ("the two big brutes of the world," as he called them) had "made mistakes in foreign policy," he concluded: "We believe in progressive capitalism, not socialism." This cautious approach, a retreat from the few socialist planks of the 1948 campaign, disturbed most radical delegates as well as the Communist minority. But Congressman Marcantonio whipped all factions into line to hold party unity, and Wallace's diluted platform was accepted.[1]

This unity was short lived. When the Korean war erupted in June and President Truman pronounced it indisputable proof of the Soviet Union's drive for world domination, Wallace made a startling shift in support of American intervention. The Progressive party's national committee refused to assign blame to either North or South Korea until an investigation had been completed and called for an immediate cease-fire by both sides. Wallace rejected the statement and resigned from the party. Soon he was backing Truman's massive rearmament program and sanctioning atomic bombing in the Far East if military strategy required it.

Wallace's defection in 1950 sealed the collapse of the Progressive party. It had produced no other leader who could rouse a national audience against the cold war. Most Progressives voted for Democratic nominee Adlai Stevenson in 1952; Vincent Hallinan, the Progressive candidate and a flamboyant San Francisco lawyer who represented Harry Bridges, polled a dismal 140,000 votes. The Communist party had little influence among Progressives at this point, but soon branded the 1952 campaign a mistake. The Progressives never put up a presidential candidate again.

Still, in strictly local races with sharply delineated issues, the Progressives could produce sizable returns at the polls. In California in 1950, they drew 600,000 votes for a Communist on a nonpartisan ticket, running for state superintendent of public instruction. Again in 1952, they polled 560,000 votes against Senator William Knowland in obvious protest against his fanatical support of war on the Chinese mainland.[2]

In New York, the ALP's senatorial candidate in 1950, black historian Dr. William E. B. Du Bois, polled 220,000 votes. Thus in two states alone that year, radicals won almost a million votes.

The outbreak of the Korean war on June 25, 1950, provided the final rationale for Truman's claim that Soviet aggression necessitated stifling the Left at home. But was the war dictated by the Kremlin?

The first reports to General Douglas MacArthur's headquarters in Tokyo had South Korea initiating the attack—although they were probably garbled. Truman himself, announcing the war at 4 P.M. on June 26, implied that the Korean conflict was a purely civil war and that the Russians might help end it. If the Kremlin had dictated or even had foreknowledge of the war, why had Russia continued its boycott of the UN Security Council and forfeited its veto of the UN resolutions supporting armed intervention?

On the other hand, Nikita Khrushchev's memoirs document Russia's involvement in the North Korean attack. He recalled that Kim Il Sung of North Korea had visited Stalin and "wanted to prod

South Korea with the point of a bayonet." Stalin supposedly agreed to a speed-up of North Korean armaments. The memoirs are considered authentic by most experts, but there is no proof Khrushchev reported the Stalin interview accurately.[3]

President Truman never sought or gained a declaration of war from Congress. He always insisted that the "police action" in Korea (eventually producing at least 130,000 U.S. casualties) came under his powers as commander-in-chief, but there were no solid precedents—previous incursions by the Marines into Latin America hardly involved an equal risk of international confrontation and atomic war. Even conservative Republicans like Rep. Frederick R. Coudert, Jr. (Rep., N.Y.), soon questioned the "devastating" precedent his fellow members had set by "remaining silent while the President took over the powers specifically reserved for Congress in the Constitution."

General MacArthur and the "preventive war" advocates seized on Korea as the perfect wedge to obliterate Communism in China, and perhaps Russia. But as U.S. Eighth Army troops plunged northward, Peking warned the Indian ambassador that China "would not sit back with folded hands and let the Americans come up to the border." With deliberate provocativeness, however, MacArthur attacked the Changjin reservoir and announced his "win the war" assault on November 24.[4]

MacArthur's army was overwhelmed by the Chinese counter-offensive, which recrossed the parallel in late December and recaptured Seoul on January 24, 1951. MacArthur's messages to Washington became almost hysterical, demanding the right to bomb China, invade the mainland with Chiang's troops, and even use the atomic bomb.

In a desperate attempt to force the war into China, MacArthur pressured Congress through his ally, Rep. Joseph W. Martin, Jr. (Rep., Mass.), the House majority leader. The general's letter to Martin, read on the House floor, attacked presidential policy and insisted, "If we lose the war to Communism in Asia, the fall of Europe is inevitable." By appealing to Congress over the President's head, the general challenged Truman's authority—an act of sheer insubordination. "I had to choose between MacArthur and the Constitution," Truman concluded. On April 11, 1951, the President fired MacArthur.[5]

The dismal war dragged on, bringing at least 75,000 more U.S. casualties after truce talks started in July. Ironically, Dwight D.

Eisenhower, the Republican candidate who dangled peace before an exhausted public, finally secured a truce on July 27, 1953 with the same dividing line between North and South set after World War II.

The Korean war converted the United States into an armed anti-Communist state, economically primed for war, and molded to conformity against radicalism and dissent. The $181 billion spent on Korea and the armed forces up to 1953 had guaranteed prosperity, with far more to come in the new buildup. In 1950, corporation profits after taxes soared 67 percent. "Cold war demands, if fully exploited, are almost limitless," stated David Lawrence, editor of *U.S. News & World Report.*

The "wipe-out-Russia maniacs"—as a *Nation* correspondent called them—were strongly entrenched at the highest White House and Pentagon levels. Secretary of Defense Louis Johnson spoke out for "preventive war." Secretary of the Navy Francis P. Matthews wanted first strikes against the Soviets. "It would win for us a proud title—we would become the first aggressors for peace," he insisted. The commandant of the Air War College advocated dropping the A-bomb before Russia had the chance to develop its own arsenal.[6]

On July 17, 1950, at the peak of the Korean hysteria, Julius Rosenberg, a 32-year-old machine shop owner, was arrested in New York for conspiracy to commit espionage. The Smith Act trials had never mentioned espionage. Not one of almost 150 Communist leaders on trial would ever be charged with it. There was no charge in any courtroom then or since that any Communist party official had spied for a foreign power. But the administration needed to convince the public that the Soviets had instigated the Korean war and that a network of American spies was abetting the Soviet drive for global domination. Nothing could be better timed than the indictment of two alleged Communists, Rosenberg and his wife, Ethel (arrested shortly after him), who were accused of a conspiracy that threatened the foundations of American security.

Federal Judge Irving Kaufman, in sentencing the Rosenbergs to death on April 5, 1951, would exploit the conspiracy thesis with pejoratives rarely heard from the bench: "I believe your conduct . . . has already caused, in my opinion, the Communist aggression in Korea with the resultant casualties exceeding 50,000, and who knows but that millions more of innocent people may pay the price of your treason." This was the judge's personal opinion; no evidence had been introduced in court to substantiate it.

Kaufman assumed that the Rosenbergs had passed A-bomb secrets to the Russians, and that possession of these secrets fortified the USSR in its support of the North Korean attack. Yet the government had never produced evidence that the defendants had turned over any secrets about anything to anyone.

Moreover, the prosecution's case rested on oral evidence—there was no proof in black and white. The Rosenbergs would be convicted and executed on the words of one couple—Ethel's younger brother, David Greenglass (who got off with a 15-year sentence, subject to parole in five years), and his wife, Ruth (named as co-conspirator but never indicted or punished in any way). Another defendant, Morton Sobell, Julius's classmate at the College of the City of New York, was sentenced to 30 years on the testimony of a single witness, Max Elitcher. The key witness, Harry Gold, whose unsupported oral testimony established the conspiracy, had never met the defendants and was never cross-examined. Although Gold in a previous trial had admitted becoming "tangled in this web of lies," the jury never learned of this pathological lying. None of the accusations about espionage in the whole Rosenbergs-Sobell trial was corroborated nor subject to possible refutation.

Unfortunately, the defense lawyers only proclaimed the innocence of the Rosenbergs but never challenged the government's assertion that a crime had been committed, as described by Gold and the two Greenglasses. Further, the defense never seemed to understand the far-reaching nature of the legal doctrine of conspiracy.[7]

Only after the *National Guardian*, a radical, non-Communist journal, uncovered chinks in the evidence in a series of articles by reporter William A. Reuben would the public question the process of justice. Two thousand clergymen protested the death sentence. The National Committee to Secure Justice in the Rosenberg Case maintained a 24-hour picket line around the White House. The Communist party, which nervously avoided any connection with the Rosenbergs until late 1952, joined the international mass movement of outrage. The U.S. embassy in Paris was besieged by angry crowds. London demonstrators far outnumbered the protesters during the Sacco and Vanzetti trial of 1927. During the brief interval of the stay after June 16, 1953, granted by Justice Douglas but overridden by the full Supreme Court, 21,000 telegrams urging clemency flooded the White House.

On the evening of Friday, June 19, the Rosenbergs went to their

death in the electric chair at Sing Sing prison. Protesting their innocence, they called themselves "the first victims of American fascism."

Since then, flaws in the government's case have been analyzed and
much essential evidence challenged in William Reuben's book, *The
Atom Spy Hoax,* in Walter and Miriam Schnier's *Invitation to an
Inquest,* and John Wexley's *The Judgment of Julius and Ethel
Rosenberg.* The government's case has been defended principally by
Louis Nizer's *The Implosion Conspiracy,* Oliver Pilat's *The Atom
Spies,* and Jonathan Root's *The Betrayers.* But with all this torrent
of debate, the essential fact remains: no documentary evidence has
proved the Rosenbergs guilty of committing any unlawful act. They
were convicted solely for *conspiracy* to commit espionage; not for
treason, and as a result, they were denied the constitutional safeguards mandatory in treason trials. New government documents
released after 1975 under the Freedom of Information Act tend to
support the view that their rights were denied.[8]

The Smith Act trials, loyalty oaths, alien deportations, the trial of
the Rosenbergs—all were part of a blueprint planned before the
advent of Senator Joe McCarthy. President Truman could foster his
Fair Deal image through FEPC and civil rights' planks while he laid
the groundwork for repression. Having unleashed the anti-Communist furies, the President now blamed their excesses on McCarthy.

McCarthy carried the crusade against Communism to its zenith
through ruthlessness, terror, and deceit. In pursuit of "subversives"
in the State Department, he demanded the ouster of John Paton
Davies, whose only mistake was a decade of honest appraisal of
Chiang's corrupt régime and of successful Communist organizing in
rural China. Although Davies's security file had been reviewed and
cleared nine times, McCarthy forced Eisenhower's secretary of state,
John Foster Dulles, to fire him.

After repeated promises to reveal "the top Russian spy" in the
State Department, McCarthy branded Professor Owen Lattimore of
Johns Hopkins University as "Hiss's boss in the State Department
ring" and "chief architect of Far Eastern policy" responsible for our
"loss" of China. Lattimore had never been a regular employee of the
department, but Eisenhower ordered him indicted. Lattimore fought
back through the courts and was finally vindicated in June 1955.[9]

When Dr. J. Robert Oppenheimer had his security clearance

removed in 1954 after a probe by a panel of the Atomic Energy Commission, the case became the symbol of a new level of madness. How could a scientist who led the team that developed the atomic bomb and maintained secrecy during World War II, be excoriated as a security risk?

There was more to this attack than making a youthful radical of the 1930s an object lesson for dissenters of the 1950s. It centered on Oppenheimer's supposed opposition to the H-bomb. He was being pilloried for his role on the General Advisory Committee of the Atomic Energy Commission, which included such notable scientists as Dr. James Conant, Dr. Lee DuBridge, and Dr. Enrico Fermi, and which voted unanimously in October 1949 against the superbomb. Although Oppenheimer supported H-bomb research once Truman insisted on it, he had to be punished for his earlier humanitarian misgivings about a weapon for global annihilation.

Humiliated and dishonored after he lost his clearance, Oppenheimer returned to the Institute for Advanced Study at Princeton. Seven years later, he was awarded the Enrico Fermi Award, the highest honor the U.S. government can bestow on a scientist.[10]

The essence of McCarthyism was to build a nightmare system that made the irrational a commonplace, to convince the public that believing in socialism was equivalent to acting as a Soviet agent. A Jackson, Mississippi, front-page editorial demanded: "Why the hell go to Korea to hunt Communists when the hunting is good on home grounds?" An air force lieutenant named Milo Radulovich was stripped of his commission for violating a service regulation against close association with "Communists or Communist sympathizers." His guilt, it turned out, was associating with his father and sister, who read a Serbian-language newspaper published in anti-Stalinist Yugoslavia. This evidence—never revealed at the lieutenant's hearing but finally broadcast on Edward R. Murrow's "See It Now" CBS-TV program—resulted in Radulovich's reinstatement.

When reporters from the *Capital Times* on July 4, 1951, asked people on a Madison, Wisconsin, streetcorner to sign a petition—which happened to be a copy of the Bill of Rights—all but 1 of 112 thought it some kind of subversive document that could lose them their jobs and refused to sign. McCarthy labeled it a "typical Communist stunt."

The aim of McCarthyism was not just to destroy the right but the will to dissent. The House Un-American Activities Committee called an endless succession of witnesses, particularly entertainment notables whose humiliation would fascinate the public. HUAC's purpose was to make the witness bend and break before the system.

A prime example was Larry Parks, who had achieved Hollywood stardom in "The Al Jolson Story." Pleading with the committee to let him "save that little bit of something that you live with," he tried to salvage his career by naming 12 friends as Communists. The attempt failed. Admitting that "I am probably the most completely ruined man that you have ever seen," he suffered a physical collapse, saw his future picture contracts canceled and the Veterans of Foreign Wars boycott those films already released.

Only a few stood up to HUAC without the destruction of their careers. Lillian Hellman, the playwright, told HUAC: "I have nothing to hide from your Committee and there is nothing in my life of which I am ashamed. But to hurt innocent people whom I knew many years ago in order to save myself is, to me, inhuman and indecent and dishonourable."[11]

The antiradical strategy achieved its ultimate form in Congress. The first of three laws attacking the right of dissent was the Internal Security Act of September 1950. Known as the McCarran Act after Senator Pat McCarran, it was essentially the old Mundt-Nixon bill assured passage by the hysteria of the trials. It ordered the registration of any organization or group performing "any act which would substantially contribute to the establishment within the United States of a totalitarian dictatorship." Under such vague and sweeping language, the attorney general had the power to order the registration of almost any group considered "communist action" or "front." Could "substantially contribute" include the streetcorner sale of a Trotskyist journal? Could it mean a five-dollar contribution to a legal defense fund labeled Communist-dominated?

Seven liberal Democrats, including Senator Paul Douglas of Illinois, compounded this repressive measure by arguing that the bill did not "go far enough" and adding an amendment giving the President power to incarcerate "dangerous" citizens in concentration camps in times of emergency. The liberals supposedly intended the amendment to discredit the bill, but their strategy backfired. The Republicans pushed the amendment through quickly. Senator Humphrey even wanted another amendment banning collective bargaining with "Communist-infiltrated" unions, which could have been used to decimate the union movement. This addition was withdrawn after pressure from President Truman, who skillfully played both sides of the issue. He called for an Internal Security Act in his message to Congress on August 8, 1950, then vetoed the bill to appeal to liberals. The act was passed over his veto.[12]

The McCarran-Walter Act of 1952, also passed over Truman's veto, provided for the arrest of noncitizen "subversives" without warrants, jailing without bail, and deportation to any country that would accept them. As a result, European scholars lecturing at American universities were often humiliated by being ordered out of the country on the flimsiest pretext of radical associations.

The Communist Control Act of 1954 went far beyond the two previous McCarran Acts, making individual Communist party membership per se a crime. It was undoubtedly unconstitutional on many counts, certainly for its conflict with the Smith Act. The Communist membership clause had been rammed through by liberal senators. For the first time in United States history, members of a political party would be indictable for the mere act of affiliation.[13]

One of the most distasteful aspects of McCarthyism was the enthusiasm with which many liberals, intellectuals, and former Marxists adopted its aims, if not its methods. While deploring Senator McCarthy personally, they supported some of the worst excesses of the cold war and joined in the destruction of dissent. They were absolute in their condemnation of Communism as unmitigated evil and monolithic conspiracy. There was little understanding of the divergent path to socialism already taken in Yugoslavia. There was virtually no support for coexistence; even after Eisenhower himself saw the possibility of diminishing tensions at the Geneva conference of 1954, many intellectuals awaited a final apocalyptic struggle between Moscow and the West.

These intellectuals, in fact, were often part of the alliance that molded the cold war. In the name of the "free world," they became eager tools of the holy crusade. As former radicals and even Communist party members, they played their new roles with a pure and special fury that often characterizes the disillusionment of apostates. "You are prepared to surrender the world to the Communists," retorted Professor Sidney Hook of New York University to a suggestion of compromise in his debate with Professor Stuart Hughes of Harvard.

Hook, a former Marxist, became an important symbol of the anti-Communist liberal strategy because of his leadership of the American Committee for Cultural Freedom. His book, *Heresy,* Yes,

Conspiracy, No, rejected all compromise. He condemned Thomas Mann's often-repeated stand: "I am neither a Communist nor an anti-Communist." No gradations of choice were possible, since Hook and his followers usually defined "cultural freedom" as whatever best served the interests of the United States government.

In developing his thesis that tolerated heresy (the old-fashioned soapbox speaker whose miniscule audience could do no harm) but forbade conspiracy (the Communist party and its fellow travelers), Hook drew a shaky line. It was not the speech of Communist members that made them dangerous, he insisted, but their acts and organizational ties. Their ties made them "a para-military 5th column of a powerful state, ready to strike, whenever their foreign masters gave the word." Once Hook established the world-conspiracy thesis, he proceeded to dismiss the First Amendment as glibly as McCarthy. No right under the Constitution is "absolute," he proclaimed, even the right of free speech, "when it endangers rights of equal or greater validity." Consequently, no Communist member should be allowed to teach since he is part of the world conspiracy (although mere belief in Communist principles can be tolerated).

This denial of "absolute" constitutional rights, of course, was the very bedrock of McCarthyism. If more valid rights—the security of the nation against the Soviets—took precedence, almost any injustice or suppression could be perpetrated in the name of the "free world." Once Communists were denied the First Amendment, the way was paved for suppressing socialists, radicals, militant unionists, and indeed all dissenters.[14]

The consequent erosion of First Amendment protection certainly contributed to the fate of the Socialist party. From a vote of about 140,000 for Norman Thomas in 1948, it dropped to a pitiful 18,000 in 1952 without Thomas as its presidential candidate.

Americans for Democratic Action, despite its anti-Communist vehemence against the Progressives in 1948, would still be tarred by McCarthy's cronies in Congress. The ADA, Rep. Kit Clardy (Rep., Mich.) told a HUAC hearing in 1953, "followed a party line almost identical in many particulars with the Communist party line, did it not?"

Even the American Civil Liberties Union limited the right of dissent to those who repudiated Communism. In its membership test for 1954, it only accepted applicants "whose devotion to civil liberties is not qualified by adherence to Communist, Fascist, Ku Klux Klan or other totalitarian doctrine." This sentence remained on the membership form until 1967. A similar clause, affecting "leadership and staff", dated back to 1940.[15]

Perhaps the most tragic result of Hook's thesis was the surrender of the American Committee for Cultural Freedom to the CIA and other agencies. The committee became as much a tool of the government's propaganda line as the American Communist party was for the Soviets. Hook and his associates accepted anyone with violent anti-Communist credentials—Whittaker Chambers, James Burnham, and other members who consistently praised McCarthy. They supported the State Department policy of refusing visas to many intellectuals whose links to Communism were never substantiated. When 360 prominent Americans petitioned the Supreme Court to overthrow the Internal Security Act of 1950, ACCF ridiculed the petition as a "whitewash" of the Communist party. The executive director wrote a crude defense of McCarthy's long and vitriolic harassment of Lattimore.

The final debasement of ACCF was the revelation that it had been financed for 16 years by the CIA and that two of its key figures, Melvin Lasky, editor of the magazine *Encounter,* and Michael Josselson, were CIA agents. Between 1961 and 1966, the CIA siphoned more than $430,000 to ACCF through a foundation front. The CIA's purchase of *Encounter* as a mouthpiece of American propaganda made a "mockery" of intellectual freedom, admitted Stephen Spender, the English poet who was one of its editors. "The whole wretched business seemed inescapably to point to the conclusion . . . that 'cultural freedom,' as defined by its leading defenders, was —to put it bluntly—a hoax," Christopher Lasch observed.[16]

The Socialist party was sadly depleted by its frequent allegiance to the cold war. Norman Thomas, who had made a world tour for the Congress of Cultural Freedom in 1952, secured funds from the CIA for ACCF and for his own Institute for International Labor Research (although he probably did not know the money's source). Subscribing to the world-conspiracy thesis, he backed armed intervention in Korea and favored atomic weapons to maintain the peace. Rejecting suggestions from his own supporters—like the veteran pacifist A. J. Muste, who advocated unilateral disarmament—that the party remain neutral in the East-West struggle, Thomas backed the corrupt Diem régime in South Vietnam and did not oppose U.S. intervention in Southeast Asia until 1965.

In 1952, Thomas abandoned the Socialist ticket for Adlai Stevenson. In 1956, the Socialist presidential candidate polled about 2,000 votes. A year later, when the Socialist party reunited with the Social Democratic Federation, there were barely 1,000 members.[17]

Two non-Communist groups that steadfastly opposed McCarthyism and the cold war were the *National Guardian,* a journal founded in 1948, and the Catholic Worker movement. Generally Marxist in viewpoint, the *Guardian* disagreed with the Communist party on many issues. The Worker movement had been founded in 1933 by Peter Maurin, a French peasant philosopher, and Dorothy Day, a radical writer and Catholic convert. Its newspaper, *The Catholic Worker,* at one time reached a circulation of 100,000. Day had written for *The Masses;* her roots were in the IWW and Marxism. She had visited Russia and wrote sympathetically about its achievements as well as its faults.

But Day and the Catholic Workers could never join the Communists or any Marxist party, disagreeing "with our Marxist brothers on the question of the means to use to achieve social justice, rejecting atheism and materialism in Marxist thought and in bourgeois thought. . . ."

Although devoutly religious, the Workers were scorned, or at best tolerated, by the Catholic hierarchy and often were attacked by lay Catholics on picket lines or when selling their newspaper. As natural allies of militant unionism, the Workers supported the strike of Catholic gravediggers in 1949, which Francis Cardinal Spellman of New York bitterly fought and eventually broke. Day would later criticize the cardinal's politics, particularly his Christmas trips to the Vietnam front. "Words are as strong as powerful as bombs, as napalm," she insisted. "How much the government counts on those words, pays for those words to exalt our own way of life. . . ."

The "personalist" philosophy of the Workers—that the primacy of Christian love should be infused into the process of history, even by a single, significant act—was expressed in protests against the cold war and atomic bomb. In June 1955, during New York City's annual air raid drill, a handful of Workers, joined by other war resisters, sat on benches in City Hall Park and refused to take cover. Their arrest in defiance of the Civil Defense Act, they told the judge, symbolized a small act of penance for the Hiroshima bomb. Each year they continued the protests, often spending 30 days in jail, until 1,000 protesters turned out in 1960 and the city gave up its miniature war game.

Federal tax offices were picketed, Workers proclaiming they would not help finance the H-bomb and napalm warfare. "I am not helping out in this plain murder," Ammon Hennacy stated. He combined fasting with picketing at Atomic Energy Commission sites across the country and was run out of town by the police at Cape Canaveral, Florida. Taking a back route into an Omaha missile base, he handed out the *Catholic Worker* until ejected; then he climbed the fence again at an unguarded spot and was arrested and jailed for six months.

Karl Meyer, another Worker who had been jailed for going over the fence at Omaha, would conceive a "Peace Pilgrimage" to Moscow in 1961. His group walked from Chicago to New York, then flew to Europe; on arrival in Moscow, they distributed leaflets as "an opening of reconciliation." The Workers would be among the first to burn their draft cards in defiance of federal law, a protest that became the symbol of the peace movement, producing thousands of "burners" at demonstrations across the country. Workers in Milwaukee would enter draft headquarters, seize the board records, and burn them in the street. Hennacy, who attended mass daily and often prayed for the souls of Sacco and Vanzetti and the Rosenbergs, liked to quote a phrase: "Two thousand years of Mass and all we've got is poison gas."[18]

By 1955, big labor had virtually abandoned all opposition to McCarthyism and the cold war. Between January 1953 and March 1954, a critical period of repression, only one passing reference to Senator McCarthy appeared in the United Steelworkers monthly magazine. When a Sauk City, Wisconsin, editor started to collect recall-petition signatures in his "Joe Must Go" campaign, neither the Wisconsin State AFL or CIO organizations would touch the petitions (although 335,000 signatures were quickly collected elsewhere).

Buffeted by the campaign of the Chamber of Commerce and other business interests to ban the closed shop and union shop through so-called right to work laws, the labor federations soon had their contracts binding a worker to his union weakened or dissolved in 17 states. The AFL and CIO seemed to stake their hopes for renewed militancy on merger. Merger talks had started soon after Phil Murray died in 1952 and was succeeded as CIO president by Walter Reuther. The marriage became official in December 1955. Yet, as the dominant partner, the AFL soon imposed its conservatism on the combined federation. Mike Quill of the Transport Workers protested that George Meany, the new president, was only "slightly to the Left" of Senator William Knowland.

Meany was so vehement in seeking the destruction of the Soviet Union that he could sacrifice labor's independence with the bizarre offer of a "nonaggression pact" between business and labor, enabling both to concentrate on the anti-Communist crusade. The offer was rejected.[19]

But Meany quickly allied the AFL's agents overseas with the cold war machinations of the CIA. Amply supplied with CIA funds, these agents worked "even with unions whose leadership was semi-fascist," paying Italian workers to break the strike of a Left union at Marseilles, as Ronald Radosh has pointed out. In Latin America, AFL-CIO agents constantly helped to smother social ferment. In the Dominican Republic, Meany backed a military junta in the overthrow of Juan Bosch, a social democrat, and vilified Bosch and other nationalist factions as Communists. Meany also hailed the landing of U.S. Marines, who made certain the junta controlled the country.[20]

One of the few survivors of radical unionism, the United Electrical Workers, came under increasing attack from the government's Subversive Activities Control Board, which tried to strip it of bargaining rights. But after four years of legal jockeying, the UE demanded in court that the government's charges of Communist infiltration be dismissed and won its case.

By 1955, raids and defections had shrunk the UE to a membership of 140,000. It had survived the 108-day Square D company strike in Detroit, when imported scabs turned the picket lines into a battleground, and held together during the 299-day Westinghouse strike in Philadelphia, one of the longest in labor history.

Now the AFL-CIO merger and a new Communist party line abandoning radical unions in an attempt to penetrate the labor federation brought the UE to its final crisis. Influenced by better pay and security in the AFL-CIO, and probably by the new Communist line, four UE district presidents and dozens of business agents and staff deserted the UE for the combined federation and took 50,000 members with them. It would be years before the UE, once the most powerful radical base in the country, could regain respectable influence and a membership of 180,000.[21]

By 1955 most radicals had either been exhausted by McCarthyism and the cold war or incorporated into the anti-Communist partnership of government and business. Henry Wallace, the first symbol of dissent against the cold war, retired in disillusionment to his 115-acre farm in Westchester County, New York, and even endorsed Eisenhower for the presidency in 1956. Summing up his Progressive candidacy in an article for *Life* magazine, he complained that the Communists had "ruined my campaign and destroyed the efforts of a great many truly patriotic Americans." Still, he clung to his old vision "not only of coexistence, but of competitive coexistence" at a time when Republican bombast threatened to drive Russia back to its pre-1939 borders.

As the Vietnam war intensified, Wallace increasingly criticized the government's Far East containment policy and renewed his contacts with Progressive associates. C. B. Baldwin, his former campaign manager, came to visit after Wallace was stricken with amyotrophic lateral sclerosis, a rare disease of the nervous system, at age 76. The mounting disaster in Vietnam had reinforced the wisdom of his 1948 platform. Having lost muscle coordination, including the power of speech, he told Baldwin by writing on a blackboard: "We're like Icarus. We're flying into the sun." A week or so later, on November 18, 1965, Wallace was dead.[22]

Vito Marcantonio remained unshaken in his radicalism. Returning to law practice after his defeat for Congress, he defended Dr. Du Bois and five other officers of the Peace Information Center who had been charged by the government in 1951 for failing to register as foreign agents. A dinner to raise defense funds for Du Bois, now 83 and recently fired for his radicalism after a brilliant career with the NAACP, had been scheduled for a prominent New York hotel. When the hotel cancelled and both speakers reneged, the affair had to be moved to a Harlem night club. Marcantonio proved in court that the government had failed to link Du Bois and the Peace Center with any foreign power, and the U.S. district judge granted a motion of acquittal.

Although Marcantonio's political relations with the Communist party were already strained, he became its defense counsel when it was ordered to register under the Internal Security Act of 1950. He also defended William L. Patterson, executive secretary of the Civil Rights Congress, which had been labeled a subversive organization by the attorney general. Patterson had been called before the House Select Committee on Lobbying Activities to produce CRC records. In an angry debate, Rep. Henderson Lanham (Dem., Ga.) called him "a god damned black son of a bitch" and tried to attack him physically. Still, the full House cited Patterson for contempt. When Marcantonio's defense produced a hung jury at the contempt trial, the federal judge asked the government to drop charges, and it complied.[23]

By 1954, the three-party coalition behind James Donovan, who had made a dismal record in Congress as Marcantonio's replacement, began to fall apart. Marcantonio's soundings showed that he probably had the votes to regain his seat. Launching the new "Good Neighbor" party, he secured enough petition signatures to place his candidacy on the November ballot. But rushing across New York's City Hall Park in the rain on August 9, 1954, he collapsed on the sidewalk from a heart attack and died. His briefcase holding the new petitions slithered into the gutter.

Although Marcantonio had requested a Catholic burial, Francis Cardinal Spellman (who would shortly honor Senator Joe McCarthy at a testimonial breakfast) refused a requiem mass in any Catholic church or a resting place in consecrated ground. Twenty thousand people filed through an East Harlem funeral home to view the body. Dorothy Day's Catholic Worker center on New York's Lower East Side broke the cardinal's injunction and held a requiem mass.

In Congress, those who had opposed Marcantonio bitterly now called him "truly a good American" who had "stood for the preservation of fundamental liberties" and singled out "his ever ready sympathy for the poor and downtrodden." House Speaker Sam Rayburn (Dem., Tex.) rated Marcantonio one of the three greatest parliamentarians he had ever known.[24]

Although he was vilified as a mouthpiece of the Soviet Union, Marcantonio's radicalism was rooted in a fundamental faith in the American dream. He possessed the uncompromising moral wrath of the abolitionists. Like William Lloyd Garrison, he insisted: "I will not retreat a single inch—AND I WILL BE HEARD!" Unfortunately, the anti-Communist state of the 1950s allowed few to be heard.[25] Radicalism was at a low ebb, but the rising black ferment in the South promised a resurgence. The black rebels would soon find their own revolutionary path, independent of the ideology of the Old Left.

· 8 ·

The Montgomery Bus Boycott
1955

The first meaningful black revolt since World War II broke out in Montgomery, Alabama, on December 1, 1955, over a seemingly trivial incident on a city bus. After an exhausting day at her department store job, Rosa Parks, a 42-year-old seamstress, boarded her bus downtown and sat just behind the section reserved for whites. At the next stop, six whites entered the bus. Following Alabama law, the white driver expanded the white section and ordered Parks and other blacks to give up their seats and stand in the crowded Negro section in the rear. The others complied; but when Ms. Parks refused to move, the driver called the police and had her arrested.

Rosa Parks's resistance set off a black boycott of the Montgomery bus lines that lasted 382 days. It was a pragmatic step, the result of decades of oppression and degradation that had brought the black community to open rebellion. The boycott produced the first effective black resistance by an entire Negro community of 50,000; and by striking at the core of the southern system of racial exploitation, it soon enflamed far more radical revolts.

The Montgomery boycott, and succeeding southern revolts, seem strangely remote from the orthodox Left. They spring from immediate oppression, disconnected from the Marxist mainstream of 1945 to 1955. At the same time, they have certain roots in the orthodox Left that cannot be ignored. Nationalism, separatism, and even "Black Power" originated long before 1955. While Montgomery was a cutoff point, a new beginning, an outburst of fresh and tumultuous forces infusing the black struggle with incredible energy, it must also be examined as part of a logical evolution. And the obvious starting point of that evolution is the fury of southern blacks against a system that had hardly changed despite the promises of the New Deal and Fair Deal.

The southern system imprisoned the black community. In the few

103

months before Rosa Parks's demonstration, a 15-year-old girl had been pulled off a bus in handcuffs and jailed for refusing to give up her seat. Five women and two children had been arrested on similar charges. A driver had slammed the door on a blind man and dragged him along the road. Blacks had been beaten by drivers, and one was shot in a scuffle.[1]

Such small terrors were only the surface portents of greater violence. Forty-five lynch-murders took place in the South within 18 months of the end of World War II. Just before the Montgomery boycott, Emmett L. Till, a 14-year-old from Chicago visiting relatives in Mississippi, had been found in the Tallahatchie River with a 70-pound cotton gin fan tied around his neck with barbed wire. His alleged crime was whistling at a white woman. Two white half-brothers indicted for the murder were quickly acquitted. "We have for 80 years as a nation widely refused to regard the killing of a Negro in the South as murder, or the violation of a black girl as rape," commented W. E. B. Du Bois.

The right of voter registration had been consistently blocked not only by legalities like the poll tax but by violence. In June 1950, six blacks had been pistol-whipped in Saint Landry parish, Louisiana, for trying to register, and another black who had sued in federal court for his registration rights was killed by a deputy sheriff.

A Miami, Florida, black, who had led the registration drive, had been killed in the bombing of his house on Christmas Eve, 1951. Four blacks were killed in Mississippi in 1955, among them a minister who had tried to register and vote. No convictions resulted.

Even outside the South there was violence. A mob of 3,000 in Cairo, Illinois, had stopped a black family in 1951 from moving into their recently purchased house. When 70 black students in the same city were admitted to a previously all-white school, shotgun blasts ripped the home of one NAACP official; a bomb damaged the home of another.[2]

The prospects for change had remained generally unfulfilled. An effective FEPC had been stopped by Senate filibuster from 1946 to 1950, and even a diluted version couldn't get through in 1952. President Truman had abolished racial discrimination in the armed forces by Executive Order 9981 in 1948. But the promise of this gesture was fulfilled only when the demands of the Korean war forced the secretary of the army to integrate the induction procedures of black and white troops.

Only in the courts, through persistent suits by the NAACP's legal division under Thurgood Marshall, had real progress been made. The U.S. Supreme Court decision in the *Gaines* case mandated that the University of Missouri either supply separate and equal facilities for blacks in graduate and professional schools or admit them to existing schools. The Universities of Oklahoma, Texas, and many others admitted blacks after 1948.

The U.S. Supreme Court in 1950 had also prohibited the use of curtains and signs to separate black dining-car patrons on the railroads, and in 1953 it closed the remaining loopholes in the laws against restrictive housing covenants. That same year the Court enforced an 1873 statute forbidding racial discrimination in District of Columbia restaurants.

On May 17, 1954, came the epochal *Brown* v. *Board of Education of Topeka* decision through which a unanimous Court overturned the "separate but equal" doctrine, the basis of school segregation. Affecting 17 southern and border states with laws mandating segregation, and other states where segregation had been practiced by subtler means, *Brown* was slightly strengthened in 1955 by the ruling that integration proceed "with all deliberate speed."

Still, the *Brown* decision produced a counterattack by White Citizens Councils, and the abolition of public schools in frantic opposition to the court order by many southern counties. As late as 1961, only 7 percent of southern blacks were attending integrated schools —a figure actually closer to 1 percent when border states and the District of Columbia are excluded.[3]

With such injustice, the question is why open revolt was delayed so long. Part of the reason was the middle-class character of early organizing, and its gradualist approach—the voter registration campaign of the late 1930s, followed by Henry Wallace's Progressive candidacy; the Southern Conference for Human Welfare, formed in 1938 by united fronters to advance the economic conditions of Negroes; training centers for integrated leadership like Highlander Folk School in North Carolina.

The gradualist approach was particularly represented by the NAACP, dominated by a centralized, hidebound board. Dr. Kenneth Clark, the black psychologist, called its local branches "generally archaic and generally ineffective." At a NAACP convention in Florida in 1952, one southern delegate protested: "To hell with these social gradualists, these time-not-ripers who say to take it easy! I'm not willing to follow any man who wants to go easy for me winning my freedom."

There were scattered movements to organize sharecroppers, black and white, like the Southern Tenant Farmers' Union supported by Norman Thomas's Socialists. Perhaps the most militant was the Alabama sharecroppers rebellion, organized mainly by the Communist party in the 1930s. But none of these reached the mass of black workers. None had the staff or finances to expand their programs effectively.

Only the CIO, which announced a grandiose organizing drive in 1947, possessed the forces, money, and skill to offer southern blacks a convincing blueprint of economic and social progress. The vision was short lived. Most of the organizers sent into the South were whites. They concentrated on forming white unions rather than integrated unions, with paltry success at that. The real enthusiasm for the campaign had come from the CIO Left unions, whose treasuries were depleted by their own struggle for survival after 1949. Thereupon, the CIO hierarchy, already pressured by southern white locals like the Steelworkers, gladly ditched the whole project.[4]

The Communist party made the most determined effort to radicalize blacks, focusing national attention on its defense of the "Scottsboro boys" and other legal cases in the 1930s. Organizing through the National Negro Congress and other fronts, particularly after the increasing status blacks gained in the armed forces during World War II, the Communist party achieved results far more creditable than generally recognized. It pioneered in pushing blacks for political office, finally electing Benjamin J. Davis, Jr., to the New York City Council in 1943. It also pushed blacks for high union posts like Ferdinand Smith in the Maritime Union. In the 1930s, blacks won complete equality in the NMU, Marine Cooks and Stweards, and other Left unions.

The Communists' southern showpiece was North Carolina, where black and white organizers built Local 22 of the Food, Tobacco & Agricultural Workers (CIO) into an integrated union of 10,000. Its many black officials, although largely non-Communist, were soon branded "communist-dominated." Still, the union lost bargaining rights in a labor board election at R. J. Reynolds's Winston-Salem plant by only a handful of votes. The party also had reasonable success with a segregated black AFL local of tobacco workers at Durham, an integrated CIO local of furniture workers at Thomasville, and other tobacco workers in North and South Carolina. The party was instrumental in forming the coalition that elected a black minister to the Winston-Salem City Council in 1947, probably the first since Reconstruction, and in the coalition that elected a black alderman in Chapel Hill.

No Communist vehicle had more impact than the Southern Negro Youth Congress. A training ground for young blacks, it experimented as early as 1941 with confrontation techniques, staging a sit-down on the benches of a Birmingham park where blacks could walk but not sit. Paul Robeson sang to an integrated SNYC meeting at Alabama's Tuskegee Institute in 1942, a milestone since even black organizations had always adhered to segregated seating. SNYC spawned many future radical leaders. Angela Davis's mother was active in Birmingham; Martin Luther King was strongly influenced by former SNYC members in Montgomery and Birmingham.[5]

The Civil Rights Congress, a Communist-led organization that resulted from the merger of the National Negro Congress and other groups, also established a creditable record in its defense of black defendants. CRC first intervened for the "Trenton Six," who had been arrested for murder of a New Jersey storekeeper in 1948, prodding NAACP and ACLU to handle some of the cases. Four of the six were acquitted, one died in prison, one was resentenced.

CRC also defended the "Martinsville [Va.] Seven," indicted for raping a white woman. When years of appeals to the Supreme Court were denied, the Seven were executed in February 1951. Again CRC defended Willie McGee, convicted of raping a white woman in Laurel, Mississippi. Two convictions were reversed by the state supreme court. The U.S. Supreme Court stayed the execution three times but refused to dismiss or review the case. McGee was executed in 1951.

CRC's most publicized campaign was a petition, signed by prominent non-Communist as well as Communist blacks, titled, "We Charge Genocide: The Crime of the Government against the Negro People." Recording almost a century of lynching and murder virtually supported by state and local officials, the petition was presented to the UN Secretariat in New York by Paul Robeson and to the General Assembly in Paris in 1951 by William L. Patterson, head of CRC.[6]

With all its pioneering, however, the Communist party never surmounted its flawed dogma. Its basic concept of "self-determination," the right to form an independent state in the Black Belt, locked southern members into insoluble conflicts. Self-determination artificially divided the South from the rest of the country, irritating many blacks by the concept that they had to stay in the South to struggle for nationhood since the CP opposed nationalist movements elsewhere. Communist officials never grasped the growing hunger of blacks to win power for themselves within the system.

Further restricted by the dogma that black liberation had to be part of the total class struggle, the party blotted out the possibility of Dr. Doxey Wilkerson's "unique solution." He had insisted as early as 1946 that the party failed to recognize the revolutionary potential in the struggle of submerged peoples. Whether in the South, Africa, or China, Wilkerson saw these struggles, no matter how different their approach to socialism, as a more significant force than orthodox class warfare.[7]

Junius Scales, the Communist chairman in North Carolina and an early rebel against the party line, constantly urged broad coalitions. Although top Communists ridiculed the NAACP, he had joined it as a student in 1938, urging it steadily into more aggressive civil rights action. Not until 1959 did the party abandon its self-determination dogma to hail the NAACP's "heroic leadership." Emerging from the cold war, it proclaimed "a mass policy in Negro freedom's cause" and urged enthusiastic alliance with the NAACP, Americans for Democratic Action, and other liberal groups.[8]

It was too late. The same rigidity that had crippled the CIO Left in the expulsion fight of 1949–50 depleted the party in the South. The Communist failure was particularly disturbing in North Carolina. Scales, the son of a millionaire lawyer who served three terms in the state senate, had worked since youth in textile mills as a volunteer CIO "colonizer," probably the only high party official in the South with extensive factory experience. His forebears, settling in the South in 1623, included the head of a company which owned all Kentucky and part of Tennessee at the time of the Revolution. Others had been a governor of North Carolina, a chief justice of the state, and a federal judge.

From 1948 on, national party headquarters converted Tobacco Workers Local 22 and other bases into an instrument of party foreign policy. "Every week we'd get new orders—pass a resolution against the Marshall Plan, raise money for Italian steel strikers, demonstrate against the Berlin airlift," Scales recalled. "They were going crazy lining up public support against the White House. They wanted the millennium. They couldn't seem to realize that Local 22 was more concerned with bread-and-butter issues than Berlin, that the first job was to get blacks and whites working together without tearing them apart over the cold war."

The white union leadership, much of it non-Communist, soon broke under the pressure and drifted away. The black leadership and membership was largely wiped out when Reynolds Tobacco conveniently eliminated their jobs through automation.

Scales also clashed with the Communist leadership appointed by New York. For years before 1948, the southern party chief was a New York white man, a Columbia graduate, which was particularly ironic given Foster's "white chauvinism" campaign. Then the command was turned over to blacks, principally James Jackson, the son of a wealthy druggist in Richmond, Virginia, a college-educated product of the Youth Congress. Jackson insisted on a conspiratorial party with underground meetings and secret hideouts. Scales struggled to hold a mass base.

Finally arrested by the FBI in November 1954, Scales was dragged through trials and retrials that lasted seven years. Most previous Communist indictments had come under the "conspiracy clause" of the Smith Act, whose legality was strained to the limit by the time the California *Yates* case reached the U.S. Supreme Court in 1955. Attorney General Herbert Brownell, therefore, reached for a desperate tactic to climax the anti-Communist campaign—the "membership clause" of the Smith Act. Scales would be indicted not for advocating the overthrow of the government but for the mere fact of party membership. No one had ever been jailed on such a charge.

Found guilty in federal district court, Scales fought the decision to the Supreme Court, which reversed the conviction and sent the case back to the lower courts.

Meanwhile, following a bitter split in Communist ranks, Scales quit the party in 1957. Yet Brownell was determined to make the membership clause hold up in court, and J. Edgar Hoover insisted that an ex-Communist had to repudiate his past and testify exhaustively on party membership, which Scales refused to do. After reconviction, the Scales case was argued twice before the Supreme Court, which voted five to four to uphold conviction.

Scales received a six-year sentence, longer than any of the previous Smith Act defendants. In October 1961, he entered the Lewisburg Penitentiary in Pennsylvania. He was released when a campaign headed by Norman Thomas persuaded President John F. Kennedy to pardon him on Christmas Eve 15 months later.[9]

The Communist party never dealt with the "nationalist-integrationist duality" in black communities. These two forces divided the black movement from the start, haunting not only the Communists but almost all their successors from the young militants of the Student Nonviolent Coordinating Committee (SNCC) to the Black Panthers.

At its simplest, nationalism involves proud awareness of blackness, symbolized first by the adoption of African dashikis and Afro hairstyles, later by militant symbols like the Black Power salute. Nationalism also involves the development of a distinct black culture —a theater, for example, that has freed itself from the thinking and stereotypes of the white stage. Nationalism in politics had to become an independent force, creating its own leadership and its own techniques for leading the black masses toward liberation.

The career of Dr. William E. B. Du Bois summed up the conflicts between nationalism and integration. One of the few black graduates of Harvard with a Ph.D. before the turn of the century, and subsequently a professor at Atlanta University, Du Bois organized the first militant protest against the teachings of Booker T. Washington. Dominating the black world after Reconstruction, Washington accepted the separate-but-equal doctrine and pinned his hopes for equality on vocational training. Du Bois's "Niagara movement" in 1905, which demanded full equality immediately, led four years later to the founding of the NAACP. As editor of NAACP's magazine, *The Crisis,* Du Bois was considered by A. Philip Randolph of the Sleeping Car Porters "the most distinguished Negro in the United States."

Du Bois rejected Communism during the 1920s and 1930s, even voting Republican in 1916 and 1920. But his nationalist tactics so jarred the NAACP that he returned to teaching in 1934, only to be brought back to the NAACP 10 years later. This time he clashed with its executive director, Walter White, who backed Truman and became consultant to the U.S. delegation at the UN. Du Bois, a Henry Wallace supporter who attacked White in *The Crisis* as a Truman puppet in the cold war, was subsequently fired.

Moving to the left, Du Bois became vice-chairman of the Council on African Affairs with Paul Robeson as chairman. He helped organize the World Peace Conference in 1949, headed the Peace Information Center (which led to his indictment), and ran for the Senate from New York in 1950 as the American Labor party candidate. He attacked the United States, which he called "drunk with power," for "leading the world to hell in a new colonialism," and branded the "widespread conviction that war is inevitable" as the "most sinister evil of this day."

Du Bois, a pioneer nationalist, thus became linked to the Left, whose line at the time was primarily integrationist. The administration harassed him by removing his passport in 1951—it was returned by a Supreme Court decision in 1958. The NAACP harassed him further by prohibiting local branches from sponsoring his lectures and pressuring black newspapers to turn down his articles and boycott his name. "A great silence has fallen on the real soul of the nation," he told the Community Church in Boston.

Then, as he emerged from the shadow cast by the cold war—his ninetieth birthday in 1958 was celebrated by 2,000 at New York's Roosevelt Hotel, and his bust by William Zorach was installed at the New York Public Library's Schomburg collection—Du Bois took his final, ironic steps. In 1961, he joined the Communist party. And he then gave up his U.S. citizenship and moved to Ghana, where he died at the age of 95.[10]

If Du Bois, as a scholar turned activist, hardly reconciled his nationalism with the Communists' foreign-policy demands, Paul Robeson grappled with a more crushing dilemma. His fame as an artist added immeasurably to the development of nationalism. Yet his contribution was weakened as his fame became submerged in political propaganda against the cold war.

Robeson's achievements made his name a byword internationally, like Joe Louis in boxing or Jackie Robinson in baseball. Robeson had a stature on stage, screen, and in the concert hall that no black had ever possessed. He was lionized in London and much of Europe, as well as in New York. The Soviet Union even named a mountain after him.

The son of a Princeton, New Jersey, minister, and the great-greatgrandson of a baker who supplied Washington's troops at Valley Forge, Robeson entered Rutgers College in 1915 and became probably the best all-around athlete in the country. He won 13 varsity letters in four sports and was twice named All-American end in football. He made Phi Beta Kappa in his junior year and was chosen valedictorian of his graduating class.

Virtually untrained as an actor, he reached stardom a few years later in 1924 in Eugene O'Neill's *All God's Chillun.* By 1926 he was acclaimed on the New York concert circuit, specializing in Negro music. Living mainly in London in the 1930s, close to the intellectual circles of H. G. Wells and Harold Laski and accepted as an equal by the English aristocracy, he made eight movies in Britain and Hollywood. He also starred on stage in *Porgy and Bess, Showboat,* O'Neill's *The Hairy Ape* and *Emperor Jones,* and *Othello,* which had one of the longest runs in Shakespearean history.

All this time he was enlarging his knowledge of African music and history. Under the influence of his wife, Eslanda Goode, an anthropologist, he studied 20 languages, including the Swahili and Bantu group, and was elected to the board of *The American Scholar.*[11]

Robeson's politics focused on black oppression. His enthusiastic reception in Moscow in 1934—he would send his son to a Russian school—convinced him that the Soviets had become the paragon of racial equality, a conviction he kept somewhat naïvely two decades later despite considerable evidence that the Russians were stifling some minority cultures. He increasingly attacked the brutality of America's treatment of black people, refusing to appear at concerts, in Baltimore in 1944 for example, without integrated seating. His southern campaign with Henry Wallace in 1948 produced the first decisive challenge to the segregation system.

His effectiveness in the black movement, however, was already complicated by his increasing attachment to the Left. In 1946, he testified under oath before California's Tenney committee that he was not nor ever had been a Communist party member. But HUAC and other congressional probers subpoenaed him repeatedly. To protest against the rising tide of investigations, he refused to answer any further questions on Communist links.

Already blacklisted by 1946, he found his bookings increasingly limited to radical groups. He thus became a double target: both for the hate-Russia fanatics and for southern legislators dominating Congress, who saw him as the quintessence of the "uppity Nigger" and strove to crush him.

His most flagrant sin in the eyes of cold war hardliners was to extol Soviet superiority in race relations against American failures. He caused an uproar when he announced at the World Peace Congress in Paris in 1949: "It is unthinkable that American Negroes should go to war on behalf of those who have oppressed us for generations against the Soviet Union which in one generation has raised our people to full human dignity."

Robeson's insistence on the respect due black people was fundamental to his political thinking. The indignities he had suffered molded his radicalism. Once when he was leaving his hotel to sing at a soldout concert in Saint Louis, the elevator man ordered him to use the service car. He referred to this moment frequently. His own pride became a symbol of the larger, black consciousness he wanted for his people.[12]

Soon Robeson's political entanglements virtually blotted him out of the American scene. He was the only two-time All-American not honored in the Football Hall of Fame. Langston Hughes's *Famous Negro Music Makers* and *Who's Who in America* failed to list him in this period.

No other American of international prominence, white or black, staked his reputation so completely on opposition to the cold war. Robeson's problem was that he was always fighting on two fronts: as a black, against the oppression of his race; as a political propagandist, who hewed to the Communist line, against the hate-Russia campaign that he believed was drawing us into war. His encompassing vision could not separate the black struggle from the East-West conflict. The two seemed indivisible to him.

Robeson's tragedy as an artist in the 1950s, but his achievement in the long run, was that he dared to take on a concept too far ahead of its time. With the Vietnam war, however, the connection between black oppression at home and colonialist exploitation abroad became a serious concern for American radicals and liberals. Robeson might well have become a heroic figure to the anti-Vietnam resistance had he not been slowed down by illness. As it was, the New Left, and eventually a much wider audience, came to understand his lonely struggle by the late 1960s. His reputation was vindicated in plays and books about him, and the sales of his records jumped.

Even before then, his fervent nationalism had had a profound influence on the development of resistance in the South. His refusal to sing in segregated halls intensified southern rebellion. His emphasis on African music and folklore, and the critical praise that his work achieved, quickened the pride of black audiences. Above all, his courage—he sang before an integrated audience of 15,000 in North Carolina at the peak of the anti-Communist hysteria in 1951 —stirred black communities to realize that resistance must come from blacks alone.[13]

While these links to Marxist roots should not be exaggerated, the Montgomery boycott was certainly influenced by prior organizing.

The forces building toward Montgomery were complex and divergent. As early as 1947, the Congress for Racial Equality (CORE), which was hardly radical then, sponsored an early "freedom ride" through Virginia, North Carolina, and other upper South states. The CORE protesters were integrated, with blacks sitting in the front of buses and whites in the rear. Some who refused to move their seats spent 30 days on a chain gang.

Despite its generally conservative, middle-class membership, a few NAACP chapters were developing radical tactics. E. D. Nixon, for example, a former president of the Alabama and Montgomery NAACP, had started a registration drive among blacks in 1944. Robert Williams in Monroe, North Carolina, pushed his local NAACP toward armed confrontation in 1955. There was constant interaction between middle-class blacks and radicals. Just a few months before the Montgomery boycott, in fact, Rosa Parks visited the Highlander Folk School, whose training program had a decided Marxist slant. Two veteran Marxists would be part of the Reverend Martin Luther King's inner circle during the boycott. This interaction would reach into other states—Daisy Bates, for example, who would lead the school-integration struggle in Little Rock, Arkansas, in 1957, came out of the 1948 Progressive campaign.

The boycott, therefore, was the outgrowth of a long process in which many shades of political opinion fused. Nixon and his associates had been debating the strategy for at least a year while the anger of the black community approached the breaking point. Rosa Parks's defiance was hardly accidental; her political experience and unimpeachable character made her ideal for the role. Similarly, King had taken over his Montgomery pulpit at the opportune moment. Nixon later recalled: "Well, we was doing things before Rev. King had ever finished school, come out of school. . . . The Movement didn't spring up overnight. It came up that particular night because we found the right person."[14]

Montgomery was important because it was totally a black concept, a black confrontation—not the product of a White House executive order or pressure from northern liberals. By shifting the emphasis from court challenges to direct action, the boycott introduced a new approach in the South.

Further, the boycott established the first mass base of revolt, involving every black down to the smallest child. The Montgomery blacks achieved radicalization by organizing themselves for the struggle—the day-by-day mechanics of running a substitute shuttle service with taxis and private cars was an extraordinary logistic feat in itself. The blacks became further radicalized by developing a new type of leadership, pledged to confrontation, under the Rev. Martin Luther King; and by maintaining a rigid discipline of nonviolence during a year of beatings, shootings, and bombings.

The morning after her arrest, Rosa Parks telephoned the Reverend Ralph Abernathy of the First Baptist Church and E. D. Nixon. She had known Nixon well during her own years as a NAACP officer. His militancy had been tested in organizing for the Sleeping Car Porters, and by running for office in Montgomery, the first black candidate there since Reconstruction. Although the city administration soon characterized the boycott as a NAACP "plot," Parks and Nixon had simply found a formula that many blacks had long searched for.

Nixon, Abernathy, and other leaders agreed to call a protest meeting on December 3, 1955. Attended by an overflow crowd of 5,000, it proved the depth of local anger. After speeches by almost every black minister in the city, and one white minister, King concluded that blacks were "tired of being segregated and humiliated, tired of being kicked about by the brutal feet of oppression." When the Montgomery Improvement Association (MIA) was formed for a one-day boycott of city transportation, King was elected president after Nixon turned down the office.

The son of a prominent Atlanta minister, King was just 26 years old and only recently called to the Dexter Avenue Baptist Church. He was a small man, 5 feet 7 inches tall, but his broad shoulders and muscular neck reflected tremendous power. After Morehouse College, he had become assistant pastor in his father's church. He had taken three years of graduate study at Pennsylvania's Crozer Theological Seminary and had received his Ph.D. in philosophy at Boston University. Married to the former Coretta Scott, an Antioch graduate and musician, he still was working late each night completing his doctoral dissertation as the boycott started.

Standing on his porch at 6 A.M. on Monday, December 5, King saw bus after bus roll by without a single black rider. Most passengers had grouped together in black-operated taxis, bicycled, walked, thumbed rides, or even rode mule-back. At another mass meeting that night, the MIA, realizing the power of 25,000 black riders, voted a permanent boycott to force the city to seat black passengers on a first-come, first-served basis. Now MIA had to create not only a substitute system of transportation but the cohesion and discipline to support it.

King's genius molded a minor protest into massive resistance and gave a philosophic base to the black revolt. Drawing on the teachings of Christianity, Hegel, and particularly Gandhi, King preached rebellion against an evil system—not passive resistance but active, nonviolent resistance. Its aim was not to defeat the white community but to defeat injustice; not to humiliate opponents but to gain their understanding. King's "soul force"—he couched his grander concepts in the language of old-time hymns and spirituals—required that the pain and problems of the boycott be accepted without violence or retaliation. At Montgomery and constantly in the future, he knew how to wage a national struggle in the disarmingly attractive guise of love and forgiveness.

"This is only a conflict between justice and injustice," King insisted. "We are not just trying to improve Negro Montgomery. We are trying to improve the whole of Montgomery. If we are arrested every day; if we are exploited every day; if we are triumphed over every day; let nobody pull you so low as to hate them."[15]

Organized around the churches with two mass meetings a week and 300 cars operating from 46 pick-up stations, the boycott remained almost 100 percent effective. After Parks was found guilty and fined $14, negotiating sessions with the city proved fruitless. Startled that a supposedly docile black community could maintain the boycott, officials first tried to break their unity with a fake settlement statement. Then on January 24, 1956, Mayor W. A. Gayle announced his get-tough policy. King was arrested for driving at 30 miles per hour in a 25 miles-per-hour zone, and other MIA leaders were pulled in on similar pretexts.

Gayle and the city commissioners ceremoniously joined the White Citizens' Council, an obvious invitation to violence by fanatical segregationists. Threats against King's life increased. His phone would ring at midnight, and a voice would warn: "Listen, nigger, we've taken all we want from you; before next week you'll be sorry you ever came to Montgomery."

On the night of January 30, when King had left his family alone at the house, a bomb was thrown on the porch, splitting a pillar and breaking the living room window. A crowd of 1,000 supporters quickly gathered on the street outside. Many blacks already kept guns at home, and they had come armed. One spark could have set off a riot. "They were ready to meet violence with violence," King recalled later. But he calmed them and sent them home, insisting, "We must meet hate with love." Even when dynamite was thrown at Nixon's house shortly after, King refused to arm himself, although he allowed unarmed guards and the floodlighting of his house at night.

Pushing his get-tough policy to a climax, the mayor unearthed an ancient antiboycott law, enjoining restraint of trade, and secured an indictment against King and more than 100 MIA leaders. King's case, the first, was tried in late February. The courtroom was packed with supporters wearing cloth crosses and the inscription, "Father, forgive them." Convicted in March, King was fined $500 or 386 days in jail at hard labor.

While the case was on appeal, city officials harassed the boycott further by banning black taxis for the car pool, lifting the licenses of volunteer drivers, and pressuring insurance companies to cancel their coverage.

King's lawyers, meanwhile, had consulted a white couple, Virginia and Clifford Durr, old friends of Parks and Nixon. Clifford Durr, who had been a prominent New Deal official, lawyer, and Henry Wallace supporter, was now ostracized in Montgomery for his radicalism. He aided King's suit to overthrow the state's laws on segregated buses. On June 4, 1956, the federal district court declared these laws unconstitutional under the Fourteenth Amendment. The weary boycotters saw the end at last. Although city officials appealed the decision and made a final attempt to destroy the car pool by arresting King and others for running a bus company without franchise, the Supreme Court on November 13 upheld the lower courts and abolished segregated public transportation.[16]

On December 21, 1956, King and other black leaders boarded the first city bus at the front and seated themselves wherever they chose throughout the bus. It was still too early to celebrate. Within a week, a young woman rider had been attacked, another shot in the leg, numerous buses struck by bullets. In early January, two ministers' homes and four churches were bombed. Later that month, more bombings struck black homes and a cab company stand, and smoldering dynamite was tossed at King's porch.

Although seven whites were arrested and all signed confessions, the jury declared them not guilty. "The office of the President was appallingly silent," King noted, urging that "an occasional word" on "the need for complying with the law might have saved the South from much of its present confusion and terror."

It would be months before unsegregated transportation was accepted by Montgomery and the enormity of this revolt penetrated the South. The boycott, publicized by newspapers and television throughout the world, gave King an international reputation. More important, it gave the black South a radical and politically explosive tool. Massive resistance henceforth would be adapted in many forms to future confrontations.[17]

· 9 ·

The Soviet Dream Disowned
1956-58

The failure of Communism as the driving force of the American Left —"the first secular world religion," Lewis Feuer called it—followed the Khrushchev revelations on Stalin and Soviet intervention in Hungary in 1956. The debacle reached far beyond the Communist party and its dwindling membership that had fallen to 20,000 or 30,000 in 1955. Orthodox Marxism also lost its hold on its traditional breeding grounds in labor and the universities. Disillusioned by the Soviet Union, battered by domestic repression, the students lapsed into a "silent generation." Even moderate dissent collapsed—the Student League for Industrial Democracy (SLID), a branch of the Socialist party, reportedly declined to 150 members at six colleges. Such moderate organizations as the NAACP and the Young Democrats dissolved at City College in New York, once the hotbed of radicalism, when the administration required them to file membership lists.[1]

Two Stanford University student leaders described their class in 1958 as "potentially the worst generation this country ever had." A year later, Clark Kerr, the new president of the University of California, concluded that the students "are going to be easy to handle. There aren't going to be any riots."

The working class abandoned liberalism as well as its limited class outlook in the 1956 elections. Almost half of all union members, and two-thirds of nonunion workers, voted for President Eisenhower. Organized labor's commitment to the Negro had virtually disappeared. There were 1.2 million blacks in the AFL-CIO, but they held almost no important offices. One out of every eight Auto Workers was black, but although the UAW still boasted a liberal image, there was not a single black on the executive board.[2]

The decline of the American Communist party coincided with improved relations between the Eisenhower administration and the

119

Soviet Union. Nikita Khrushchev's régime concluded a long-sought peace treaty with Austria in May 1955. Both Russia and the United States pulled out its occupation troops, and Austria became a neutralist base between East and West. Then came the heralded summit meeting between Eisenhower, Khrushchev, and Prime Minister Anthony Eden of Britain at Geneva in July. Afterward, Khrushchev announced that "neither side wants war"—perhaps the first Soviet admission that America was not committed to aggression—and pledged his country firmly to "peaceful coexistence."

Furthermore, the Kremlin announced a cut of 1,200,000 in its armed forces, renewed its plea at the UN for a nuclear weapons ban, and dissolved the Communist Information Bureau (Cominform), the symbolic vehicle for Communist expansion around the globe.

Eisenhower, on his part, concluded: "Since the advent of nuclear weapons, it seems clear that there is no longer any alternative to peace." Far less belligerent toward the Russians than Truman, he successfully stifled the preventive-war advocates. The public's vigorous impulse toward peace was revealed in a Gallup poll showing 51 percent in favor of inviting Khrushchev to the United States, only 31 percent opposed, the rest undecided.[3]

The U.S. Supreme Court, too, had sharply reversed the erosion of individual liberties of the McCarthy era. In the *Young* decision, it halted a 10-year flood of firings by ruling that only federal employees in "sensitive" positions could be ousted as security risks. In *Emspak* and two related cases, the Court broadly interpreted the right of witnesses to claim protection under the Fifth Amendment before congressional committees. In *Sweezy,* the Court overruled "an invasion of the petitioner's liberties in the areas of academic freedom and political expression" by prohibiting a state legislature from delegating its interrogating powers to a local official. In *Watkins,* the Court held that Congress had no power "to expose for the sake of exposure" and severely limited procedures that inquisitors had followed for years.[4]

The decreasing tensions of the cold war might have led to a revived Communist party with a unique socialist approach to American problems had the Communists not been devastated by an unexpected blow. On December 21, 1955, *Pravda* celebrated the seventy-sixth anniversary of the late Joseph Stalin's birth with a front-page picture and the usual paeans of adulation. Only two months later, in a secret speech before the 20th Congress of the Russian Communist party, Khrushchev branded Stalin a tyrant and murderer and demolished an idol enshrined with Lenin in Soviet mythology.

The Khrushchev revelations tore the American party apart. "Stalin had been like a god to us—his decrees perfect and undebatable," John Gates, editor-in-chief of the *Daily Worker* recalled. Still, the blow might have had its constructive rather than negative aspects if the movement to rebuild the party on a less rigid Stalinist basis, quietly pushed by the "Gates group" in recent years, had not been blocked by the Foster faction. Gates wanted to use the Stalin debacle to turn the party in new directions. Foster clung to the rigid dogmas of the past.[5]

Khrushchev's "secret speech" to the top party leadership on February 24 and 25, 1956, created even more havoc. This speech was printed in full by the New York *Times* on June 5 from a copy secured by the State Department and reprinted by the *Daily Worker.*

According to the *Times* analysis, the Kremlin now considered Stalin a "savage, half-mad, power-crazed despot" whose reign had been enforced by "terror, torture and brute force." Khrushchev charged that Stalin planned to execute most of the Politburo leadership just before his death and laid full blame on the dictator for concocting the "doctor's plot" of 1953, a supposed attempt, mainly by Jewish doctors, to murder a number of Kremlin leaders by medical means. Stalin got his confessions by "cruel and inhuman tortures" in a "brutal violation of Socialist legality," the speech concluded.

Whatever the Kremlin's motivations—possibly the demands by technocrats and professional classes to end the stagnation of Soviet economy and government brought on by decades of one-man tyranny—the charges overwhelmed Communists here and abroad. Day after day the *Daily Worker* was filled with a flood of breast-beating, disillusion, and guilt. The paper became a psychiatric couch, an orgy of self-examination. Why had the Stalinist terror been allowed to develop? What, if anything, had Khrushchev and other officials done about it? Should not some of the blame fall on the present leadership? The novelist Howard Fast, who would shortly resign from the Communist party, concluded that "millions of human beings share my disgust at this idiotic behaviour—wicked, uncivilized, but above all, idiotic."[6]

The Stalin denigration spurred the Gates group to focus its demands for drastic party change on the draft resolution to be considered by the national convention the following year. The group drew its strength from the *Worker* staff, the New York State organization with about half the party's membership, and California, as well as many Midwest states. Gates, a stocky, blue-eyed, driving man, had been a top official of the national committee for a decade, a Communist since the age of 17 in 1931, and a fulltime organizer since 19. He had left college to organize steelworkers in Ohio for the party; achieved a notable record as political commissar of the Abraham Lincoln Brigade with the rank of lieutenant colonel, the highest rank of any American in the Spanish civil war; and served as a master sergeant in combat with the U.S. army paratroops in World War II.

At the 20th Congress, Khrushchev had enunciated three concepts seemingly in conflict with traditional Soviet philosophy: first, that war between capitalism and communism was "not fatalistically inevitable," and that "peaceful coexistence" was essential; second, that socialism could be won through constitutional means rather than the violent overthrow of the capitalistic structure—a concept stressed at the Smith Act trials but never corroborated by Moscow; third, that there could be many roads to socialism with different conditions in each country.

But such changes did not go far enough in meeting what Gates called a "profound crisis." Demanding a "fully democratic socialism" independent of Soviet dictation and applicable to American dynamics, Gates insisted that the deification of Marx and Lenin was as harmful as the deification of Stalin. As if this rejection of the Kremlin was not shocking enough, Gates also wanted the name of the party changed.[7]

One of the most sensitive issues pressed by the Gates group, soon labeled "revisionists" by Foster, was the ravages of anti-Semitism in the Soviet Union. The facts on the 1952 executions of Jewish anti-Fascist committee members, comprising most of the Jewish leadership in Russia, had leaked to some individuals through a small Jewish paper in Warsaw. The American party ignored reality. "We had implicit faith in Stalin, and could not believe the executions had taken place," Max Gordon of the *Daily Worker* explained. Although Khrushchev's secret speech finally admitted that the "Doctors' plot" was "fabricated from beginning to end," Khrushchev attacked Stalin's treatment of minorities, but never mentioned Soviet anti-Semitism. Now, the Kremlin's continuing evasions, and the American party's failure to demand a reversal of Soviet policy, was branded a "horror" and "political bankruptcy" by the dissidents, many of whom were Jewish.[8]

But the final crisis for the American party came from Eastern Europe. In June 1956, the workers of Poznan, Poland, took to the streets in angry riots that left hundreds dead and wounded. One of a series of open rebellions against Stalinist policy, it produced a reform government under the veteran Communist Wladyslaw Gomulka, who had stood almost alone against Stalin for years and had just been released from prison.

Spurred by this upheaval, Hungary carried reform almost to the stage of revolution. On October 23, 1956, workers, students, and intellectuals swarmed into the streets of Budapest to celebrate the achievements of Gomulka and to demand a new leadership under Imre Nagy. Khrushchev himself removed the Stalinists the next day and installed Nagy as prime minister.

After convincing the Kremlin to withdraw Russian troops from Budapest, Nagy initiated some startling policies. He conferred with Joseph Cardinal Mindszenty, an archreactionary, who urged that private property be returned on November 3. He sought to sever his country from the Warsaw Pact, the anchor of Soviet policy in Eastern Europe, and to make Hungary a neutralist state on the Austrian model.

Moscow would later claim Nagy seemed unable or unwilling to contain the riots that broke out in Budapest again on November 4. Moscow would also charge that what started as a reformist revolt would become a counterrevolution of "white terror"; that many supporters of the former fascist dictator, Admiral Nicholas Horthy, an ally of Hitler's, had infiltrated the country from West Germany; and that arms had been supplied the rebellion by outside governments, including the American CIA. Although none of these accusations was substantiated, it is clear that Cardinal Mindszenty returned to Budapest on November 4, hailed by many of the rebels; and that the Voice of America, an arm of the U.S. government, encouraged hopes of American support, replaying on radio the "liberation" promises of Secretary of State Dulles.

The Kremlin ordered Russian tanks back into Budapest and replaced Nagy with hardliner Janos Kadar. This overreaction was Khrushchev's critical mistake. Russian tanks mowed down the demonstrators. By November 15, all opposition was stamped out, and 80,000 refugees fled to Austria. Although the White House first seemed on the point of armed intervention, Eisenhower limited his aid to food and medicines and the immediate admission of 21,500 refugees into the United States—probably convinced that reinforcement of the demonstrators would have caused their massacre and perhaps world war.[9]

The brutality of the Soviet tank forces split the American Communists irreconcilably. A section of the national committee under Foster's domination defended the use of troops as essential to stopping a "fascist Hungary." The Gates group felt the revulsion of most Americans. "The action of the Soviet troops in Hungary," concluded the *Daily Worker,* "does not advance but retards the development of socialism because socialism cannot be imposed on a country by force."

Charney, the New York State chairman, denied that the threat of a fascist coup was real enough to warrant the Soviet invasion. Despair flooded the party's ranks; hundreds of members quit each week. Gates told associates, "For the first time in my life, I am ashamed of being a Communist." The Marxist journal *Monthly Review* concluded: "Any claim the Soviet Union had to moral leadership of the world socialist movement is now extinguished."[10]

In the midst of their acrimonious differences over Hungary, Foster now declared open warfare on the Gates group. He predicted its program would bring nothing more than a "managed economy" and "progressive capitalism"—ironically, the same targets Henry Wallace had blueprinted in 1948. Foster constantly linked the program to Browderism and "American exceptionalism," two ghosts that had haunted the party for decades. Above all, he accused Gates of trying to turn the party into an ineffectual "educational association."

The fate of the party was supposed to be settled at the sixteenth national convention on February 9, 1957, the first convention in seven years.

Yet the convention settled almost nothing. It approved a "peaceful, constitutional, democratic road to socialism," safeguards for the right of dissent, and new methods for electing leadership that would make the party more responsive to the will of the membership. Then it turned around and passed a resolution opposing transformation of the party to a "political or educational association."

Foster's final step was to crush Gates himself and his *Daily Worker* base. Just before Christmas, the national committee announced it could no longer guarantee the money to subsidize the paper, and that publication would be suspended on January 13, 1958. Gates and the rest of the staff resigned from the party shortly afterward, joined by such national committee members and influential officials as Abner Berry, Fred Fine, Sid Stein, and Dr. Doxey Wilkerson. The party had shrunk to an estimated 5,000 members through this final act of suicide.[11]

It was the end of a dream, a dream built on the infallibility of the

Soviet Union as the supreme model of what Marxism could create. Stalin had brought Russia through the onslaught of World War II and had raised her from the ruins. Compressing hundreds of years into a few decades, Russia had reached a level of economic production, science, technology, and education not far below the standards of the United States. Whatever reservations some American Communists had along the way—the purge trials of the 1930s, for example—were written off as aberrations in the laws of historical evolution. "The Communists offer one precious, fatal boon: they take away the sense of sin," Murray Kempton observed.[12]

To the faithful, of course, the party offered far more. It gave even the most inconspicuous member a feeling of power, a link with the Soviet juggernaut supplying unlimited hope that the same miracle would be reproduced in his own country. It also gave each member a home and a web of political, personal, and often business associations that filled and fed his life, providing a security never found before.

Communists came to believe they were living at the center of history and at the heart of their times. Through a highly structured, international party, they were convinced of their ability to reshape society. Their identification with the working class was virtually a religious experience. Their commitment was passionate and unquestioning—their lives were dedicated to a system they believed was the only one that guaranteed workers justice and human dignity.

A Communist organizer who spent four years with the California fruit pickers summed up these aspirations in an interview with Vivian Gornick:

Day by day people were developing, transforming, communicating inarticulate dreams, discovering a force of being in themselves. Desires, skills, capacities they didn't know they had blossomed under the pressure of active struggle. And the sweetness, the generosity, the pure comradeship that came flowing out of them as they began to feel themselves! They were—there's no other word for it—noble. . . . It was my dream of socialism come to life. I saw then what it could be like, what people could always be like, how good the earth and all the things upon it could be, how sweet to be alive and to feel yourself in everyone else.[13]

Certainly most American Communists—though not all—joined the party for similar idealistic motives. It was this very idealism that eventually drove them out. Tito's Yugoslavia, the proof that the Soviets did not own the one path to salvation, opened cracks in their faith. But it was Stalin himself, the creator of an "unprecedented orgy of murder," as Howard Fast put it, the god turned devil, the caricature of everything that communism should mean, who finally destroyed their faith. The butchery in Hungary, the slave-camp revelations, and anti-Semitism completed the process.[14]

When revisionists insisted that much of Soviet Marxism had become irrelevant to American problems, the mold that had held the Left together for a hundred years was broken. The old belief that social engineering could bring Utopia through a master plan lost its power.

For most leaders like Max Gordon, who had joined the Young Communist League at the age of 18 in 1928 and devoted himself almost entirely to the movement after graduation from New York's City College in 1931, these were wrenching, despairing years. "Although the party's increasing isolation, particularly from the unions, had been debated frequently among us since 1951," Gordon recalled, "it was the total horror of Stalin's record that shook the foundations of our faith and made us feel like moral outcasts. How could we explain to ourselves that such manic actions could have occurred in what our theory taught us had to be an ideal social order? How could we explain our support for, and our past efforts to justify Stalin's tyranny?

"Many of us only got through that year or two because we thought we could change the party and rebuild it to fit the ideals we had started with. The daily discussions on the *Worker* and New York State committee kept us going. It wasn't until after the national convention in 1957 that I and others realized nothing could be changed. No matter what resolutions were passed, they became tied up in endless wrangles and factional struggles killing the party from the inside."

Humanity had been squeezed out of Marxism. "I left because the all-embracing system conceived by Marx became a closed system under Stalin, a system that substituted dogma for reality and disowned man himself as a factor in shaping his existence," Charney concluded.[15]

· 10 ·

The Black Rebellion Begins
1960-62

Massive resistance by southern blacks became an organized movement on the afternoon of February 1, 1960, when four black students from North Carolina Agricultural and Technical College walked into nearby Greensboro and sat down at the lunch counter of the Woolworth's store. Although refused service and insulted and roughed up by white patrons, the students sat there until closing time. The next day they came back, a dozen students this time, and sat down again. By April, the "sit-ins" had spread to 78 southern cities and towns, resulting in the arrest of 2,000 students. Within a year, the sit-ins blanketed the South, involving a spontaneous army of 50,000 to 70,000 youths in more than 100 localities. At least 3,600 went to jail, often for months.

It was the first time that black bodies had formed a wall of resistance. The students were called "black bastards," splattered with plates of food, kicked, frequently beaten. In prison, they were tortured with electric cattle prods and "wristbreakers." But although their lives were constantly in danger, no one ever struck back. When attacked, they went limp. When reviled, they stayed silent. Following the policy of nonviolence that King had used so effectively in the Montgomery bus strike, the students developed it into an even more effective confrontation that changed the South.[1]

In contrast to the Marxist vision for a total overthrow of bourgeois society, the black revolt concentrated on immediate, specific targets. For the South, these targets may have seemed radical. But as rights long constitutionally guaranteed, they were conservative.

While the Silent Generation watched at white universities, these sit-ins, and the "freedom rides" that followed, were almost completely a product of black campuses, drawing a scattering of veteran leaders like King, and occasional white leadership from the Congress for Racial Equality.

The black revolt drew youths as young as 14 and 15 from surrounding communities. They were a new breed, brash in their independence of the old-line black groups, determined to keep control in
their own hands, defiant of the southern oligarchy.

"Each kid who went said he was willing to give his life," reported
John Lewis, soon to become national chairman of the Student Nonviolent Coordinating Committee. They were mainly children of the
working class or the lower middle class. Their fathers were laborers
and janitors, their mothers maids and seamstresses. They had
reached college through scholarships and their own hard-gained
earnings. Lewis, a divinity student, was the only one of ten children
of a poor Alabama family to finish high school. Henry Thomas, an
early freedom rider, raised with nine other children in a Georgia
shack by a drunken stepfather, worked as a road laborer before
winning a scholarship to Howard University. The faded blue jeans
that quickly replaced the ties and white shirts of the first sit-ins
symbolized SNCC's link to the working class.

A small segment of the black revolt, as it happens, came from Left
backgrounds. Julian Bond, an initiator of the Atlanta sit-ins later
elected to the Georgia legislature, was the son of Horace Mann Bond,
a board member of the Southern Negro Youth Congress and dean
of education at Atlanta University. Some freedom riders were the
products of the Workers Defense League, an ally of the Socialist
party. The CORE staff included a few Socialists.

But these exceptions brought hardly any Marxist influence to the
black revolt. Its unswerving policy in the first five years was a total
rejection of previous ideology, almost as if the youths resented the
dogmas of the past, the incessant factions and dissensions.[2]

This clean break explains the time lag between Montgomery in
1955 and the sit-ins of 1960. The student rebels, inspired as they were
by King and by the Fellowship of Reconciliation's workshops in
nonviolence in 1958, still wanted no dominance by their black elders
or their Marxist predecessors, and needed those years to solidify their
ranks around new strategies. Any violent shift in historical forces
needs a concentrated buildup of frustrations and anger, and a group
whose expectations have long been stifled. Black college youths, with
their minds and emotions stirred by the expectations of the classroom, were the obvious shapers of rebellion.

Their anger had grown with each new lynching and with the
mounting reaction of southern whites against the Supreme Court's
desegregation decision. Four years after her application, and despite

a federal court order, mobs still stopped Autherine Lucy from entering the University of Alabama in 1956. More violence at Clinton, Tennessee, that same year blocked the admission of black students into the white high school until December. President Eisenhower had to call up the 101st Airborne Division to force the entry of nine black students into Little Rock, Arkansas, Central High School in September, 1957. At the height of the crisis, six Alabama whites, out to "get some niggers" they didn't even know, castrated a black man with a razor blade and poured turpentine into the wound.

By the spring of 1960, there was still not a single black student in white schools in Alabama, Georgia, Louisiana, and South Carolina; and only 34 in North Carolina, 98 in Arkansas, 103 in Virginia, and 169 in Tennessee.[3]

Shortly after the Greensboro sit-ins of February 1, 1960, students expanded their confrontation to the streets, welcoming arrest. A thousand paraded through Orangeburg, South Carolina, in March; and after a hundred arrests filled the city jail, 400 more were packed into an open stockade. Another thousand paraded through Tallahassee, Florida; 750 through Marshall, Texas, where the demonstrators were assaulted with fire hoses and tear gas. So many demonstrators crowded the courtroom, halls, and stairs at the student trials in Raleigh, North Carolina, that the fire chief closed the building and moved the trial to a 3,000-seat auditorium.

The sit-ins spread to municipal libraries, bingo halls, swimming pools, and movie theaters. A student coalition in 13 Texas cities formed long lines at white movie theaters; each time they were refused a ticket, they got back in line and started the process again.

With the cry of "Fill the jails," the next step was the "jail-in"— thousands of students refusing bail and voluntarily going to prison. It started in Tallahassee, Florida, when five students were sentenced to 60 days. Singing "Before I'll be a slave, I'll be buried in my grave," nine out of ten students arrested at Rock Hill, South Carolina, chose jail. Almost all of 145 arrested Fisk University students at Nashville added a hunger strike to their jail-in tactics.[4]

In Atlanta, students ran the sit-ins like a military campaign, sending separate squads to 10 restaurants at the same time, driving the police frantic as new squads rushed to replace those just arrested. Struggling to keep up with student militancy, King was arrested for sitting in with 51 students on October 19, 1960. The judge ruled he had violated his parole on a charge of driving without a license and sentenced him to four months at Reidsville state prison. It was the height of the Kennedy-Nixon election campaign. When reporters asked Nixon to comment on the severity of the sentence, he shrugged off their questions. Kennedy, however, called Coretta King from Chicago, telling her he would do anything to help; and his brother Robert telephoned the judge to insist on the minister's constitutional right to bail. As a result, not only King's father but thousands of other blacks switched their votes to the Democratic line.

Former President Truman, on the other hand, commented on a television show: "If anyone came to my store and sat down, I'd throw him out." After Truman insisted he'd been misquoted, a replay of the station's tape confirmed the statement, and turned up an additional comment: "I don't think they're all students. I think this [the sit-ins] was engineered by the Communists. . . ."

Truman, who had contributed substantially to the origins of McCarthyism, thus aligned himself with the anti-Communist gambit of southern extremists. Black students were constantly accused of being "directed by the Communist party," as the Birmingham *News* put it. "Is there a master plan, Soviet inspired, behind the racial incidents so widespread in America today?" the paper asked in its six-part series. When students published a manifesto on the Atlanta sit-ins, Gov. Ernest Vandiver of Georgia labeled it a "leftwing statement." During the freedom rides, Senator James Eastland of Mississippi branded Jim Peck, a white CORE official, as a "Communist agitator and organizer of the most dangerous kind."[5]

The movement actually was fiercely independent of outside control. The students welcomed advice but not dictation. CORE, which had been organized nationally in Chicago in 1943 around the principle of nonviolence and had experimented with sit-ins in Los Angeles and elsewhere shortly afterward, was asked to send organizers to North Carolina in early February. The NAACP and King's Southern Christian Leadership Conference, obviously jockeying for influence, attended a conference of students leaders on February 16, 1960, and an even more important meeting with representatives of 56 southern colleges on April 12 to 15, organized by Ella Baker of SCLC.

Here, James M. Lawson, who had been expelled from Vanderbilt University's divinity school at Nashville for joining the sit-ins, called the NAACP a "black bourgeois club." Lawson and other students, unhappy with King's moderation, consequently formed SNCC to promote a more militant approach.

With its national chapters, CORE was instrumental in establishing picket lines at Woolworth's and other chain stores across the country, adding considerable economic pressure to the sit-ins. In New York, picket lines spread to 69 Woolworth stores in three weeks, the International Ladies Garment Workers Union alone supplying 800 pickets. Harvard and other neighboring colleges picketed 12 Woolworth's in the Boston area.

As a result of CORE's identification with the sit-ins, it doubled its national chapters to almost 50 by the end of 1960. Buoyed by press coverage, its fund raising produced $144,000 by June and another $110,000 by the end of that year.[6]

The economic boycott by southern blacks—they gave up all Easter shopping—also lent potent support to the sit-ins. Black patronage constituted an estimated one-fourth of all Woolworth sales in 300 southern branches. In Charlotte, North Carolina, alone, blacks spent an estimated $150 million a year.

The impact on Woolworth's business was soon apparent. Its March sales in 1960 dropped almost 9 percent from the previous March. CORE claimed that Kress's sales in four southern states had been slashed 15 to 18 percent.

As a result, the sit-in movement soon broke down most restaurant segregation throughout the South. Nashville integrated lunch counters in six stores in May 1960. The Hot Shoppes in Virginia followed in June; Knoxville and Greensboro chain stores in July; 28 variety stores in Miami in August. Atlanta chain stores and department stores held out for 18 months. But by the spring of 1961, lunch counters and restaurants in 140 southern cities had surrendered to the sit-in campaign.[7]

Rather than lose momentum, CORE decided to expand massive resistance with the more drastic technique of freedom rides. Following the model of an earlier trip in 1947, the riders—seven black and six white—aimed to penetrate the Deep South by bus, breaking state laws on segregated seating and segregated restrooms and restaurants along the way. The time for this offensive seemed ripe since the Supreme Court had just prohibited segregation in interstate travel in *Boynton* v. *Virginia* in December 1960.

After training at CORE's center in Virginia, the riders left Washington, D.C., on May 4, 1961. They included James Farmer, the new national director of CORE; John Lewis, already arrested five times in the sit-ins; and a number of black students from the sit-in movement. The whites were generally older. James Peck, a CORE staffer, jailed as a pacifist in World War II, was the only veteran of the 1947 trip. Albert Bigelow, a 58-year-old architect and former naval commander turned pacifist, had recently taken his ship, *Golden Rule,* into the prohibited zone of the Pacific in a protest against atomic testing. Walter Bergman, a retired school administrator, and his wife were both over 60. Although the Left had virtually no influence on the black student rebellion, at least four of this group were Socialists or close to the old Socialist parties.

Sensing that this invasion would produce far more violence than the sit-ins, the riders had appealed to President Kennedy for protection of their constitutional rights. The Justice Department thereupon alerted the Birmingham police force, among others. Still, the ride proceeded with almost no incidents until two members were beaten by a mob in the white waiting room at Rock Hill, South Carolina. At Anniston, Alabama, on the way to Birmingham on May 14, a mob attacked the Greyhound bus with chains and iron rods, breaking windows and slashing tires. The bus then developed a flat tire a few miles out of Anniston, and part of the mob, following in cars, hurled bricks through the windows and set the bus afire with incendiary bombs, destroying it completely. As the riders fled the bus, one black student received a crushing head blow; twelve had to be hospitalized for smoke poisoning. "The hoodlums were shouting 'Heil Hitler' and 'Sieg Heil,' " Bigelow reported.[8]

Freedom riders on another Trailways bus were attacked on board by eight men who tried to oust black students from the front section. When Peck and Bergman came to their assistance, they were beaten. (A few months later, Bergman would suffer a stroke, possibly as a result of his injuries.) As this bus pulled into the Birmingham terminal, an angry crowd surrounded it, inflicting head wounds on one black student, and sending Peck to the hospital with severe cuts on his face and scalp. Although alerted, no police appeared for at least 10 minutes. The Justice Department later found the police planned this delay. All rioters arrested turned out to be Klan members.

Although the riders agreed to go to Montgomery, no driver would take them. Even when they decided to fly directly to New Orleans for a church meeting ending the CORE phase of the trip, another mob and bomb threats at the airport forced a six-hour delay while John Siegenthaler of the Justice Department arranged a special flight.

The supermilitants at SNCC refused to be stopped. John Lewis, Henry Thomas, and a new contingent of black students from Nashville negotiated until May 20 to find a bus to take them. Governor

John Patterson of Alabama, who had pandered to the Klan in his election campaign, ostensibly pledged the riders' safety. But arriving at the Montgomery terminal, 19 riders were met by a mob of 300. Lewis was smashed to the ground by baseball bats. Battered and unconscious on the floor, William Barbee, a black student at Nashville's American Baptist Theological seminary, had to wait 20 minutes for a black ambulance—no white personnel would treat him—to take him to a hospital. Even a writer and a photographer from *Life* were beaten, and Siegenthaler was knocked unconscious on the street. The Associated Press reported it took 20 minutes for the police to arrive, and the rioters, now numbering a thousand, could not be dispersed for two hours. "A total breakdown of law enforcement," *Newsweek* called it.[9]

President Kennedy sent 600 federal marshals to the city under Deputy Attorney General Byron White, later a Supreme Court justice. Forced to take some responsibility by pressure from the White House, Governor Patterson called up the National Guard and declared martial law on May 21, 1961. Still, when a mob of 1,000 surrounded the First Baptist Church that night, where Dr. King was speaking, and lobbed rocks and teargas bombs into the building, there were almost no police on hand. The mob was only checked by 150 marshals.

Farmer, who had been attending his father's funeral, arrived in Montgomery a few days later, and CORE, SNCC, and SCLC combined their forces for an all-out assault on Jackson, Mississippi. After integrating the Trailways restaurant, 26 riders left Montgomery by bus on May 24, escorted by state patrol cars and helicopters. All were arrested on arrival at Jackson for using the white waiting room and toilets, some beaten for refusing to say "yes, sir" to the police.

Riders poured into Jackson—65 over the first weekend, 328 by the end of the summer—to be arrested with conveyor-belt regularity. Black students from nearby Tougaloo College, who had sat in at the city library, immediately went to jail. A large contingent from Jackson State College for Negroes, parading through town the next day, were dispersed with police dogs and tear gas. Riders from the North, including whites like the Reverend William Sloane Coffin, Jr., the Yale chaplain, many Jewish rabbis, and 15 Episcopalian priests, among them the son-in-law of Governor Nelson Rockefeller of New York, arrived at Jackson and were immediately arrested.[10]

Almost all chose jail rather than bail; some got sentences of four months. Once the city and county jails filled up, the riders were sent to Parchman state penitentiary, whose death row and electric chair served the worst criminals. Fourteen women riders, confined in a 13-by-15-foot cell and sleeping on damp concrete floors, annoyed the guards so much with incessant singing they were thrown in a sweat box. When the men used singing as a technique of protest, they were tortured with wrist-breakers and cattle prods.

Mississippi courts set exorbitant bail to deplete movement funds; CORE alone spent $140,000 on bail and legal fees. The defendants usually ended their voluntary jail-in after 39 days, the last day they were still eligible to appeal their cases. Fortunately, NAACP's legal defense fund now assumed a large share of these costs, and with increasing press coverage, CORE raised $228,000 during the summer of 1961.

The freedom rides proved astonishingly effective. Both Greyhound and Trailways removed their whites-only signs from Montgomery terminal restaurants in June 1961. Under prodding from the Kennedy administration, the Interstate Commerce Commission on September 22 imposed prohibitive fines against segregation in interstate travel. The crucial test came in McComb, Mississippi, when a federal court ordered the removal of whites-only signs. With 40 FBI agents and local police controlling a hostile mob, six freedom riders successfully desegregated the bus terminal in December. It would take until 1965 for the Supreme Court to reverse the convictions of freedom riders. But despite pockets of harassment, particularly in Albany, Georgia, the freedom riders for all practical purposes forced an end to segregated travel by late 1962.[11]

Robert Williams, a strange and aberrant figure in Monroe, North Carolina, whose 14,000 population was about one-quarter black, built a movement in this period that challenged the nonviolent tactics of SNCC and CORE. Although an NAACP officer, his base was always the working class. While claiming to oppose "violence for its own sake or for the sake of reprisals against whites," he would soon become a symbol for armed force, a precursor of the violence that would sweep the black world a few years hence.

An ex-Marine with three years of college, six feet tall and 240 pounds, Williams returned to Monroe in 1955 to find the NAACP chapter had dwindled to six members. Recruiting from factories and pool halls, he was elected president after putting together a large and militant membership that integrated the town library in 1957. Refused the use of the white swimming pool even one day a week, although black youngsters had to travel 25 miles to swim at Charlotte, he campaigned for a black pool, then for admission of his sons to the local white school.

When the Klan struck back with frequent parades of cars through the black section, firing at the homes of Williams and his vice-president, Williams decided on a unique approach. He took out a charter from the National Rifle Association, purchased guns legally, and fired back. Interestingly, when an Indian settlement nearby dispersed a Klan motorcade with similar gunfire, the national press covered the story with tolerant amusement.[12]

Williams further enraged the city by his intervention in two local trials. He brought a black lawyer, Conrad Lynn of New York, to defend two boys, eight and nine years old, in the noted "kissing case." The boys were charged with assault on three white girls a few years younger and confined to a reformatory on 14-year sentences. Although the facts remain obscure, the worst that probably happened was that one boy whose mother had worked for the family of one of the girls greeted his old friend with a kiss, and the children then imitated a television kissing game. The imprisonments produced indignant headlines throughout Europe, 15,000 petition signatures against the verdict in Rotterdam, and demonstrations at American embassies in London, Paris, and other cities. Governor Luther Hodges released the boys after three months in February 1959.

In another trial, Williams championed the cause of a pregnant black woman who fought off rape by two whites, with a white neighbor as witness to prove it, and of a mentally retarded black man charged with rape of a white woman. The courts exonerated the whites and jailed the black defendant. Since federal and local governments refused to protect his people, Williams bitterly told reporters, they "must meet violence with violence, lynching with lynching." Disturbed by the statement, and explaining that "there can be no issue of self-defense for this has been a cardinal principle of the NAACP since its organization 50 years ago," NAACP headquarters suspended Williams in June 1959. Williams insisted on the right of self-defense, but the NAACP said he had called for "aggressive, premeditated violence."

Even self-defense was a revolutionary program. During the sit-in and freedom-ride period, there were occasional beatings but no serious violence in Monroe because, Williams claimed, "we'd shown the willingness and readiness to fight to defend ourselves." But violence broke out in June 1961, when the Williams group, supported by freedom riders, began to picket a white picnic area and demanded that the city hire more blacks and desegregate the schools. Klan members fired on pickets from the trees, and Williams claimed the police gave no protection. On June 23, Williams's car was forced off the road, and almost over an embankment, by cars that he identified for the police. No arrests were made.[13]

Two days later, Williams's car was blocked at an intersection by another car and surrounded by a mob of 2,000, crying, "Kill the nigger, burn the nigger." As one man approached him with a baseball bat, Williams took a carbine from the seat—carried legally under state law if not concealed—and threatened to shoot anyone who came closer. A policeman ordered Williams to drop his weapon, but with a friend covering a second policeman with his pistol, Williams refused to move until the state police broke up the mob and escorted him to safety.

Late that afternoon, a crowd of 2,000 attacked the picket line, beating freedom riders and forcing Williams's guards to return to the black district. At 6 P.M., a cavalcade of cars invaded the district. Williams's guards stopped one car and took the driver, Bruce Stegall, a known Klansman, and his wife to the Williams home. With whites shooting into black homes from their cars, and blacks returning the fire, the area was soon surrounded by police cars. Williams "stressed to his followers that any violence should be only defensive, and that there should not be any retaliatory violence," David Morton, a freedom rider from Minneapolis, reported.

Convinced he would have a hostile white jury if arrested, Williams decided to escape to New York. There he found he had been indicted not on a civil rights charge but on a federal charge of kidnapping. The indictment did not explain why the Stegalls had been driving through the black area to begin with, or how their detention in the midst of gunfire from both sides was kidnapping.[14]

Williams, now the symbol of resistance for young black nationalists, started on a curious odyssey that would cover the revolutionary gamut. One group of his northern supporters were mainly Trotskyists; another group, pro-Communist. Williams himself moved impartially from camp to camp.

At first he settled in Cuba, enjoying the friendship of Fidel Castro, making short-wave broadcasts to the United States for the Revolutionary Action Movement (RAM) of which he was chairman, and supposedly supervising the military training of blacks. HUAC accused Williams of fomenting a Chicago riot in 1965. He traveled to

North Vietnam, still claiming to be a non-Communist, and settled in China for three years. In 1969, he abandoned China, successfully reentered the United States, and—somehow fighting off extradition to North Carolina on the kidnapping charge—joined the staff of the University of Michigan's Center for Chinese Studies.

Once he had fled the United States, Williams dropped all pretense of self-defense. His program became "a unique form of urban guerilla warfare" with the black revolutionary "ambushing and seizing arms from the enemy oppressor." The firebomb was the black's "most effective weapon." The black riots in Newark and Detroit in the 1960s were "merely skirmishes of protest." He envisioned a flaming conflagration in black ghettos across the land. "Burn, baby, burn," he announced, was "the most noble cry to come out of America since the Boston Tea Party."

Williams's concept of revolution was essentially nihilistic. Although he once announced that "the only hope for us seems to be socialism," he had no concrete program to offer, and even the Communist party rejected him. Still, his struggle in North Carolina and his later teachings would have a profound impact on the exploding forces of black liberation. Many black nationalists, including the Black Panthers, would incorporate aspects of his violent credo into their own.[15]*

*All charges against Williams were dropped in 1976 when the prosecution stated that its key witness was too ill to testify.

· 11 ·

Building a Black Base
1961-63

On August 29, 1961, a SNCC field secretary named Robert Moses accompanied two black residents of Amite County, Mississippi, to the registrar's office in an attempt to qualify them to vote. Moses was promptly attacked by the sheriff's cousin, then visiting the office, and beaten badly. One important result of this incident was that Moses filed charges for assault and battery—probably the first time a black had brought charges against a white man in the state since the Reconstruction era. More significantly still, it marked the beginning of the voter registration drive throughout the South, a new direction in the black revolt, and the search for a power base that would consume much of SNCC's and CORE's forces for the next few years.[1]

In its brief existence, SNCC had concentrated on massive confrontations—the sit-ins and freedom rides that had already desegregated a large part of the eating and travel facilities in the South. But people like Moses were beginning to think this wasn't enough. The system had to be changed at the roots of power. Eating in a white restaurant touched only the periphery. To get at police brutality, at jobs, at schools, SNCC had to find a way to control the sheriff's office, the school hierarchy, the county machine. SNCC's immediate strategy was to develope power through the ballot box.

The decision did not come easily. It was hammered out through days and nights of bitter debate at the SNCC staff meeting in early August, 1961. Even then, it was a compromise between old and new —the final report settling on a dual program of both massive confrontations and voter-registration drives.

The extent to which registration symbolized power in the South was demonstrated by Amite statistics—there was only one registered black out of 5,010 blacks of voting age. In 13 of 69 Mississippi counties, where figures were available, not one black had been al-

138

lowed to register. Among the rare exceptions, Pike County had 207 blacks registered out of 6,936 eligibles.

This outcast status in politics was accompanied by similar economic degradation. More than 90 percent of Amite blacks had no heating facilities or indoor toilets. In Leflore County, whites made up only a third of the population but owned 90 percent of the land. A SNCC worker in Canton reported: "Many of the houses were constructed of unpainted weathered boards, looking as if a light breeze would bring them tumbling down. Front steps were rotting, and milk crates served as porch furniture. The rooms were dark, often lighted only from the fireplace or by kerosene lamps. In one house two bulging paper bags were tacked high on a wall. Here Sunday clothing were [sic] safe from mice. Walls were plastered with old newspapers."[2]

Organizing against this system, Robert Moses would become virtually a legend—"among the greatest human beings who have ever walked the face of the earth," Dick Gregory, the comedian, called him. Thirty years old, stockily built, with light brown skin, large tranquil eyes behind thick glasses, and a languid voice that formed words with almost pedagogical care, Moses reflected an unshakable calm. "He could walk into a place where a lynch mob had just left and make up a bed and prepare to go to sleep, as if the situation was normal," a SNCC worker observed. Walter Stafford of SNCC, later a Hunter College professor in New York, considered him "the main stabilizing influence of the movement." Joyce Ladner of SNCC, who also became a Hunter professor, described him as "gentle and humble, never asking anything. But his magnetism brought out the best in people."[3]

Moses was one of the few SNCC staffers who had not been reared in the South. Born in Harlem, he excelled both academically and athletically at Stuyvesant High School, won a scholarship to Hamilton College, where he majored in philosophy, and took his master's degree at Harvard in 1957. He taught mathematics at Horace Mann, a New York private school, until the sit-in movement drew him to Mississippi in 1961.

The first pressure brought against blacks attempting to register was the threat of losing their jobs. School teachers, particularly vulnerable as public employees, were often fired. Sharecroppers were forced off their land, even those like Anderson T. Thomas who had worked the same Ruleville plantation for 30 years. Fannie Lou Hamer of Ruleville, who had picked cotton since she was six, was evicted after 18 years for leading a group of 26 to register. Sixteen bullets were fired into her house. "They beat me and they beat me with long, flat blackjack," she testified. One official said, "You're going to wish you was dead."

Leflore County officials tried to stop registration by cutting off the federal surplus food program. Thousands of blacks came so close to starvation that black students at Michigan State University and other campuses had to run a steady shuttle of food trucks from the North.

The main weapon against registration was fear and violence, not only from night riders of the Klan but organized methodically by sheriffs and other state officials. "Most of the people are so afraid that they will not open the door to us," reported Charles Sherrod, the registration coordinator for southwest Georgia. "Half the time, though, we were just sitting up because we were afraid someone would try to kill us after we went to bed," wrote Anne Moody from Canton, Mississippi, in 1963 when many workers were already keeping guns for self-defense. "Doris slept so lightly I would just touch her and she would jump up, grabbing for the rifle."[4]

At first, however, SNCC workers adhered rigorously to nonviolence. When attacked, they took a defensive position on the ground, curled up in a ball, legs together, protecting their head with their arms. A week after his first beating in August 1961, Moses returned to the Amite courthouse with Travis Britt, who was attacked by a group of whites shouting, "Shall we kill him now?" Britt recalled that one "just kept hitting me and shouting, 'Why don't you hit me, nigger?' I was beaten into a semi-conscious state." On September 6, another SNCC worker at Tylerton was ordered out of the registrar's office at gunpoint. As he turned to leave, the registrar beat him on the back of the head with the pistol butt.

Herbert Lee, a farmer who had worked closely with SNCC and publicly announced his support of registration, was shot to death by State Representative E. H. Hurst in late September while seated in the cab of his pickup truck at Liberty, Mississippi. The sheriff reported Lee had tried to hit Hurst with a tire iron during an argument. That afternoon, a coroner's jury decreed the shooting had been self-defense.

Moses, having learned that other black farmers had witnessed the shooting, searched for days to identify them and found one, Lewis Allen, who could repudiate the self-defense plea. A federal grand jury was called in October, but Allen told Moses he could not present the real facts without federal protection, which was refused him. Later a deputy sheriff accused Allen of contacting the Justice Department. In February 1964, Allen was found dead on his porch, his face and body riddled with buckshot.[5]

Shortly after the Lee killing, a black body, weighted with stones and never identified, was found in a nearby river; and two young girls were shot from a passing car and gravely injured. In February 1963, Moses and two associates were traveling by car near Greenwood, Mississippi, when they were splattered by 14 bullets. Three hit James Travis in the head and neck, reaching the spinal cord, but he survived. In June that year, Medgar Evers, state head of the NAACP, had just returned from a SNCC meeting when he was murdered in the driveway of his Jackson, Mississippi, home.

William Moore, a white Post Office employee from Baltimore and a CORE member, announced he would make a one-man protest march from Chattanooga to Jackson in the spring of 1963. He got only as far as Gadsden, Alabama, when he was murdered by gunshots from the roadside. CORE and SNCC immediately announced a Memorial Freedom Walk to follow Moore's route. They wired President Kennedy, asking for protection, but got no response. On May 3, at the Tennessee-Alabama line, they were attacked by a mob of 1,000 people. They assumed a self-defense position on the ground, but Alabama state police beat them with nightsticks and cattle prods, and took them to jail where they remained for a month, refusing bail.[6]

Moses and SNCC had concentrated the registration drive on Mississippi in 1961, but CORE soon joined them, and the drive spread to other southern states. It received an enormous boost in April 1962 with an injection of funds from the North, mainly $870,000 from the Field Foundation, Stephen Currier's Taconic Foundation, and the Stern Family Fund. The money was administered by the Voter Education Project (VEP) of the Southern Regional Council.

The Mississippi campaign was run by an umbrella organization called the Council of Federated Organizations (COFO), which included SNCC, CORE, King's SCLC, and the NAACP. But SCLC's role was slight; and the NAACP was represented mainly by Aaron Henry, the Clarksdale pharmacist, as president. SNCC not only dominated the executive committee, with Moses as director, but staffed four out of five congressional districts in the state, with CORE staffing the fifth.

The SNCC radicals, as many had feared when they debated the

advantages of a registration drive as opposed to mass confrontations, now became increasingly dependent on the White House. They had foreseen the problems of working within the system—President Kennedy principally wanted voter registration for his own purposes and undoubtedly influenced some of the major funding. The President's advisers considered voter registration less volatile than mass confrontations. Besides, there was a good possibility the Democrats would benefit from the votes of most new blacks registered.

SNCC's goals were different. It expected to use registration to build power bases, to heighten the radical consciousness of black communities, and to develop local black leadership. These aims were increasingly frustrated by conflicts with the liberal establishment.

SNCC rejected the politics of the past, refusing to get enmeshed in pro-Communist or anti-Communist ideologies. Its only policy was "nonexclusion"—a refusal to exclude Marxists, Communists, or any brand of radical. Consequently, when it found itself desperately short of legal help, it had no hesitation in accepting volunteers from the National Lawyers Guild, labeled Communist-dominated in the McCarthy era. The NAACP refused Guild lawyers. Even CORE, whose New York headquarters and dependence on white membership and white financial support made it more cautious than SNCC, condemned the Guild. In 1964, the National Council of Churches prohibited the ministers it sent to Mississippi from using Guild lawyers. The syndicated columnists Rowland Evans and Robert Novak called SNCC that year "substantially infiltrated" by Communists.[7]

Such red-baiting, however, was inconsequential compared to SNCC's failure to get Justice Department protection for the civil rights of its workers. The FBI's attitude was so discriminatory that blacks considered FBI agents, who generally ignored the brutalities of local sheriffs and police, their enemies. Despite constant appeals to the Justice Department and meetings with Burke Marshall, the assistant attorney general in charge of civil rights, there were only two occasions prior to the Voting Rights Act of 1965 when the administration took legal action to protect registration workers.

The first, according to a study by Pat Watters and Reese Cleghorn, occurred in Leflore County, Mississippi. After the shooting of Jimmy Travis in February 1963, the burning of four black-owned buildings near registration quarters, shooting attacks on SNCC workers in March, and finally the burning of the COFO office, the Justice Department went into federal court for a restraining order. But even this attempt to protect the right to register and to assemble for peaceful demonstrations fizzled. The injunction was dropped when local officials promised to obey the law.

The arrest of three white men by the FBI for interfering with voter registration at Itta Bena, Mississippi, in June 1964 again had little more than symbolic effect. The administration's position was weakened by its appeasement of southern politicians. Kennedy's appointments to the federal bench consistently included rabid segregationists—one of them, District Judge William Harold Cox, compared blacks in the registration drive to "chimpanzees." And despite an 80-year prohibition in the United States Codes against segregated federal juries, the administration made no effort to enforce the law, virtually ensuring that blacks would be judged by all-white juries.

Despite these obstacles, the registration drive produced promising results. In 11 southern states between April 1, 1962, and November 1, 1964, 688,000 blacks were added to the registration rolls for a total of 2,174,200 registered, or 44 percent of those eligible. Georgia now had 44 percent of eligible blacks registered. On the other hand, hard-core resistance remained in Alabama, which had only 23 percent registered, and in Mississippi, which had only 6 percent.[8]

Living constantly with death changed SNCC's attitude toward nonviolence. By 1963, many SNCC offices posted armed guards at night, and workers slept with guns by their beds. Even CORE officials admitted that nonviolence as a guiding principle was hardly discussed at meetings anymore.

Everyone insisted that arms meant only self-defense. But there was a narrow line between a shot fired in defense and further shots that led to violence. Self-defense thus became an integral part of the radicalization of SNCC, and guns inevitably led to revolutionary rhetoric.

The self-defense principle reached its most organized form in Louisiana through the Deacons for Defense and Justice, which claimed 50 to 60 chapters throughout the South. The Deacons patrolled 24 hours a day, often exchanging gunfire with night riders. After James Farmer, CORE's national director, led 400 marchers through Bogalusa, he testified he "benefitted from the protection the Deacons had provided." But King criticized the Deacons, which created increasing tension between him and the radicals.[9]

Charles Evers, brother of the assassinated NAACP chairman in Mississippi, went beyond the self-defense principle in a Nashville, Tennessee, speech in 1964. Concluding that "nonviolence won't work in Mississippi," he insisted: "If they bomb a Negro church and kill our children, we are going to bomb a white church and kill some of their children." Evers later claimed he had been misquoted, but the black reporter for the Nashville *Banner* had a 15-year record for accuracy.[10]

SNCC's early radicalization had almost no roots in Marxist teachings, although Stokeley Carmichael, James Forman, and a few others read Marx and Lenin. Moses described one SNCC staffer as a "revolutionary by necessity," implying that the daily struggle against an unyielding, monolithic system forced workers into increasingly radical positions. Their demands were urgent—in Maryland, Gloria Richardson insisted, "We want it all, here and now."

SNCC workers described themselves as "guerrilla fighters" long before the concepts of Frantz Fanon from the Algerian war entered the terminology of white student radicals. One observer thought the Greenwood, Mississippi, office looked "like a front company headquarters during wartime." SNCC would eventually develop a close identification with Castro's guerrillas in Cuba. It practiced complete self-denial. Its staff, which reached perhaps 250 at its peak (there was no formal membership, only the thousands that joined its projects), was paid a survival wage of $10 a week.

Yet SNCC vigorously rejected the centralism of Castro's régime. Its mood was anarchistic. Despite a few titles and a headquarters staff at Atlanta, it vehemently opposed the leadership principle. Decisions were made at staff meetings, with debates often going on all night and meetings lasting for days.

SNCC had a mystical, almost transcendental faith in the inherent goodness of the poor. The typical SNCC clothing showed this identification—blue jeans or overalls, the flat-topped, broad-brimmed straw hats of the black field workers, the bulky shoes of the laborers. Almost a religious order in its total commitment, SNCC stressed the ability of southern blacks to organize and govern themselves. Its philosophy was to build local cadres among laborers and sharecroppers, to develop independence and pride. "The people are also our teachers," SNCC preached.[11]

This interaction was exemplified in the voter-registration schools to train applicants in the complex questionnaires used to block Negro registration. When 15-year-old Brenda Travis and five of her high school friends staged a sit-in at McComb, Mississippi, they were arrested and received sentences of eight months to a year at the state school for delinquents. Spontaneously, a hundred other students organized a protest march and were refused readmission to school after suspended sentences unless they pledged to take no part in further demonstrations. Eighty refused to sign. Moses thereupon enlarged the registration school for them with a whole range of high school classes, and this academic facility became the prototype of the Freedom Schools of 1964.

SNCC had no use for sentimentality, living existentially from day to day, glorifying direct action. Despite the increasing influence of black nationalism in its ranks, it clung in those early years to the concept of integration, and its picket lines proclaimed in song "black and white together."

Such contradictions often produced a combination of romanticism and hardheadedness in projects like the "mock election" of 1963. Since the few Mississippi blacks registered were excluded by trickery from white primaries, SNCC decided to put up its own candidates on its own ticket. Aaron Henry of NAACP was chosen by caucus to run for governor; the Reverend Edwin King, the white chaplain of black Tougaloo College, for lieutenant governor. It was essentially an exercise in organization, since 93,000 blacks, who voted in November at simulated polling booths, of course elected no one. On the other hand, this outpouring of political pride—voters tramping for miles to cast a dummy ballot—had a hardheaded purpose. It trained blacks to think politically. It formed the base of a real party organized in 1964. It led the way to the Mississippi Freedom Democratic party, which would challenge the political titans of the state and President Lyndon Johnson himself at the Atlantic City Democratic convention the next year.[12]

CORE and SNCC committed their forces to the sit-ins and protest marches attempting to integrate all public facilities in McComb, Mississippi. Two young whites from the North—Tom Hayden, a recent graduate of the University of Michigan, and Paul Potter of the National Student Association—were beaten on the streets. Hayden would shortly be jailed in Albany, Georgia. Both represented the vanguard of the white New Left, which allied itself with the black radicals. Both would become prominent in Students for a Democratic Society (SDS), which established Friends of SNCC units and raised money for SNCC on campuses across the country.

CORE focused on Louisiana, particularly Baton Rouge and Plaquemine Parish. When David Dennis, a sharecropper's son and

CORE field secretary, was arrested with 22 students for picketing in violation of the state's new antidemonstration law, two thousand students from Southern University marched eight miles to the parish jail where the demonstrators were held. The police dispersed them, more than 50 were arrested, and the university eventually barred most from returning to campus.

James Farmer came from CORE headquarters in New York to lead a mass march on Plaquemine on August 19 and September 1, 1963. Born in Texas where his father had been the first black Ph.D. in the state, Farmer held degrees from Boston University and Harvard, helped found CORE in 1942, worked for the NAACP, and returned as CORE's national director in 1961. Louisiana state troopers, mounted on horseback, charged Farmer and the student demonstrators with billy clubs and cattle prods, forcing hundreds to flee to the Plymouth Rock church and parsonage nearby. Then the troopers saturated both buildings with tear gas and high-pressure hoses. The troopers searched all night for Farmer, who had hidden in a funeral home. The demonstrators managed to smuggle him out in a funeral hearse with two armed men following in a car behind.

CORE, strong in North Carolina, staged mass demonstrations in Greensboro and Durham in 1963, concentrating on Howard Johnson restaurants. By fall, almost all Johnson restaurants in the South had been desegregated, but many North Carolina public facilities held out until passage of the Civil Rights Act of 1964.[13]

The main confrontation of those early years came in Albany, Georgia. On December 10, 1961, four SNCC workers, including James Forman and Tom Hayden, took the train from Atlanta to Albany, where they were arrested in the white waiting room and jailed. Two SNCC veterans, Charles Sherrod, 22, and Cordell Reagan, 18, proceeded to organize the Albany Movement from a coalition of women's clubs, businessmen, and student groups.

On December 16, King led a march of 250 to city hall. By August 1962, 1,000 had been jailed, two black churches burned, and a black café owner shot to death for "resisting arrest." A black boycott of the bus line was so effective that the line went out of business.

King and three others were found guilty of parading without a permit, obstructing the sidewalk, and disorderly conduct. They went to jail in July for 45 days rather than pay $178 in fines. What happened then added to the growing tension between King and SNCC radicals, who accused him of trying to take over at Albany after SNCC had done all the organizing.

King was released from jail after a day or so—one bigrapher says he was "ejected"—when an unidentified source paid his fine. The Kennedy administration may have pressured Albany officials, although this has never been verified. King led another prayer vigil on July 27 and was jailed again for two weeks. Except for registering about 500 blacks, the Albany Movement had accomplished little by the end of the summer.[14]

After its early gains, the movement could not seem to shake hard-core pockets of resistance without federal intervention. This principle was tested in September 1962, when federal courts ordered James Meredith, a nine-year veteran of the air force, to be admitted to the University of Mississippi. Attorney General Robert Kennedy provided federal marshals to accompany Meredith to the campus. For almost a week, Governor Ross Barnett turned them back with a wall of state troopers and sheriffs.

Keeping 20,000 army troops in reserve, Kennedy ordered 400 marshals to take Meredith to the administration building on September 30. A mob of about 3,000 attacked the marshals with rocks, Molotov cocktails made from Coke bottles, concrete benches, and even a bulldozer. Since the marshals were allowed tear gas but no ammunition, Kennedy eventually had to call on army units to subdue the campus. Two people were killed; 168 marshals were injured, including 28 wounded by sniper bullets. But on Monday morning, Meredith enrolled at the university.

King now decided on a major confrontation. The place selected was Birmingham, Alabama, the most segregated large city in the nation, where Police Commissioner T. Eugene "Bull" Connor had terrorized blacks for 23 years.

The campaign opened on April 3, 1963, with marchers penetrating downtown areas until a local judge issued an injunction against all demonstrations. King defied it with a march on Good Friday, April 12, and he and 53 others were arrested. On Easter Sunday, blacks swarmed to white churches, but only 4 churches out of 21 admitted them to services.

After Connor broke up demonstration after demonstration with high-velocity fire hoses, thousands of school children joined the march on May 2, some groups almost reaching the steps of city hall. With a thousand more joining the next day, black schools were virtually deserted. Television news programs across the country showed Connor's fire hoses slamming small children against the walls and sidewalks and snarling police dogs lunging at children's throats. It was "revoltingly reminiscent of totalitarian excesses," the New York *Times* commented.

With 2,000 in jail and Birmingham on the brink of chaos, civic leaders opened negotiations with blacks on May 8. But a few days later, a bomb demolished the front of the house of the Reverend A. D. King, Martin's brother. Six more bombs exploded in black areas. As blacks poured into the streets, setting stores on fire and destroying cars, hurling rocks and bottles at the police who ran for cover instead of firing back, the revolt entered a new phase. The Reverend Wyatt T. Walker, a King associate, tried to calm the demonstrators by preaching nonviolence, but a voice from the crowd demanded, "Look what nonviolence got you!"[15]

Governor George Wallace sent 700 highway patrolmen and deputy sheriffs to Birmingham. Armed with rifles, they surged through the Negro districts, shoving and clubbing bystanders with billies and gun butts. The negotiating committee, with Burke Marshall of the Justice Department playing an advisory role, finally came up with a set of token compromises, including desegregation of some downtown stores and the hiring of a few blacks in sales positions. But relative calm was not restored to the city until the Supreme Court ruled on May 20 that Birmingham's segregation ordinances reflected an unconstitutional public policy. Even then, authorities indicted 14 blacks in June under a statute passed in 1830 after the Nat Turner rebellion for "inciting the colored people to acts of violence and war against the white population."

The instant impact of continuous television coverage at Birmingham brought to the nation the immediacy of the black revolt. On June 19, President Kennedy, pressured by the Birmingham crisis, announced he would send a sweeping new civil rights bill to Congress. SNCC and CORE took only a limited part in organizing, but they had strong links to the city's poor and pressured King into increasingly aggressive tactics. The administration tried to moderate King; he, in turn, realized the value of White House cooperation. In fact, the administration tried to stop all demonstrations in early May when they seemed to be getting out of hand.[16]

Birmingham marked a dividing line between King's nonviolent strategy and the emerging violence of the ghettos. SNCC still wanted its alliance with SCLC, but its criticism of King's policies increased. There were factions in SNCC that felt that ghetto blacks were ready for uprisings; and outbreaks in many cities a few months after Birmingham supported this view.

The grand March on Washington of August 28, 1963, bringing an estimated 250,000 people to the capital, also reflected the division between moderates and radicals. It had been conceived by A. Philip Randolph of the Sleeping Car Porters as a demonstration of support for Kennedy's civil rights bill. It was a product of the liberal-labor coalition, which remained convinced that black demands could be satisfied within the system. Its leaders were King, Roy Wilkins of the NAACP, Bayard Rustin of the War Resisters League, Reuther of the Auto Workers. Many unions joined the march, but George Meany of the AFL-CIO refused to endorse it.

Administration advisers feared riots around the White House, so almost 6,000 police were put in the streets, and 4,000 troops were stationed nearby. Agnes E. Meyer, owner of the Washington *Post* and *Newsweek,* predicted "outbreaks of violence, bloodshed and property damage." The only problem, as it turned out, was traffic congestion.

SNCC and CORE, however, protested that the march had become a joint effort with the administration to pass a bill—James Forman attacked the "sell-out leadership of the March"—rather than a demand for jobs and total freedom. Yet John Lewis and Floyd B. McKissick, heads of the two organizations, agreed to speak. Lewis hammered in his speech at the urgency of the revolution: "We want our freedom and we want it now."

Lewis's speech, in fact, focused its attack on the President. "Which side is the government on?" he demanded. "The revolution is a serious one. Mr. Kennedy is trying to take the revolution out of the street and put it into the courts."[17]

SNCC became bitter when Rustin, Randolph, and religious leaders, including Archbishop Patrick O'Doyle, forced Lewis to cut the most provocative sections of his speech. "We shall fragment the South into a thousand pieces, and put them back together again in the image of democracy," Lewis had written in his draft. "We will make the actions of the past few months look pretty."

Despite this censorship, the march was a day of jubilation, the largest gathering in the history of the civil rights movement. A caravan of 200 cars came from North Carolina, 450 buses from New York City, 30,000 people from Philadelphia. An 82-year-old man biked from Ohio; another man roller-skated from Chicago; 12 CORE members walked from Brooklyn. Josephine Baker flew in from Paris in the uniform of the Free French, and other celebrities included Lena Horne, Marlon Brando, Burt Lancaster, about 150 members of Congress, and Marian Anderson. She sang for the huge crowd, which gathered at the Washington Monument and then flowed to the Lincoln Memorial a mile away.[18]

The high point was King's "I have a dream" speech. "I have a dream that one day on the red hills of Georgia, sons of former slaves and the sons of former slaveowners will be able to sit down together at the table of brotherhood," he declared. The speech has become part of American folklore, but not everyone was convinced by its lilting images. Anne Moody, who had driven up from Mississippi, "sat there thinking that in Canton we never had time to sleep, much less to dream." Julius Lester, a black writer, noted that "most black folks just dreamed about eating," and called the march "a grand therapy sermon." More acidly, Malcolm X dubbed it the "Farce on Washington" which had turned black anger into "chic" with a "Kentucky Derby image." All it did was "to lull Negroes for a while."

Such reservations seemed more justifiable a few weeks later. While Governor Wallace's state troopers still rode the streets of Birmingham under Confederate flags on Sunday, September 15, a bomb exploded in the black Baptist church on 16th street, filled with Sunday-school students. Four girls were killed, twenty-one injured. Before the day ended, the toll rose to six. A black youth was shot in the back by police; a 12-year-old boy was killed by two white youths.* Hearing the news on the radio back in Mississippi, Anne Moody wrote in her diary, "You know something else, God. Noviolence is out."[19]

After less than four years of organizing, SNCC and CORE had produced one of the most effective instruments for social change in American history. Now they turned to increasingly revolutionary rhetoric. But the risks were great. Once they went beyond voter registration and became a separate political force, they could lose the financial backing of northern liberals and the White House's limited support. Yet SNCC, in particular, saw an even greater risk of stagnation if it stayed subservient to the liberal coalition. By 1964, relations in SNCC between moderates and those who called themselves revolutionaries, seemed strained beyond repair.

*In November 1977, Robert E. Chambliss was convicted in Montgomery of first-degree murder of the four girls and was sentenced to life imprisonment.

·12·

Summer of Decision 1964

"There's not even a sharp line between living and dying, it's just a thin fuzz," the SNCC lecturer told a meeting of volunteers who had gathered in early June 1964 at Oxford, Ohio, for intensive training before leaving for Mississippi. The volunteers were well aware of the risks in Mississippi Freedom Summer, an ambitious plan to make a dent in the bastion state of segregation by sheer force of numbers. "I've got cannonballs in my stomach," a volunteer commented.

John Doar of the Justice Department emphasized that Washington could not protect them—"We can only investigate." J. Edgar Hoover had already expressed his aversion to the movement, calling King the "most notorious liar in the country." Even when Hoover visited Jackson, Mississippi, on July 10, under pressure from President Johnson, to open a statewide FBI center with 153 agents, he stated brusquely: "We most certainly do not and will not give protection to civil rights workers. The FBI is not a police organization."[1]

The presence of 500 to 600 volunteers, mainly white, would obviously add a new impetus to SNCC's campaign, since much of the staff was close to exhaustion after four years. Some critics categorized the volunteers as "guinea pigs"—although staff lecturers in Ohio constantly urged them to return home if they had any doubts about their durability. SNCC also wanted to focus the attention of the country on the Mississippi struggle in order to hasten passage of a strong civil rights bill, now being pushed by President Johnson following Kennedy's failure the year before. The infusion of hundreds of young whites—some from prominent families, including the son of Congressman W. Donlan Edwards (Dem., Cal.)—would attract the interest of the press. And despite the hazard of increasing black-white tensions, this infusion could step up the campaign for northern money. SNCC's projects already cost $750,000 annually. Yet money was so tight that its staff often went without their subsistence wages for weeks.

Above all, SNCC's objective was to organize its first significant power base, the black Freedom Democratic party, which they hoped would oust the all-white Democratic regulars at the National Convention in August. SNCC wanted everything that summer. Its favorite song was "99-1/2 Won't Do."

The volunteers had come across the country, primarily from college campuses and from secure, often prosperous backgrounds. Ellen Lake came from Radcliffe; Bruce Payne from graduate studies at Yale; Mario Savio, from the University of California at Berkeley, where he would shortly assume a different role in the first major campus rebellion; and a Queens College student, Andrew Goodman, from New York. His name in nationwide headlines would become synonymous with the aspirations and tragedy of that summer.

The volunteers had to finance themselves—$150 each for transportation and living expenses, and a $500 pledge of bail money in case of arrest—and many felt intense family pressure to give up the project. Kay Prickett, for example, a senior at Southern Illinois University at Carbondale, was told by her 70-year-old maternal grandfather, a southerner, "You can choose between the niggers and me." Kay's mother, on the other hand, while frightened for her daughter's safety and trying to persuade her not to go, stated: "I was in tears the whole last week, but I was proud of her."

Many volunteers gave up their personal lives to join the project. One woman used her college graduation money to finance the summer. Another took the funds she had saved for a European trip. A third arrived in Ohio on her wedding day, jilting her fiancé when she found his commitment did not match hers.[2]

Robert Moses told the volunteers: "Mississippi is unreal when you're not there, and the rest of the country unreal when you are." The volunteers would have medical help—a hundred doctors sent into the state by the Medical Committee for Human Rights. Legal protection would come from teams of lawyers supplied by the National Lawyers Guild, ACLU, NAACP's Legal Defense Fund, and other organizations. Four hundred ministers and rabbis were being sent by the National Council of Churches, but the hope that a clerical presence might diminish violence was rudely shattered a few weeks later when Rabbi Arthur Lelyveld of Cleveland was badly beaten at Hattiesburg.

Moses was still at the Ohio training session on June 22 when a staff worker approached him on stage, whispering briefly. Squatting on his haunches, Moses remained bent over, rocking back and forth in anguish. Then he announced, his voice flat and unemotional, his eyes bleak behind thick glasses, that two staff workers and a summer volunteer had been missing since the day before.

Rita Schwerner, 22, painfully thin, dressed in faded blue shorts, came to the blackboard and wrote the names of the missing three and the place—Philadelphia, Neshoba County. One of the missing three was her husband. Another Andrew Goodman, 20, had been sitting in the same auditorium only a few days before and stationed in Mississippi a bare 24 hours.

Goodman had been sent to Meridian, a city of 50,000 not far from the Alabama-Mississippi line. On Sunday, June 21, he drove with two coworkers to inspect a bombed-out church near Philadelphia, the site of frequent registration meetings. Michael H. Schwerner of Brooklyn, N.Y., 24, also white, had studied at the Columbia School of Social Work and had been attached to the CORE office since January. His close friend, James E. Chaney, a 21-year-old black Mississippian, also belonged to CORE. They inspected the church and then were stopped in their blue Ford station wagon about 3 P.M. by Deputy Sheriff Cecil Price, who took them to the Philadelphia jail on a speeding charge. Four black witnesses later swore that Price had shot the right rear tire. Price later testified that he had released the three on bond about 10:30 that night.

At 6 P.M., SNCC headquarters notified the FBI and State Highway Patrol that the three were definitely missing. But it was not until 6 A.M. the following day that four FBI agents entered the case; not till 9:30 that night that agents reached Philadelphia; not till June 25 that 200 sailors from the Meridian air station were assigned to the search.

The lure of a $25,000 reward finally produced clues from a white informer in Philadelphia. On August 4, the three bodies were found. Later testimony showed that the young men, after release from jail, had been seized in a wild car chase by a local mob, mainly Ku Klux Klan members. Schwerner had been shot through the heart, then Goodman, both without a struggle. Chaney, who had probably been beaten with chains, put up a brief struggle and was shot three times. "At least I killed me a nigger," one Klansman reportedly said. After examining Chaney's body, Dr. David Spain, a New York medical examiner, testified, "In my twenty-five years as a pathologist, I have never witnessed bones so severely shattered."[3]

The bodies had been taken to a dam site six miles from Philadelphia and buried in a trench dug by bulldozer along the length of the dam. The blue station wagon was driven 15 miles away, doused with diesel fuel, and burned. The mob then gathered at the local courthouse square in Philadelphia where a Mississippi state official announced, "The one who talks is dead, dead, dead."

At Chaney's funeral, David Dennis of CORE cried: "If you go back home and sit down and take what these white men in Mississippi are doing to us . . . if you take it and don't do something about it, then God damn your souls!" The murders quickly concentrated national attention on Freedom Summer. But even that had its ironic side. As Rita Schwerner observed, "If he [her husband] and Andrew Goodman had been Negroes, the world would have taken little notice of their death."[4]

Five blacks had already been killed in Mississippi between January and May 1964 without any serious investigation by authorities. After a black storekeeper was beaten by two policemen in Canton on May 29, and a bomb exploded outside CORE headquarters, James Farmer pleaded vainly for an appointment with Attorney General Robert Kennedy. Only after the Chaney-Goodman-Schwerner murders would President Johnson order the FBI to give unofficial protection to civil rights workers.

As it was, the FBI did not arrest 21 Neshoba County men, including Sheriff Lawrence Rainey and Price, until December 4, and Gov. Paul B. Johnson, Jr., refused to allow the state attorney general to bring charges because of inadequate evidence. The Justice Department thereupon called a federal grand jury in Meridian, which handed down an indictment against 18 men for conspiracy to violate constitutional rights. Federal Judge William Harold Cox tried to reduce the charge to a misdemeanor until the Supreme Court reversed him. A jury subsequently found seven guilty, including Price. They were given sentences of three to ten years in jail. Rainey and the others were acquitted. It was the first known occasion that an all-white jury in the state had convicted white defendants in a civil rights case.[5]

The threat of death that hung over Freedom Summer intensified the shift toward violence. In Greenwood, two brothers, Silas and Jake McGee, tried to buy tickets to a white movie theater. On July 25, shots were fired into their house. Joined by their half-brother, Clarence Robinson, a 6-foot 6-inch paratrooper home on furlough, they invaded another theater only to be attacked by 200 whites. Jake was hit in the eye and had to be taken to the hospital. SNCC cars that followed him were fired on. White cars blocked the hospital driveway when Jake tried to leave after treatment. The sheriff only agreed to escort him home after intervention by the Department of Justice.

The next night, more blacks tried to gain admission to a white restaurant, and Silas was shot through the left side of his throat while sitting in a car. From that point on, young blacks guarded SNCC offices around the clock with guns. "I'm saying that you only resort to violence after you have done everything possible to avoid it," Robinson told a SNCC meeting.

Natalie Tompkins, a volunteer from Melrose, Massachusetts, staying with a farm family 10 miles outside Canton, recalled: "It [was] like an armory, rifles in every room." The volunteers' only lifeline to summon aid was a black grocery store four miles away, but they lost that when the sheriff told the grocer he'd be in trouble if the white girls used his phone. All told that summer, 80 volunteers were beaten and 3 wounded in 35 shootings. Thirty-five black churches and 31 homes were burned or bombed.[6]

Working in rural areas of wooden and tin shacks, where women cotton pickers made $2.50 a day, one white volunteer wrote, "Living conditions are so terrible, the Negroes here are so completely oppressed, so completely without hope, that I want to change it all NOW." Most volunteers established close links to the local families with whom they lived. "This is Nancy, my adopted daughter," one black woman always introduced her summer guest. The volunteers gradually adapted to the terror that SNCC lawyers could do little to alleviate. After her arrest and jailing, Sally Belfrage requested, "We want to see our lawyer." The deputy sheriff replied, "Your lawyer's in jail." Bruce Payne, who had been beaten by four whites and later fired upon in a frantic car chase, concluded, "The very horror of Mississippi is that terror and violence have come to seem normal and natural. . . ."

In the North, Freedom Summer brought increasing references to retaliation. At a New York Town Hall forum in June, David Susskind, the moderator, observed, "I have never heard such carefully couched calls for violence and bloodshed in a long time." He quoted another panelist, John Killens, a black author, as saying, "We haven't had a bloody revolution, we need a revolution."[7]

Despite daily terror, the Mississippi registration campaign pushed ahead—Stokely Carmichael and his partner alone registered 600 people.

One aim of the freedom schools established that summer was to prepare blacks for political leadership. The schools also aimed at furthering the education of all age groups. With no compulsory-education law in Mississippi, the average black attended school for only six years, usually in split sessions wedged between chopping and picking seasons in the fields. A black education cost the state half what it spent on a white child, but in places like Yazoo County, only a fourth or less of white expenditures.[8]

Classes were always linked to the movement. French teachers conjugated, "We love freedom." Math classes centered on practical examples of installment buying. Farmers were taught about un-tapped federal sources of financial aid. The most popular course was black history. Directed by Staughton Lynd, a Yale professor and Quaker who had taught at a black college and a rural Georgia cooperative, the freedom schools opened 47 branches with 2,165 students by the end of the summer.

The sudden influx of hundreds of white women volunteers into Mississippi black communities provoked the expected sexual tensions—"the typical attitude of the Southern white is that obviously I'm sleeping with Negro guys," a University of California undergraduate observed in her diary. After a meeting at a black church, a white woman volunteer asked a local youth to drive her a quarter of a mile to a grocery store to buy a pack of cigarettes. The trip took 10 minutes, but the next day the police spread the word the two had been kissing in the front seat, and, under pressure from the sheriff, the youth was fired from his job.[9]

Similar tensions were already affecting the internal dynamics of SNCC and CORE. Black demands that CORE should be a completely black organization erupted in the Newark chapter as early as 1961. The chairwoman of the New York chapter in 1962 opposed Farmer's appointment as national director partly on the grounds that he had a white wife. The Detroit chapter almost broke apart over the role of white members.

In SNCC, whites held only a limited number of staff positions, but they were always southern whites of remarkable ability. Robert Zellner, son of an Alabama Methodist preacher, had been beaten and jailed as much as anyone in the movement, including a Louisiana charge of criminal anarchy that brought four weeks' imprisonment before the indictment was dropped. Ralph Allen was arrested in

Americus, Georgia, for "inciting an insurrection," a capital offense in that state. He spent four months in jail without bail and with the threat of death over his head until a federal court ruled the insurrection law unconstitutional.[10]

Still, the issue plagued SNCC increasingly, particularly when black staffers developed more companionships with white volunteer women than the white men developed with black women. It also affected SNCC's political polarization. Cleveland Sellers, the program secretary, noted a growing split between two factions he called the "stars" and the "hardliners." The first group, led by Moses, was mainly college-educated, part-white and part-black, and clung to the integrationist concept. The second consisted almost entirely of blacks who would shortly demand a "black power" orientation.

None of these issues, however, diluted the main objective of Freedom Summer, the organization of the Mississippi Freedom Democratic party (MFDP). Founded at Jackson on April 26, 1964, it had 60,000 members throughout the state within a few months.

The MFDP contended it was the only legal representative of the national Democratic party and that its delegates must be seated at the national convention in August. It argued that the vast majority of blacks had been unlawfully prevented from registering in the Democratic party, and that even those registered had been blocked by fraud from voting in the precinct meetings of the Democratic regulars on June 16. These meetings were generally held in secret at private homes, resulting in tight control by a handful of whites in each precinct. By contrast, the MFDP had hundreds of blacks at each open precinct meeting, and 2,500 delegates at its state convention. But even more important in terms of party legality, the Democratic regulars announced on June 30 that they rejected both the national platform and President Johnson. Many state leaders, in fact, supported Senator Barry Goldwater (Rep., Ariz.), the Republican presidential candidate.

After Americans for Democratic Action and key delegations like New York backed MFDP's claim, the struggle to unseat the Mississippi regulars came to dominate the Atlantic City convention.

Meanwhile, the anger in northern ghettos triggered a new explosion. President Johnson had tried to head it off with his promise of the "Great Society" in May 1964 and his Office of Economic Opportunity (OEO), which had just started trickling funds into poverty areas. But Johnson's "unconditional war on poverty" raised expectations that were never met. Only $800 million was allotted in the first fiscal year, and $1.5 billion starting in July 1965, before the Vietnam war eroded such social programs. About one of every two nonwhite families remained below the poverty level of $3,130 annual income (the OEO estimate for an urban family of four), compared with only one family out of five among whites.[11]

Many CORE chapters sought to force more poverty funds out of the administration with tactics that the national office generally opposed. At the opening of the New York World's Fair in April, for example, Brooklyn CORE staged a "stall-in" of cars on surrounding roads that resulted in 300 arrests.

President Johnson thought he had mollified discontent with the passage of the Civil Rights Act of 1964. The most concrete result of murders and confrontations in Birmingham and Mississippi, the act prohibited discrimination in theaters, restaurants, and other public accommodations, in employment and union membership, and in federally supported programs. The President signed it into law on July 2. Ironically, a wave of rioting broke out in New York and other cities within two weeks.

On July 16, a black youth of 15 who had been attending summer school about a mile from New York's Harlem, was shot to death by Lieut. Thomas R. Gilligan. The police officer, then off-duty, claimed the youth had threatened him with a knife. Gilligan said he had fired one warning shot before killing the boy. On Saturday, July 18, CORE held a protest rally in Harlem and marched on the local precinct headquarters to demand Gilligan's suspension. When scuffles broke out, Inspector Thomas V. Prendergast ordered CORE leaders arrested, shouting, according to a report from a CORE official: "I've had enough of this. Get them niggers." As the crowd started throwing bottles and bricks, police rushed out of the station house, supported by arriving members of the Tactical Police Force, and attacked the blacks. The inspector "lost his head," James Farmer concluded.

The riots grew over the next five nights, reaching their peak after the funeral service for the slain youth. Squads of steel-helmeted police fired steadily at rooftops from which missiles were being hurled. "There were hundreds of cops running in circles, and they were all shooting," a reporter noted. A businessman, owner of the same store for 27 years, complained, "When I tried to put out a fire in front of my building, I was hit with a club by the cops." In the first night of rioting, 15 blacks were shot, one fatally, and 116 injured, including 12 policemen. Farmer thought the police "behaved badly" and described it as a "blood bath."

Certainly police brutality in Harlem had contributed to the riot, but the growth of black nationalism had some impact. Addressing a crowd at one point, Jesse Gray, leader of militant rent strikes, called for "a hundred dedicated men who are ready to die for Negro equality." A woman shouted, "Let's bomb them. Let's get bombs and destroy them." When Bayard Rustin, whose moderate viewpoint was well known, tried to calm the crowd, he was hooted down with cries of "Uncle Tom."

The Progressive Labor party (PL), an extremist Marxist faction organized in 1962, had concentrated on Harlem in recent months. Its newspaper, *Challenge,* stated: "There is no lawful government in this country today. Only a revolution will establish one." A black detective who had infiltrated PL's Harlem Defense Committee testified it had distributed leaflets on the production of Molotov cocktails. William Epton, PL's local black leader, supposedly told one meeting, "We will not be fully free until we smash this state completely. . . ." Six days after the riot subsided, Epton called for a protest march through Harlem. But all black organizations, including CORE, opposed the march and warned of renewed bloodshed. The city obtained a restraining order against the march, and only a handful showed up.[12]

New York City officials and the Police Department were determined to prove that the riot had been triggered by Communists, ignorant that PL and the Communist party were bitter antagonists. "A five-month investigation by dozens of top detectives, working in close cooperation with the FBI, has disclosed widespread Communist infiltration—so much so that they command 1,000 young fanatics dedicated to violence," the New York *Daily News* reported on July 22. On the Senate floor that same day, Sen. James Eastland (Dem., Miss.) extended the anti-Communist attack to Mississippi and the Freedom Summer volunteers, claiming he had proof of the "red record of white workers."

Epton was arrested on July 25 and was indicted in August for criminal anarchy and advocating the overthrow of New York State. Almost a dozen PL members were cited for contempt for refusing to testify. In December, Epton was convicted, largely on the evidence of an undercover police agent, and jailed.

The use of PL as a scapegoat ignored the basic cause of the riot: it occurred not only because of police overaction and misconduct, but as Farmer pointed out, "because ghetto conditions manufactured

social dynamite; because a legitimate case of police brutality, symbolic of a million other brutalities, came along to light the fuse.
. . ." The mass migration to the North after 1940, when 75 percent of blacks still lived in the South, had produced black majorities in the District of Columbia and Newark. More than a third of the populations of Baltimore, Cleveland, Detroit, and Saint Louis was black. These ghettos held a new breed of militant, instantly in touch with the southern struggle through television and their own organizations.[13]

As a result, riots became the principal outlet for ghetto protest, and the Harlem outbreak quickly spread to Brooklyn and Rochester, New York; to Jersey City, Patterson, and Elizabeth, New Jersey; to Chicago, and to Philadelphia. "Temple University in Philadelphia," one witness noted, "looked like bombed-out, war-time Berlin."

Fearful that the riots could produce a white backlash against his administration, President Johnson called black leaders to the White House and convinced King, Wilkins, and Whitney Young to issue a statement urging "a broad curtailment, if not total moratorium of all mass marches, picketing and demonstrations until after Election Day, November 3." SNCC and CORE refused to go along with the moratorium.[14]

The trend toward urban violence had been shaped earlier in Cambridge, Maryland, a small city on the eastern shore. It seemed like an unexpected site for a bloody struggle that would bring the city close to civil war. But until bridges were built to shorten the trip to Baltimore, Cambridge resembled Mississippi, a rural outpost dominated by a white aristocracy and rigid patterns of segregation modeled on the Deep South.

SNCC had moved into Cambridge early in 1961 with sit-ins and demonstrations at movie theaters and restaurants. The leader of the Nonviolent Action Committee, probably the first woman to achieve this status, was Gloria Richardson, a graduate of Howard University. Her family had lived in the area for generations. The power structure allowed one black official, and her grandfather had represented the black ward on the city council. But Richardson, who wore green military dungarees on every picket line, represented a new philosophy. A supporter of Malcolm X and the Black Muslims, she preached armed self-defense. After two years of fruitless demonstrations, police beatings, and jailings (Richardson herself went to jail 12 times), Cambridge would become the first city where SNCC members openly carried hunting guns, which were allowed under state law.

The increasing skirmishes and gunfire between the white community of 8,000 and the black community of 4,200 had reached the danger point by June 1963, when Gov. J. Millard Tawes sent in the National Guard. Despite military command posts on every corner, white gangs roamed the black district at night. Richardson told a reporter she could no longer "control 2nd Ward residents who have turned to violence."[15]

On July 12, the "eighteen-month-old war," the Baltimore *Afro-American* reported, "finally exploded . . . and unchained violence swept the streets of Cambridge." The incident that set it off was the arrest of a 17-year-old black, accused of having a paring knife in his possession. Chanting "Freedom, Freedom," the Baltimore paper said, crowds of "heavily armed" blacks surged into the streets. Two cars, crowded with armed whites, raced back and forth through Pine Street, the Negro business center, with guns blazing at windows and doorways. From rooftops and windows, blacks fired back. The gun battle lasted over an hour, and "bullets literally rained on the county seat of Dorchester county."

Armed clashes continued for two weeks—six people shot in the first three days. Richardson telegraphed President Kennedy, requesting he come to Cambridge to "avert civil war," but the only response was an increase in the number of guardsmen.[16]

The National Guard preserved an uneasy truce until the spring of 1964, with armed blacks holding a defense perimeter around their district. "Black men in Cambridge usually slept during the day, and patrolled the community at night," Richardson remembered. But the truce was broken by the arrival of Governor Wallace of Alabama, the most aggressive spokesman for segregation since the Birmingham confrontation, now campaigning for presidential delegates in the Maryland primary. Six hundred blacks marched to the meeting to protest his presence. A detachment of guardsmen met them at the edge of the white district, advancing with drawn bayonets and firing gas cylinders that filled throats and stomachs "like burning acid," Cleveland Sellers of SNCC recalled. The blacks stood firm; shots were fired. Stokely Carmichael, badly hurt, was rushed to a hospital. Richardson and dozens of others were arrested and held at the Pikesville armory for two days.

Cambridge would be plagued by riots during the next few years, but 1964 was the dividing line, a point when many black radicals decided that the movement would have to be forged in blood. "I thought 1964 was the time for revolution," Richardson observed. "The blacks were ready for it."[17]

Malcolm X admitted that "in the white man's press," he had become "a symbol—if not a causative agent" of violence. Black Muslim influence had grown sharply for a year or two before the 1964 riots. The Muslims preached a fanatic nationalism, complete separation of blacks from whites, a sovereign black nation in the West on lands they demanded the government deed them. They hammered incessantly at hatred of the white man—he was the devil, total evil. They repudiated the United States and refused to serve in the armed forces. They rejected Christianity—their religion was Islam.

"This is a real revolution," Malcolm insisted in 1964. "I'm for violence if nonviolence means we continue postponing a solution to the American black man's problem—just to avoid violence."[18]

Black Muslim membership was estimated at 50,000 to 250,000, but its impact reached every ghetto. There were three mosques in New York City alone, parochial schools in Chicago and Detroit, a university in Chicago, hundreds of Muslim restaurants, barbershops, and stores. Part of their strength came from rabid discipline; they disdained smoking, liquor, drugs, prostitution, and dressed with exemplary neatness. Respected by social workers for their rehabilitation of black prisoners, they were rarely involved in crime. Malcolm himself converted to Islam during a 10-year jail sentence for theft.

Malcolm's audience was the poor and oppressed. A spellbinding speaker, he reached them with vivid, uncomplicated words, cutting through the "chains on black minds like a giant blowtorch," Julius Lester noted. Malcolm's aim was to restore the black man's pride, his shattered manhood. Even black liberals who disliked him took a secret pleasure in the way "he frightens the white man." He was an extremist, tearing down one society but with little plan for replacing it, at least until the last year or so of his life. As he counseled Alex Haley, coauthor of his *Autobiography,* when Haley's brother became a state senator: "Tell him that he and all the other moderate Negroes who are getting somewhere need to always remember that it was us extremists who made it possible."[19]

The chief lieutenant of Elijah Muhammad, founder of the Nation of Islam in the United States, Malcolm broke with his mentor in March 1964, after 13 years. Probably he was forced out. As editor of the sect's newspaper, controlling its propaganda, and crisscrossing the country constantly on speaking engagements, Malcolm became far better known than Muhammad. Further, he had quietly criticized Muhammad for immorality after two of Elijah's former secretaries claimed in court he had fathered their children. Malcolm was evicted from his New York house, owned by the Muslims, and predicted that his former associates would plot his murder. He and his followers immediately organized their own Muslim mosque in Harlem and the Organization of Afro-American Unity.

Just before this rupture with the Muslims, Malcolm X had gone through a climactic personal crisis during a pilgrimage to Mecca, the sacred fount of the Islam religion. Meeting Islamic leaders of all colors, even blue-eyed whites, he had been transformed at Mecca by a "radical alteration in my whole outlook about 'white' men," he wrote. "The true Islam" had shown him that a "blanket indictment of all white people" was wrong. He even revised his views on inter-marriage, now regarding it simply as a personal matter. "No one who knew him before and after his trip to Mecca could doubt that he had completely abandoned racism, separatism and hatred," Ossie Davis, the black actor, concluded.[20]

Rejecting the Muslim position that a white political party was so evil it must be totally boycotted, Malcolm went to Selma, Alabama, at SNCC's invitation to aid voter registration. He was no longer simply an American black nationalist. He now became a black inter-nationalist, preaching that the fate of the African black was insepara-ble from the American black, and that colonialism abroad and rac-ism at home could only be destroyed through the destruction of capitalism. He adopted the rhetoric of the social revolutionary, al-though he never lived to define his vague Marxist leanings.

Addressing an audience at New York's Audubon ballroom on February 21, 1965, impeccable as always in a seersucker suit, Mal-colm was shot down by at least three gunmen sitting in the front rows. Sixteen shotgun pellets or revolver slugs were found in his body. Although he had predicted an assassination plot and con-stantly asked for police protection, none of the 20 policemen, head-quarters said were guarding the meeting could be accounted for by members of the audience. Only one of the presumed killers—chased by members of the audience—was caught by police. Since Malcolm had his own personal guards, and the audience had been screened, the killing must have been carefully plotted by those who had gained Malcolm's confidence. He left four young daughters and a pregnant wife, but no savings or insurance.[21]

Malcolm's fiery nationalism not only helped create the mood for riots in Harlem and elsewhere but led to the confrontation at Atlantic City, the bloodshed at Cambridge, Maryland, and Black Power risings that followed. SNCC, and later the Black Panthers, would revere Malcolm's teachings. After his death, many radicals abandoned their nonviolent philosophy for good.

Lyndon Johnson, consumed as no other President before him by the need to win the 1964 election by the greatest landslide in history, made the Atlantic City convention an imperial celebration. He had scheduled it for August 27, the week of his birthday. A giant 44-foot-high portrait of himself hung above the stage, dominating the consciousness of delegates. The only holdout from the Johnson bandwagon was a shaky coalition of New Left whites, pledged to go only "Part of the Way with LBJ," or not at all, and the Mississippi Freedom Democratic party.

The MFDP delegation of 64 blacks and 4 whites, representing 850,000 unregistered voters of the state, had come to the national convention with high hopes of being accepted as the legal party. They had pledged to sign loyalty oaths to the Democratic party. The Mississippi regulars had refused. The regulars, as Richard Rovere pointed out in *The New Yorker,* "had scarcely any more claim to be seated . . . than a delegation of Republicans, Communists or Prohibitionists."

In addition to support from nine key delegations, including New York and Michigan, 25 Democratic members of the House, and labor blocs such as the United Auto Workers, the MFDP had the moral authority of a cause that both Kennedy and Johnson had championed. The delegation was final proof that segregated blacks could organize at a grass-roots level, that the radicals of SNCC could work through the democratic process and secure their rights by democratic means.

Further, the MFDP already had the support of at least 11 members of the credentials committee, the vote needed to get the issue on to the convention floor. "I have only an hour to tell you a story of moral agony that could take years," Joseph L. Rauh, Jr., former chairperson of ADA and counsel for the UAW, told the credentials committee hearing. His witnesses, capped by the bittersweet eloquence of Fannie Lou Hamer, a symbol of black emergence from poverty to political involvement, caught the emotions of the television audience.[22]

When the MFDP issue seemed certain of reaching the floor, Lyndon Johnson stepped in. He was determined to avoid a floor debate that could jar the unanimity of this orchestrated machine. He probably clung to the notion that enough Mississippi regulars might still take the state for the Democratic party, or at least that they had to be placated to hold other Deep South delegations. His hunger for complete mastery of the party overcoming his previous support for the black movement, Johnson insisted on a disturbing compromise. He agreed to accept two token delegates from the MFDP as long as all the regulars were seated.

Johnson rammed through his compromise with the kind of relentless political muscle he had perfected in years of Senate leadership. Senator Hubert Humphrey, almost certain to be Johnson's vice-presidential choice, was put on notice that his candidacy depended on stopping the MFDP. Administration pressure on the credentials committee—a threatened loss of federal judgeships and poverty program money—reduced support to four votes. Walter Reuther of the UAW, a heavy contributor to King's SCLC, swung him to the compromise, and undoubtedly pressured Rauh.

The full force of the labor-liberal bloc—Senator Wayne Morse (Dem., Ore.), Rustin, Wilkins, King, and Rauh—was thrown against the MFDP. But although Aaron Henry and Edwin King sat with the Alaska contingent as delegates-at-large, the MFDP caucus, led by Hamer, Robert Moses, and James Forman, rejected compromise. "We didn't come all this way for no two seats," Hamer retorted.[23]

In a last-ditch attempt to sway the convention, MFDP delegates borrowed floor passes from sympathetic delegates, filtered onto the convention floor, and took over the seats of the Mississippi regulars. But it was a maneuver of desperation. The convention approved the compromise. Even then, only three Mississippi regulars signed a loyalty oath and took their seats; the rest walked out. Johnson carried 44 states on election day, winning 486 electoral votes to 52. Except for his own state of Arizona, Goldwater won only five states, all in the Deep South, including Mississippi, which the President had tried so frantically to appease.

When the newly elected Congress met on January 4, 1965, the MFDP tried again. It had run three candidates that fall against the regulars—Hamer, for example, against Jamie Whitten, seeking his thirteenth term in a district where a shade over 4 percent of Negroes were registered. The MFDP election, of course, was extralegal, a mock election held before November 3. But it showed that the Mississippi radicals still clung to the electoral system.

Sponsored by Congressman William Fitts Ryan (Dem., N.Y.), the MFDP consequently challenged the seating of four incumbent Democratic regulars and one newly elected Goldwater Republican on January 4. The House, however, by a majority of 127 votes authorized the Speaker to administer the oath of office to the regulars. Again on September 17, 1965, although by a smaller majority of 85 votes, the House rejected another MFDP challenge to the right of the Mississippi delegation to its seats.[24]

Atlantic City was a testing ground for black radicals, a crucible of disillusion. They had tried to work within the system, to maintain a coalition with the Democratic party. Now they were convinced that the President's poverty funds were basically a ploy to buy off black militancy and break the back of the movement. They were convinced that the liberal-labor alliance was more concerned with power politics than the morality of the MFDP cause, and had assumed the right to define the limits of radicalism.

The years of agony that had gone into building the MFDP possibly affected their judgment—for the Civil Rights Act of 1964, followed by a stronger act in 1965, provided considerable progress toward their goals. But the injustice done at Atlantic City seemed to show that the system was so corrupt it could never work for them. As President Johnson increasingly failed in his pledges to stop the Vietnam buildup, and poverty funds were slashed under the pressure of Vietnam arms, Atlantic City took on added significance. Large segments of the movement abandoned coalition politics and openly broke with the system. By 1965, many would become committed revolutionaries.

· 13 ·

The New Left and the Berkeley Uprising 1960-64

On May 13, 1960, hundreds of students waited for admission to the hearing room of the House Un-American Activities Committee (HUAC) at San Francisco's city hall. Two thousand had rallied in Union Square the day before to protest the hearings. Now the police ordered the students to leave after admitting only a handful and packing the room with HUAC's own supporters, granted special white cards. But the students sat down on the floor instead, an action reminiscent of the black sit-ins that started in North Carolina only a few months earlier. As in the southern movement, the California students sang "We Shall Not Be Moved."

Unrolling fire hoses, the police focused heavy streams of water on the recumbent bodies. Some of the students fled from the barrage before the police moved in on the others with their clubs swinging. At least 150 students were dragged down a long flight of marble stairs, their heads and spines striking the steps, the women often pulled by their hair. Many lay bleeding or unconscious in pools of water at the door. "Never in twenty years as a reporter have I seen such brutality," a New York *Post* correspondent observed.

This day, soon called "Black Friday," marked the end of almost a decade of campus retreat from political action during the McCarthy era. It also marked the opening confrontation of a new political movement among middle-class white students that would eventually become the New Left.

Black Friday represented a strange fusion of past and present. The claims by HUAC and the police that the demonstrations were a Communist plot seemed like a McCarthyite scenario. Even the rhetoric belonged to 1952—Congressman August E. Johansen (R., Mich.) in a HUAC-produced film on the confrontation described the students as "toying with treason" and "hand-picked by the Communists to do the work of the Communists."[1]

There were, of course, a few Communists involved, who openly identified themselves. But the overwhelming majority of the demonstrators—5,000 turned out on the last day—were moderate and even nonpoliticized students from the University of California at Berkeley and other Bay Area colleges who were simply determined to stop the red-baiting excesses of HUAC. They had the backing, in fact, of 300 Berkeley faculty members and of the *Daily Californian,* the student newspaper.

HUAC and the police were equally unsuccessful in proving that the Communists had tried to start a riot and crash their way into the hearing room. Sixty-two of 63 students arrested on Black Friday were exonerated in court immediately, and one a year later. Their trials showed that the students had taken nonviolent positions on the floor, and that the attack and subsequent struggles had been initiated by the police.

The real issue, however, was not Communism at all. Black Friday was the starting point of the New Left because of HUAC's attempt to use the red-baiting tactics of the past against the new black revolt in the South. Berkeley had become a center of support for the black sit-ins and freedom rides. The CORE chapter, as well as the socialists and other youth factions of the Old Left, had not only raised money but had kept constant picket lines around Woolworth's and similar chain stores to break down their resistance to integration of their southern stores. The students were particularly infuriated because many of those subpoenaed by HUAC were civil rights leaders in the Bay Area. HUAC, therefore, had only a token interest in the few known Communists. Its purpose was to crush the alliance between campus activists and the black revolt, and its technique of red-baiting SNCC, CORE, and even Martin Luther King would be stepped up over the next few years.

The links between the Old and New Left were modest but still important. The Marxist factions on campus, it is true, had dwindled away. The Communist Labor Youth League folded in 1957; the Young Socialist Alliance (Trotskyists) and the Young People's Socialist League (Socialist party) had miniscule memberships.

Yet Berkeley, more than any other campus, retained a radical tradition that made it an obvious springboard for the New Left. Many of its faculty had participated in Left politics of the 1930s and 1940s, producing a fusion of two generations that was particularly effective in civil rights and antinuclear protest. Further, the campus had a secondary tier of support: both the hippie-beatnik world of San

Francisco and the nonstudent world of Berkeley. Hundreds of militants from the thirties had settled nearby, feeding on the cultural ferment of the university, frustrated by past defeats, obviously longing for rejuvenation through a new struggle.

Above all, the first stirrings of the New Left were molded by a sizable contingent of children of the Old Left, who had come to Berkeley because of its radical tradition as well as academic standards. These so-called red-diaper babies—somewhat of a misnomer since most parents had long split with Communism—brought considerable political sophistication to the campus. David Horowitz, for example, then a Berkeley undergraduate, read the *Worker* as a boy at home and was sent by his parents to Communist summer camps. Michael Rossman, another undergraduate, had a Bolshevik grandfather in Russia who had been imprisoned and exiled by the czar.

Such red-diaper babies dominated the leadership of SLATE, a campus political party organized in 1957 with a membership ranging from moderates to Maoists. SLATE put up one of its moderates for student body president in 1959 and got him elected. It also capitalized on the energies unleashed by the HUAC demonstration to call a conference at Mount Madonna Park, California, in the summer of 1960. Mount Madonna probably ranks as the first nationwide gathering of the budding New Left. Tom Hayden, who had helped start VOICE, a political party at the University of Michigan patterned on SLATE, would spend the summer of 1960 at Berkeley digesting radical politics. Hayden, who came from a middle-class Catholic background and would join SNCC in the South that fall, represents a further link between the ferment on white campuses and the black revolt.

The early New Left rejected Stalin and almost all orthodox ideology. "What struck me immediately," Horowitz observed, "is that my generation didn't give a damn about Stalin. How could we deal with Stalinism? Only by emphasizing moral issues in place of ideology, only by taking a moral view of both America and the Soviet Union. When we opposed nuclear testing, we demonstrated against both American and Soviet testing." Rossman concluded that the "trademark of the new radicals is a primitive moral ideology."[2]

The early New Left became a constant search for moral symbols. One symbol at San Quentin prison in San Francisco was Caryl Chessman who had been tried for rape but faced execution because the state had convicted him on a technical charge of kidnapping. Held on death row for 11 years, Chessman gained wide support through the moral quality of his books and articles among not only opponents of capital punishment but also Quakers and other humanists. In April and early May 1960, these groups, joined by hundreds of California students, held daily vigils outside the prison, determined that each individual must protest injustice through a personal act of defiance. When the state supreme court refused a stay and Chessman was executed on May 2, the students outside the jail "stood shaking with rage and frustration," Horowitz recorded.

Similar personal acts of moral defiance were aimed at the Reserve Officers Training Corps at Berkeley, another reminder of the past since the students of the 1930s had also focused on ROTC. In October 1959, Fred Moore, Jr., son of an air force colonel, staged a two-day fast on the steps of a Berkeley building to demand the transfer of ROTC from a compulsory to a voluntary course. Seven thousand students signed a petition in support, many picketing the ROTC drill field.

The peace movement, in which the anti-ROTC campaign became an important facet, provided further continuity between radical pacifists of an earlier generation and the New Left. Dr. Linus Pauling, the biochemist, winner of the Nobel Peace prize in 1954 and later in 1962, announced that 11,000 scientists world-wide (almost 3,000 of the Americans) had signed a petition opposing nuclear testing. Senator Eastland had his Internal Security Subcommittee investigate Pauling and portrayed his campaign as a Communist front.

The National Committee for a Sane Nuclear Policy (SANE), founded in 1957 by such liberals as Norman Cousins of the *Saturday Review*, Eleanor Roosevelt, and Norman Thomas, achieved enough influence through its 130 chapters to attract the attention of U.S. Senator Thomas J. Dodd (D., Conn.), who accused it of being Communist-infiltrated.

One organizer of SANE's Madison Square Garden rally in New York had indeed been a member of the American Labor party and Wallace's 1948 campaign. But he refused to discuss Communist affiliation with SANE's leadership. SANE thereupon fired him and passed a resolution disqualifying members or chapters adhering to "communist or other totalitarian doctrine." Objecting to a revival of McCarthyite tactics, a number of prominent board members, including Pauling, and about half the New York chapters (constituting about half the national chapters), resigned from SANE, crippling the organization.[3]

The most important figures for the early New Left were radical pacifists like A. J. Muste and David Dellinger, grouped around *Liberation* magazine, the Fellowship of Reconciliation, and War Resisters League. They generally opposed capitalism as well as war and practiced nonviolent direct-action tactics. They aided the protest by Albert Bigelow and his crew, who tried to sail the *Golden Rule* into the H-bomb test area of the Pacific in 1958 and were jailed for 60 days. At the same time, the *Phoenix,* commanded by anthropologist Earle Reynolds, actually penetrated the test zone.

At the Omaha Intercontinental Ballistic Missile base in 1959, a group including the 75-year-old Muste climbed the fence to protest nuclear weapons and ended up in jail. Another group boarded nuclear submarines at New London, Connecticut, in 1960.

Campus radicalization received further impetus from the Student Peace Union (SPU), founded by Midwest socialists and pacifists in 1959. It would soon have 5,000 members and 12,000 subscribers to its bulletin. It would turn out 1,000 students at Harvard and 3,000 at Berkeley for its demonstrations. In fact, much of the New Left's eventual resistance to Vietnam and the draft was foreshadowed in this period. Tom Cornell, a young Catholic Worker, burned his draft card in 1960, the first of thousands of burnings that were to become symbols of resistance. Peter Irons, a socialist, sent back his draft card in 1960, the first to advocate this technique in the SPU bulletin. Eventually he would serve 26 months in prison for draft refusal.[4]

Much of the early mood of the New Left—as well as some shock troops—came from an underground subsociety that had gathered in colonies like San Francisco's North Beach, Los Angeles's Venice, and New York's East Village. This underground rejected America's materialist, industrialized, and conformist society as well as its sexual repression and bourgeois values in family and culture. Its inner-directedness produced an addiction to mysticism and Zen Buddhism. Its troubadors were Allen Ginsberg, author of *Howl,* and at first Jack Kerouac, who reflected a nostalgia for the open road of the Wobblies that had been suffocated by the neon jungle of suburban shopping strips. Its growing bitterness and despair led to the harsh satire of Lenny Bruce, and finally to the hard-drug mania of William Burroughs.

The New Left kept some of this subsociety's trappings, particularly its dress, its sexual freedom, its aversion to all puritanism and hypocrisy. But the two movements had no basic common ground. The beat world rejected politics and had generally disassociated itself from society.

The New Left, by contrast, met reality head on, whether at HUAC hearings or antinuclear demonstrations. Its moral vision of change, like the black revolt, depended on personal commitment and direct action. Until 1964, the New Left, in fact, was decidedly reformist and convinced that American institutions could be made to reflect proclaimed ideals. Only when the New Left began to lose hope for modifying the system did it turn to drastic political alternatives. This process of disillusionment was shaped by the cold war and hastened by Vietnam.

United States strategy of intervention in many countries that seemed to threaten the government's containment policy provided justification for the New Left's anti-imperialist analysis. In Iran, the CIA plotted the overthrow of Prime Minister Mossadegh in 1953 after he announced the nationalization of the country's oil. Gulf Oil Corporation would secure a major oil lease under the new régime, and Kermit Roosevelt, the local CIA chief, would become a Gulf vice-president in 1960. Similarly, the CIA supported the 1954 coup against the left-liberal government of President Jacobo Arbenz Guzman of Guatemala, who intended to nationalize United Fruit Company lands. General Walter Bedell Smith, director of the CIA, would become a board member of United Fruit.

After the first flush of campus enthusiasm for the Kennedy administration, the Cuban invasion brought added disillusionment. Eisenhower had intervened in 1960 in Guatemala, where a naval task force maintained a tottering right-wing régime that provided the training base for the Cuban invasion. Kennedy approved the Bay of Pigs operation, planned by his predecessor, though he was still assuring the public a week before D-Day that U.S. forces would never move against Castro. The use of Cuban exiles with U.S. arms, trained by the CIA, hardly alleviated this deceit. Ambassador Adlai Stevenson's UN denial of American involvement, which had thus far been kept from him, compounded the spiraling hypocrisy.[5]

Student groups, particularly at Berkeley, were important in the Fair Play for Cuba Committee; and as news of the invasion spread on April 17, 1961, more than 1,000 rallied in protest at Berkeley's central plaza. Five days later, 2,000 gathered in San Francisco's Union Square. Edwin H. Pauley, chairman of the university's Board of Regents and an important Democratic fund raiser, blamed these protests on Communist infiltration of the student body. This, of course, was a serious misrepresentation of the growing concern with nuclear gambles of both superpowers, reflected by another demonstration of 5,000 from the Student Peace Union and Students for a Democratic Society in front of the White House in February 1962.

In the Dominican Republic, U.S. troops supported a military coup against President Juan Bosch, elected democratically in 1962 by a coalition of peasants, urban poor, and the lower middle class. In British Guiana, AFL-CIO funds, probably linked to the CIA, instigated a lengthy dock strike in 1963 that toppled the socialist prime minister, Cheddi Jagan, who was accused of trying to bring his country into the Cuban orbit.

The New Left insisted that both the USSR and the United States had to share equal blame for the Cuban missile crisis that fall. Whatever Khrushchev's rationale for planting his ICBMs 100 miles from the Florida coast, whatever Kennedy's rationale for going to the brink on October 24 and halting Russian freighters near Cuban waters, many students grasped for the first time that someone might actually push the nuclear button.[6]

Students for a Democratic Society (SDS), which was to become the unifying force of the New Left, had sprung from a virtually moribund unit of the Socialist party. A few of the more adventurous students, seeking more campus identity, insisted on a change of name to SDS in January 1960. Following a conference at the University of Michigan in May attended by Bayard Rustin and other civil rights leaders, SDS secured a grant of $10,000 from the United Auto Workers and opened a dingy office on New York's East 19th street.

Its only concrete function at first was to support the black revolt. Most of its members belonged to CORE chapters or Friends of SNCC, and its first field secretary, Tom Hayden, made his reputation reporting to SDS from the South. Hayden had attended the University of Michigan on a tennis scholarship, became editor of the student newspaper, and was drawn to militant politics as a member of VOICE. His dark, brooding eyes, sharp-hewn features, and restless ambition to give direction to increasing student unrest would help him rise quickly in the SDS hierarchy.

The statistical importance of the campuses was becoming obvious. There were 3,789,000 in colleges and graduate schools in 1960. With admissions rising sharply, there would be 7,852,000 by 1970. "We must have a try at bringing society under human control," Hayden wrote in an SDS memo in early 1962.

This concept formed the basis of the *Port Huron Statement,* probably the most significant document to come out of the early New Left. At the UAW vacation camp in Port Huron, Michigan, between June 11 and 15, 1962, SDS had gathered together delegates from about 10 functioning campus chapters, as well as from SNCC, CORE, Campus ADA, Student Peace Union, and a few observers from religious groups. Significantly, SDS followed SNCC's nonexclusion policy and accepted young Communists and organizers of the William E. B. Du Bois clubs, which were Communist-oriented.

Much as it has been acclaimed as a new vision for radicals, the *Port Huron Statement* was essentially middle-class thinking. Yet its stinging opposition to the cold war, its demands for the downgrading of NATO, and its condemnation of the military-industrial complex caught the mood of the dawning student rebellion.

It intentionally rejected specifics, refusing the demands of some delegates for inclusion of words like "socialism" as too reminiscent of past factions. Its great strength, in fact, was its attempt at an encompassing philosophy that would attract large numbers of students. "We would replace power rooted in possession, privilege or circumstances by power and uniqueness rooted in love, reflectiveness, reason, and creativity," it declared. "As a social system we seek the establishment of a democracy of individual participation."

There was something curiously old-fashioned about this emphasis on classic individualism. What was new, however, perhaps the most radical section of the manifesto, was the demand that everyone must control the *decisions* and *resources* on which their lives depended. The manifesto introduced new slogans—"participatory democracy" and "decision-making . . . by public groups"—to express this aim.[7]

These slogans seem to differ little from the blueprint already used by SNCC to develop community organization among the powerless against the governing elites. Yet Todd Gitlin, who joined SDS at Harvard in 1962 and became its president the following year, considered Port Huron radical in values if not specifics. Participatory democracy for him implied a socialist type of society. Lewis Feuer, a professor of philosophy at Berkeley in those years, gave a more drastic interpretation. The subheading for "participatory democracy", in his book on this period, *The Conflict of Generations,* is titled "Lenin Updated."

The "participatory democrat," as Feuer interpreted the phrase, had "no use for elections, votes, parliamentary procedures; his basic argument is that since the masses are nonparticipant, the elite activists must act on their behalf." Feuer called it "Lenin's theory of revolutionary action by a small, dictatorial elite translated into the language of the 'nonviolent movement.' "[8]

But the New Left's early development hardly seems to justify this leap from Port Huron to Lenin. The humanistic language of Port Huron, its almost pathetic pleading for a real democracy, were to be translated into a desperate, often fumbling search to find the right forms for decision making at a community level. The Economic Research and Action Projects (ERAP) provided the principal form at first. Like SNCC's Freedom Democratic party, ERAP concentrated on building community participation and local leadership through elections, community pressure, and established democratic channels.

Rather than elitism, SDS's weakness in this period was that endless debates and struggle for consensus made its leaders insular and indecisive. Its basic mood was closer to anarchism than to authoritarianism.

SDS had its first blow-up over its nonexclusion policy and seating of Communist observers. When SDS, calling the old factions "sectarian nonsense," voted to seat Communists, the group's Socialist party mentors were furious. In a bitter confrontation in New York, Michael Harrington (whose study of poverty, *The Other America,* would soon make him a celebrity) joined the Socialist elder statesmen in attacking SDS. Dropping the exclusion clause, Harrington pointed out, would estrange liberals upon whom the thesis of coalition politics depended.

When SDS refused to back down, the Socialists cut off its funds, seized its mailing lists, and took over the SDS office by changing its locks. Kirk Sale in his history of SDS reports Hayden's angry response: "It taught me that social democrats aren't radicals and can't be trusted in a radical movement." Eventually, Harrington would apologize for his stand, and through the intervention of Norman Thomas, among others, the dispute was patched up. But SDS recognized that its dependence on the Socialists had become a temporary convenience.[9]

SDS's immediate problem was the search for a power base. Starting from scratch as a movement of moral protest with no tradition to guide it, spontaneous and existential in its thinking, unable to grasp the possibility of the campus as a class vehicle until the Berkeley uprising in late 1964, SDS went outside the campus for its organizing base. It saw real glamour elsewhere. In order to show its strength, it wanted instant results. Thus, the New Left indulged in a pendulum process, trying each approach until it reached its limits, then testing another. From 1960 to 1964, it concentrated on the black revolt, supporting SNCC and CORE with campus units, pouring an increasing number of workers into the South. But by 1963, SDS foresaw the end of the black alliance and moved into northern slums with its Economic Research and Action Project.

The New Left thought it could gain unity with the masses through the black struggle, and in fact, make blacks the "vanguard" of the working class. Supposedly, the New Left could turn the "lumpen" poor into the real proletariat and make the slums rather than the factory the centers for social change through ERAP.[10]

ERAP, a questionable concept at best, was opposed by some SDS leaders like Alan Haber, the first president. It originated with a $5,000 grant from the Auto Workers. (SDS was then still reformist enough to cooperate with an AFL-CIO union that had cooperated in the cold war.) ERAP's most workable formula was to combine a campus-based group with a nearby black community like Chester, Pennsylvania, a city of 63,000 that was 40 percent black. The students came from Swarthmore, a small Quaker college. Many had proved themselves as SNCC volunteers elsewhere. In November 1963, nearly 100 joined local blacks in a series of picket lines and marches that led to the arrest of 57 after violent clashes with the police and also secured economic and political gains for the blacks.

In Chicago, where the project was known as Jobs or Income Now (JOIN), students opened storefront offices on the North Side, handing out leaflets on unemployment insurance lines and organizing protests against unemployment. In Newark, New Jersey, ERAP promoted marches against police brutality and forced increased slum repairs and garbage collections. All told, SDS established 10 projects by the summer of 1964, including Baltimore, Boston, Cleveland, Oakland, and Hazard, Kentucky.[11]

At least this experiment among the poor gave SDS a chance to apply its theory of participatory democracy. But it soon found that full employment could not be won on a local level, and that struggles over a new traffic light or garbage collection did not go to the core of people's lives. By the end of 1964, certainly by 1965, SDS had to admit that ERAP, except for a few projects, was a failure. "The greatest mistake was that it took us off the campus," Todd Gitlin admitted.

By the fall of 1964, the army would have almost 24,000 troops in Vietnam. A conference of radical student groups met at Yale University that March to debate methods of halting the Vietnam buildup. The decision was for mass demonstrations. On May 2, 1,000 students marched to the United Nations in New York for speeches attacking United States imperialism. Similar meetings were held in Boston, San Francisco, and Madison, Wisconsin. Out of this day came the May 2 Movement (M2M).

SDS had supported the demonstrations and founding of M2M, and one of its members, Russell Stetler of Haverford College in Pennsylvania, became its first chairman. He was from a conservative, working-class background, but the Cuban missile crisis jarred him into political activity. He first joined Student Peace Union, then formed an SDS chapter. By 1964, he was collecting money for medical supplies for the National Liberation Front in South Vietnam. It probably marked the first open identification between student groups and the Communists.

Although Stetler was not a Progressive Labor member, PL dominated the board of M2M. PL had been founded in New York City in July 1962 by a group that had either resigned or been purged from the Communist party as ultraleftists. Its chairman, Milton Rosen, a former member of the Communist national committee, was its chief theoretician. The editor of its paper, Fred Jerome, was the son of V. J. Jerome, who had run the cultural division of the Communist party. Its Harlem chairman, William Epton, had come through the Young Communist League.

With its bitter opposition to the Communisty party, which it considered counterrevolutionary, with its rigid Marxist-Leninist doctrine, centralized bureaucracy, and conspiratorial, secret meetings, PL now represented the hard line on the Left. It demanded incessant class struggle. It championed the Chinese revolution—the Communist party charged PL received funds from Mao.

Actively supporting ghetto violence, Fred Jerome stated in 1964 that "armed Afro-Americans inside the great ghettos, too, were ready for revolution." One PL member, who deserted the party, claimed in the *Saturday Evening Post* that PL kept an arms cache in New York and intended to "launch a reign of terror," a charge never proved. But when coal miners struck in Hazard, Kentucky, in 1963, PL sent its organizers with a station wagon of guns. The organizers, however, were run out of town before the guns were discovered.[12]

PL demanded discipline and robotlike cadres. It was almost puritanical in its ban on beards and marijuana, its attacks on Bob Dylan and other avant-gardists who were considered decadent. It ridiculed the moral ideology of the New Left and used SDS to recruit students for its factory cadres, which it considered the real battleground.

With this wide divergence in purpose, it may seem puzzling that SDS allowed M2M, largely a PL front, to make such inroads into its campus chapters. The SDS nonexclusion policy, to be sure, tolerated any radical group. But the basic reason was the Vietnam war. M2M had already made itself the spearhead of anti-Vietnam resistance. In addition to demonstrations, it had started a petition campaign among male college and high school students and by early 1965 had 1,000 signatures on its "We Won't Go" petitions.

Most important of all, PL was the only radical organization to advance a sharply defined anti-imperialist analysis of the war. It insisted that United States intervention on the basis of protecting a presumed democratic government in South Vietnam and blocking a Chinese takeover of Southeast Asia was a sham. The real purpose, it claimed, was to build a new sphere of neocolonialism in an area of rich, natural resources and to fill the vacuum left by French withdrawal.

In early August 1964, the Tonkin Gulf incident seemed to affirm PL's analysis. The Pentagon reported that three North Vietnamese PT boats had attacked the destroyer, *U.S.S.Maddox*, which supposedly was patrolling in international waters in Tonkin Gulf. Later investigation showed the *Maddox* had actually been cooperating with a South Vietnamese naval attack close to shore. Neither the *Maddox* nor a second destroyer was damaged, and there was serious doubt which side fired first. But the White House portrayed the incident as a flagrant example of Communist aggression, and Johnson asked Congress for a resolution giving him virtually blanket approval to wage war without a congressional declaration of war. Only a few voices like Senator Morse condemned the resolution as unconstitutional. It passed the House without a dissenting vote, and Johnson signed it on August 7, 1964. Eventually the Tonkin Gulf resolution would give both Johnson and Nixon legal justification to escalate Vietnam into a catastrophic war.[13]

The New Left's first target had been racism. Now it saw that racism was closely linked to neocolonialism in Vietnam, Africa, and elsewhere. Its hostility to liberalism mounted as the liberal establishment continued to back the Vietnam war. Its moral revulsion rose against a society it considered increasingly corrupt. Its conviction that the system had failed would be epitomized in the Berkeley uprising with its scornful slogan, "You can't trust anyone over thirty."

This rejection of the past has occasionally been defined as a "conflict of generations" resulting from the process of alienation. This disillusionment with an older generation holding dominant economic and political power has been labeled "de-authorization." But such terms exploit only the nihilistic side of the student movement.[14]

Richard Flacks, Kenneth Keniston, and other researchers have found that New Left youth, far from being driven by an unconscious rage to destroy the "de-authorized" father, were often close to their parents, and that their values were generally shaped by what they had learned at home. Their parents tended to be well educated, often liberal, occasionally radical. Comparing the fathers of activist students with those of nonactivists, Flacks found them significantly more liberal-radical.

Rather than being trapped in a turmoil of destructiveness and self-destruction, these activists, Leonard L. Baird reported, seemed "practical rather than 'romantic' " and "aggressive, self-confident, progressive and well-organized." Seymour L. Halleck found them "more emotionally stable" than other students. Flacks concluded that the activists excelled academically as a group more than nonactivists.[15]

To replace the centralized authority and rigid dogma of the Old Left, the New Left created a mystique of individualism, self-help, and self-reliance. It stressed localism and decentralized decision making, "a belief that ultimate salvation must come on an individualistic basis," as Martin Duberman pointed out.

Greg Calvert, soon to become SDS national secretary, and Carol Neiman called it a "revolution about our lives." They recognized the pitfalls of alienation but asked: "Is it possible to build a movement on the basis of love, eros, and life affirmation, or are we condemned to live out the bourgeois values of repression, guilt, self denial and self hatred, which are the daily fare of life in this society?"

"We're making changes in society with our own two hands," Michael Rossman expressed it. "That's a new feeling for my generation."[16]

By rejecting the standard political apparatus after the disillusionment of Atlantic City in 1964, the New Left leaped from moral exhortation to direct action. Lacking an ideology that could transform its moral wrath into public programs, it depended on keeping society in a constant state of crisis. Its political practice was essentially shock.

The Berkeley uprising during the fall of 1964 was the first important example of this technique. For the first time, the student movement would make the campus its battleground, paralyze the functions of one of the great universities, and virtually seize control. The anger of white radicals had reached a point where thousands could be drawn into direct confrontation with the armed authority of the state. Berkeley climaxed the developmental stage of the New Left.

The immediate issue was free speech, and the student groups behind the uprising called themselves the Free Speech Movement (FSM). As in the HUAC riots of 1960, the students had suddenly been thwarted in their efforts to help SNCC and CORE, only this time the enemy was the university.

Picket lines and sit-ins throughout the Bay Area in 1964 had confronted stores, automobile showrooms, and hotels with a demand for more black jobs and better pay. In 1964 alone, 1,300 students had been arrested. Senator William Knowland, the archconservative publisher of the Oakland *Tribune* and a member of the university's board of regents, had become so disturbed that he pressured college officials for a crackdown. The students retaliated by picketing his newspaper plant.

The radicals had come to view the university as a symbol of the oppressive corporate state. The university administration had come to represent a corrupt society. For some extremists, Berkeley had become Mississippi. It was a far-fetched analogy in many ways, yet the links between the Pentagon and the university were obvious. The federal government paid $246 million to Berkeley to operate three giant atomic installations, and $175 million more for military-connected research. With its growth as a resource facility for the armed forces and aircraft and oil corporations, Berkeley was depicted in the radical analysis as a "public utility" for war and neoimperialism.

The makeup of the board of trustees, and its manipulations against student protest, represented everything the New Left despised. Pauley, who had made his fortune as an oil speculator, and Catherine Hearst of the Hearst publishing company, symbolized the anti-Communist policy behind Vietnam. Jesse Tapp of the Bank of America, the nation's largest bank, had helped finance the California aircraft industry.

Berkeley with its 27,000 students—but still just one of seven campuses of the University of California—was seen by the radicals as a giant factory. "A factory that turns out certain products needed by industry and government," Mario Savio, an FSM leader, called it. The university was no longer an educational center, but a highly efficient industry, producing for the state and its Vietnam policy "an enormous number of safe, highly skilled and respectable automatons," Bradford Cleveland wrote in a SLATE pamphlet.[17]

New Left students hated the omnipotent bureaucracy that had developed at Berkeley. The campus had been dehumanized. Many professors, drawn to the prestige and high pay of research, appeared only for occasional lectures and were even more remote than administrators. The undergraduate saw himself as a number, a minute cog. His whole world was reduced to his identifying IBM card which he had to carry everywhere. One of the key slogans of the uprising was: "I am a UC student. Please don't bend, fold, spindle or mutilate me."

Mississippi Freedom Summer had stepped up the process of radicalization. Much of the New Left leadership was trained by SNCC in the South and suddenly left without a revolution of its own. The New Left suffered from isolation in the white world and remained a stepchild to the far more glamorous battles of Mississippi and Alabama. The need to re-create parallel circumstances of confrontation is reflected in student rhetoric. Rossman, like the first freedom riders, exults that white radicals have put "our bodies on the line." Berkeley becomes a microcosm of the revolution; and when the students seize one building, Rossman elevates it to "one-half acre liberated by our presence" where "we acted out our universe in miniature."

The university set off the uprising on September 14, 1964, when Dean of Students Katherine Towle banned student tables on a small strip outside Sather Gate, long used by SNCC and CORE to raise money and recruit personnel. The ban may have had some basis in an old university rule. But the strip had been considered off-campus, and a committee of the Academic Senate, the faculty's parliamentary body, criticized the "vagueness of many of the relevant regulations."[18]

When 18 student groups, including the Goldwater Republicans, protested the ban as a denial of First Amendment rights, they gained

only minute concessions. Some groups then defied the ban by returning their tables to the strip, and five names were taken for disciplinary action and ordered to report to Sproul Hall, the administration
building. Instead, 500 angry students showed up, insisting they were
equally guilty, and started a sit-in that lasted till early morning,
October 1. The university suspended the original five and three
student leaders.

A trivial incident, probably triggered by pressure from regents
determined to eliminate controversial politics from the campus, had
grown into a confrontation. The administration showed a surprising
inability to compromise, and its case had flimsy constitutional
grounds. "Any regulation of speech which turns entirely on the
'lawful' or 'unlawful' character of off-campus conduct *advocated on*
campus would probably constitute an unconstitutional regulation of
content," ACLU lawyers observed. This infringement of free speech
seemed odd for a university recently awarded the Meiklejohn Prize
for academic freedom by the American Association of University
Professors. President Clark Kerr himself had garnered something of
a liberal reputation in 1959 by eliminating the loyalty oaths that had
crippled Berkeley in the previous decade.

The administration bumbled further on October 1 when the FSM
staged a rally to protest the suspension of the eight, and campus
police arrested a former graduate student who was manning the
CORE table. At this point, an incident became an uprising. One
student lay down in front of the police car to which the arrested
student had been taken. Others followed. From that afternoon until
the next evening, the police car and its prisoner were held hostage
for more than 30 hours by at least 3,000 students.

This marathon produced the uprising's first spellbinding speaker,
Mario Savio. Born in New York in 1942, the son of a machine-punch
operator, Savio had attended Manhattan College on a scholarship,
transferred to Queens College, and then to Berkeley, where he
achieved an almost-perfect 3.9 grade average. Tall, with sandy, friz-
zled hair, he had joined the Young People's Socialist League briefly,
read Marx, abandoned Catholicism, and taught in a Mississippi
freedom school a few months before. "I'm tired of reading history,"
he wrote a friend. "I want to make it."[19]

Now the university threatened open violence by summoning 643
police officers and state units to break up the demonstration by force,
but a settlement was finally reached late on October 2. The FSM
agreed to release the car in return for negotiations and a faculty-
student committee of investigation.

Though the FSM proved to be abrasive negotiators, President Kerr inflamed the temporary peace even more with an injection of red-baiting. In a statement in a local Hearst newspaper on October 3, repeated by a Hearst columnist a few weeks later, Kerr charged that "the majority of the demonstrators were not students and that up to 40 percent of the hard-core leaders were adherents of the 'Mao-Red China communist line.'"

Kerr later insisted he had been misquoted. The published facts had also been badly twisted. Of the 60-member FSM executive committee, 58 were students, as were all of the 12-member steering committee except a former graduate student not registered at the moment. FSM's coalition of 22 organizations included a handful of Maoists, but it also had Goldwater conservatives and religious groups.[20]

When Chancellor Edward Strong insisted on pressing charges against four students, FSM called a mammoth rally on December 2. In his climatic speech, Savio equated the university with a machine —a machine that "becomes so odious, makes you so sick at heart, that you can't take part. . . ." He demanded that students put their "bodies against the gears, against the wheels and machines, and make it stop until we are free." It was hyperbole, of course but close enough to the students' perception of an academic factory as surrogate for an oppressive state to convince them that the machine had to be challenged. The method, again reminiscent of the black revolt, was to take over Sproul Hall. An estimated 1,500 marched into the limestone, pillared administration building to establish in that frantic night a sort of counterculture—"autonomous learning collectives" ranging from law and strike tactics to music instruction by Joan Baez.

When most students refused the university's plea to leave by 3 A.M., the police removed them by force, dragging them "down the steps by their shoulders and in some cases their heels," the San Francisco *Chronicle* reported. "Take 'em down a little slower, they bounce more that way," the *Chronicle* quoted one policeman. Reporters noted that trained riot police sought out student leaders, "their boots landing heavily on heads, arms, shoulders and legs"; and that most officers removed their badges to avoid identification and covered windows and stairwells to obstruct photographers and television crews.

Eight hundred and fourteen were arrested, almost 600 eventually indicted on trespass charges, many for "resistance" as well. They served an average of two months in jail. Despite accusations that many demonstrators came from hippie communes, 84 percent were students, teachers, research assistants, or university employees; the rest mainly wives or husbands. One study showed only 5 percent belonged to radical groups.[21]

On December 3, FSM countered with a general strike, supported by two-thirds of the teaching assistants. FSM had fulfilled its threat to stop the machine, although a few observers claimed about half the classes met. On December 7, President Kerr offered his first meaningful compromise to a meeting of 13,000 faculty and students.

The next day, a crucial meeting of the Academic Senate gave overwhelming support to almost every FSM demand. By a vote of 824 to 115, the faculty resolved that the "content of speech or advocacy should not be restricted by the university." Professor Feuer tried to limit the resolution's scope with an amendment, "provided that it is directed to no immediate act of force or violence. . . ." But it was defeated 737 to 284.

The student body gave similar backing to FSM's demands when student government elections swept all seven SLATE candidates, pledged to FSM, into office.

On January 2, 1965, the removal of Chancellor Edward Strong and appointment of Professor Martin Meyerson in his place achieved the objectives of the uprising. Meyerson immediately established new rules that allowed student groups to set up tables, raise money, and solicit for political action on campus. Two days later, the first rally under the rules was held on the steps of Sproul Hall. President Kerr lamented: "We fumbled, we floundered, and the worst thing is I still don't know how we should have handled it."[22]

Perhaps the saddest part of this admission is that Kerr and so many others never recognized the seriousness of the issues behind the uprising. Some critics have claimed that it was originated and controlled solely by political extremists and supported mainly by crackpots and drug addicts. While these groups certainly attached themselves to FSM, as they would to almost every New Left movement, most students rated highly by academic and motivational standards. One study shows that of all undergraduates arrested, 47 percent had better than a *B* average. Of graduate students arrested, 71 percent had averages between *B* and *A*. Twenty were Phi Beta Kappa members; eight, Woodrow Wilson fellows; fifty-three, National Merit Scholarship winners.

Sheldon S. Wolin and John H. Schaar, professors of political science at Berkeley, concluded that "the vast majority of students shared the goals of FSM, and a near majority also supported their direct action tactics." While a few reports dispute this conclusion, Richard H. Somers, another Berkeley professor, found in his study that "as many as one third of the 27,000 students on campus supported not only the goals, but also the tactics of the demonstrators, and that another third, while rejecting the tactics, supported the goals."

Analyzing the opinions of 230 students five years later, the Knight newspaper chain reported that 84 percent would have joined the uprising and followed the same tactics if they had to do it over again. Only 9 percent criticized FSM tactics.[23]

The dilemma of the New Left was to become something more than an adjunct to the black movement. The Berkeley uprising brought a university to its knees and radicalized the campus. But the New Left would never achieve importance until it could make the public understand the connection between Berkeley and the Vietnam war. It was only when Berkeley students a few years later sat on railroad tracks to block troop trains headed for the embarkation port that the New Left emerged as a coherent movement with a focused objective. The Berkeley uprising shocked the country, but its larger meaning remained blurred.

· 14 ·

From Civil Liberties to Ghetto Riots 1965

"It was the Atlantic City convention, not SNCC, that produced Black Power," in Stokeley Carmichael's analysis. The bitterness created by the failure to seat the Mississippi Freedom Democratic party sharply altered the tactics of SNCC and CORE in 1965. It destroyed any hope of continued cooperation with the liberal-labor coalition and increasingly divided SNCC from moderates like King. The black radicals were losing their faith in the workability of the system. The coming bloodbath at Selma, Alabama, would intensify the process. "Many are trying to decide whether the white man's soul is worth saving," as Aaron Henry, the Mississippi leader, described the mood.[1]

The Harlem riot had just demonstrated that even with the vote, northern ghettos contained as much rage as the South. Fire bombs and gunfire foreshadowed more serious armed confrontation. Black radicals were shifting toward a policy of separatism, enunciated by Malcolm X, and SNCC in particular became convinced that liberation depended on building power bases in the South.

Selma was the next turning point after Atlantic City. SNCC had done the grinding, day-by-day organizing there since 1961. Selma was the center of 19 Alabama Black Belt counties. Some had no blacks registered at all. Selma had 1 percent registered. In early 1965, SNCC groups suffered 3,300 arrests in their registration campaign.

When Martin Luther King decided to launch a march from Selma to Montgomery that would bring national attention to the deadlock, SNCC protested. It always favored organizing over showmanship, particularly when lives were endangered. But SNCC finally made up the core of 500 marchers that headed for the Pettus Bridge on March 7, 1965, only to be mauled by state troopers on horseback. A white Edmundite priest named Father Maurice Culetta thought that "the Pettus Bridge was Calvary." At the bridge, he had just lifted into his

186

arms a black girl with her face smashed in.

President Johnson blamed Governor George Wallace for the blood-letting and arranged through his representatives for a second "token" march.[2]

The arrival of at least 400 white clergy from the North, including a Protestant bishop and Catholic nuns, as well as white radicals like Mario Savio with a California contingent, expanded the March 9 protest to 2,000. At the Pettus Bridge, mounted troopers and Sheriff Jim Clark's posse attacked with bull whips, chains, and tear gas. King knelt for a few moments in prayer, then turned and led his followers back to Selma. SNCC insisted it had never been informed of this planned retreat, which it called a "sellout" to the administration.

The tensions between SNCC, King, and the administration rose with the death toll. Jimmie Lee Jackson, a veteran registration worker, had been shot dead near Selma on February 18. James J. Reeb, a white Unitarian minister from Boston, was beaten to death on March 9. In August, a white Episcopalian seminarian from New Hampshire, Jonathan M. Daniels, would be killed by a part-time deputy sheriff.

King finally secured a federal court order protecting the march to Montgomery. When Gov. Wallace told the President he didn't have enough forces, Johnson called up 1,800 National Guardsmen and sent hundreds of federal marshals.

The march took off from Selma on March 21 with 3,200 people. When it reached Montgomery on March 25, there were 25,000, probably the largest southern demonstration yet staged. After rallying on the state house lawn, once the capitol of the Confederacy, participants were transported back to Selma or points along the route by volunteers. One of them, Viola Gregg Liuzzo, wife of a Detroit Teamsters Union member and mother of five, was making her last trip of the day when a car drew alongside her. A passenger, later identified as a Ku Klux Klan member, fired a .38-caliber pistol into her head, killing her.[3]

Selma shocked the country and became an important factor that summer in the passage of a new civil rights bill. In the short run, King's strategy of massive demonstrations was producing results. But the violence unleashed by Wallace and Sheriff Clark would work two ways. Tom Kahn, then a young socialist anxious to preserve the liberal coalition, later an AFL-CIO official, concluded that "Selma had made SNCC violence-prone." It pushed the black radicals toward separatism. It hardened their disillusion with the democratic process and the dependence on the liberal-labor coalition, a disgust already evident at SNCC's staff meeting at Atlanta in February 1965.

The core of the problem was whether the black movement would remain linked to the Johnson administration. Established leaders like Bayard Rustin considered it essential. "The future of the Negro struggle depends on whether the contradictions of this society can be resolved by a coalition of progressive forces which becomes the effective political majority in the United States," he wrote in *Commentary* in early 1965.

But resolving contradictions was no longer enough for black radicals. They wanted more than society was grudgingly offering. They wanted a *new* society.

White radicals like Staughton Lynd warned of the dangers of cooption. Ruston's thesis, Lynd stated, would simply "assimilate Negro protest to the Establishment just as labor protest was coopted at the end of the 1930s. . . ." Greg Calvert of SDS insisted that coalition politics would "perpetrate the illusion of democracy and freedom" and lead to "public powerlessness."[4]

SNCC agreed. At its Atlanta meeting, it took a decisive step in breaking with the past. Instead of struggling for power within the Democratic party, as it had done in Mississippi, it would build its own party in Lowndes County, Alabama, which it hoped would be the first of other bases in the Black Belt. Thus, SNCC broke with reform and moved closer to revolution—as Sellers put it, "searching for the pulse of the revolution."

Critics of SNCC generally viewed this course in old ideological terms. When a few SNCC officials met with Attorney General Nicholas Katzenbach at the White House a few months before, they were disturbed by his incessant attack on SNCC's dependence on the National Lawyers Guild, which he called Communist-dominated. James Wechsler of the New York *Post* accused SNCC of "staging an uprising against the major civil rights blocs" led by a "fragment of Communists," Chinese (rather than Russian) in orientation.[5]

These labels were vastly oversimplified. SNCC, to be sure, had a vague Marxist tinge by 1965, mainly from Forman, Carmichael, and the Howard University "group," its leading theoreticians. Walter Stafford described it as "philosophical Marxism, a mixture of many things besides Marxism." Jean Wylie recalled, "We read Marx, but were really looking for an alternative to capitalism."

This alternative was not Marxism but black nationalism, separatism, and an increasing hunger for immediate results. This strategy, embodied in the Lowndes campaign, was put forward in SNCC by the "hardliners." Their opponents, on the other hand, dubbed the "stars," generally favored the tradition of nonviolence and integration. The growing split largely determined SNCC's direction for the next few years. It may also have caused a baffling personal crisis and the withdrawal of Robert Moses from SNCC.

In a ceremony before the whole SNCC staff at Atlanta's Old Gammon Seminary, almost a "sacred ceremony," as Sellers saw it, Moses began the strange process of erasing his past. It was symbolized by his change of name. Henceforth, he would drop his last name, and call himself Parris, his middle name. A bottle of wine was passed around the room as though to confirm his new identity. Dorie Ladner, a close associate, was distraught when Parris (Moses) passed her by with the wine, as well as others close to him. Her sister, Joyce Ladner, recalled, "No one really understood it."

His closest friends could only suggest that Robert Parris (Moses), obviously exhausted and brooding about the recent death of his father, had cut himself off from the movement because people had used him "as a crutch." He soon made the final break by leaving for Africa and settling in Tanzania to teach school. He did not return to the United States until 1976, when he entered Harvard graduate school to take his doctorate in philosophy.[6]

But the disappearance of Parris (Moses) had deeper meaning. He had always been the main force in the conservative faction. Some considered him a reactionary, unwilling to move to the next stage of SNCC's development. His de-emphasis of the individual and commitment to organizing the rural poor had come into conflict with the new "structured" approach of the Lowndes campaign, the swing to nationalism and separatism preached by Forman and the hardliners. When Forman's position had been accepted at the Atlanta meeting, Parris possibly felt that his usefulness had ended.

The anarchist mood of SNCC's early years was fading. Forman as executive secretary ran a highly disciplined headquarters at Atlanta. (John Lewis had been re-elected as chairman, and Sellers as project chairman.) The staff reached a peak of about 250 in 1965; the budget reached $800,000. Although contributions from the Auto Workers and other liberal unions would soon be wiped out by SNCC's anti-Vietnam stand, stars like Harry Belafonte and Sidney Poitier helped raise considerable funds for another year or so.

SNCC's mood now was absolutist. Unable to accept what it considered the dragging pace of coalition politics, it demanded rapid social transformation beyond the limits of the welfare state. It had spent considerable blood in Mississippi and failed. Three hundred years of oppression produced an urgency few whites could understand. The beatings and deaths at Selma, and the trials that pardoned most of those indicted for these deaths, intensified the bitterness. Thus, SNCC reached for extreme solutions, often out of touch with reality. Knowing that extremism could bring a white backlash, it still determined to give up half-measures and strive for power.[7]

The cynicism of black radicals was directed toward the Voting Rights Act signed on August 6, 1965. It had been passed by a congressional coalition of Republican liberals and the administration's own liberal-labor vote, spurred by the horror over Selma. In his address to Congress urging passage, the President even borrowed black rhetoric, crying at the climax, "And we shall overcome!"

The act undoubtedly was a substantial achievement. It set up a system of federal examiners to make certain that no one eligible was denied the right to register and vote—but only in those states and countries where less than half of the eligibles had registered. It banned literacy tests and other devices long used to block the registration of blacks. It forbade discrimination in federally aided programs. Among other provisions, it directed the United States attorney general to bring suit against local poll taxes (those in federal elections were prohibited in 1964 by constitutional amendment).

But the administration dallied in putting the act to work. Instead of hundreds of registrars in the South, there were only about 50 by the end of the year. Many counties such as those in Southwest Georgia didn't get examiners until 1967. As a result, only 16,000 blacks were registered in Georgia in the first six months. It took a whole year to get a thousand registered in Neshoba County, Mississippi.

Black radicals saw the act as another example of tokenism. Yet it would gradually have its effect. By the end of 1966, 18 months after the act was passed, black registration in Alabama and South Carolina had risen to 51 percent of those eligible, and in Mississippi to 33 percent. Between August 1965 and 1970, black registrants in 11 southern states rose from 1.5 million to 3.5 million.[8]

The radicals, however, were unimpressed by a potential vote five years hence. What value was the vote without immediate jobs, health care, and union membership? In 1962, infant mortality among blacks nationwide was 90 percent greater than among whites. Unemployment among black teen-agers had reached a frightening 26 percent.

Union organization in the South had been at a standstill since 1948 when the CIO abandoned its drive—sharecroppers in 1965 generally made three dollars a day. (Even in the North, many unions still barred blacks, particularly in the construction industry.) Johnson's Great Society trickled funds into a few states, the Child Development Group in Mississippi giving food and school transportation to 9,000 rural children. Black radicals claimed many programs simply perpetuated the subordination of blacks to whites and speeded up the selling out of civil rights workers. One black leader complained, "The old militants are taking the sugar tit."

The SNCC staff in Mississippi concentrated on labor organization. Sharecroppers, cotton workers, and tractor drivers were organized into the Mississippi Freedom Labor Union, which signed up 1,325 members. But when 350 sharecroppers (making $300 to $400 a year, the day laborers even less) went on strike for higher wages, the plantation owners broke the strike by evicting them. Homeless, they thought they had a refuge in the deserted barracks of the Greenville Air Force base, but the military too forced them out. By August, only a handful remained on strike.

The SNCC team that moved into Lowndes in late 1965 had reasonable cause for cynicism. In March 1965, not one black was registered in the county. Farmhands earned three to six dollars a day, maids four dollars a day. Despite the Supreme Court's integration decision over a decade earlier, schools remained rigidly segregated, and black children only completed a median of 5.1 school years. About 85 white families owned 90 percent of the land; and of 800 white men in the county, over two-thirds were gun-carrying deputy sheriffs. It had well earned its title of "Bloody Lowndes"—Ms. Liuzzo being the most recent victim.

By exploiting an ancient quirk in the Alabama law allowing any group to establish itself as a party when it got 20 percent of the primary vote for candidates for county office, SNCC set out to organize the Lowndes County Freedom Organization. Its symbol became the Black Panther, a fierce animal that struck back with particular savagery when backed into a corner.[9]

Stokeley Carmichael headed the project. Carmichael had survived over 25 jailings, including 49 days in Mississippi's infamous Parchman State Reformatory after the 1961 freedom rides. He had a cocky, infectious smile, and burning eyes. His once-lean face had puffed out from a constant diet of "starch fat" and greens on which the poor depended. He had a reputation for icy courage under police attack—"Look, man, I've been to 17 funerals since 1961," he'd say. Howard Zinn described him rushing "cool and smiling through Hell, philosophizing all the way."

He could be tender with young recruits, harsh with opponents. "He terrifies me and exalts me at the same time," one associate declared. There was a network of supporters across Mississippi—dubbed Friends and Admirerers of Stokeley Carmichael—who sent him frequent gifts of cigarettes and shaving cream.

Born in Trinidad in 1941, he had been brought to Harlem at the age of 11, where he ran with the gangs, stole, and smoked pot. His father, a carpenter and cabdriver, and his mother, a maid, moved the family to the Bronx, a mainly white area where they eventually bought a house. Stokeley had earned impressive grades at the elite Bronx High School of Science. One of his close friends was Eugene Dennis, Jr., son of the Communist Party leader, who introduced him to Marx. Soon Stokeley was moving in white socialist circles and attending Park Avenue and Greenwich Village parties. His soft, lilting, Trinidad accent was enveloped by gutter Bronx, spiced with Yiddish, and in turn, converted to a southern drawl when he joined SNCC. In Lowndes County, he enjoyed taunting the sheriff in Yiddish: "Kish mir tuchas, baby."

Turning down scholarships to white universities, he chose Howard and affiliated with a radical group that soon dominated SNCC. He was an astute political debater, not a theoretician like James Forman. Robert Lewis Shayon, the radio critic, later called him "quietly rational." Others considered him a hip Malcolm X. All through Howard, he would take off weeks and months organizing with SNCC in Cambridge, Maryland, and Mississippi. He turned down a scholarship for graduate study to go full-time with SNCC in the summer of 1964. Distinguishing himself in registering rural blacks, he was soon put in charge of Mississippi's 2nd Congressional District at Greenwood.[10]

Carmichael brought to Lowndes the pick of SNCC's staff, many from the "Howard group"—Courtland Cox, Charles Cobb, Cleveland Sellers, Ed Brown (brother of Rap), Marion Barry (who became mayor of Washington, D.C. in 1979), and John Wilson (later city councilman in Washington). He also patterned his tactics on Greenwood. The seeds of black nationalism had been sown there when he refused white staff workers, and he continued this policy at Lowndes. When local blacks wanted an integrated ticket for the Black Panthers, Carmichael insisted, "You're all black, ain't you, so what's wrong with an all-black slate?"

Starting with about 13,000 eligible blacks to register, and little help from federal registrars, the Panther party met stiff opposition. Sharecroppers were evicted from their homes if they registered; maids fired from their jobs. The county courthouse suddenly raised the filing fee for black candidates for sheriff and other offices from the previous $50 to $900. The influential Baptist Alliance, dominated by middle-class blacks, pressured its membership to vote with the regular Democrats. The Democratic party used the press and radio to convince blacks that no votes would be counted except the Democratic line. Some SCLC officials, sensing the danger to integrationism if the nationalist-separatist position took hold, quietly opposed the Panthers.

Still, by a relentless door-to-door campaign, the Panthers registered about 600 by primary day. Ejected from the Hayneville Courthouse, they met at the foot of the steps to organize their party and nominate a slate. Almost every man carried a gun.

By election day in November 1966, 2,758 blacks had been registered—enough to win in an honest ballot. With only about 1,900 eligible whites, 2,823 white names had been recorded on the registration books for 1966. There was also the problem of black defections. Many black fieldhands trudged to the polling booths—to vote white. One of them told Cox: "When you pay my wages, I'll vote your way." Cox concluded later: "We just hadn't dealt with the economic pressures."[11]

It was the first vote for black candidates in Alabama for 75 years, but the pattern could not be reversed that quickly. The Panther candidates—sheriff, tax assessor, and other county offices—all polled about 41.5 percent of the vote. The campaign had lacked money from the start—northern liberals were scared off by the black nationalist trend. There had never been a total commitment from SNCC. The black-middle class and clergy had been driven by extremists into the Democratic fold. This was the political pattern that would emerge in most southern states—not black nationalism, but an increasing coalition of black and white moderates in the Democratic party.

Thus, the blueprint for a black base in one Alabama county, the forerunner of other bases throughout the Black Belt, had been stalled. Lacking a coherent revolutionary strategy, the radicals had overemphasized the importance of registration. Day laborers lacked the independence to stand against the landowning class. Blacks had to have more land, more shops and cooperative economic units, more alliances with poor whites through union organization, before they could successfully use politics to gain control of their communities. "Participatory democracy" could never succeed in a vacuum.[12]

As late as April 17, 1965, Paul Potter, the president of SDS, would urge in a Washington speech: "We must name that system. We must name it, describe it, analyze it, understand it and change it." Potter had purposefully avoided using "capitalism" as the word for oppression. It was, he explained, "an inadequate description of the evils of America—a hollow, dead word tied to the thirties."

But what exactly were the white radicals trying to change? Their most productive work had been in the South as adjuncts of SNCC and CORE. But the growth of black nationalism had ended this phase. Berkeley had made a tentative step at naming the system— Savio's academic "machine," the university as a tool of industry, the Pentagon, and American imperialism. But would paralyzing the Berkeley campus affect Potter's "evils"?

Obviously not, and this was the New Left's dilemma. Until it confronted the meaning of Vietnam, until it made the link between the war and racism and American intrusion into the Dominican Republic, Guatemala, and Vietnam, white radicals would lack a structure around which to organize.

Like the blacks, the New Left had been shaken by the President's refusal to seat the Mississippi Freedom Democrats at Atlantic City. It had been even more embittered by Johnson's betrayal of his campaign peace pledge—"We seek no wider war," he had promised. Yet in February 1965, only a month after inauguration, he opened a campaign of air bombing against North Vietnam, committing the first American ground troops to defend bases for the air force. Soon he doubled draft calls to 35,000 a month, increasing our Vietnam forces from 25,000 to 200,000 by November 1965 in order to escalate the land and air war.

The rising death toll of North and South Vietnamese civilians accentuated the racist nature of a war that considered Asian villagers as likely a target as the military—the Pentagon insisted the two could

) During government's trial of 12 top Communist party officials on conspiracy charges in 1949, ympathetic pickets surround Manhattan's federal courthouse. Communists were convicted, but ur escaped jail temporarily by going underground. (Photoworld)

) Former Vice President Henry A Wallace, red from Truman cabinet in 1947 for oppos- g President's hard line against Soviets, ran oorly as Progressive party peace candidate in 948 with Communist backing. (PCA)

3) Julius Emspak, Albert Fitzgerald, James Ma-tles (left to right), leaders of radical United Electrical Workers, Testify against Taft-Hart-ley bill before Senate committee in 1947. Bill damaged all unions, particularly Communist officials. (UEW)

4) Communist party officers Eugene Dennis and Benjamin Davis, first black elected to New York City Council: (third, second from right), at Union Square reviewing stand for 1950 May Day parade. (Photoworld)

5) Communist party trials and nationwide anti-Soviet hysteria cut huge turnouts of previous May Days in New York to a few thousand marchers in scattered clusters in 1950. (Photoworld)

) American Labor party, largest U.S. radical party, startled Democrats by electing Leo Isacson to
Congress from Bronx in 1948 special election. Isacson (light jacket, center) leads pickets for price
controls. (Photoworld)

) Congressman Vito Marcantonio, ALP head; black singer Paul Robeson; and Isacson (left to right)
at Washington demonstration against Mundt-Nixon bill in 1948. Expanded bill, passed later, restricted Communists and radicals. (Guardian)

8) Martin Luther King, Jr. (left, with wife), famed for organizing Montgomery, Alabama, bus strike, on way to jail in 1962 for demonstrations at Albany, Georgia. Also jailed: Ralph Abernathy (right, with wife). (Guardian)

) H. Rap Brown, chairman of SNCC, lauds "guerrilla warfare" during Cambridge, Maryland, riots 1967. Brown was hit by shotgun pellets soon after. (Guardian)

0) Student Nonviolent Coordinating Committee's demand for revolutionary "Black Power" draws ousands on Mississippi march in 1966. Highway patrolmen attack marchers at Canton in mount- g civil rights clashes bringing many deaths. (Guardian)

11) After President Lyndon B. Johnson orders air bombing of Noth Vietnam, Students for a Democratic Society, largest New Left organization, rallies almost 25,000 in Washington to stop the war. (Guardian)

13) As New Left violence mounted in 1969, University of California at Berkeley students seized university property for "People's Park." Police battled radicals on May 15 to retake park. (Guardian)

4) After government indicts "Chicago Eight" for conspiracy to riot during 1968 Democratic Convention, demonstrators protest trial on September 24, 1969. Five guilty verdicts were overturned by higher court. (Guardian)

12) American deaths in Vietnam reached 23,000 when priests Philip Berrigan (left), his brother, Daniel Berrigan, and seven others raided Catonsville, Maryland, draft office and burned records on May 17, 1968. (Guardian)

15) Revolutionary Black Panther party had frequent shootouts with police. Here, chairman Huey Newton greets followers after release on bail in August 1970 on charges of killing policeman in 1967. (Guardian)

16) After SDS split in 1970, extremist Weather faction tries to stop Vietnam war with street battles. Chicago "Days of Rage" in September was last action before Weather went underground.

17) Anti-Vietnam demonstrators, from pacifists to ultra-Left, pour into Washington in April 1971, following nationwide strikes over Cambodian invasion. (Guardian)

18) Vietnam veterans, opposing war, march past Lincoln Memorial on way to White House on April 19, 1971, led by William Wynan (left) of New York and James Dehlin of Flushing, Michigan. Both lost legs in war. (Guardian)

19) Prison racism becomes Panther target when 27-year-old George Jackson, jailed since 18 for $18 robbery, is killed by guards at San Quentin, California, in possible frame-up on August 21, 1971. Jackson, author of best-selling *Soledad Brother,* is buried from Oakland church under Panther Banner. (Guardian)

20) Women's movement makes abortion rights, guaranteed by U.S. Supreme Court, a key issue after Catholic hierarchy organizes against abortion. Buffalo, New York, demonstrators demand Medicaid abortions for poor on March 31, 1979. (Guardian)

not be separated. World War I had produced only 5 percent civilian casualties; World War II, 45 percent; the Korean war, 80 percent. But an estimated two or three North Vietnam civilians would die for every enemy soldier.[13]

In late March 1965, students and faculty on many campuses— often with SDS and pacifist sponsorship—fashioned a new instrument, named the "teach-in," to bring the war issue into public debate. It started at the University of Michigan and spread quickly to Columbia, Oregon, Berkeley, and such previously uninvolved campuses as Marist College in Poughkeepsie, New York. All told, almost 120 campuses participated.

A teach-in would start at night and run into the early morning. Berkeley's would last 36 hours with an audience of 12,000. The sponsors tried to get speakers on all sides of the issue. But pro-Vietnam speakers frequently boycotted the debate, and the State Department often reneged on its commitment for speakers until the administration grasped the groundswell running against it. In May, the President ordered "truth teams" sent to many campuses.

The climax was scheduled to be a national debate on television on May 15 with McGeorge Bundy, the President's national security adviser, defending the Vietnam war. When Bundy dropped out, using the Dominican crisis as an excuse, the debate was postponed to June 21. The administration justified the Marine invasion of the Dominican Republic on various grounds: first to evacuate Americans and defend American property; then as a "defensive" force; finally to cooperate in the overthrow of a moderate socialist, Juan Bosch, whom the President considered Communist-controlled. "The affluent society is in need of an enemy against which its people can be kept in a state of constant psycho-social mobilization," Herbert Marcuse contended.

By their sheer size and number, the teach-ins made dissent legitimate and focused attention on the war as nothing had done before. They ensured that the campuses would now be the base of that dissent, and made thousands of new converts for SDS. U.S. Senator Thomas J. Dodd (Dem., Conn.) claimed that the teach-ins and anti-Vietnam movements were exploited "for purely Communist purposes."[14]

The Communist label was also used against SDS by seemingly thoughtful critics. Having grown to 52 chapters, SDS felt strong enough to announce an anti-Vietnam march in Washington for April 17, 1965. Peace groups like the War Resisters League and Women's

Strike for Peace asked to join, and the coalition soon included black radicals as well as the Communist party and Du Bois clubs. Many liberals were horrified, and A. J. Muste, Bayard Rustin, Norman Thomas, and 19 others issued an attack on the inclusion of Communists (although Muste and Thomas later apologized). Campus ADA boycotted the march. SANE refused to supply speakers. The New York *Post* warned of "attempts to convert the event into a pro-Communist production."

The march turned out 20,000 to 25,000 at the Washington Monument. Students came from Maine and Iowa, Tulsa and Toronto, from perhaps 100 campuses. Paul Potter urged "massive civil disobedience all over the country that will wrench the country into a confrontation with the issues of the war. . . ." The demonstrators marched on the Capitol, halting at the steps; Staughton Lynd speculated that "even had some been shot or arrested, nothing could have stopped that crowd from taking possession of the government."[15]

In this vision of revolution, Lynd, of course, was indulging in the rhetoric that often marred the New Left. Still, SDS was in fact growing at a phenomenal rate—it would have 124 chapters by December, and Nathan Glazer, the sociologist, estimated it could rouse 10 to 20 percent of a campus when the issue was right. But it still had no official policy on the draft. It hesitated to commit itself too quickly to a one-issue campaign on the war. It lacked internal organization—the National Office was chaotic and had limited contact with chapters, and almost no control.

This situation was changing with a rapid influx of membership and leadership from the Midwest and Southwest, people from small-town Protestant families with no radical traditions. It had started with the presidency of Paul Potter, a graduate of Oberlin who had grown up on an Illinois farm. It developed further at the national convention in Michigan in June with the election of Carl Oglesby as president and Jeff Shero as vice-president. Oglesby's father had come from a South Carolina farm, ending up in the rubber mills of Akron, Ohio. His mother was from Alabama. He was not steeped in Old Left factionalism or theory. Shero, a Texan, who had made his SDS chapter a strong force at the University of Texas, had worked for SNCC in many southern states.

SDS had just moved its national office to Chicago. Now it climaxed the break with its old-line socialist sponsors by eliminating the anti-Communist clause in its constitution.

The new régime gave grudging support to the October demonstrations planned by the new National Coordinating Committee to End the War in Vietnam, but SDS's only step toward blocking the draft was to urge students to apply for conscientious-objector status. At the national council meeting in December, even a resolution that backed immediate withdrawal of troops from Vietnam was defeated. SDS was still vacillating badly, uncertain whether its base was on the campus or in an alliance with the Marxist Left, fearful that a bold Vietnam stand would take it away from other radical priorities.[16]

SDS, in fact, built up its JOIN project in Chicago to prove that the crisis was in the community. JOIN became the last gasp of the ERAP model. It attempted to unite welfare and tenant groups with other representatives of the poor like the Young Lords (mainly Spanish-speaking youths) and the Young Patriots (mainly southern whites).

Other groups in the New Left had already taken the Vietnam initiative from SDS. The Vietnam Day Committee, founded in the San Francisco area by Jerry Rubin, then a graduate student at Berkeley, demanded immediate withdrawal of American troops, recognition of the National Liberation Front, and impeachment of President Johnson. In May, it distributed leaflets to Vietnam-bound troops, attacking "this nightmare war." In early August, its followers clustered on the tracks in front of troop trains headed toward Oakland's embarkation center for Vietnam. The protesters leaped out of the way at the last minute, but it was a pioneering action in the use of resistance to stop the war.[17]

On August 9, the National Coordinating Committee (NCC), serving as an umbrella for all anti-Vietnam groups, staged a march of 5,000 in Washington. But it was only a warm-up for NCC's Days of Protest over the weekend of October 15–16, which drew about 100,-000 people in 100 cities.

In New York, 20,000 paraded on Fifth Avenue. David J. Miller, a young Catholic Worker, burned his draft card at the Whitehall Street induction center—the first burning since Congress had made it a federal crime—and was arrested by the FBI.

Despite SDS reluctance to support the Days of Protest, at least 50 chapters helped organize the demonstrations, and the press generally conveyed the impression that SDS had sparked these massive gatherings. As a result, new memberships soared, and the leadership negotiated a role for itself in the November 27 demonstration that SANE had called for Washington.

Overcoming SANE's traditional anti-Communism, SDS won

agreement that the march would be open to all groups. As president, Carl Oglesby represented SDS in addressing a crowd of 25,000 to 40,000, reversing the vacillation of recent months with a blunt speech that named the enemy as "corporate liberalism." "This country, with its thirty-some years of liberalism, can send 200,000 young men to Vietnam to kill and die in the most dubious of wars, but it cannot get 100 voter registrars to go into Mississippi," he noted. In a fore-warning of violence, he predicted that "revolutions do not take place in velvet boxes." SDS had now moved to the "theory and practice of revolution for the United States," Oglesby concluded later.[18]

But had it? Until SDS fused Vietnam and a comprehensive analy-sis of the corporate state, until it adopted outright resistance to the war through disruptive direct action, it could never rouse many people beyond the campus. SDS was still searching for an ideology.

Black radicals had opposed Vietnam before the New Left. Mal-colm X stressed the connection between Vietnam and America's racial imperialism on his return from Africa in the summer of 1964. SNCC workers in McComb, Mississippi, also linked domestic and overseas racist policies. After the death in Vietnam of 23-year-old John D. Shaw, a participant in early SNCC demonstrations, they urged that blacks refuse the draft: "No Mississippi Negro should be fighting in Vietnam for the white man's freedom until all Negro People are free in Mississippi."

In December 1965, SNCC officially opposed blacks registering for the draft. One of the first to be indicted for refusing to register in South Carolina was Cleveland Sellers, who attacked the racist makeup of his state's draft board, which had only one black among 161 members. Carmichael also announced he would go to jail rather than enter the army, and SNCC pickets would shortly surround the Atlanta induction center, chanting, "Hell no, we won't go."

After the shooting of Samuel Younge, Jr., in Alabama in January 1966 (described in the next chapter), SNCC declared: "Sammy Younge was murdered because United States law is not being en-forced. Vietnamese are murdered because the United States is pursu-ing an aggressive policy in violation of international law." SNCC stressed the extreme disproportion of blacks—60 percent—called up by the draft "to stifle the liberation of Vietnam, to preserve a 'democ-racy' which does not exist for them at home." It was also pointed out that the percentage of blacks killed in Vietnam—21 percent—

was twice as high as the proportion of blacks in the United States population.

As public relations director for SNCC, Julian Bond had issued the Younge statement which supported resistance to the draft. He had just been elected to the Georgia House of Representatives. When an Atlanta *Constitution* headline announced, "SNCC Leader and Legislator Backs Draft Card Burning," a special committee of the legislature concluded that Bond had betrayed his country, and the House refused to seat him. Running for the same seat in a special election in February 1966, Bond was reelected. A federal court then ruled that the general assembly had the right to set qualifications, denying a seat to a member, but Bond appealed to the Supreme Court, which ordered him seated.[19]

CORE soon followed SNCC's anti-Vietnam stand. At its 1965 convention, it passed a resolution demanding immediate withdrawal of American troops. But James Farmer, the national director, considered the resolution bad tactics and forced it to be tabled—although he personally opposed the war. With Floyd McKissick as director in 1966, CORE not only condemned the war but pledged its support to all draft resisters.

Martin Luther King lagged a little behind. In July 1965, he issued a bland call for a "negotiated settlement even with the Vietcong." A year later, he came out for an immediate end to the war and led 45,000 peace marchers in a demonstration at Chicago's city hall.

King had moved his base to Chicago in the fall of 1965 to focus on ghetto problems, but he kept Vietnam in the limelight by constantly asking at rallies, "Do we love the war on poverty, or do we love the war in Vietnam?" His Chicago campaign, dubbed "Operation Breadbasket," demanded open housing and more and better jobs. Poorly organized, it claimed to have produced 800 new or upgraded jobs in the first months, but its gains affected the middle class far more than the poor.[20]

Still, King's move had special significance. It indicated that the anger of the ghettos now equaled that of the South. Harlem had been a signal in 1964. The real explosion would come in Watts, the black ghetto of Los Angeles, on August 11, 1965.

If black radicals in the South approached violence cautiously, Watts demonstrated overnight that violence was the language of the ghetto. The Watts riot, sparked by a minor arrest for alleged drunken driving, eventually spread over 50 square miles and resulted in 34 deaths (25 of them blacks), 1,032 reported injuries, almost 4,000 arrests, and an estimated loss of $40 million with 200 buildings totally destroyed.

The cry that spread through Watts—"Burn, baby, burn!"—reflected the long-dammed fury against ghetto oppression. The fury was directed above all at police brutality, a long history of beatings and humiliation, often for no discernible reason. Its special target was Police Chief William H. Parker, whose department included only 4 percent blacks and who had long been known for his bigotry. "We're on the top and they are on the bottom," he remarked during the riot.

The looting and assault on fire trucks attempting to reach a blaze symbolized the hatred against white merchants who had long exploited Watts, hiring blacks below minimum wage but charging more for their products than in other areas. The ghetto had also been penalized by bungled poverty programs; a high unemployment rate; no hospital (the closest was 12 miles away); and inefficient public transportation, which required numerous bus changes and often two hours of travel each way for blacks to reach jobs in other areas. (Only 14 percent of Watts families had their own cars).

The defeat of the Rumford Fair Housing Act by popular referendum only a few months before had produced growing bitterness. Watts residents had voted about 90 percent for the act; 80 to 90 percent of whites in surrounding areas opposed it.

The link between the northern ghetto and southern revolt was demonstrated in Watts. Observers recorded that teams of rioters— "a collective celebration in the manner of a carnival," one sociologist called it—often shouted as they hurled their rocks and bottles: "This is for Selma . . . This is for Birmingham!" The detailed press coverage of black deaths in the South had unified black communities across the country. The northern black had previously only participated through money or clothes. Now he could have personal revenge, if not on the Alabama plantation owner, at least on the white merchant around the corner.[21]

One sociologist concluded that blacks saw the riots "as a means of attacking the 'system.' In short, they are participating in a social movement that may or may not reach revolutionary proportions."

Another study found that 65 percent of blacks considered themselves "isolated and powerless." Watts became their vehicle for communicating with white society.

Although Mayor Samuel Yorty of Los Angeles would blame Communist agents for the riot, and other officials spoke of a minority of "hoodlums" in Watts, the evidence contradicted both theories. The McCone Commission, appointed by Governor Edmund G. Brown, later reported nothing to support the conspiracy theory. Two sociologists, David O. Sears and T. M. Tomlinson, found that "support for the riot was far more extensive then the public had been led to believe, numbering about a third of the area's adult residents, though a majority did disapprove of it." Their studies showed that 58 percent of the residents "foresaw predominantly beneficial effects . . . an expression of protest by the Negro community, as a whole, against an oppressive majority." The studies concluded: "Many viewed the riot in revolutionary or insurrectional terms. . . ."[22]

At least 10,000 blacks had taken to the streets of Watts, and 10,000 National Guardsmen had been called up to suppress them, before the riot ended a week later. Violence in the South and in urban ghettos had become the end result of an historical chain, the product of action and reaction. The process had produced both Chief Parker and black nationalism and had moved many blacks to the stage where insurrection became a distinct possibility. Neither SNCC nor any radical group initiated Watts. But thousands of shotguns and pistols were stored in Watts because they had proved essential to survival in Selma and Albany, and blacks believed their lives depended on them.

The Watts riot convinced SNCC that the ghettos were a tinderbox. SNCC began to think about moving northward, but first it had to clarify its nationalist objectives. It started to do this late in 1965 when the "Atlanta Project" began work on a "Position Paper on Race," perhaps the most crucial policy statement SNCC ever made. One line from the statement, which would change the course of the whole black movement, began: "If we are to proceed towards true liberation, we must cut ourselves off from white people. . . ."[23]

· 15 ·

Into the Streets: Black Power and Antiwar Resistance 1966

The election of Stokeley Carmichael to replace John Lewis as chairman of SNCC at the May 1966 staff meeting signaled the ascendancy of black nationalism. The meeting—"there was never anything like it, it lasted almost a week," one participant recalled—adopted the Atlanta position paper. "We reject the American dream as defined by white people, and must work to construct an American reality defined by Afro-Americans," the paper explained.

This paper, while granting the past contribution of whites, rejected them from future organizing and envisioned black-run communities. "We must form our own institutions, credit unions, co-ops, political parties, and write our own histories," the paper declared. SNCC's new nationalism also called for an end to coalition politics: "There can be no talk of 'hooking up' unless Blacks organize Blacks and White people organize Whites."[1]

These positions, in effect, converted SNCC from reform to revolution. The trend toward black nationalism and separatism was never in doubt. But the leadership choice between Lewis and Carmichael involved a bitter vote. Lewis had been chairman almost from the start, and his record of beatings, jailings, and courage was unrivaled. But he clung to nonviolent, integrationist, and coalitionist ethics that had now been discarded. He was a board member of SCLC and close to King, whose moderation irked radicals. More immediately, Lewis insisted on attending the White House conference on civil rights in June, boycotted by SNCC as a symbol of administration-dominated coalition politics.

Still, Lewis was elected on an early ballot, but many of the staff had been at outside meetings, and a new vote was called. Carmichael later claimed that opposition to Lewis had been building through the night, but that the radicals had never agreed on a candidate. Others insist he sought the position openly.

On the final ballot, Carmichael was elected chairman and Ruby Doris Robinson executive secretary. As a small concession, Jack Minnis, a white and close ally of Carmichael's at Lowndes, was chosen for the executive committee along with John Lewis. But Lewis resigned from SNCC a few weeks later.

SNCC had started on a new and risky road to nationalism, separatism, and violence. "Once it threw off its liberal and labor allies, SNCC would become more extremist with each defeat," Tom Kahn noted. Dorothy Healey, a former Communist official, conceded that SNCC may have gained immediate strength by building on black pride and nationalism but insisted, "Blacks always need alliances in the long run. SNCC had neither alliances nor program after 1966."

Yet SNCC had taken the risk with considerable forethought. To continue on its previous course, it believed, would have meant becoming a slightly more militant version of King's SCLC, and eventually being coopted by the Democratic coalition. It decided on the Lowndes approach of southern power bases both as a model of nationalism and a defense against cooption.[2]

SNCC had been trying to establish a base around the Tuskegee Institute in Alabama for at least a year before the murder of Samuel Younge, Jr., on January 3, 1966. Younge, a SNCC organizer, had been shot by a gas station proprietor while trying to use the white waiting room, and his killer was subsequently declared not guilty by jury trial. Despite a march of 3,000 angry students on city hall, the Tuskegee Civic Association, mainly representing black university and business circles, held to its traditional alliance with white moderates. Even when Lucius Amerson, a former army paratrooper, was chosen the first black sheriff since Reconstruction in November 1966, and a few other blacks were also elected, SNCC considered this integrated slate of moderates little more than tokenism.

The nationalists wanted independence from white control, an end to subordinate status, an intensification of group pride, and above all, their own political, economic, and cultural institutions. Their aim was not to achieve white middle-class standards for their children but to build the black community—"rejecting this racist-integrationist trap," as Alvin F. Pouissant, the Harvard psychiatrist, said.[3]

The cultural nationalists claimed that their objectives were more attainable. A leading spokesman, Ron Karenga, considered the militants "hung up on the myth of revolution" and insisted cultural institutions had to precede politics and economics. Karenga's followers at the University of California at Los Angeles, where he had taken an M.A. in political science, wore African dashikis, studied African languages, and demanded courses in black studies at every university. Their emphasis was obviously more on the African past than the Afro-American present, but it helped to raise black consciousness.

Another prominent cultural nationalist, LeRoi Jones, who adopted the African name of Imamu Amiri Baraka, expressed intense black anger. A graduate of Howard with an M.A. in comparative literature from Columbia, he wrote plays like *The Slave,* which dealt with cataclysmic race war and orgies of antiwhite vengeance. He preached the inevitability of guerrilla warfare; Irving Howe called him the "pop-art guerrilla warrior." But his poetry and plays attained considerable popularity, and in 1965 he received $40,000 in federal funds for the black theater group he established.

Karenga's group, which called itself US, competed with the California Black Panther party in a struggle to control the black studies department at UCLA in 1969, where a Panther was mysteriously killed. Two members of US were convicted but served only brief jail sentences, leading Karenga's critics to label US as informers.[4]

The basic flaw in the cultural approach, as SNCC saw it, was that it only touched the periphery of nationalism. The costumes and hairstyles only created an aura of progress detracting from the real struggle. The culturists, SNCC feared, would simply become brokers between the ghetto and capitalism, between the white ruler and the black ruled. As it turned out, the dashiki and other African trademarks were adopted not only by the black middle class—often as substitute for involvement—but by white trend-setters as well. White manufacturers would make sizable profits from African products.

SNCC's search to carry nationalism beyond Lowndes and the South to northern ghettos found an unexpected solution on June 5, 1966. James H. Meredith, who had fought successfully four years before to gain admission to the University of Mississippi, was on the second day of a lonely march from Memphis to Jackson, Mississippi. Its purpose, he announced, was to prove that a black could go unmolested anywhere in the South. With a Bible in one hand, and accompanied only by a few friends, state troopers, and newsmen, Meredith had gone two miles beyond Hernando, Mississippi, when a white man stepped out of the bushes along the road and fired three shotgun blasts. Seventy pellets were removed from Meredith's body at a Memphis hospital, but he suffered no serious injuries.

The Meredith march suddenly assumed nationwide significance:

further proof, despite Meredith's faith, that southern blacks still lived in constant peril. Black leaders from every organization—Carmichael, King, Roy Wilkins, Whitney Young, and Floyd McKissick, the new head of CORE—rushed to Meredith's bedside. There they agreed that the march would continue under their sponsorship as an affirmation of resistance.

But the SNCC leadership saw a special opportunity to push nationalism to the forefront through television and media coverage. It drew up a bristling "Radical Manifesto" which CORE approved. "We had King in the middle and Wilkins and Whitney Young on the right, and our problem was to move King to the left," Carmichael recalled. King deplored the language but was won over. Wilkins and Young dropped out.

At a Memphis rally that night, Carmichael unveiled a sample of his new nationalism. "I'm not going to beg the white man for anything I deserve," he told an appreciative crowd. "I'm going to take it." Michele Wallace, a young black writer, noted: "Stokely was the nightmare America had been dreading—the black man seizing his manhood, the black man as sexual, virile, strong, tough and dangerous."

The mood intensified as the march, drawing hundreds and soon thousands, entered Mississippi. SNCC had worked the area for years and knew almost every house on the route. It had assembled its top organizers, who turned out crowds at every stop. There was a new type of song: "Ho-ho, whatta you know, White folks gotta go." There were new signs attacking racism in Vietnam, one based on heavyweight champion Muhammad Ali's slogan: "No Vietcong ever called me Nigger!" And there was Carmichael's jabbing, slashing style, reminding the crowds that 40 blacks had been lynched or murdered in Mississippi in the previous three years, and that "we have been saying Freedom for six years and we ain't got nothin.' "[5]

At Greenwood, SNCC decided to encapsulate its militant nationalism in one phrase that would seize the imagination of every black and stir a furor in the press. Willie Ricks, whose evangelical delivery had given him the title of "reverend," coined it and tried it out first on an audience of high school students. "What do we want?" Ricks cried. "BLACK POWER!" The students picked up the phrase and shouted it repeatedly.

Greenwood had been Carmichael's headquarters, and an overflow crowd came to the city park. "We had planned it all," Carmichael recalled. "King was away at a television taping. McKissick was in another county. We knew civil rights was dying, and that Black Power would bring the movement to a new stage, and give blacks a new concept of themselves."

Carmichael had just been released from jail after his arrest for trying to erect tents for the marchers on a black school's playground. Standing on a flatbed truck, he announced:—"The only way we gonna stop them white men from whuppin' us is to take over." Then he demanded, "What do we want?" He paused a moment, and cried: "Black Power!" The crowd picked up the chant as Carmichael demanded again and again, "What do we want?" And the crowd roared back each time: "BLACK POWER!"

The same words would be heard incessantly on the rest of the march to Jackson, and the press, which recognized an exploitable issue, would immediately recast SNCC in the image of Black Power. King saw the movement threatened. At Yazoo City on June 22, he spent five hours with the SNCC and CORE leadership, pleading with them to alter the phrase to Black Equality. They refused to budge.

At Canton the next day, there was an open split in the movement when the police again forbade marchers to pitch their tents on the playground of a local black school, and SNCC and CORE voted against King's opposition to fight it out with the police. With machine guns mounted on nearby rooftops, the police sprayed the area with gas, and charged the crowd of 2,500. "People were lying all over the field unconscious, even women and children," Pouissant remembered. "Stokeley was badly gassed, and Andy Young and I had to drag him away. It was mayhem—the police didn't give a damn."

At Jackson, where the march ended on June 26, with 25,000 walking the last few miles, the split widened appreciably. SNCC and CORE passed a resolution to exclude the NAACP from the final rally on the state house grounds, and King opposed it. The press played up the split. Thus, the Meredith march had become the movement's Rubicon. Black Power embodied the mounting radicalism of SNCC, CORE, the Deacons, and other militants; it would destroy the unity of the civil rights era, terrify many whites, and lead to an increasing backlash of repression.[6]

King insisted that the "most destructive feature" of Black Power was "its unconscious and often conscious call for retaliatory violence." Carmichael's inflammatory language fanned such accusations—"I have never rejected violence," he announced a few days after the march. King held fast to the basic principle of his career: "If every Negro in the United States turns to violence, I will choose to be that one, lone voice preaching that this is the wrong way."

King also defined Black Power as "an implicit and explicit belief in black separatism," which he considered "no solution." Wilkins of the NAACP declared, "No matter how endlessly they try to explain it, the term 'black power' means anti-white power." The NAACP voted at its convention in July to sever all links with SNCC and CORE, which made the break between moderates and radicals official.[7]

In the turbulent debate that went on for at least a year, Carmichael only confused the issue by combining strident and conciliatory statements. He urged blacks to get their share of the wealth from white capitalism even if it meant "tearing down their system." At the same time, he interpreted Black Power in economic terms: "Ultimately, the economic foundations of this country must be shaken if black people are to control their lives." He saw Black Power as a lever to "bargain from a position of strength."[8]

Black Power was a confused clarion call, specific only in giving blacks a sense of urgency. It could mean violence in ghetto riots, or revolution to the ideologues. It could mean more community control, and a fairer share of incomes and jobs. It was a paean to black pride aimed at stirring nationalism in the ghettos.

Black Power was also a stand against American colonialism. It would help black radicals identify with emerging Third World uprisings against imperialism, racism, and capitalism. SNCC officials would soon travel frequently to Africa, Cuba, and Puerto Rico and seek to ally American blacks with Third World positions at the United Nations.

The immediate impact of Black Power on CORE was apparent at its July 1966 convention. It had been completely integrated from its founding over two decades before. Now almost 70 percent of the delegates were black. The most prominent resignation came from 68-year-old Lillian Smith, the Georgia author of *Strange Fruit* and longtime advocate of civil rights, who was dying of cancer but complained that "adventurers, nihilists, black abolitionists and plain, old-fashioned haters . . . have finally taken over." The National Action Council had only one white member left. CORE had always been a membership organization, but whites were virtually eliminated from cities like Boston and Kansas City where they had formerly held prominent posts. Within a year, the word, "multiracial" was removed from the national constitution.

The mood at the convention mirrored the Meredith march. One field secretary said the message of Watts was that blacks refused "to walk peacefully to the gas chambers." McKissick, chosen national director by the separatist bloc, defended revolution as a constitutional right. "Many good things have occurred for blacks as a result of violence," he would point out, calling for black separatism as "a nation within a nation."[9]

With 38 riots in 1966, including Chicago, Cleveland, and San Francisco (compared with 7 the year before), a significant number of blacks seemed to agree with McKissick. A Louis Harris poll reported that 41 percent of black leadership and 34 percent of black rank and file believed that "riots have helped" the Negro.

But Black Power and violence would also bring an increasing number of whites to support political repression. President Johnson gave repression a thinly veiled sanction when he reminded blacks that they only made up a tenth of the country. Police Commissioner Frank Rizzo of Philadelphia, long known for anti-black harassment, was not as subtle, exclaiming after Black Power demonstrations, "The only thing we can do now is buy tanks and start mounting machine guns."

SNCC had just built its first northern bases in Philadelphia and New York—the North previously supplied only student support and fund raising. On August 11, 1966, Rizzo sent police squads with machine guns to raid what he claimed was a "dynamite plot" in four supposed SNCC offices. After arresting four men, Rizzo announced that a serious incident had been averted. Actually, there was only one SNCC office, and three of those arrested were not on SNCC's staff. Branding it a "frame-up," SNCC showed that the dynamite had been found in a non-SNCC apartment and that the only staff member involved had been beaten by a white group, probably police, a few days before. All charges were quietly dropped, but Rizzo had effectively stalled organizing in the Philadelphia ghetto.[10]

Mayor Ivan Allen, Jr., of Atlanta also seemed determined to drive SNCC's national headquarters from the city. The trouble started on September 6 with the shooting of a black car-theft suspect by a white policeman. A crowd gathered quickly, pelting the police with bricks and bottles. The mayor tried to climb to the top of a car to address the crowd but was toppled to the pavement, unhurt.

SNCC sent a sound truck through the black district to announce an organized protest, and Carmichael himself canvassed from door to door. After a few days of clashes between police and blacks, the tension reached a climax when a black was shot by a white man in a passing car, and 12 SNCC workers and 60 other blacks were arrested. The Atlanta *Constitution* attacked SNCC as "openly committed to a destruction of existing society," and Carmichael certainly abetted this image by threatening to "tear this place up." There may have been ample provocation for such rhetoric, but it only gave the city administration an excuse for further repression, which began with Carmichael's arrest for inciting to riot under an old state antiriot statute. He now had a possible 10-year sentence over his head.

The Johnson administration used a variety of repressive techniques. In September, the Internal Revenue Service demanded a list of donors, but SNCC fought the order in the courts and won. The draft was used not only against officials like Sellers but against SNCC's medical service. Dr. Pouissant, head of the service, was reclassified from 2A to 1A and ordered to report to a Texas induction center. On the same day his associate, Dr. Robert Smith, got the same orders. SNCC was convinced that an informer had been feeding names to the government.

The FBI and other agencies probably infiltrated SNCC as early as 1964. "Everything we did—our meetings, our demonstrations— were known to the police long before they were announced," Pouissant recalled. "The police employed blacks who had been in previous trouble with the law, giving them money, food, and immunity from old prosecutions in return for information and disruptions. It became obvious that wild and irrational disruptions—unrelated to our strategy—could only be traced to police plants."

Once the administration and FBI had set the mood, Rizzo in Philadelphia and Mayor Richard Daley in Chicago let their police forces go unchecked. King, who had been leading open-housing demonstrations in Chicago, called them off when white counterdemonstrations attacked blacks with little interference by the police. Robert Lucas, the Chicago CORE chairman, organized new marches in July that resulted in two black deaths. As final proof of the white backlash, Congress scuttled the Civil Rights Bill of 1966, which would have given the black movement its cherished goal of open housing.[11]

At its June 1966 national council meeting, SDS voted unreserved support to the Black Power position of SNCC and CORE. Yet it had come as a blow. The New Left's most creative role had been to bolster the black movement. Now whites had been cast adrift, leaving the New Left more disoriented than ever.

The mounting resistance to the Vietnam war provided the only consistent synthesis of theory and action for the Left. When President Johnson came to New York on February 23, 1966, to accept the Freedom House award at the Waldorf-Astoria, 4,000 chanting pickets, mainly from pacifist groups, ringed the hotel. Jim Peck, the veteran pacifist who had paid $25 for a ticket, stood up on his chair as the President started to speak, screaming "Peace in Vietnam" repeatedly until Secret Service men shoved a napkin in his mouth and hustled him out of the room.

During the International Days of Protest on March 25 to 26, proving the strenth of the resistance, approximately 100,000 people marched in 80 cities, 50,000 in New York alone. Counterprotesters broke up marches in Boston and Oklahoma City. Still, Louis Harris polls showed that approval for the President on Vietnam had dropped from 63 percent in January to 49 percent in March.

When Selective Service in May announced a new policy of reclassification based on college class rank and a special exam for all deferred students, SDS initiated sit-ins at the University of Wisconsin, San Francisco State, and elsewhere. University of Chicago students took over the administration building for a few days. SDS and SNCC issued a joint statement demanding the end of the draft. SDS also printed 500,000 copies of a satiric four-page exam, distributed at exam centers and meant to sharpen a student's perspective on the war.

SDS, unfortunately, had failed to make it clear that resisters to the draft would pay their penalty. One SDS organizer, Jeff Segal, would shortly be sentenced to four years in jail for refusing induction. Peter Irons of New Hampshire SDS would be sentenced to three years. But many members of SDS still considered its resistance too moderate, and eight students in the Yale chapter planned a large-scale turn-in of draft cards in July.

When Secretary of Defense Robert McNamara arrived at Harvard for a speech on November 7, 1966, 1,000 students surrounded his car and refused to let him keep his speaking date until the police stopped a near-riot. Comparing his antagonists with his own student days at Berkeley, McNamara snapped: "I was both tougher and more courteous. I was tougher then and I'm tougher now."[12]

The Justice Department named the Du Bois clubs as a Communist-front organization in March. A few days later, both the clubs' national office in Brooklyn and the San Francisco office were wrecked by bombs, and after the national office reopened in Chicago, it was robbed of its mailing lists and tax records. Another bombing destroyed the Vietnam Day Committee headquarters in Berkeley.

The New Left, like the blacks in Lowndes County, had still not given up on electoral politics. In Berkeley, Jerry Rubin ran for mayor with Vietnam Day Committee (VDC) backing, placing second in a field of four, and getting 22 percent of the vote.

In the June Democratic primary for the House of Representatives seat in the Berkeley-Oakland area, 30-year-old Robert Scheer, managing editor of *Ramparts* magazine and a VDC leader, ran against Jefferey Cohelan, the incumbent. Cohelan was a veteran union official and former city councilman, rated highly as a liberal by Americans for Democratic Action. But he had backed the President solidly on the war, and Scheer made peace in Vietnam his prime issue.

The New Left produced 1,000 volunteers and registered 10,000 new voters. Still, there was a serious split in its ranks. The radicals felt the campaign was drawing too much money and energy from community organizing and would result in little but old-fashioned coalition politics. As a result, Jerry Rubin and many radicals dropped out, and the campaign depended increasingly on Old Left groups who favored liberal-labor alliances.

Scheer was never able to win over the white working class in Oakland, except for a few unions. And black nationalism, as well as red-baiting (his campaign coordinator was an avowed Communist), caused him trouble in the Oakland ghetto.

Still, Scheer drew 57 percent of the ghetto vote on election day, and his overwhelming margin in Berkeley gave him 29,393 to 35,921 for Cohelan, an impressive showing.[13]

The Scheer campaign accentuated the wavering policies of SDS. The National Office and Berkeley chapter, scorning electoral politics and the Democratic party, had neither taken a position on Scheer nor given the slightest support. On the other hand, Paul Booth, SDS national secretary, and other SDS veterans like Tom Hayden and Clark Kissinger had been instrumental in forming the National Conference for New Politics, which would throw considerable effort behind antiwar candidates in 1966. The uproar over Booth's role almost forced his resignation before the end of his term in June.

By fall, SDS had almost 250 chapters, with a national membership of some 6,000 and a chapter membership around 25,000. But with the influx of Midwest members ("Prairie Power," as it was called), the anarchist tradition became even more influential.

In fact, at the national convention in Iowa at the end of August, the National Office was downgraded and increasing control given local chapters. The president had always been limited to one term; in 1967 the offices of president and vice-president would be abolished.

Prairie Power gained final ascendancy in 1966 with the election of Nick Egleson as president, Carl Davidson as vice-president, and Greg Calvert as national secretary. The old guard had been pushed out for good. But the task of organization and continuity was more critical than ever. Davidson himself admitted that as much as 90 percent of the membership was new undergraduates too easily attracted by the "hippie, Bob Dylan syndrome"; that the "super-intellectuals," mainly busy graduate students, made up 5 to 10 percent; and that the real organizers were a minute fraction.[14]

Desperate to give SDS more structure and continuity, Davidson came up with a lengthy blueprint at the convention calling for a "student syndicalist movement." Like the late nineteenth-century French syndicalists, who wanted worker control through an economic federation of worker groups, Davidson visualized a federation of student unions, based on the campus but organizing strikes and boycotts in the surrounding community to link students and workers into a permanent radical force.

But as an editorial in *Studies on the Left* noted, all blueprints—whether under the name of "participatory democracy" or "syndicalism"—were meaningless unless based on the complete elimination of private ownership of the means of production. SDS was not ready for Marxism or other radical ideologies, however. Socialism was still the forbidden word. The Davidson paper stirred considerable debate but no decision.

The New Left has "no theory of society, no theory of social change, and no understanding of the nature and promise of socialism, "complained Eugene Genovese, a Rutgers university professor who raised a political storm in New Jersey at the teach-ins by espousing a Vietcong victory.

Dominated by its revulsion to ideology on one hand, and a mystical faith in permanent protest and confrontation on the other, SDS searched for a "new proletariat to take the place of the class that failed," as Michael Harrington put it. SDS had cut itself off from the past and thus never profited from the successes and failures of the Old Left. SDS had largely ignored the organized working class, influenced both by the writings of Herbert Marcuse and by the inflexible cold war politics of George Meany and the AFL-CIO. SDS could never surmount its anarchist roots, its constant experimentation that would take it from ERAP to syndicalism to the "New Working Class Theory" unveiled in 1967. Each experiment attempted a new synthesis of theory and program that was almost a caricature of the last. When SDS finally moved toward Marxism a year or so hence, it would be a "cheap, simple-minded Marxism," Todd Gitlin observed.[15]

At best in 1966, its most coherent concept of a proletariat revolved around the emerging Third World movements. It saw the Vietnam intervention as aimed solely at tightening the military ring around Communist China, and cold war anti-Communism simply as a mask for "Free World" imperialism, which sought indirect control of other economies in order to find market and investment outlets for America's surplus capital. America's investments abroad, as a result, had grown from $17 to $125 billion since World War II.

Dean Acheson had argued years before that a loss anywhere means a defeat everywhere, which provided the logic for the administration's domino theory. This logic demanded continued escalation and American intervention around the world, whether openly in the Dominican Republic or Lebanon, or covertly through the CIA in Indonesia or Latin America. Thus, the United States transformed the cold war against Russia into a struggle against revolutionary and nationalist movements of the Third World. Often allying itself with reactionary régimes, particularly in Latin America, American policy stifled any type of social change. To preserve the status quo, Washington had spent $800 billions on armaments since 1945.

The New Left suffered not only from its dependence on the black radicals, but from its inability to resolve the priorities between theory and practice. As late as the Columbia riots in 1968, SDS was split between the "Praxis Axis," which wanted an ideological base for each step, and the "Action Faction," demanding a spontaneous and volatile uprising that could be fitted later to theoretical planning.[16]

This failure to find a new proletariat and develop a coherent social theory around it made the New Left turn to Herbert Marcuse. In his disillusion with the working class as a revolutionary force, Marcuse had built his philosophy around marginal groups. Society could only be shaken, he believed, by the outcasts and outsiders, rebellious students, outraged poor, alienated hippies, oppressed blacks, the unemployed and unemployable. Both Marcuse and the New Left considered organized labor at the moment only a handmaiden of the liberal corporate state. Both attacked the Soviet system as a distortion of Marxism—its overwhelming bureaucracy and technocratic centralization often leading to worse forms of repression than capitalist society.

Born in Berlin in 1898, a refugee from Nazi Germany in 1933, Marcuse, who taught at Harvard, Yale, and Columbia before the University of California at San Diego, espoused a utopian vision of liberated man. It was a vision that drew essentially on Marx and Freud, for Marcuse tried to make a synthesis between socialism and psychoanalysis, to add a Freudian dimension to the Hegelian-Marxist tradition.

Concerned with the theme of alienation in Marx and Hegel, Marcuse accepted Freud's pessimistic assumptions on repression but tried to build a system turning repression into human fulfillment. Liberation for Marcuse meant the achievement of "libidinal rationality"—the release of erotic energy from the impositions of capitalism and technocracy. His objectives were moral and aesthetic. He saw politics as a framework for individual liberation, as the New Left said in its slogan, "A liberal wants to free others, a radical wants to free himself."

In *One-Dimensional Man* (1964), a work that would have profound impact on the New Left, Marcuse argued that democratic capitalism has made us "sublimated slaves" mistaking servitude for freedom. People are forced by the system to "find their soul" in high-powered automobiles, split-level homes, and household gadgets. The increasing success of technocracy further advances the repressive power of the state. The development of machines to maximum profitability through automation intensifies the irrationality of human labor and alienation. The system thus imposes what Marcuse calls "surplus repression," abetted by the sexual and social controls of law and custom. The price of ever-mounting affluence, and the illusion of power and success spewed out by advertising and the media, becomes more centralized control and repression.

Sexuality as well has been harnessed to the demands of the system. Marcuse found the sexual permissiveness of recent years a sham, serving only to "desublimate" repressed tensions and to pacify "one-dimensional" man into accepting a stifled and unfulfilled existence. Marcuse went along with Freud in the need for repressing damaging biological drives. But he condemned "surplus repression" as a device of capitalist domination.

Marcuse had trouble moving from the philosophic level to political strategy. He asserted the dual reality of existence: everything that "is" can be transformed into what it "could be" if its potentialities were realized. If freed from surplus repression, people could advance to a stage of revolutionary consciousness, an essential step for radicals after 1965. Black Power, to cite one example, aimed at raising nationalist consciousness—a vision beyond civil rights that stirred blacks to seek economic, political, and social power greater than the gradualism offered by the corporate state.

Once freed from surplus repression, society, as Marcuse saw it, has the potential to transform its sublimated drives into creative, joyful, and affirmative work. Industrial man can find this potential in the very technocracy used to alienate him. The abundance produced by science and technocracy obliterates the need for joyless labor. When man controls his own machines instead of being manipulated by them—a constant theme in the New Left—he can shape a world in which personal fulfillment supplants alienation and the Puritan ethic.

This, of course, is a nebulous vision. Marcuse never tells us how such a world will be organized, nor whether a small team of automakers, following their product through to completion instead of being chained to the unending repetition of one minute step on the assembly line, can achieve more beauty in their lives than the high-paid unionist enjoying his backyard swimming pool.

Nor does Marcuse, disillusioned with the working class as a radical force, provide any specific instrument for social change to replace the old Marxist parties. He extols direct democracy, the overthrow of institutions dominating our lives, and the reintegration of the worker into a liberated community that smacks of the New Left's "participatory democracy." He envisions students and intellectuals as the shock troops of radicalization, voicing the hopes and needs of the silent masses and prodding them into action. He defends the natural right of resistance to oppression—by violence if other means fail. He proposes a potential alliance of students with professional and technical workers.

But when all Marcuse's visions were weighed against the immediate crisis, he admitted that students and intellectuals could not produce a revolution on their own. After the student uprising in Paris in 1968 almost brought France to the edge of revolution, Marcuse was asked about the possibility of revolution in America. "Absolutely not," he replied. "Because there is no collaboration between the students and the workers, not even on the level on which it occurred in France." He concluded: "I cannot imagine . . . a revolution without the working class."[17]

Thus Marcuse gave the New Left no synthesis of theory and action. It was still a movement without a technique of revolution. Aware of this failure, SDS established a Radical Education Project to produce a revolutionary blueprint. But the Progressive Labor party moved first. In February 1966, it dissolved the M2M group, its previous front, and ordered all PL members to join SDS. With its rigid Marxism, its student-worker alliance, and Maoist principles that made it known as the "Mao Now" crowd, PL was confident it could provide the technique of revolution. Its first step was to take over SDS.

At its December 1966 meeting, SNCC completed its transition to nationalism with the ouster of whites from its staff. Whites could hold administrative jobs or remain in Friends of SNCC units. But they were barred from the staff as policy makers or organizers. The "Zellner compromise"—proposed later by Bob Zellner, a veteran white organizer, and allowing whites to stay on staff if they worked in poor, white districts—was defeated.

Carmichael insisted that even whites as skilled and dedicated as Zellner were superfluous. "They could no longer open up an area like Lowndes," he explained, "but could only go in after we'd made a base."

Dr. Pouissant saw deeper problems in "white paternalism and superiority," particularly involving sexual relations. Whether rational or not, a few extremists claimed there were informers among white volunteers; and even a veteran officer like James Forman roused some hostility because of his white wife.

SNCC, in effect, was involved in a parallel crisis to the New Left. Like SDS, it was unable to come to grips with socialism and so had turned to nationalism to reach the ghetto masses. It was searching for its own instrument of revolution, its own proletariat. Failing to understand that nationalism was not inherently radical but could take bourgeois forms as in the case of the Muslims, SNCC would make nationalism into a surrogate socialism.[18]

Meanwhile, even SNCC had hardly noticed that a new organization had risen in the ghetto. Ironically, this group of black outcasts in the Oakland, California, slums had borrowed its name, the Black Panthers, from SNCC's party in Lowndes. Founded in October 1966, its chairman was Huey P. Newton, 24; its minister of defense, Bobby Seale, 30. Although both had some college education and read widely, their constituency was the "wretched" of the slums (they admired Frantz Fanon's writings), the "lumpen" that Marx considered untrustworthy. Unlike SNCC, they adopted a hybrid Marxist-Leninist program from the start but fused it with black nationalism. Rejecting SNCC's anarchist spirit, they built a rigid, disciplined party, forbidding the use of liquor and drugs while on duty, always wearing the prescribed uniform: a black beret, black leather jacket and pants, and a blue turtleneck shirt.

Newton was born in Louisiana on February 17, 1942, son of a railroad brakeman and Baptist preacher, the youngest of seven children. "My father's father was a white rapist," he noted. Eager for education, he read Chinese philosophy and poetry at the urging of an older brother. When his family moved to Oakland, he tried to register at the superior Berkeley High School from a sister's address but was detected and forced back to a technical institution at Oakland. After graduating from Merritt, the local two-year college, he took one year of law school, which convinced him he was unsuited to the profession; yet the brief training provided an invaluable asset in Panther tactics.

Newton had met Seale at Merritt College, where they organized the Soul Students Advisory Council, their first experiment in nationalist politics. Seale had spent four years in the army, the last six months in the stockade for protesting a racial incident, and had done time in California jails for minor burglaries and petty larceny. They became close friends in 1965 when Seale briefly joined the Revolutionary Action Movement.

A disciple of Malcolm X, Newton decided by 1966 that nationalism, and SNCC's call for Black Power, needed a unique approach in the ghettos. The prime enemy of black pride, the most immediate symbol of oppression, was the Oakland police. Their harassment, friskings, searches, and beatings kept the city's blacks, Chicanos, and Chinese (about half the 450,000 population) in terror.[19]

Newton believed that the only way to make the police respect the rights and dignity of blacks was to meet force with force. Each Panther on duty would carry a loaded, unconcealed gun—legal under California law at that time except in automobiles, where only a handgun could be kept loaded. While black radicals in the South, particularly the Deacons, owned guns to defend their homes and meetings, the Panther strategy was to patrol the streets constantly. They had designated themselves an armed agency to protect the community, to put the police on notice that if a black were mistreated or a home invaded without legal warrant, black protest would be backed up with bullets.

Panther cars frequently tailed police cars. If the police stopped for an unwarranted questioning or frisking, the Panthers would watch at a distance. Newton always carried his law books in his car, ready to read the appropriate passage applying to a citizens' rights. "At times they drew their guns and we drew ours, until we reached a sort of standoff," Newton explained.

Newton took severe risks. Once the police surrounded him with drawn guns while he was sitting in his car in front of the Panther office on 58th Street. Newton got out, unarmed. While a crowd gathered, he upbraided the police, calling them "pigs" and one of them, a "Georgia cracker." The use of such epithets was part of an intentional policy to treat the police with the same scorn they had long applied to blacks.

The street patrols, were only one aspect, albeit the most publicized, of Panther policy. Newton and Seale had developed a philosophy that amalgamated numerous Marxist teachings in a package called "the 10 Points." They advocated a proletarian revolution cutting across racial lines. Although fervent nationalists, they believed in alliances with the white Left. They sought and received considerable help from white lawyers, educators, and other radicals in their programs.

In their concept of a disciplined party, the Panthers were strict Leninists. They called themselves the vanguard; their slogan was, "Panther Power to the Vanguard Party."

Their nationalism was pragmatic. While demanding liberation for the "black colony" in the "white mother country," Newton held that even five or six black states could not survive surrounded by white, capitalist America. He shrewdly opposed "an enclave-like situation where we would be more isolated than we already are now."

While advocating a cultural as well as political revolution, the Panthers were equally pragmatic in condemning the limiting objectives of Karenga's US. It was absurd to think that wearing a dashiki or taking a black-study course would make you free. The Panther minister of education called rigid culturists "reactionary and insane and counter-revolutionary." Newton particularly opposed the culturists' hatred of anything white. Criticized once for holding a door for a white woman, he retorted, "The white girl's not attacking me. She's not brutalizing me."[20]

The Panthers altered orthodox Marxism in other respects. Like SNCC, they saw the "colony" at home as an integral part of revolutionary and nationalist struggles in the Third World, whether Algeria or Cuba, whether Marxist or only borderline Marxist. These struggles, they explained, further heightened black militancy here. Their analysis of neoimperialism, their opposition to the "expansionist, racist war in Vietnam," paralleled the positions of other black and white radicals.

In an effort to provide a minimal economic base in the slums, they would establish a free hot-breakfast service and a free clothing store for poor children. These services obviously strengthened their community ties. Later, they would establish a school of enough merit to draw many black students from the public schools.

The "10 Points" in addition, demanded that all imprisoned blacks —victims of a prejudiced jury system—should be released immediately. Future trials should only be held by the black communities themselves. Black people should be exempt from military service since they had no obligation to "defend a racist government that does not protect us." The points concluded: "We want land, bread, housing, education, clothing, justice and peace."[21]

Within three years, these demands had roused such support in the ghettos that the Panthers could claim chapters in 30 cities. They had moved the revolt to a new stage. They had established permanent armed confrontation with the police, a continuing guerrilla warfare that was, in effect, a struggle for control of the ghetto.

· 16 ·

Guerrilla Warfare
1967

After almost two years of laborious organizing in Lowndes County, SNCC seemed on the verge of establishing its first important power base in the South. It had lost the 1966 elections by only 600 to 700 votes and undoubtedly could have won the next elections. An influx of federal registrars was making it easier to get fieldhands to the polls and diminish the intimidation by white planters. SNCC probably could have gone on to take control of other counties, or work with moderates as it had at Tuskegee, to advance the "black nation within a nation" concept. Yet SNCC abandoned this strategy in 1967 and pushed into the northern ghettos. In effect, it tried to turn itself overnight into a national organization.

What had brought such a momentous shift? What had caused SNCC to give up community organizing among rural counties and gamble on chaotic ghetto politics, where its previous expertise counted for little?

The principal momentum for the shift came from Watts and each succeeding riot. SNCC became increasingly convinced it had to shape the anger and rebellion of the ghettos. Suddenly fearful of being buried in remote areas of the South, it determined to join the mainstream. Impatient for power, escalating its demands for immediate results, SNCC saw itself as the driving force of the whole black movement. "We had a choice of working in a few Southern counties, or building black consciousness and nationalism in the ghettos. I still think we made the right choice," Stokeley Carmichael concluded in 1977.

The decision had an element of desperation. With increasing repression by the federal government and local police, SNCC wanted the greatest national impact in the few years possibly left to it. "There is no way to go but up or under," Forman said then.

At the same time, the decision was influenced by the raised expec-

220

tations of the Meredith march. The introduction of Black Power as a national issue had made SNCC, and Carmichael especially, into media figures. Carmichael was in constant demand as a speaker in late 1966, traveling feverishly to address overflow crowds at campuses and black rallies. His own ambitions and ego thus became a factor. Highly skilled at using the media for his own image and SNCC's nationalistic ends, Carmichael decided that SNCC had to attack all oppressive institutions. Some critics thought Carmichael had been converted from an organizer into a "media freak" and that his marriage to Miriam Makeba, a prominent singer of African songs, confirmed this change. Tom Hayden felt that the SNCC leadership could not stand being isolated from black workers in the ghettos, and "the move North was a way of consolidating their power."

The cutoff of white liberal money after the Black Power ruckus also convinced SNCC it had to seek new funding elsewhere; moving North, it hoped, would help its chances with the black urban bourgeoisie. In addition, there was considerable pressure from Friends of SNCC units in the North, and from Old Left supporters, both black and white, to draw SNCC programs to their own areas and make themselves an immediate part of the glamour. Further, SNCC had lost its southern rural character—most of the staff was now from the North.

But impelling as all these factors seemed at the time, they still should not have overridden the opposing arguments. "It was absurd to think we could accomplish the same things in Philadelphia as in Mississippi—just sheer fantasy," Julian Bond observed. "We failed to develop a clear ideology."

"Harlem was so split politically—not just Democrats and Republicans, but Marxists, Muslims, and other factions—that SNCC could never build a base there," commented Gloria Richardson, who opposed the move. "We had no roots, no programs that had a realistic chance."

"The great danger of leaving the South was diffusion," noted Jean Wylie of SNCC. "We had no analysis of where to begin." Further, Bayard Rustin and other powerful voices in liberal-labor circles didn't want SNCC in New York or other cities, and they had enough influence over antipoverty agencies and money to raise severe obstacles. SNCC, in fact, had almost no previous organizers in the North; its offices there were mainly for fund raising. Its staff, already shrunk by the money crunch, numbered fewer than 100, at times only 60 or so. Few of the early veterans remained on staff, and they were exhausted. "Some people freaked out from the violence. Some people were battleweary . . . they went into shock," Ivanhoe Donaldson recalled. Forman's health, in particular, was failing. "The New York chapter never developed, the staff simply fell apart," Pouissant concluded.[1]

Except for a handful who stayed with the Mississippi Freedom Democratic party and local projects in other states, most of the SNCC staff chose to gamble on the North. They turned to a kind of political guerrilla warfare. Their model was the long-drawn struggle at Cambridge, Maryland, but they failed to realize Cambridge was far more a southern town than northern ghetto. Within a year or two, the results would prove disastrous.

The Panthers in Oakland, meanwhile, expanded their hold on the ghetto. When State Representative Don Mulford of Oakland introduced a bill into the legislature—obviously aimed at the Panthers—to prohibit the carrying of loaded weapons in incorporated areas, 30 Panthers journeyed to Sacramento and held a press conference of protest inside the State House. Television cameras and newsmen crowded around the Panthers, and suddenly they found themselves on the Assembly floor. They would claim it was an accident, but probably they had arranged it. Legislators were horrified to have guns in their chamber, and guards hustled the Panthers into an adjoining room and disarmed them. Later, they insisted on their legal rights to have the guns returned and won their point. The uproar gave the Panthers their first national exposure and aided ghetto recruitment, despite passage of the Mulford bill in July.

The Panthers achieved further attention that spring with their latest recruit, Eldridge Cleaver, author of *Soul On Ice,* a raw, brutal, yet often poetically eloquent account of black degradation in Cleaver's ghetto and prison years. Cleaver had met his first Panthers shortly after release from Soledad prison and called them "the most beautiful sight I had ever seen." He had been given a job on *Ramparts,* which carried sections of the book. Newton made him minister of education almost immediately. He was undoubtedly overawed by having a best-selling author, a star of the literary circuit, in the party.

Born in Arkansas in 1935, Cleaver moved with his family to the Los Angeles ghetto, where he grew up hustling pot, playing football for his high school team, and dabbling in petty theft. His first arrest came at 15. Out on parole, he made enough money from pot to live expensively, often with white women. He had an athlete's build, with powerful shoulders, and catlike movements, giving him an ease and confidence that approached elegance. A reporter described the "startling green irises" of his eyes and thought they inspired "instant feelings of confidence and warmth." Cleaver would claim in his book that most relations with white women involved rape rather than seduction, for he had decided to politicize sexuality and made each rape an "insurrectionary act." Charged with assault and rape in 1957, he was returned to jail for a 2-to-14-year sentence.[2]

Reading omnivorously, he became a convert to Malcolm X, joined the Muslims, and started writing himself. He sent some essays to Beverly Axelrod, a noted San Francisco lawyer whose name he had picked at random from the newspapers. She passed the essays to Edward Keating, publisher of *Ramparts,* where they were polished and edited by Paul Jacobs and David Welsh. These essays, with further additions, became *Soul On Ice.*

While Axelrod struggled to get Cleaver out of jail, a strong attachment grew between them. "And having recognized each other, is it any wonder that our souls hold hands and cling together while our minds equivocate, hesitate, vacillate, and tremble?" he wrote her. Although he had been eligible for parole in two years, he was not released until December 1966, after serving a nine-year sentence. The Axelrod-Cleaver romance soon faded when he met Kathleen Neal, the 23-year-old daughter of a black college professor. They were married in 1967.[3]

Huey Newton had expected Cleaver that year to edit *The Black Panther,* the organization's newspaper, and run educational seminars for members and recruits. But Newton complained that Cleaver's editorial work was sloppy and that Cleaver preferred the glamour of radio and television appearances to community education. Cleaver had long moody spells; his repressed anger flared up at the slighest irritation. Further, he frequented the bars of San Francisco's Haight-Ashbury and Berkeley's Telegraph Avenue, and Newton, who insisted the Panthers stay off drugs, found that Cleaver was "attracting hippies and Yippies to the Party." Newton would conclude years later that "Eldridge lived in a fantasy world" and was "in search of a strong manhood symbol." But that, of course, was hindsight, and Newton had already made Cleaver the Panther's main spokesman.[4]

SNCC, too, was having its leadership problems. Carmichael as chairman had been making increasingly inflammatory statements favoring armed struggle and violence. Ruby Doris Robinson, the executive secretary, felt this rhetoric put unneeded pressure on field organizers, hindered fund raising, and would lead to further repression. She even introduced a motion to silence him for six months, but it was never passed.

Carmichael's personal flamboyance also upset the anarchist traditions of the staff, which lived on a subsistence level. When he and his wife, who made large singing fees, looked for a house in Washington, D.C., the press reported they had bought a $70,000 property. Carmichael insisted they had only examined the house, but the real estate broker had mistakenly reported it to the press as a completed sale. Still, the split in SNCC reached a point by the fall of 1967 where many of the officers and staff wanted to expel Carmichael. But Forman stopped expulsion on the grounds it would remind the black community of the destructive feud between Malcolm X and Elijah Muhammed.[5]

In May 1967, Carmichael had already been replaced as chairman by H. Rap Brown. Carmichael claimed he wanted to return to organizing. His close associate, Cleveland Sellers, also declined to run again.

Brown, supposedly Forman's candidate, was a "street fighter," more like the ghetto-bred Panthers than the Howard University group that dominated SNCC. Born in Baton Rouge, Louisiana, in 1943, he worked as a ditchdigger while at Southern High School, and carried a gun (stolen from a sporting goods store) from the time he was 14. He attended Southern University briefly and was expelled for taking part in the sit-ins. He followed his older brother, Ed, to Washington, D.C., where he joined Carmichael, Cox, and other members of the Howard group in SNCC. By 1963, he was a veteran of Cambridge, Maryland, street fights. He worked under Carmichael in Alabama, eventually taking over as SNCC's project director. His violent record, he claimed, kept him out of the army: "I'd already told 'em that if they gave me a gun and told me to shoot my enemy, I'd shoot Ladybird [Johnson]."[6]

With little ideological training, Brown insisted that "books don't make revolutionaries" and scorned many of the "bootleg preachers and coffee-house intellectuals" among black nationalists. Despite earlier staff unhappiness with Carmichael's rhetoric, Brown proved that he could outdo him. When police broke up a SNCC rally at Prattville, Alabama, in June 1967, Ku Klux Klan members surrounded a house where the staff was staying, and shots were fired from both sides. Brown announced to the press that SNCC accepted the attack by "racist, white America as a declaration of war." He added later: "I preach a response to violence. Meet violence with violence."

Five Texas Southern University students who tried to form a Friends of SNCC unit had already been charged with murder that June. The students had rioted when SNCC was banned from the campus, and 500 police, firing 6,000 rounds, had invaded two dormitories. A policeman had been killed, supposedly by a dormitory sniper. But SNCC, stating that the building had no doors or windows where the sniper was said to be stationed, charged that the bullet had come from another policeman.[7]

The level of warfare was escalated further in Cambridge, Maryland. Brown had just arrived from the Newark riot to address a protest rally on July 24, 1967. The brutality and death toll at Newark had heightened the tension in Cambridge. "In a town this size, three men can burn it down. That's what they call guerrilla warfare," Brown told his jittery audience. "I know who my enemy is and I know how to kill him." He urged them to "burn this town down if this town don't turn around."

Brown's next words, taped by the police, came even closer to direct incitement. Referring to a half-burned black school that had been condemned 12 years earlier and set afire twice since June, Brown told the audience, "You should've burned it down long ago." SNCC insisted he was alluding to the previous fires, not advocating immediate arson. However, about 12 shotgun blasts were fired at Brown as he walked other blacks home, and he was hit in the forehead by a pellet. Armed whites raced through the streets of the black district in their cars, firing wildly. A black youth and a white policeman were wounded, and blacks began shooting back. By early morning, flames raged out of control through the area. The black school had been burned to the ground—the fire department contended it was too risky to answer the alarm. More than 700 National Guardsmen had to be rushed to Cambridge to control the outburst.[8]

Although Brown left town for Washington well before the fires started, the district attorney charged him with inciting riot and arson. The police chief called it a "well-planned Communist attempt to overthrow the city government."

Carmichael, of course, was no longer SNCC's spokesman, but he also raised the rhetoric a notch. "In Newark we applied war tactics of the guerrillas," he observed. "We are preparing groups of urban guerrillas for our defense of the cities." No one bothered to ask whether "we" meant SNCC specifically or the ghetto rebels in general. But national and local law officers, unconcerned about the point, now considered Rap Brown their prime target.

Because Brown had crossed state lines, the Cambridge charge became a federal one, and he was arrested by the FBI on July 26 at Washington airport. He claimed he was flying to New York where his lawyer, William Kunstler, had arranged to turn him in. Released by federal authorities, he was rearrested by Virginia as a fugitive from Maryland. Brown furthered the confrontation by announcing that Newark and Cambridge were just "a dress rehearsal for real revolution."

The consequent cycle of arrests produced a legal maze that would not be disentangled for years. After a speech in Dayton, Ohio, in August, he was charged by the city with "criminal syndicalism." Later in August, while flying from New Orleans to New York, he was charged with carrying a weapon across state lines while under federal indictment—although he had checked his plastic-wrapped carbine with the plane's pilot. He was jailed again in Virginia in September, released on bail, and rearrested in New York in February 1968 for violating bail terms that restricted him to the southern district of New York. (He had flown to California to see his lawyer, he claimed.) Returning to New Orleans, where the original warrant had been issued, he was jailed on $100,000 bail, and fasted for 43 days until bail was reduced to $30,000.[9]

The furor over Brown obscured the fact that neither he nor SNCC played any detectable role—except in Cambridge—in the immediate wave of ghetto riots. There were bloody outbursts that spring and summer in Cleveland, Washington, D.C., Omaha, Boston, Louisville, Kentucky, and Montgomery, Alabama, among other cities. No SNCC staff seems to have been present at any riot except Rap Brown at Newark, New Jersey. The only corroboration of Carmichael's prediction of "urban guerrillas" was a *Life* magazine report on a "sniper organization" whose members "belonged to a group formed by young civil rights workers in Mississippi in 1965." When the reporter asked why so few police had been hit by snipers, a spokesman replied, "Why kill for no reason?" He added, "The important thing is our people know we're here."

While SNCC undoubtedly moved the ghettos toward black nationalism and gave an ideological sanction to violence, the Newark riot on July 12, 1967, like Watts and others, appeared to be completely spontaneous. The degradation and anger were too deep to need organized leadership. Unemployment among blacks and Puerto Ricans, who made up 52 and 10 percent respectively of the Newark population, had reached twice the national rate. The city had the highest percentage of bad housing, the highest crime rate, and the highest maternal mortality rate in the country. On the police force of 1,400, there were only 250 blacks; among New Jersey's 1,200 state troopers, only five blacks. CORE had requested a civilian review board on police brutalities two years before, but had been turned down by Mayor Hugh Addonizio, representing the ruling Italian-American faction.

While the causes of the Newark riot hardly differed from other cities, the retaliatory fury of the police was unequaled elsewhere. Following the deaths of a police officer and fireman, with no clear evidence of the circumstances, the police seemed bent on almost ritual acts of revenge. One black youth, for example, had 45 bullet holes in his body. The police sprayed black homes with unremitting gunfire. Two women, one caring for three grandchildren, were killed in their apartments. The death toll eventually reached 27, including six women and two children. The American Civil Liberties Union concluded that the police "seized on the initial disorders as an opportunity and pretext to perpetrate the most horrendous and widespread killing, violence, torture and intimidation."[10]

The Detroit riot erupted on July 23, 1967. What made it different was the extent of guerrilla operations. Blacks used automatic weapons and tracer bullets. The Kercheval area was controlled for 36 hours by rooftop snipers, the police and military driven out while waiting for reinforcements. Eighteen blocks of 12th Street and three miles of Grand River Avenue were burned to the ground. Unlike Watts and other riots, the combat zone was not confined to the black ghetto but spilled over into white areas, with poor whites joining the looting.

Eventually, President Johnson sent 4,700 army paratroopers to assist 3,000 Detroit policemen, 500 state troopers, and 2,000 National Guardsmen (poorly trained for such duty, and as in most riots, so trigger-happy they fired at anything that moved). Army tanks had to rescue 100 soldiers and police besieged by snipers in two station houses. With 43 dead and 2,000 wounded, the riot probably represented the greatest internal violence since the Civil War. It was the peak year of ghetto violence: 75 major riots took place in 1967 compared with 21 in 1966.

James Forman of SNCC would call it "a revolution where we are part of the vanguard process that seizes and holds power." The public, too, seemed to believe that radicals were instrumental in the riots—45 percent of whites polled attributed the revolts to "Communist backing," "outside agitators," and "minority radicals" in a Harris survey.[11]

All elements of the New Left, from SDS to the peace movement, sought power in the streets in 1967. A new slogan—"The streets belong to the people"—symbolized this shift. Huge crowds—350,-000 to 500,000 nationwide, perhaps 250,000 in New York, and 75,-000 in San Francisco—turned out on April 15 for the Spring Mobilization against the War in Vietnam. The black flag of anarchism, the red flag of communism, and National Liberation Front banners were sprinkled throughout the marches. Although few black students remained in SDS, "Spring Mobe" brought together a broad spectrum of support. In New York, Dr. Benjamin Spock spoke from the same platform as Stokeley Carmichael. By focusing on Vietnam, SDS was finally reaching a new constituency.

It had not come easily. The SDS National Council, in fact, only gave grudging approval. The impetus came from local chapters, pushing the movement "from protest to resistance," as Greg Calvert called it. Cornell University in particular organized draft-card burnings, soon an important vehicle of resistance. In New York's Central Park on April 15, Gary Rader, a veteran of the elite Green Beret units from Vietnam, led the ceremonial burning of 175 cards, while the surrounding crowd shouted, "Hell No, We Won't Go!" In October, 1,400 cards were burned or returned to federal authorities during "Stop the Draft" week.[12]

Todd Gitlin saw the expulsion of the military from all campuses as a "national synthesis" despite indifference at the SDS convention. Columbia SDS organized 800 students to oust military recruiting from its buildings. At Harvard, a Dow Chemical Company recruiter was held captive for nearly 12 hours by a student mob.* At Brown, Pennsylvania, Indiana, and Stanford, at scores of campuses across the country, students blocked military and defense recruiters, often clashing with the police in the process.

When the new chancellor of the University of Wisconsin promised

---

*Dow was the principal manufacturer of napalm.

to protect all recruiters, at least 3,000 students forced the Dow Chemical man out of the Commerce building on October 18, 1967, and battled with the police in bloody, rock-throwing skirmishes. Sixty-five students and seven policemen ended up in the hospital, but most of the campus, including the student newspaper and conservative groups, backed the confrontation, and the chancellor soon resigned.

By the time of Stop the Draft Week, the New Left had made street action its accepted strategy. These were no longer casual demonstrations, but planned and coordinated attacks. In Oakland, most participants wore helmets and carried makeshift shields. They traveled in small, disciplined units, four or five grappling with a policeman from the rear if he tried to arrest one of their members. On October 17, 3,000 surrounded the military induction center at Oakland. Almost 100 fought their way inside; at least 20 were injured and many arrested. Ten thousand surrounded the induction center on October 20. Coached in "mobile" warfare to avoid a head-on clash with the police, they threw up quick barricades to stop army buses reaching the center and overturned cars to block the streets. Constantly melting away when the police attacked and reforming elsewhere before the police could reach them, they controlled large areas of Berkeley and Oakland for four hours.[13]

Oakland was a dividing line for the New Left. Nonviolence had been replaced once and for all by warfare in the streets. Carl Davidson, SDS's interorganizational secretary, concluded a bit optimistically that November: "The events of this summer marked not only the possibility, but the beginning of the second American Revolution."

Long dominated by anarchist politics and its disdain for Old Left labels, SDS, too, was edging toward a Marxist ideology to direct its day-to-day functioning. The first step was the presentation at a Princeton conference in February 1967 of the "New Working Class Theory," a strained attempt to apply Marxist class analysis to immediate needs. The New Left had been searching for a new working class to replace industrial workers and unions. Drawing on C. Wright Mills, André Gorz, Marcuse, and other theoreticians, SDS claimed to have found this new class in a curious amalgam consisting of three groups: technical and professional workers, including clerical and sales forces; industrial workers at the highest technical and pay levels; workers in the social sciences from artists to social workers, teachers, and physicians.

SDS's thesis was that these groups could be radicalized by a student "vanguard" (Old Left terminology slipping in at last), and that by moving off the campus to clerical offices and technical laboratories, the New Left could break out of its isolation. It was a flimsy thesis, abandoned almost before it was tested. But it had some importance in the internal politics of SDS, representing a bulwark against the Progressive Labor party.

In the midst of SDS's hectic growth—it now exceeded 250 chapters—PL was the only faction that could claim a sharply defined program. For many, therefore, its Maoist rigidity and mechanical Marxism-Leninism filled an ideological vacuum. Its "Worker-Student Alliance" cut deeply into SDS that summer with a "Vietnam Work-In," placing students in temporary factory jobs and carrying the antiwar, anti-imperialist message to the assembly lines.* With mounting strength at the local level, particularly in Boston, New York, and Chicago, PL increasingly took over SDS chapters. By the December national council meeting, it controlled about a quarter of the delegates. In effect, PL pushed SDS toward Marxism by forcing it to build its own Marxist front against PL domination.[14]

The New Left had taken increasing hold on most campuses. By the 1967–68 academic year, at least 75 percent of American universities had been hit by serious demonstrations. When a study was made of 2,250 students at the University of Wisconsin who had signed a "Declaration of Responsibility" after the Dow Chemical riot in 1967, 47 percent classified themselves as anarchists, communists, New Leftists, or under other radical labels. A *Fortune* magazine poll in 1968 found that 20 percent of all students were potential supporters of the New Left.

The makeup of the New Left had also altered. A large proportion now came from "Middle America," from small-town, working-class, and even Republican and southern backgrounds. There had been a sharp increase of Protestant and Catholic students as opposed to Jewish and "secular" youths.

A contributing factor to campus disillusionment was the revelation in *Ramparts* in March 1967 that the National Student Association (NSA), a prestigious coalition of campus organizations, had been controlled for years by the CIA. Based on material from a former NSA officer, the article cited specific payments—$2 million

---

*The New Left turned out an additional 20,000 or so volunteers, many from SDS, in perhaps 500 "Vietnam Summer" projects aimed at disrupting the war.

in one instance, $250,000 in another—that had been channelled by the CIA through respectable foundations. This money not only provided NSA with a lavish Washington headquarters and a half-million-dollar annual budget but made it virtually an arm of U.S. foreign policy.[15]

The radicalization of the campuses was only a partial indication of the strength of the New Left, which took in a much broader cultural base described by Theodore Roszak as the "counterculture." This world of hippies had expanded considerably since taking root in New York's East Village and San Francisco's Haight-Ashbury in the early 1960s. Drawing on all social and economic groups, not just upper-middle-class rebels, it represented a concerted attack on American bourgeois values. It stressed drugs and liberating sexuality and was a revolt against puritan morality and technocratic discipline. Its romantic pastoralism—its communes surviving on basic necessities, its flower children—was a protest against materialism and affluence run amuck.

Folk-rock festivals and "happenings" celebrated the yearning for emotional release and fulfillment. Dr. Timothy Leary, fired from Harvard for testing hallucinogenic drugs on students, preached a mystical and ecstatic pseudoreligion of sensual pleasure based on "consciousness-expanding" drugs like LSD. Psychedelic drugs were part of the search for new perceptions and sources of wisdom, a search that rejected reality and western rationalism for an inner world of heightened awareness. Sexuality, Zen Buddhism, and mysticism became routes toward achieving meaning for each existential moment. Sound and light systems, combining rock music and acid-dropping with the pop-culture mainstream, aimed at raising the senses to a pitch of ecstasy. Allen Ginsberg's poetic chants, booming repetitive hurricanes of sound, explored the same sensual nerves. Ginsberg's "Human Be-In" brought 20,000 hippies to San Francisco's Golden Gate Park in January 1967, and the "Summer of Love," attracting thousands more to Haight-Ashbury a few months later, put the country on notice that the counterculture was a national phenomenon.

Paul Goodman, author of *Growing Up Absurd* (1960) and an apostle of utopian anarchism, contributed to the participatory democracy and early humanism of the New Left. He preached spontaneity in art, love, and politics—values adopted both by campus radicals and SNCC organizers in the South. Utopian communities—whether farm cooperatives or urban communes like the "Diggers"

in California who supplied the hippies with free food and clothing
—became a significant life-style that lasted into the 1970s.

This life-style above all else united the hippies and the Left. Its
most obvious badges—blue jeans, flowing hair, beads—were as common to Berkeley's SDS as Haight-Ashbury's subculture. The hippies
also supplied a reservoir of manpower for political picket lines. Antiwar demonstrations always had their ration of holy men and mystical chants. At the Pentagon demonstration in October 1967, a number of witches, warlocks, saints, sorcerers, and shamans circled the
military's headquarters determined to "levitate" it from its foundations and win the "mystic revolution," as the *East Village Other*
called it.

Yet the hippies never made consistent political allies. Their fundamental premise was antipolitics. They wanted to change perceptions,
not political reality. Their otherworldliness divided them sharply
from the street fighters of the New Left, who had come to see power
as indivisible from violence.

Only the Youth International Party (Yippies)* of Abbie Hoffman
and Jerry Rubin, which wanted to destroy the system by showing its
absurdity, really linked the two movements. The Yippies were
psychedelic clowns, pinioning their political targets in the media
through a national theater of the absurd. On May 20, 1967, the
Yippies arrived unnoticed at the visitors gallery of the New York
Stock Exchange and began throwing handfuls of five-dollar bills to
the trading floor. Brokers scrambled with unashamed ferocity to
retrieve them, turning the floor into bedlam and stopping the ticker
tape. After being ousted, the Yippies danced in front of the Exchange
and burned a five-dollar bill while onlookers groaned in horror.
Hoffman explained on television that it was a celebration to mark the
"end of money" and to publicize the Yippies' thesis that "Property
is Theft."

The Yippies staged a different version of their act before the House
Committee on Un-American Activities. Rubin appeared in the marble hearing room dressed as a soldier of the American Revolution
and tried to distribute copies of the Declaration of Independence.
Another time, he carried a toy rifle and wore a Mexican bandolier
of bullets, cow-bells on his wrist, and brief Vietcong pajamas, claiming that the chairman of HUAC "couldn't take his eyes off my
painted tits." When Hoffman appeared in a commercially manufac-

*Its name, probably coined by *Realist* editor Paul Krassner, was not adopted officially until
1968.

tured shirt with red and white stripes on a field of blue, the Capitol police arrested him for mutilating the flag.

The Yippies aimed at total dissolution of authority—in effect, rampant anarchy. Hurling their irony at every form of repression, they tried to recruit an increasing circle of revolutionary actors in revulsion against the "Pig Nation." They concentrated on a cultural revolution, the toppling of old structures. They sought to involve people in experience, not to persuade them. Rejecting the nuclear family as well as all institutions of control, they saw themselves as a threat to the consumer economy. Rubin slyly claimed himself a Marxist—"We follow in the revolutionary tradition of Groucho, Chico, Harpo and Karl." Because the press wanted comic relief to balance the grimness of the New Left, it cooperated in making the Yippies into successful vaudeville.[16]

The problem of racism in the New Left came out into the open at the National Conference for New Politics at Chicago on August 31, 1967. It had been called to bring some unity to the multiplying offshoots of radicalism, possibly a third party in 1968. In particular, it wanted renewed dialogue between the black and white Left. But its beginnings were hardly auspicious. Neither SNCC or CORE were represented officially, although SNCC would dominate the Black Caucus, and Julian Bond was one of two chairpersons. Of about 3,600 registered delegates, representing considerable elements of the Old Left as well as New, only about 400 delegates were black. Only 9 of a 25-person steering committee, and only 6 of the 24-person executive board, were black. The conference's sponsorship, in fact, was more liberal than radical, and Dr. King was picked as the keynote speaker. Except for a few older members like Tom Hayden, SDS ignored the conference.

In the richly carpeted grand ballroom of the rococo Palmer House, James Forman of SNCC quickly set the challenging tone of the Black Caucus. Escorted to the platform by a flying wedge of bodyguards who swept all whites from the speaking area, Forman announced, "We're going to liberate you whether you want to be liberated or not." The Black Caucus then put forth a 13-point program which it said must be accepted without change. The most startling point was the demand for half the votes at the convention, although blacks made up a little more than 10 percent of the delegates. No less controversial, however, was Point 5, which condemned the "imperialist Zionist war," the six-day war between Israel and the Arab states in June. Forman had already attacked Israel in the SNCC *Newsletter* as an "extension of United States foreign policy," and this added attack would virtually cut off SNCC's remaining contributions from the white community. The Reverend Hosea Williams, one of Martin Luther King's principal aides, flew in to lobby the Black Caucus and softened the anti-Zionist resolution slightly.

But the demand for half the votes at the convention stirred an agonizing debate in which guilt and self-contempt paralyzed the white delegations. Speaker after speaker deplored the insignificance of the New Left and confessed its dependence on the black radicals. One Michigan delegate, not untypical of the rest, called whites "just a little tail on the end of a very powerful black panther" and agreed to accept any terms "to be on that tail—if they'll let me." Todd Gitlin of SDS admitted, "They forced down whitey's throat the plain truth that the movement's momentum is mainly black. . . ."

The black radicals, to be sure, had suffered most of the deaths and daily punishment for eight years, and unquestionably made up the core of the movement. Yet, their insistence on degrading their allies —the points were approved by a three to one majority—raised a serious question of tactics. The maneuver gave no practical gains to the blacks. In fact, the New Politics Conference disbanded soon after. There was no permanent structure to control, if that had been the Black Caucus's aim. There was not even a decision for a national third party in 1968. The delegates left the whole issue of electoral politics up to each local group. In the end, the Black Caucus produced only bitterness and the impression that mania for power dominated all its relations.[17]

As if to make up for its orgy of guilt at Chicago, the New Left planned an assault on the Pentagon on October 21, 1967, as the violent finale of Stop the Draft Week. In previous days, street fighters had attacked induction centers in Oakland and other cities. Carl Davidson of SDS insisted, "We must tear them down, burn them down if necessary." Admittedly, such admonitions were softened quickly to placate liberals and peace groups in the "Mobe" (the National Mobilization Committee to End the War, an umbrella group of antiwar forces). There was no equivocation about the New Left's intentions. This was planned and purposeful guerrilla warfare to harass the government's military headquarters and slow down the Vietnam war.

The preliminary ceremonies started peacefully. A group of 400 professors, clergy, and representatives of the arts gathered at the Department of Justice on October 20 to give almost 1,000 draft cards (or copies of burned cards) to the attorney general, who refused them through an aide.

Black radicals turned out in considerable force in Washington. John Wilson, head of SNCC's anti-Vietnam committee, called it the "only existing institution in the country where black and white people can work together."

Rap Brown, and Lincoln Lynch of CORE, spoke at the press conference announcing the event. At the Lincoln Memorial before the Pentagon assault, Ella Collins, Malcolm X's sister, addressed a crowd of at least 125,000. Many blacks dropped out at this point, one explaining, "We do not want to be slaughtered playing Indian outside the White Man's fort." But Norman Mailer was impressed by the way black contingents "moved through the New Left with a physical indifference to the bodies about them, as if ten blacks could handle any hundred of these flaccid whites. . . ."

Allen Woode, stationed in a security unit at the Pentagon, later wrote in *Ramparts* magazine that the government feared black radicals would incite a riot among the city's blacks and destroy Washington. To forestall this possibility, 2,500 troops slept in the Pentagon all week, backed up in the surrounding area by 2,500 National Guardsmen and 1,500 metropolitan police, with 25,000 other troops ready to be flown in from other camps.[18]

But as soon as the march left Lincoln Memorial on October 21 and headed for the Pentagon, the crowd of 125,000 shrunk to 75,000, and the street fighters took over. The hard core consisted of SDS and New York's "Revolutionary Contingent," many of whom wore fencing jackets and motorcycle helmets. Leaving the main march, they cut through the woods between the Potomac River and the Pentagon, feinted toward troops at the north and left of the Pentagon, reached the north parking lot, and rushed across the mall. One unit of perhaps 2,500 to 6,000 broke through a line of soldiers and surged up the left ramp of the Pentagon to a lightly guarded smaller entrance. Another unit of similar size reached the central plaza and entrance stairs. A handful, possibly 25, managed to get past the military police and raced into the Pentagon corridors, where they were quickly corralled and arrested by federal marshals. The rest formed a sort of beachhead, holding their positions for 32 hours.

Mike Goldfield of the University of Chicago SDS claimed: "Possibly, if there had been any leadership or organization of the attack, most of us would have made it into the Pentagon." But this was pure fantasy. Greg Calvert of SDS gave a more accurate appraisal: "A thousand people would have been killed if they attempted to storm those lines unarmed."

As it was, the brutality of the Pentagon defenders, particularly the marshals, far exceeded expectations. After midnight, paratroopers from the Eighty-second Division replaced the MPs and drove a wedge through the protesters, smashing heads and faces with their gun butts. Marshals with billy clubs reached through the troops, dragging away those sitting on the ground, often women, beating many of them unconscious. David Dellinger, a Mobe organizer, estimated that 1,400 were beaten and gassed, 7,000 arrested.[19]

If the Pentagon assault failed to disrupt the nation's military head-quarters, it proved that the New Left had adopted a new level of violence to stop the war. There was an increasing tempo to the disruptions in Boston, Indiana, Ohio, and across the country that fall. When Secretary of State Dean Rusk came to speak in New York on November 14, a crowd of 5,000 to 10,000 turned mid-Manhattan into a shambles. Mark Rudd and Ted Gold of Columbia SDS, who would gain further notoriety shortly, were among those arrested for "incitement to riot." For a few days in early December, the New Left concentrated on closing the Army induction center at Whitehall Street. Dr. Benjamin Spock, who had resigned as cochairman of SANE to join more militant groups, got himself arrested by trying to crawl through police barricades. But despite clashes with the police and 581 arrests, the induction center remained functioning.

A group of Catholics, mainly priests and former priests centered around the Berrigan brothers, tried another approach. On October 27, 1967, Father Philip Berrigan and three others entered Selective Service headquarters in Baltimore and poured blood over the files to make them illegible. In May 1968, Father Daniel Berrigan, Philip, and seven other Catholic priests and laymen destroyed 378 draft files at Catonsville, Maryland. Majorie Melville, a former Catholic nun married to Thomas Melville, a former Catholic priest, announced that she "had to accept jail as testimony of my opposition to my country's military intervention in Latin America and Southeast Asia." Both had worked for years with the Guatemala Indians.

Hundreds of draft files were destroyed in Boston in June 1968; perhaps 10,000 files were burned in Milwaukee; 75,000 files were destroyed in the Bronx, and thousands more in Queens. Father Nick Riddell rented a room in a Chicago building housing 34 Selective

Service boards, broke into the draft office through a window early Sunday morning, and burned 20,000 files.

The Berrigans and others, arrested and tried, based their defense on the charter of the International Military Tribunal, which convicted the Nazi war criminals at Nuremburg. The charter had laid down a principle of "individual responsibility" for participating in "inhuman acts committed against any civilian population." Orders from higher authority could not relieve one of this responsibility, the charter ruled. Now the Berrigans proclaimed the same principle. American troops were bombing and napalming women and children in Vietnam; the Berrigans insisted they were opposing the higher authority that ordered such atrocities. The courts, however, allowed no parallel between Germany and Vietnam. The Berrigans and others went to jail.[20]

As violence increased, it was inevitable that federal and local governments would intensify their repression. In July and August 1967, 10 members of SDS's national staff in Chicago—a "police state," as they called it—were arrested on flimsy charges. The FBI increased the number of agents and informers inside the New Left. William R. Divele, who spent four years as an FBI informer, later turned against his former employers and confessed to naming 4,000 radicals. In July, President Johnson ordered the army's intelligence units to extend its spying to political groups. At least 10 university administrations, including Berkeley and Duke, admitted to channeling records of left-wing students to the FBI. This was undoubtedly a small sample of the informing done by campus officials.

Many city and state governments built up huge arsenals against potential riots—Newark spent $300,000 on armored cars and bulletproof helmets. The army added 10,000 riot troops to the 15,000 already on duty. There was so little sympathy for ghetto wretchedness in the summer of 1967 that the House of Representatives voted down an antirat bill by 207 to 176, with one southern member taunting it as a "civil rats" bill. "I see a ghetto perhaps cordoned off into a concentration camp," Dr. King predicted shortly before his assassination in 1968. "We may be witnessing the beginning of a totalitarian state not only for black people but for all Americans," Julian Bond, now seated as a Georgia state senator, warned.[21]

The expulsion of Congressman Adam Clayton Powell, possibly the most powerful black in America, from the chairmanship of the

Education and Labor Committee, and eventually from his House seat, appeared to many as repression in a different guise. Admittedly, Powell flaunted the courts by dodging a New York libel suit against him. By putting his estranged wife on his payroll and traveling openly with his women friends, particularly on lavish weekends at Bimini, he jarred the sensibilities of House members, who often indulged in similar practices but generally kept them out of the press. Still, the punishment vented on Powell seemed excessive to the point of racism. He was, after all, an Olympian figure for the black world. Although the courts restored his seat, his power had gone with the chairmanship. "So when they stripped him of his power," Eldridge Cleaver observed, "they were castrating a black man who was in a position to help us."

In the long run, much of the repression fell on the Black Panthers in Oakland. They represented the main ghetto challenge to police authority. Their policy of countering force with force went to the core of police brutality, long the dominant grievance among black communities. At first, the Oakland police tried to cripple the Panthers with raids and petty arrests. But as the Panthers gained increasing confidence among blacks and established new chapters in other cities, the police concluded they had to be crushed. The obvious target was Huey Newton himself. The technique—since the Panthers knew their law—was to provoke a shootout, and the first of many around the country occurred in Oakland on October 28, 1967.

Driving home from a party around 4 A.M. with another Panther, Newton was stopped by a police car and asked for his license and registration. He produced them, explaining his car belonged to a woman friend. Officer Herbert Heanes started to write a ticket for reasons never explained in court. Newton protested, showing the appropriate paragraphs in his law book. In his version, the officer pushed him, forcing him to his knees. "As I started to rise," Newton recalled, "I saw the officer draw his service revolver, point it at me, and fire." Newton remembered "a rapid volley, but I have no idea where they came from."

The bullets, whoever fired them, killed another officer, John Frey, from a second patrol car, and wounded Heanes. Newton himself had four bullet holes in his abdomen, one in his thigh.

The next thing Newton remembered was being at Kaiser Hospital, five miles from the shooting, his hands and feet handcuffed to a gurney that stretched his stomach wounds so that the pain was unbearable. He was then transferred to East Oakland County Hospital, where, Newton claimed, his feet were shackled to the bed, and the police tortured him, shaking the bed every time he tried to sleep and holding a shotgun at his head.

The jury indicted Newton for the murder of Frey, assault on Heanes, and kidnapping of Dell Ross, a black bystander allegedly forced by Newton to drive him to the hospital. At the trial, the prosecution claimed that Newton had pulled a pistol from his jacket pocket or shirt and killed Frey, then grabbed Frey's gun and continued shooting. Yet Heanes had testified before the grand jury he had never seen a weapon in Newton's hand. Charles Garry, the San Francisco lawyer representing Newton, stressed that this alleged pistol of Newton's had never been found or put in evidence. In fact, Heanes's gun was the only one found at the scene, but the two cartridge cases lying in the street had not come from it. Garry also brought out ballistic proof that the bullets in Frey's and Heanes's guns were lead, not the copper-jacketed type used by the revolver Newton supposedly owned and fired. The prosecution had to avoid the implication that the two officers had shot each other or that an unknown person did the shooting.

Newton was held in jail nine months between indictment and trial, an inordinately long time. Meanwhile, the "Free Huey" campaign became the focus of the black movement, stirring so much anger that the New York Panthers alone recruited 800 new members in a month. The Panthers wanted alliances with the New Left and had started making them long before the shootout, although Newton admitted he was "vehemently attacked by black students for this position. . . ."[22]

Other militant black groups often made similar alliances. In the Milwaukee ghetto, the "Commandos" (predominantly black and one of a growing number of independent groups unaffiliated with SNCC, the Panthers, or other national organizations), were led by a 36-year-old white Catholic priest, Father James E. Groppi. They concentrated on passing an open-housing law. After it was rejected by the city's common council by 18 to 1, Groppi and the Commandos marched 2,000 blacks into white areas night after night, sparking frequent skirmishes. The mayor banned night marches, but the Commandos continued them, battling with the police as well. "The black man has a right to use violence if other techniques don't work," Groppi insisted.

By mid-1967, the line between radicals and moderates in the black movement became further blurred as Martin Luther King moved leftward. His stand against Vietnam approached the stridency of SNCC and the New Left on April 4, when he labeled the United States "the greatest purveyor of violence in the world" and demanded "somehow this madness must cease." He recognized the economic basis of ghetto unrest in his Poor People's Campaign and supported economic planning that seemed only a few degrees removed from socialism. King, in fact, was making a belated but determined attempt to mold the civil rights and antiwar movements, and black radicalism, into a common front.

The Black Power Conference in Newark on July 20, 1967, was the first cohesive gathering of 1,000 delegates, representing 45 mainly radical black organizations. Bayard Rustin, Roy Wilkins, and other moderates boycotted the conference, but King's SCLC, significantly, sent the Reverend Jesse Jackson. The conference focused on the "black nation" problem, calling for a "national dialogue on the desirability of partitioning the United States into two separate and independent nations, one to be a homeland for whites and the other to be a homeland for black Americans." At the same time, SNCC and the Panthers demanded United Nations membership for black Americans in recognition of their nationhood status. The radicals increasingly classified themselves as part of a revolutionary and anti-imperialist Third World coalition, a link that James Forman of SNCC stressed as a speaker at the UN seminar on colonialism in Zambia that July.[23]

Liberals saw the chance to diffuse the nationalist fervor through electoral politics. When a black candidate, Carl Stokes, showed reasonable strength in the mayor's race in Cleveland, Cyrus Eaton, a liberal industrialist, and other businessmen put sizable financing behind his campaign. The Ford Foundation, recognizing the reformist instincts in CORE, gave Cleveland CORE $175,000, which indirectly enabled it to pour added manpower into the Stokes campaign. Stokes was elected, the first black mayor of an important city. Others soon followed, like Kenneth Gibson in Newark. While this trend brought economic gains, particularly in housing, it bore little resemblance to the black power bases that radicals had once envisioned for Lowndes and the South.

A more significant phenomenon took place in the November 1967 elections in Mississippi. Although most of the SNCC staff had pulled out of the South, a few continued working with Fannie Lou Hamer and the Mississippi Freedom Democratic party. They had long played down the "nationhood" approach. Like the Panthers, they wanted white alliances. They made them inside the Democratic party. They also collaborated with the NAACP, which was far more militant under Aaron Henry than the national organization. The MFDP was still radical but recognized the value of coalition politics.

As a result, 22 blacks were elected in Mississippi for the first time since the Reconstruction era—16 on the Democratic line, 6 as independents. Not many of these offices carried real influence, perhaps just those of state representative and four county supervisors. But it was the start of a new momentum. No one could measure at this point whether armed confrontation in Cambridge, Maryland, or the Freedom Democratic party brand of electoral politics would bring more benefits to the black community. Perhaps both were essential. But the Mississippi approach was obviously more in line with American reality.[24]

· 17 ·

The Violent Year
1968

It was a year when revolution seemed more than a distant vision, when student uprisings in France paralyzed that country for weeks, stirring the hopes of the American Left. It was a year when riots swept the ghettos after the assasination of Martin Luther King, and fires burned only a few blocks from the White House. It was a year of violence on the campus—not just the seizure of Columbia University, but the threat of "Two, Three, Many Columbias," as SDS exhorted.

The Panthers had expanded their roots in the ghettos with new chapters in Chicago, Denver, Los Angeles, New York, and other cities. Their program—"seizure by the people of their own communities"—offered a bridge between the orthodox Marxist analysis of class oppression and black nationalism. Huey Newton shrewdly followed Malcolm X by extending class oppression to include all exploited peoples, white and black. "We don't hate white people; we hate the oppressor," he insisted.

The pressure on SNCC would destroy one of its last campus bases at South Carolina State College at Orangeburg. Cleveland Sellers's "Black Awareness" committee was still trying to integrate the only bowling alley in town four years after the Civil Rights Act of 1964. When students insisted on their right to bowl, the police chief closed the alley on February 5, 1968. Fifteen were arrested the next day as they rushed the door. On February 7, students took to the streets, hurling rocks at passing autos, causing Governor Robert E. McNair to call up the National Guard. The events of the next night came to be known as the "Orangeburg massacre."

The students had built a bonfire on a street bordering the campus. A line of at least 100 guardsmen, and 200 state troopers and police, advanced toward the dwindling fire. The students faced them quietly, but one suddenly stepped forward and threw something in the fire.

242

There was no warning by bullhorn, no tear gas to disperse the crowd, simply the crackle of bullets. Three students lay dead, and twenty-eight, including Sellers, were injured.

The police would claim that students fired first, but Pat Watters, a white reporter from Atlanta, could find no evidence of student weapons. Jack Nelson of the Los Angeles *Times* wrote that at least 16 of the 28 wounded students and at least one of the dead were "struck from the rear." Sellers charged, "Some were shot while lying on the ground or attempting to run away." The Department of Justice would eventually bring nine state troopers to trial for violation of civil rights, but all were acquitted.[1]

SNCC and the Panthers had already started merger negotiations that offered considerable advantages to both sides. SNCC would have gained ready-made bases in the ghettos and a reservoir of badly needed shock troops. The Panthers would have profited from SNCC's tested organizers, its more sophisticated grasp of Marxism, and above all, the national reputations and media-celebrity of Rap Brown and Carmichael.

Newton announced the appointments of Carmichael as Panther prime minister and of James Forman as minister of foreign affairs at an Oakland birthday party rally in his honor on February 17, 1968, attended by 5,000 adherents. But from that point on, nothing worked right. Carmichael, just back from a world trip on which he had irritated SNCC by criticizing some African liberation movements, was already in a power struggle with Forman and Brown and seemed to be using the Panthers to regain his control. At the rally, he upset everyone by attacking the Panther links to the New Left and by claiming that socialism and communism were irrelevant to black people. Years later, he admitted his error, insisting, "I was always for socialism. I really meant the white Left was trying to mislead the movement."

Eldridge Cleaver called it a "merger" between the two organizations. Forman argued for the term "alliance." The debate became even more strained at a SNCC meeting where the "10 Points" of the Panthers were called more reformist than revolutionary. Cleaver, in turn, characterized SNCC as "composed virtually of black hippies . . . of black middle-class students who have dropped out of the black middle-class. . . ."

Both organizations agreed to a New York meeting of the leaderships in August. One Panther, never identified, put a pistol in Forman's mouth and squeezed the trigger three times. It didn't go off and was probably unloaded. But Forman, already close to paranoia, according to Sellers, resigned his Panther position, and the whole merger or alliance collapsed.[2]

The increasing repression of SNCC and the Panthers reflected the White House's waning interest in economic and social solutions for the ghettos. The National Advisory Commission on Civil Disorders (known as the Kerner Commission after its chairman, former Governor Otto Kerner of Illinois) came out with some soundly reasoned answers on March 2, 1968. But President Johnson ignored the study he had himself ordered.

When ghetto blacks followed normal channels of protest, they got little sympathy. This was the case in Memphis, Tennessee, where 2,300 garbage collectors, badly underpaid and almost all black, had been on strike for two months. In late March 1968, Martin Luther King came to Memphis to support the strike. It was a decision based on his growing stress on the economic causes of racism, a concentration that had started with his Chicago campaign. It was also a decision that would end his life and unleash a storm of rioting throughout the ghettos.

King had already led the garbage workers in a number of demonstrations by April 4. That afternoon, he was leaning on the balcony railing of his second-floor room at the Lorraine Motel, talking to associates in the court below. In a roominghouse across the street, a sniper took aim with his scope-sighted rifle and fired one shot that penetrated King's neck, exploded against his jaw, and cut his spinal column. King died an hour or so later without ever regaining consciousness.

The assassination of the world's foremost apostle of nonviolence in this decade, and the youngest person ever to win the Nobel Peace Prize, seemed the final repudiation of King's dream of effecting social change peacefully. He had clung to nonviolence even when it meant a split with SNCC, CORE, and other radicals. He had blamed the Vietnam war for making America the most violent nation on earth; now he was the victim of violence. Despite their differences in recent years, even the most radical segments of the black movement recognized his genius. No one had equaled him in galvanizing the black community. No one had better fused the ghetto laborer and black bourgeoisie in a common front. Nikki Giovanni, the black poet, charged: "The assassination of Martin Luther King is an act of war. . . ."

There were no political overtones, and seemingly no organized leaders, when riots swept 168 ghettos and communities after King's death. Sheer rage set off the worst outburst of arson and looting in the nation's history, resulting in 46 deaths and 21,000 injuries. Almost 24,000 federal troops and 35,000 National Guardsmen had to be called to suppress the uprisings.

In Washington, 711 fires were recorded, and the White House feared attacks on government buildings. Several politicians blamed the riot on Carmichael, who supposedly had urged blacks to "get your gun." No evidence supported this accusation. In fact, Carmichael, Sellers, and other SNCC members in the city urged businessmen to close their stores and get people off the streets. But by 11 P.M., nothing could calm the gathering throngs. Carmichael, an obvious police target, went into hiding. "The uprising was completely spontaneous," Courtland Cox insisted. "You would see someone walking along the street, and suddenly pick up a brick and hurl it through a window. A minute later, a complete stranger would join him. The community just reacted with absolute solidarity."

The Panthers in Oakland and other cities were out on the streets, urging their communities to "cool it" and return home. The radicals had no desire to add more blood to the Memphis assassination. As it turned out, all but 5 of the 46 deaths from demonstrations were black.

A final note of horror would be added to King's assassination by a congressional investigation in 1976. This report confirmed earlier revelations that J. Edgar Hoover and the FBI had conducted a five-year "war" to "destroy" King, a war with "no holds barred." The FBI had tapped King's phones as early as 1963 and had offered the tapes to Washington journalists. Hotel-room "bugs" with possibly compromising conversations had been sent anonymously to Coretta King, accompanied by notes that seemed intended to drive her husband to suicide. Just a few months before the assassination, the FBI had sent its field bureaus a warning that King was a potential "messiah" who could "unify and electrify" the black nationalist movement, and ordered a campaign of obstruction against the upcoming Poor People's March. While no evidence ever linked a government agency to James Earl Ray, eventually convicted for the King murder, the counsel for the House Committee on Assassinations noted that documents "relevant to our investigations" had been destroyed.[3]

The King revelations were followed by others that confirmed a longstanding plot by the FBI and other agencies against the American Left. Much of it was illegal. The FBI's "Cointelpro" operation brought 2,370 actions against the New Left, the Communist party, the Socialist Workers party, and other radicals from 1965 to 1972. It burglarized the New York City offices of the Socialist Workers 92 times between 1960 and 1966—burglaries the New York *Times* called "raids against the Constitution." By feeding defamatory material to employers, it forced radicals out of their jobs. Professor Morris Starkey of Arizona State University, for example, was fired by the board of regents, although he denied Socialist Workers' membership. By turning over names of radical groups and individuals to Internal Revenue, the FBI had more than 10,000 singled out for special tax examinations.

Violating its charter, which forbids domestic surveillance, the CIA ran an illegal campaign, particularly against the antiwar movement, and kept files on 10,000 Americans. Army intelligence units kept files on 100,000 others through illegal wiretaps and mail openings. After his election in 1968, President Richard Nixon approved special concentration on the New Left, according to Richard Helms, a former CIA director. Helms later admitted that the CIA spied on the highly respectable National Student Association even after the CIA stopped its secret payments to that organization.[4]

The Panthers, as always, were a prime target for repression. The police broke into a Panther meeting at Saint Augustine's church on April 3, 1968, although they had no legal warrant. Just before, they had raided a Panther's home in San Francisco without search warrant. The King assassination occurred on April 4. Two days later—the dates seem more than coincidental—three Panther cars were returning from a fund-raising meeting when they parked on Oakland's Union Street, and two police cars drew up near them.

Eldridge Cleaver later claimed he had stopped to urinate, while the other cars waited. An officer ordered Cleaver to the middle of the street. Before he could arrange his clothes, Cleaver said, the police started shooting.

Cleaver and Bobby Hutton, the 17-year-old Panther treasurer, managed to reach a nearby basement. The other Panthers took refuge elsewhere. At least 1,000 rounds, as well as tear gas, were fired by the police into the basement. Hutton fired back with his shotgun. Cleaver, following the terms of his parole, claimed he carried no gun. He was eventually shot in the leg and hit in the shoulder, possibly by a tear-gas canister. When the basement timbers caught fire, Cleaver shouted that they were surrendering and threw out Hutton's shotgun and pistol. Determined to show he had no hidden weapon, Cleaver emerged from the basement naked.

Both were already blinded by tear gas when they stepped into the police floodlights. Cleaver said both had their hands raised. The police later claimed Hutton started to run. He may have been disoriented by the gas, his body possibly bent over in a sprinting position, but Cleaver also insisted the police ordered Hutton to get moving. He had just taken a few steps when they killed him with five bullets. Since there were from 50 to 100 officers in the area, it seems unlikely that Hutton tried to escape. The police version later said that the Panthers had planned to ambush the police when they originally parked their cars. But after the King riots two days before, it seems equally unlikely that the Panthers would have sought a shootout. Don Schanche, a *Saturday Evening Post* editor who investigated the Panthers for months, concluded that the shootout was "provoked by the police, not the Panthers."

Charged with three counts of attempted murder, Cleaver was jailed until a superior court judge released him on $50,000 bail. Since the state insisted he carried a gun at the shootout, he faced the added threat of reimprisonment for parole violation. Meanwhile, Huey Newton went to trial in July for the killing of Patrolman Frey the year before. The jury—with only one black—returned what could be called a "political" verdict. It judged him not guilty of assault on Patrolman Heanes but guilty of voluntary manslaughter in Frey's case. This meant Newton had fired without premeditation and under provocation. One can infer that since the evidence was weak relating to what gun killed Frey, and whether Newton even had a gun, the jury felt pressured to apply some punishment, even if minimal. Thus, Newton received a sentence of two to fifteen years in jail.[5]*

A few hours after the verdict, a police car drove past Panther headquarters in Oakland and riddled it with bullets. The headquarters turned out to be unoccupied. The two officers in the car, found to be drunk, were arrested and suspended. After three Panthers were killed by police in a Los Angeles gas station shootout in August, it seemed obvious that the Panthers were marked for extinction.

Newton's policy of white alliances thus assumed special importance. Its principal vehicle was the Peace and Freedom party, founded in March by a coalition that included the Panthers, black nationalists, the New Left, and many elements of the Old Left that

*In 1970, the district court of appeals ordered a new trial, which ended in 1971 with a hung jury. The state then dropped the case.

had participated in Henry Wallace's 1948 campaign. Its platform was as broad as possible, attempting to draw not just radicals but a sizable slice of the Democratic party Left. It called for an immediate Vietnam pullout, community control of police, schools, and other public agencies, and even touched on ecological issues and abortion rights.

Paul Jacobs, a San Francisco writer with a considerable following among the Old Left, agreed to run for the United States Senate. Tom Hayden appeared at rallies, once waving a carbine in one hand over his head. Much of the campaign money came from the Hollywood movie colony, another sentimental throwback to the 1948 campaign.

Peace and Freedom got off to an impressive start by collecting 105,000 signatures to place its candidates on the ballot. But the Panthers so emphasized their "Free Huey" campaign that many whites grumbled that the party was simply a Panther front. One critic felt the party was "a street gang going political, a gang dressed up in ideology." Another white associate complained after his disillusionment a few years later that even the most idealistic Panther program was tainted—the free breakfasts for children, he charged, were financed by pressure on local liquor dealers.

These points may have had some validity, given the shaky Panther leadership. With Newton in jail, Cleaver was virtually in control. He also became the Peace and Freedom candidate for President. Despite Newton's prohibitions, some associates said Cleaver took drugs. "He was stoned out of his mind half the time—his speeches terribly erratic," one recalled. He concentrated attention on himself rather than the party and its platform.

"Cleaver was a bad candidate," Dorothy Healey, a Communist official at the time, concluded. "The campaign was just a stage to play out his aspirations."[6]

The failure of American policy in Vietnam, and the growing strength of the antiwar movement, now pushed the Johnson administration to one of its most farcical steps. On January 5, 1968, the Department of Justice indicted Dr. Benjamin Spock and four co-conspirators for a conspiracy to violate the Selective Service Act. Since the Pentagon demonstration, the fusion between radicals and peace groups, generally known as "the Resistance," threatened the President with a common front of serious proportions. The purpose of the indictments, therefore, was not only to stop the Berrigans and others from interfering with the draft process, but to split the radicals from a much larger coalition of "respectable" people who opposed the war on religious and moral grounds.

Spock was the ideal target. Reared in the Protestant-Republican ethic of an old New England family, he had attended Andover and Yale, trained in pediatrics and psychiatry, and served as a naval officer in World War II. His book, *The Common Sense Book of Baby and Child Care,* had become the Bible of millions of American families. Translated into 30 languages, it was, in fact, the best-selling book of all time next to the Bible. Spock's quarrel with SANE made him particularly distasteful to the government. By helping to draft "A Call to Resist Illegitimate Authority," Spock was pushing other intellectuals toward resistance. He had attacked the core of Johnson's policy—"There is no shred of legality or constitutionality to this war," he exclaimed.

The other four were equally respectable: William Sloane Coffin, Jr., the chaplain of Yale and an early participant in the southern civil rights movement; Marcus Raskin of the Institute of Policy Studies in Washington; Mitchell Goodman, a New York writer; and Michael Ferber, a Harvard graduate student. By going into federal court against them, the government obviously intended to make them national examples and to warn others to mute their opposition to the war.

The prosecution focused on one issue: violation of the Selective Service Act. The defendants were not accused of a specific crime but rather of a conspiracy to commit one—for example, Coffin and Ferber had officiated at a service at Boston's Arlington Street Church on October 16, 1967, where draft cards were burned. Conspiracy was a vague and thorny legal charge—a favorite of the government's since the Rosenbergs had been sentenced to death under it in 1951. It meant that each member of the conspiracy was liable for the statements and deeds of the others, although most had not even met each other. Three defendants, significantly, did not even know about the Arlington Street service until after it happened.

At the trial in Boston that May and June, Federal Judge Francis J. W. Ford immediately ruled out any defense based on the Nuremburg principle of personal moral responsibility for opposing crimes against humanity, or any reference to the aggressive or illegal nature of the war. The defendants were not allowed to testify about their interpretation of their moral duties or legal rights under the First Amendment, and the judge's charge to the jury assumed that the defendants knew they were violating the Selective Service Act.

Thus the outcome of the trial never seemed in doubt. Perhaps the only surprise was a not-guilty verdict for Raskin. The four guilty defendants each received two-year jail sentences, and Spock and Coffin were fined $5,000 each. But the government secured few benefits from its temporary victory. The indictments and the trial itself roused considerable cynicism far beyond antiwar circles. To increase the government's embarrassment, the convictions of Ferber and Spock were overturned by the United States Court of Appeals in July 1969, and the Justice Department dropped its case against the others.[7]

The Spock trial was accompanied by increasingly violent resistance against the war—221 demonstrations were recorded by mid-June. Violence had passed the point of street clashes with the police. The extremist wing of the New Left was already organizing in communes, dedicated to the seizure and destruction of buildings. Ten incidents of bombing and burning, including ROTC facilities at Stanford and Berkeley, were reported that spring.

"Ten Days of Resistance" began on April 16, 1968, climaxed on April 26 by a strike on at least 50 campuses with 1 million students walking out of classes, the largest student strike so far. At Berkeley, it became the "Battle of Telegraph Avenue," starting as a gesture of solidarity with the recent student uprisings in Paris, and ending in a series of street fights with the police and banners claiming "Telegraph Is Ours!"

When the Chicago Peace Council and the Mobe organized a March against War on April 27, drawing 6,500 people, Mayor Daley's police charged and clubbed the demonstrators. A citizens' commission under Edward J. Sperling, president emeritus of Roosevelt College, described it as "wholesale police brutality". Daley wanted to prove he could keep Chicago pacified for the Democratic convention that summer.

The "resistance position" had become well accepted in SDS, which could count on the support of at least 135,000 students, a study by the Educational Testing Service of Princeton, New Jersey, reported. But more than 700,000 could be mobilized around key issues, particularly the war.[8]

While the tempo of violence at home increased in proportion to American commitment in Vietnam, now 549,000 troops, the New Left's effectiveness was suddenly stalled by a split in the Democratic party. In late January, the Tet offensive indicated that the United

States could never clinch a military victory. North Vietnam and Vietcong forces assaulted strongpoints in 100 South Vietnamese cities and towns and in 25 days controlled large areas of the countryside, including the Mekong Delta. American combat deaths reached 23,000.

This blow to the administration's credibility, and growing public awareness of the futility of the war, created sharp opposition in the Democratic party to the President's leadership. By December 1967, U.S. Senator Eugene McCarthy of Minnesota had decided to challenge the President on Vietnam in the 1968 primaries. He had been particularly angered by Attorney General Katzenbach's insistence that the Tonkin Gulf resolution gave the administration unlimited authority for the Vietnamese war.

Drawing his forces from the antiwar movement of New England campuses, McCarthy waged a determined campaign in the New Hampshire primary. On election day, March 12, he took 42.4 percent of the vote to Johnson's 49.5 percent. Had Republicans crossovers been counted, he would almost have defeated the President.

The results shook the White House. The President knew he had failed in Vietnam. The ghetto riots, the strength of the antiwar forces, increasing violence in the streets, the dismal showing in New Hampshire, and even more dismal prospects in the upcoming Wisconsin primary indicated to Johnson that he had lost control of the country. Ahead lay an agonizing chain of further primaries. Johnson had ruled too long at the top to undertake grueling months of campaigning at towns and whistle-stops to win back the Democratic party. He told Doris Kearns the following year: "I felt I was being chased on all sides by a giant stampede coming at me from all directions. I was being forced over the edge by rioting blacks, demonstrating students, marching welfare mothers, squawking professors, and hysterical reporters."

On the evening of March 31 (many radicals dating it as April Fool's Eve), the President announced that he would diminish the bombing of North Vietnam, that he would open negotiations with the National Liberation Front, and that he would not run for a second term. On Boston Common and in many cities, antiwar demonstrators danced in the streets, mistakenly assuming that the President's renunciation heralded an end to the war.

There was considerable irony in the New Left's contribution to this momentous decision. It had been a strong factor—no one could gauge precisely how strong—in forcing the President out of office.

Yet the Left would be damaged by the drain of its campus forces to the McCarthy camp. Thousands of SDS members who wanted above all to stop the Vietnam war, considered McCarthy's nomination a more realistic means toward their objective than making guerrilla raids on induction centers or working for the Peace and Freedom party.

SDS struggled to stop this drain. Carl Oglesby, a former president, emphasized in his "Open Letter to McCarthy Supporters" that McCarthy's liberal record was badly marred, that he had voted for the Student Loyalty Oath bill in 1959, and even for the Tonkin Gulf resolution. "We think you are afraid of your own politics, and that you are employing the McCarthy campaign as a means of making your dissent look respectable and 'legitimate,' " Oglesby wrote.[9]

Yet the drain became worse when U.S. Senator Robert Kennedy of New York, who had vacillated for almost a year on opposing President Johnson, announced his candidacy on March 16. Kennedy not only inherited the mantle from his brother the late President but appealed particularly to fringe radicals of SDS, and to black radicals as well as moderates. He defeated McCarthy in the Indiana and Nebraska primaries; lost by a slim margin in Oregon; and defeated McCarthy again both in South Dakota and California. At his Ambassador Hotel headquarters in Los Angeles on June 4, Kennedy made a victory speech to his volunteers at midnight and then left by a back corridor where an assassin, identified as Sirhan Bishara Sirhan, a native of Jordan, fired eight shots from just four feet away. One bullet entered Kennedy's brain, and he died shortly afterward at the hospital.

It seemed incredible: Robert Kennedy slain only a few months after Martin Luther King, only five years after President Kennedy. Many in the New Left considered it proof that a violent system was close to collapse. Yet the consolidation of antiwar forces around McCarthy made things even more complicated for SDS. With its emphasis on Vietnam negotiations and working within the Democratic party, the McCarthy campaign forced massive protest back to the center of politics. It weakened the link between black radicals and antiwar forces. It demonstrated the basic problem of radicalizing the liberal-labor coalition: most liberals preferred the stability of the system when it offered even a modest alternative. Eldridge Cleaver, after all, was hardly an encouraging alternative to McCarthy.

The McCarthy campaign, in addition, complicated the upcoming demonstrations against Vietnam at the national Democratic convention. In March, before the President's renunciation, the Yippies had announced a "Festival of Life" in Chicago during August. Contrasting the convention and the festival, the Yippies announced, "Ours will affirm life and man; theirs d-e-a-t-h!" The National Mobilization Committee and the Resistance also announced they would bring huge crowds to Chicago. Lyndon Johnson, the superhawk, was the obvious target for the Yippies protest against Death. Now McCarthy blurred the image and diluted the anger.[10]

In its long search to find the right combination of theory and action, SDS had reached an impasse in the spring of 1968. It could claim some credit for the shift in public opinion against the Vietnam war. Even the New York *Times,* Chicago *Sun,* and *Wall Street Journal* asked for a negotiated settlement in March. With the seizure of Oakland streets around the Selective Service center, with the bombings and burnings of campus buildings, the New Left had moved to violence as a precursor of revolution. But random violence was meaningless. SDS boasted almost 300 chapters by late March, with much of the growth on such "Middle American" campuses as Louisiana State University and Parsons College, Iowa. But it still lacked a policy that linked immediate action to revolutionary strategy.

Inside SDS, this search revolved around Progressive Labor's ambitions. PL demanded a "base-building" approach. The extremists, or "action faction" as they were called at Columbia and elsewhere, pushed for "vanguard actions" or "exemplary actions" to release "the tremendous potential of the base," as Mark Rudd of Columbia SDS explained it. This base-building versus militant action debate had plagued Columbia SDS for months, and chapters across the country would be split by the same factionalism. Progressive Labor, Rudd insisted, had become "the real right wing in the movement."

Although PL placed four of its adherents on the 10-member New York regional executive committee at its February meeting, Rudd's action faction took control at Columbia. What it wanted now was a "revolution in microcosm"—a power seizure on one campus that could attain the status of revolutionary symbolism for the whole country.

SDS's primary issue was the revelation in 1967 that Columbia was one of the chief facilities for the Institute of Defense Analysis (IDA), a consortium of universities supplying the Pentagon with vital military research. Columbia had denied its role, then retracted the denial after the proof was published.

The Institute of Defense Analysis was a focus for student hatred of the Vietnam war and the university's relationship to "corporate liberalism." IDA was both an essential instrument of the military and an outgrowth of the partnership between business and the university. An estimated 46 percent of the university's budget in 1966 came from government contracts—about a fourth of this from the military. When SDS occupied President Grayson Kirk's offices in Low Library, it found incriminating documents tying the CIA and its covert groups to American universities. Columbia's board of trustees, including officers and directors of International Business Machines, Lockheed Aircraft, and General Dynamics (all large war contractors) reflected this partnership with the military-industrial complex.[11]

An SDS petition signed by 1,700 Columbia faculty and students demanded the university sever its ties with IDA. On March 27, 150 SDS members marched into President Kirk's office with the petition, intentionally violating the indoor-demonstration ban. As SDS undoubtedly hoped, a number of students were disciplined, bringing the issue to a head.

But SDS's real skill was in exploiting a second and more explosive issue—the building of a university gymnasium in nearby Morningside Park. The park abutted Harlem and was mainly used by blacks. If the gym issue could be linked to IDA, and SDS to the black radicals, SDS could enlarge its campus base to a ghetto base. There was nothing that Columbia, or city officials, feared more than a confrontation with Harlem.

The university had not only wheedled a virtually rent-free deal from the city to build its private gym on public property but had insulted blacks by planning a separate back-door entrance for them and restricting their time and use of facilities at the gym. Further, the gym was only the latest example of Columbia's expansion in the area. In the last 15 years or so, Columbia had gobbled up 150 neighborhood buildings, evicting residents, many of them blacks and Puerto Ricans, from their homes. Thus, university racism became a primary target. After the Students' Afro-American Society (SAS) on campus seized the Hamilton dormitory, Ray Brown of SAS laid down a blunt challenge to the white radicals: "It's about time you people stopped talking about revolution and started acting in a manner that is going to bring some meaningful changes."

The stage was set by an unimaginative Columbia administration on April 22 when it announced that Rudd and five other students who had carried the IDA petition to the president would be placed on disciplinary probation. Kirk should have seen the importance of negotiations on IDA. This authoritarian punishment inflamed the campus, and SDS was able to attract 1,000 students to a protest rally the next day.

Rudd now managed to fuse black and white anger. At the end of the rally, he called for a march on the Morningside gym site, where construction had just started. The demonstrators rushed to the wooden wall around the construction and tore down part of it. One student was arrested, but a black-white front had been forged.

Rudd immediately advanced to the next stage of institutional confrontation, the seizure of campus power. He urged his followers, many blacks among them, to invade Hamilton Hall and take Dean Henry Coleman as hostage for the student just arrested. They occupied Hamilton all night, and the next morning the New York *Times* reported the seizure on the front page. Harlem leaders came to Hamilton to confer with the SAS blacks, and rumors started that Harlem radicals intended to storm the campus. Rap Brown of SNCC made these rumors a little more immediate by flying in to address a black rally and exhorting his audience: "If they build the first story [of the gym], blow it up!"[12]

The seizure of Hamilton and other buildings shortly after might not have been invested with such revolutionary significance were it not for the simultaneous student uprising in Paris. The Paris revolt came closer to overthrowing the government than any similar violence in an industrialized nation. Columbia SDS was deeply influenced by the events in France, and SDS often attempted to model its strategy on "the most surprising revolution of our time: the birth of an ultraleft," as *L'Express* described the Paris events.

Like the "IDA six" disciplined at Columbia, six students were arrested at Nanterre University in the Paris suburbs on March 22 following a demonstration against the Vietnam war. Soon 10,000 students went out on strike, occupying many buildings, and Nanterre closed down. The Sorbonne in Paris followed shortly after. Like Columbia, the uprising was both anarchistic and romantic in tone. Hundreds of "action committees" would be formed at educational institutions throughout France. Daniel Cohn-Bendit, a 23-year-old graduate student in sociology, noted that "all decisions were taken in general assembly, and all reports by the general study commissions had to be referred back to it as well." "Danny the Red," as he was called, soon became the central figure for the press.

The posters that covered Paris and Columbia reflected romantic optimism. The Sorbonne had: "Tout est possible." Columbia announced: "Lenin won. Fidel won. We'll win." The Columbia students described their occupying units as "communes" after the 1870 French revolution and settled all decisions—even cooking and toilet arrangements—at general meetings with often nerve-shattering debate. Two students were married during the occupation of Columbia's Fayerweather Hall—Andrea and Richard Eagan, called "children of the new age" by the officiating college chaplain.

The French students covered the broadest possible political spectrum—anarchists, Trotskyists, Maoists, Castroites, and Communists who had split with the party. Columbia had a similar range, and black nationalists as well.[13]

But here the two uprising begin to diverge. SDS may have envisioned Columbia students pouring into the streets and joining rebels in Harlem. But the bloodshed of the King riots was only a few weeks in the past, and no one wanted to repeat them. Besides, SNCC and the Panthers had only miniscule influence over black workers compared with the Left unions in France.

The Communist-controlled Confédération Générale du Travail and other Left unions and parties proclaimed a general strike in France on May 13. A million people marched through Paris that day, and uncounted numbers protested in other cities. No trains ran, no telegrams were delivered.

The French students forced the Left unions into a temporary alliance unique in a western democracy. By May 27, from 8 to 10 million were on strike, and the French economy was paralyzed. Then De Gaulle staved off revolution by securing the loyalty of his army chiefs, probably with the promise of freedom for officers jailed during the Algerian war. He offered the workers improved profit-sharing and social security and a guaranteed minimum wage. The Communist party and CGT announced that these offers met their demands. The Communist party was only too glad to make peace; it feared the anarchism of the "March 22 movement" as much as the Gaullists. Without the workers the movement could not survive—the uprising verified the Marxist principle that no revolution was possible without the working class.[14]

At Columbia, the New Left could not even hold its tenuous alliance with black radical students, much less make inroads into the

Harlem working class. In fact, the day after Hamilton's seizure, the blacks announced that they wanted to occupy the hall alone. The SDS contingent thereupon left Hamilton and broke into the administration building, Low Library, taking over President Kirk's office with its $450,000 Rembrandt on the wall. At least three other buildings were occupied soon after.

SDS now seemed to have the strength to secure its demands—abandonment of the Morningside gym, severance of university ties to IDA, and amnesty for the IDA six and all arrested students. But Columbia refused to budge. David Truman, university vice-president, insisted that any leniency would mean "destroying every other university in the country." Columbia obviously saw itself as the surrogate defender of higher education against the radical hordes.

Despite attempts by the Ad Hoc Faculty Committee to bring both sides together, the university refused to negotiate what seemed like negotiable demands. On April 30, President Kirk decided on force. Signing a complaint that the students were trespassing on university property, he called on the New York City police to oust them. The police "bust" turned out to be far more vicious than anyone had anticipated. Although the blacks in Hamilton had agreed beforehand to be led away in handcuffs without resistance, the white radicals were dragged from buildings, many beaten savagely. Diana Trilling, hardly an apologist for the New Left, wrote: "The brutality of the police on the morning of April 30 outraged virtually everyone who saw or heard about it." About 700 were arrested and 148 injured, including 17 policemen.

The "bust" convinced the moderate majority of Columbia students, including the Columbia Student Council, to support the strike SDS called for May 1. Here was Rudd's "vanguard action"—a minority radicalizing a far broader base. The Student Coordinating Committee, representing some 4,000 students, shut down the university completely.

When Kirk continued to enforce disciplinary action against the strike leaders, SDS occupied Hamilton again on May 21, resulting in a second police "bust" with 200 arrested and 68 injured. Three days later, SDS led a demonstration at a Columbia-owned building nearby, where the university was ousting tenants to make way for new construction. But these tactics irked the moderates, who left the coalition.[15]

Still, SDS would gain its objectives. *Fortune* magazine commented: "You can't argue with success; and SDS has yet to lose a battle." The university would shortly abandon its gym in Morning-side Park and cut its ties to IDA. President Kirk took early retire-ment under pressure, and with charges dropped against the majority of students arrested, and the reorganization of student disciplinary procedures, the university seemed completely humiliated. The tem-porary alliance between blacks and whites would have one concrete effect on educational policy—a push for "open admissions" of black and minority students that shook up institutions in New York and throughout the country.

Columbia made SDS a national byword and inspired more campus revolts than ever before. At least 40 strikes and riots took place in the next month or so—many on such sedate campuses as Marquette, Delaware State, and the University of Denver.

Columbia undoubtedly moved SDS further toward violence. Tom Hayden envisioned barricaded resistance on many campuses, prophesying that "students will threaten destruction of buildings as a last deterrent to police attacks." When SDS met in June for its national convention at Michigan State University, pictures of Lenin and Trotsky adorned the hall. A *Fortune* poll that fall would show that 5 percent of all students, or 368,000, strongly agreed to the need for "a mass revolutionary party" while 14 percent partially sup-ported it.[16]

When 25-year-old Bernardine Dohrn, a recent graduate of the University of Chicago Law School being considered for office at the SDS convention, was asked whether she was a socialist, her reply undoubtedly expressed the views of most delegates. "I consider my-self a revolutionary communist," she stated. Dohrn had worked with King in Chicago, with SDS's JOIN project, and eventually with the National Lawyers Guild, which handled most of the legal strategy for the New Left.

At the convention, Progressive Labor decided to try to gain con-trol of the national leadership. Although PL held only about a fourth of the delegates, they tied up the meetings with endless debates. Long lines waited at the microphones to speak. Everyone carried Marx or Mao's "Little Red Book" and quoted from them repeatedly. PL was denounced from the floor as "an external cadre." Tom Bell, a foun-der of the Cornell chapter, screamed, *"I'm* the communist here, not you guys from PL." In the midst of the uproar, he demanded: "PL OUT!" Many delegates picked up the chant.

In an attempt to exclude PL, the National Office for the first time put up a single slate for top officers: Mike Klonsky for National Secretary, Dohrn for Interorganizational Secretary, Les Coleman for

Educational Secretary. Klonsky, 25, was a Californian whose father had been a former Communist party official. But Klonsky called himself a communist with a small "c." The first two were elected, but Fred Gordon, two years out of Harvard and a former student of Herbert Marcuse, beat out Coleman by one vote. The elections represented the last triumph for the National Office in SDS.[17]

The New Left came to Chicago for the Democratic convention beginning on Monday, August 26, 1968. The plan, initiated by the Yippies as a Festival of Life, had been picked up by the National Mobilization Committee. David Dellinger, one of the coordinators of Mobe, was a 53-year-old, round-faced, cigar-smoking Phi Beta Kappa graduate of Yale, who had been a pacifist all his life. Although SDS scorned electoral politics, Tom Hayden and Rennie Davis, veterans of SDS, were also Mobe coordinators. As the Chicago demonstrations gained momentum, SDS's position changed. It wanted to recruit from swarms of campus volunteers coming to Chicago for Senator McCarthy. Eventually, SDS sent about 500 organizers, working out of five Chicago "movement centers."

Long before the convention, Mayor Richard Daley of Chicago announced that he had given the police orders "to shoot to kill any arsonist or anyone with a Molotov cocktail in his hand . . . and to shoot to maim or cripple anyone looting any stores in our city." Brigadier General Richard T. Dunn of the Illinois National Guard also announced that his men would "shoot to kill" to stop any rioting. These officials were determined to scare away as many people as possible, and in this they were successful. While the Yippies had fantasized hundreds of thousands in the streets, the New Left produced no more than 30,000.

Still, Daley made Chicago an armed camp. In addition to 12,000 police and 12,000 guard and federal troops, the convention hall was ringed by a chain-link fence topped by three strands of barbed wire.

The New Left insisted it came to Chicago for lawful reasons. It came to demonstrate against the Vietnam war, to pressure the convention to adopt a peace plank, to use the First Amendment right to assemble and march in an effort to gain these ends. Attorney William Kunstler, would later argue at the "Chicago Eight" conspiracy trial that "the real conspiracy in this case is the conspiracy to curtail and prevent the demonstrations against the war in Vietnam and related issues."[18]

Certainly, President Johnson was desperate to keep the convention as unruffled and unified as possible, if not for himself, at least for his surrogate, Vice-President Humphrey. The President was making a last frantic effort to solve the Vietnam impasse through Russian pressure on North Vietnam in return for United States concessions, and a summit meeting with the Soviets. Such global wizardry, he hoped, might still win him the nomination by unanimous acclamation of the convention. But the Soviet invasion of Czechoslovakia on August 22, ousting Alexander Dubceck's government which had been tilting toward the West, dashed Johnson's hopes.

The New Left had made every effort since early 1968 to secure legal permits from Chicago authorities. The Mobe and the Yippies were bounced from office to office in a vain attempt to get these permits. When they finally met with David Stahl, the mayor's administrative officer, the city would not even propose alternative locations for a rally at the convention amphitheater. The demonstrators ended up with no permits for rallies or marches that should have been guaranteed by the First Amendment.

As a result, the New Left's attempts to rally and march were roughly handled by the police. It started with a death on the eve of the convention—Dean Johnson, a 17-year-old Indian youth from South Dakota, allegedly pulled a gun on the police, and was shot in the back from a few feet away.

The police ordered the demonstrators out of Lincoln Park near the Hilton Hotel and attacked in force on Sunday evening, August 25. As they pursued demonstrators through the narrow streets of Chicago's Old Town, the police clubbed and tear gassed them, as well as diners at nearby restaurants who happened to be caught in the onslaught. When a youth pulled down the American flag from the park flagpole and ran up his own bloodied shirt as a symbol of Chicago's blood-letting, the police charged into the crowd, shouting, "Kill, kill, kill." At the intersection of Clark and LaSalle streets, the police almost went berserk, breaking into bars and hurling patrons to the streets.

Late Wednesday afternoon, August 28, the balloting took place at the convention on the peace plank. The minority plank of Senator McCarthy called for an end to all bombings of North Vietnam and the withdrawal of United States and North Vietnamese forces from South Vietnam, among other points. Hardly the strongest of planks, it was still defeated by Humphrey's commitment to go on with the war by a vote of 1567 3/4 to 1,041 1/4.[19]

Denied a permit to express their opposition to the war plank, the Mobe decided it had to go ahead with a march from Grant Park to the convention hall. Five thousand marchers were met by a wall of police and National Guardsmen. By 7:30, the demonstrators had been boxed in near the Hilton Hotel, which housed Humphrey and McCarthy headquarters. The cops pinned demonstrators and even bystanders against the side of the hotel and beat them cruelly. Some cops pursued wounded into the lobby, still flailing at them.

McCarthy volunteers brought the wounded to his headquarters on the fifteenth floor of the Hilton. For the first time, McCarthy grasped the extent of the savagery. He had tried to keep young volunteers from coming to Chicago; now he hesitated to go down to the lobby. At 9:55 P.M., as Carl Stokes, black mayor of Cleveland, seconded Humphrey's nomination, the convention was erased from the screen to be replaced on television networks by films of the bloodbath around the Hilton.

The final police action took place at dawn on Friday, August 30. Although the convention had ended, volunteers remained at the McCarthy headquarters. Police and National Guardsmen, patrolling the streets below, claimed something had been thrown from that floor. Without writ or warrant, police and guardsmen charged into the hotel about 5 A.M. and raided the fifteenth floor with clubs swinging, forcing students from their rooms. This attack continued until the police were told calls had been made to the press and Senator McCarthy. When McCarthy faced the remaining police in the lobby, they admitted no one was in charge of the raid. McCarthy vented his anger at last—only when his headquarters were invaded and his volunteers beaten.

The Chicago police had often been provoked. The demonstrators resisted police orders and fought back at times. Still, none of their provocations was commensurate with the frenzy of the police. The National Commission on the Causes and Prevention of Violence recorded 1,400 witnesses to specific instances of police brutality. It defined Chicago as a "police riot," not a riot caused by demonstrators. The toll was 100 injured demonstrators in hospitals, 625 treated at "movement medical centers," and about 668 arrested.[20]

Most police excesses were carried on national television; official brutality was no longer a southern phenomenon directed at rebellious blacks. Chicago had made it clear that organized police violence ran deep in the land. Except for a few objectors like Senator Ribicoff, even the Democratic party tolerated it.

Like Atlantic City in 1964, Chicago revealed electoral politics at its ugliest. Intensifying the bitterness of the American Left, it created a mood for violence that would go far beyond the Columbia uprising.

The Cleveland ghetto had just seen a sample of premeditated violence. On the evening of July 23, 1968, a tow truck answered a call to remove an abandoned Cadillac on the East Side near Lakeview Road. When the truck's operator was fired upon, police cars rushed to the scene. Suddenly bursts of gunfire came from an apartment building nearby. The police fired back, and in the ensuring battle, 10 people were killed, including three police officers. Of the seven dead civilians, four were identified as members of black nationalist groups.

The ambush of the police had obviously been carefully planned, the snipers well equipped with rifles and carbines. Yet there had been no turmoil in Cleveland since the riots of 1966, when four blacks had been killed. In fact, during the recent campaign of Carl Stokes, the ghetto slogan had been "cool it for Carl." Mayor Stokes now announced the arrest of Fred Ahmed Evans, a black nationalist, and Harllel Jones, leader of the Afro-American Set.

Neither man, nor his group, had any links to SNCC, the Panthers, or other nationwide organizations. This corroborated the pattern of Detroit the year before. Local nationalists had emerged on their own with ample support from their communities. Only eight days before the shootout, both Evans and Jones had marched behind the mayor in a parade marking the anniversary of the Cleveland riots of 1966. Two of their followers in the parade carried rifles slung on their shoulders.[21]

Forty-one cases of campus bombing and arson were reported in the fall of 1968, mainly ROTC facilities at Berkeley, Washington University in Louis, and the University of Washington, where students circled the blaze singing, "This is number one, And the fun has just begun." Although no links to SDS were found in most cases, an SDS member was sentenced to five years in jail for the Washington University bombing. Extremists were taking over a number of SDS chapters—the "Jesse James Gang," for example, at the University of Michigan.

At San Francisco State College, the most sustained rebellion in the history of American higher education was led by George Murray, Panther minister of education and an instructor at the college. SDS, radical unions, and teachers' groups formed part of the coalition.

The basic issue was racism. Although San Francisco State was the city's main low-cost institution, blacks and other minorities made up less than 10 percent of its student body compared with a 70 percent ratio at the city's junior and senior high schools. The Black Student Union, therefore, demanded open admissions and a Black Studies department with control over its own hiring and curriculum policies.

After Murray called for a strike on November 6, 1968, he was suspended from the faculty. Two thousand students marched out of class that day. The president closed the campus and shortly resigned. Weeks of demonstrations and police clashes followed. The acting president, Samuel I. Hayakawa, whose inflexible stand mirrored the State Board of Regents, tried to reopen the campus on December 2, backed by 650 policemen. Allowing no student rally without his approval, he leaped on a student sound truck and yanked out its microphone wires. Professor Kay Boyle of the English department, a noted author, cried: "Eichmann Hayakawa!" The president screamed back: "Kay Boyle, you're fired!"

Throughout January 1969, Hayakawa and the police sought to reopen the campus, one pitched battled following another. Although the black radicals eventually won most of their demands, 731 students were arrested, and 80 students and 32 policemen injured.[22]

In the presidential campaign that fall, Nixon and Humphrey outdid each other in their pledges for "law and order." Nixon eked out a slim victory with 31,770,237 votes to Humphrey's 31,370,533. But George Wallace drew the hard-core conservatives with 9,906,141 on the American Independence party line.

Eldridge Cleaver was not only an undistinguished alternative to Humphrey but spent most of his time on the "Free Huey" campaign. The Peace and Freedom party, as a result, failed to take many radicals and liberals from the Democratic party. A good number did not vote at all. Others, frightened at the possibility of a Nixon victory, accepted Humphrey as a slightly better hope for Vietnam peace.

With 105,000 signatures in California on Peace and Freedom nominating petitions, party analysts expected at least 300,000 votes there. But although the Panthers and New Left campaigned vigorously in San Francisco and Los Angeles, Cleaver polled only 27,707 votes. The party made no effort elsewhere. Cleaver's total vote was only 36,563. In New York State, and a few other states, Dick Gregory polled 47,133 on the Peace and Freedom line.

Cleaver added a disturbing denouement to the campaign. Fearful that he might be returned to jail for parole violation on the state's claim that he carried a gun during the Hutton shootout, he jumped his $50,000 bail and fled the country. According to Kathleen Cleaver, the bail money was put up by Godfrey Cambridge, Paul Jacobs, Ed Keating of *Ramparts,* and two others. Jacobs stated that he lost $7,000 of his $10,000. Keating undoubtedly lost more.[23]

The SDS national convention met at Ann Arbor, Michigan, on December 26, 1968, to resolve the most wracking crisis in its history. Its growth had been phenomenal: it now claimed 350, possibly 400 chapters. New applications came in so fast the National Office could not keep up with processing them. At Princeton that fall, for example, 106 out of a freshman class of 851 applied for SDS membership.

Yet SDS's internal convulsions were slowly crippling it. SDS had committed itself to Marxism but never had agreed on a theory and program.

Convinced that Progressive Labor, with its Maoist-oriented Marxism and its insistence on a worker-student alliance, would try to take over SDS, the National Office planned its own counteroffensive.

But the office represented little more than an assortment of factions, mainly held together by fear of PL. To give them coherence and unity, Mike Klonsky, the national secretary, and his associates, had developed a new position paper, known as "Towards a Revolutionary Youth Movement" (RYM). Klonsky's strategy was to beat PL at its own game, to outradicalize it, to build an ultraleft that would make PL seem timid and bureaucratic.

RYM's emphasis was on the black liberation movement as the vanguard of revolution. It insisted that blacks (and white youths as well) were a separate revolutionary entity. In contrast to PL's orthodox Marxism, which considered the working class the sole instrument of revolution, RYM encompassed a broad range of groups in the radical struggle. The Panthers and black radicals were the cutting edge. But students (junior colleges and trade schools along with the universities), working-class youth, campus unions and workers, street gangs, and every element of the outraged poor—all were considered allies of the black vanguard.[24]

The acceptance of blacks as a separate revolutionary entity, and a special position paper on women's rights, particularly galled PL. PL would not even go along with RYM's emphasis on the "oppression of women through male supremacy," since it considered women simply an oppressed part of the whole working class.

The debate raged for five days. Every argument had to be screamed in Marxist-Leninist jargon that substituted invective for analysis. The PL bloc would urge its speakers on with cries of "Mao, Mao, Mao Tse-tung." RYM supporters would retort: "Ho, Ho, Ho Chi Minh" (a presumed insult to PL, which opposed Ho's acceptance of aid from the "revisionist" Russians).[25]

The votes on the main resolutions clarified nothing. The RYM position paper was passed, as was the women's liberation resolution. At the same time, the convention approved PL's worker-student alliance. The only thing certain was that SDS had moved from a radical student organization to a tumultous and factionalized revolutionary movement. Once disdainful of Old Left clichés, SDS had fallen into all the pitfalls of the Old Left in its anxiety for doctrinal purity.[25]

It would seem logical to conclude that 1968 was the turning point of the movement. The Left had attained some degree of power. It could seize a campus like Columbia and control the streets of Berkeley and other areas for short periods. Its resistance to the Vietnam war had focused increasing public attention on the meaning of neoimperialism. But the Left was still not strong enough to build any lasting political framework without a coalition with the peace forces, and particularly the left-liberal wing of the Democratic party.

Now the Left, and SDS in particular, destroyed its last chance at coalition. By abandoning its campus base for armed struggle, the Left turned to a perverted Marxism-Leninism of despair and violence. It fell back on a crisis psychology. "I can't wait three years for revolution," one associate told Jeremy Brecher, an SDS officer in the Washington, D.C., area.[26]

Admittedly, a coalition with the peace forces and other mainstream groups would have pushed the Left toward reformism. This is the dilemma of American politics. Eventually, after furious outbursts of revolt, there comes a point where radicalism must blend with reformism if it is going to survive. The Panthers had already grasped this concept, demanding that the ultra-Left give up armed struggle for community organizing. Obviously unable to achieve a revolution in the streets, SDS could have built a lasting framework around its campus communities and the gradual development of semisocialist structures that the Panthers had pioneered. Instead, the ultra-Left chose violence and chaos over realistic aims, and the result was disastrous.

· 18 ·

The Limits of Radicalism
1969

The hesitant attempts by both black and white radicals to transform theory into long-range programs had reached a critical stage by 1969. SDS could not decide what kind of Marxist-Leninist organization it would become. It boasted that the Columbia uprising was a revolution in microcosm. But even if this formula were applied at many campuses, would it bring the country any closer to lasting radical change? The Black Panthers, too, claimed they were a Marxist-Leninist party. But were their free-breakfast programs for children a real step toward socialism?

The most specific achievement of the New Left was its obstruction of the war. Its demonstrations, and its increasing violence, had reached mammoth proportions. The National Student Association reported 221 major demonstrations at 101 colleges and universities in the first half of 1969. At least 1 million people marched against the war in November 1969. When President Nixon ordered American troops into Cambodia in May 1970, 4 million students took part in antiwar protests across the country. Many protests were violent —30 ROTC buildings burned that spring, even at presumably remote campuses like the University of Alabama.

Certainly public opinion against the war was shifting drastically. Only 31 percent of those polled in a Gallup survey in November 1969 considered themselves "hawks" on Vietnam, while 55 percent called themselves "doves." There had been 41 percent in both categories in April 1968. (The remainder in both years were undecided.)[1]

The New Left contributed something to this opinion shift. "The tragic, violent aftermath of violence and destruction on our campuses following the President's speech on Cambodia is a clear warning of the impact of New Left terrorist philosophy and advocacy of street action," the FBI told a United States Senate Select Committee. "The threat to the Nation's ability to function in a

266

crisis situation has never been more clearly drawn."

By 1970, 20 to 35 percent of all students thought violence justified, according to a Daniel Yankelovich survey. Gallup found as many as 44 percent took this stand.[2]

In the long run, however, the question was whether violence had any constructive function in developing radical programs. The New Left was still experimenting in "models" fitted to the American experience. One of the most innovative was the "People's Park" at Berkeley, California. The *Black Panther* newspaper called it "socialism in practice." This may have been an exaggeration, but like Columbia, the park had revolutionary implications.

It had been a vacant lot owned by the university, intended for a soccer field that never materialized. A coalition of radical and community groups (85 percent of 15,000 students polled backed the project) decided to convert this wasteland into "a little island of peace and hope in a world made filthy and hopeless by war and injustice," as Denise Levertov, the poet, described it. On April 20, 1969, they seized the land and began to roll out sod, plant flowers and trees, and build playgrounds. Thousands of people worked on the park for three weeks.

One community pamphlet called it an "emerging showdown between the Industrial-University machine and our Revolutionary Culture." *New Left Notes* theorized: "The question of OWNERSHIP AND CONTROL OF PROPERTY is the basis of the current struggle."[3]

When the university put up an eight-foot fence on May 15 and began to demolish the park, 3,000 supporters tried to retake it. They were met by 600 police and sheriff's deputies, using shotguns and tear gas. Standing in a group on the roof of a three-story building, probably as a mere observer, James Rector had his stomach ripped by buckshot and died four days later. Deputies swept the rooftops with gun fire, blinding Paul Blanchard, an artist, in one eye.

Governor Reagan called up almost 3,000 National Guardsmen the next day, and clashes continued for weeks, with about 100 wounded and 500 arrested. Thirty thousand supporters of the park marched on Memorial Day, including the Black Panthers, who made the march a symbol of coalition with the white Left. The main avenues were closed by barbed wire; machine guns were posted on the roofs. Berkeley had become a battle zone.

But was this so-called island of socialism a step toward radical change? What value was a symbolic struggle at this stage? The state obviously had to stand behind the principle of private property and help the university reclaim its land. By the end of the year, in fact, the university not only reclaimed the land but converted it to a parking lot.

One might speculate that if enough radicals had been willing to take up arms and risk bloodshed, they might have tied up enough troops to wear down the state's resistance. It was hardly worth the risks. And it would have required similar radical seizures at the same time on many campuses—in effect, provoking a revolutionary situation.

The New Left never came near this point. People's Park, therefore, simply radicalized the community further. This process—getting people to experiment with the techniques of socialism—was probably the limit of the Left's potential at the time. Yet its impact cannot be underestimated. A Yankelovich survey in 1969 showed that at least a third of all full-time college students supported SDS's brand of radicalism.[4]

The Black Panthers always had more defined radical objectives than the New Left. It was a highly structured party, its policy determined by a central committee. By 1969, it claimed 38 or 40 chapters in cities from San Diego and Denver to Chicago, Indianapolis, Boston, and New York. Its membership was small, probably less than 5,000, but intentionally restricted to fit its "vanguard" purpose. Its influence in the ghettos, however, was so strong that the Panthers could turn out an overflow crowd of 10,000 in 1970 in a Philadelphia hall.

Huey Newton insisted that the Panthers were a Marxist-Leninist party, following the "dialectical method" and instituting "socialist programs." But the core of the Panthers' socialism was "community survival services." Starting with free breakfasts for children, these services had been expanded to liberation schools, free clothing stores, free health clinics, free legal aid and ambulance services, and even support of sickle-cell anemia research. In the breakfast program alone, the Panthers said that 50,00 to 60,000 children were fed each morning across the country.[5]

If all this seemed somewhat remote from orthodox Marxism, Newton declared that by "unifying the black vote in this country around the survival programs," the Panthers would constantly enlarge their base among the poor. The Panthers, in fact, had abandoned armed confrontation with the police for long-range community organizing. Newton concluded a few years later: "It was very wrong and almost criminal for some people in the Party to make the mistake to think that the Black Panthers could overthrow even the police force."

Panther policy went through another shift on the nationalist issue. After the Republic of New Africa—a separatist movement demanding black control of Alabama, Georgia, Mississippi, Louisiana, and South Carolina—was organized in 1968, Newton gave it his blessing. But a year later, he disclaimed nationalism. "The Black Panther party," he announced in January 1970, "has transformed this movement into a socialist movement and we have become, not nationalists, like the Black Power movement of the past, but internationalists."[6]

Panther strategy now bore an ironic resemblance to the Communist united fronts of the 1930s. The Panthers wanted coalition with every possible ally, white radicals as well as Third World revolutionaries. Appropriately enough, their basic approach, which brought over 3,000 delegates to Oakland on July 18, 1969, was called the Revolutionary Conference for a United Front against Fascism.

All factions of SDS were represented, in addition to the White Panthers from Michigan, the Young Patriots from Chicago (mainly southern whites), and most significantly, the Du Bois clubs and the Communist party itself. The Panthers credited the Communists with much of the work on the conference, which probably involved financial help too.

Considerable Panther funding, in fact, now came from whites, particularly in Hollywood and New York. Marlon Brando, the actor, and Sidney Lumet, the director, were two acknowledged contributors. One of the younger Rockefellers donated to the Panther schools. Leonard Bernstein, the conductor, gave a party at his Park Avenue penthouse to raise money for the Panthers on trial in New York.

The Panthers, moreover, increasingly emphasized coalition with whites against the Vietnam war—"one of the most important movements that's going on at this time," Newton called it. Fred Hampton, the Chicago Panther chairman, announced that the blistering criticism of *all* whites in the 10-Point program was being modified—"we used the word white where we should have used the word capitalist."

Hampton had been the prime mover in Chicago's "Rainbow Coalition" which radicalized the Blackstone Rangers, the Black Disciples, and other black street gangs. "We're all one Army," he told a press conference in May 1969. When an off-duty policeman shot a member of the Young Lords to death, black, brown, and white radicals marched together in an antipolice demonstration for the first time. The Lords and the Latin Kings, mainly of Puerto Rican descent, ran a children's breakfast program and health clinic modeled on the Panthers'. The Lords, with a sizable chapter in New York as well, demanded Puerto Rican independence, withdrawal of United States military bases from the island, and "a society where the people socialistically control their labor."[7]

Open admissions at colleges and universities became an important issue around which black and white radicals could organize together. The violence at San Francisco State in 1968 was duplicated to a lesser degree that year at Northwestern University in Chicago, where students barricaded themselves in the administration building. In April 1969, 150 black students at Cornell University at Ithaca, New York, seized Willard Straight Hall and had arms smuggled into the building. No shot was fired, but it marked the first occasion an armed contingent held out in an Ivy League building. After 6,000 students, mainly organized by SDS, staged a supportive sit-in at the gym, the university agreed to cooperate with the Afro-American Society in a plan to increase black students and faculty. The occupying force then marched out jauntily with their guns and bandoliers of bullets.

At the City College of New York, the Black and Puerto Rican Student Coalition closed down the campus and battled police who were trying to retake the buildings, until the Board of Higher Education agreed to establish open admissions by 1970. The New York plan virtually guaranteed admission to any city high school graduate who applied. But by 1976, New York's financial crisis forced a cutback in educational funds, and open admissions were also curtailed. Some thought the plan had failed. In 1978, the dean of the humanities division resigned after charging in an article that open admissions, along with other "affirmative action" programs and hiring policies, had toppled City College from its former eminence to "mediocrity."[8]

The issue went to the core of black demands: a key avenue through which three centuries of oppression could be reversed. Only by weighting educational opportunities in favor of minority groups long denied access to college and professional training could some parity be secured. Open admissions in itself was obviously insufficient without improved teaching at the grade and high school levels, and without intensive remedial services during the college years. The standards at City College and elsewhere would also suffer in this period of adjustment. But these were sacrifices that had to be made as they had in the past for the children of many groups. Hardly radical in theory, open admissions would remain one of the most imperative black demands as long as class lines kept ghetto children from the same educational openings as others.

By 1969, the Panthers desperately needed a network of allies, for it was obvious that the federal government, as well as local police forces, had determined to eradicate them. J. Edgar Hoover had already declared: "Without question, the Black Panther party represents the greatest threat to the internal security of the country." Nixon's Assistant Attorney General, Jerris Leonard, announced in May 1969, "The Panthers are a bunch of hoodlums. We've got to get them."

Shortly afterward, the FBI in cooperation with the Chicago police engineered the cold-blooded murder of Fred Hampton, the 21-year-old chairman, and 22-year-old Matt Clark. Secret FBI memoranda, made public in 1974 as a result of court action against Chicago officials, revealed that the FBI had planted an informer at Panthers headquarters, William O'Neal, who supplied the police with the headquarters floor plan and a list of arms stored there. O'Neal may even have drugged Hampton earlier that evening to diminish his chances of escape.[9]

On December 4, 1969, at about 4:45 A.M., 14 policemen under orders from Edward V. Hanrahan, state's attorney of Cook County, burst into the front and back entrances of Panther headquarters. The police objective was to seize allegedly illegal arms. According to Hanrahan's press release, the two lead officers announced their identity, but the occupants "attacked them with shotgun fire."

In fact, much of Hanrahan's evidence on Panther resistance was faked. His pictures of Panther bulletholes in the kitchen proved to be nail holes. A federal grand jury, convened after the FBI made its own investigation, revealed that from 82 to 99 shots had been fired into the apartment by the police. Only one shot could be identified ballistically as having been fired by the Panthers. Two bulletholes entered Hampton's head from the right and from above at a 45-degree angle, indicating he had been murdered in his sleep. The grand jury called the Police Department's Internal Inspection Division "so seriously deficient that it suggests purposeful malfeasance."[10]

This damning evidence resulted in the calling of a Cook County grand jury that subsequently indicted Hanrahan himself for "conspiracy to obstruct justice." But despite the appointment of a prestigious special prosecutor, Hanrahan was acquitted. The only satisfaction the Panthers would get was seeing Hanrahan defeated at the next election, mainly by defection of the black Democratic vote.

The extraordinary lengths to which the government would go to pin a conviction on the Panthers was demonstrated in New York by District Attorney Frank Hogan, one of the best-known law officials in the country. On April 2, 1969, Hogan announced at a press conference on all television networks that a jury had indicted 21 members of the New York Panthers. They were accused of attacking four police stations during the previous fall and winter and planning to bomb Macy's, Bloomingdale's, and other department stores, as well as the New Haven Railroad tracks and the Bronx Botanical Gardens, on April 3.

When bail was set at $100,000 each, an impossible sum for the Panthers, all defendants went to jail. For five months they were kept in seven different jails, making interviews by defense attorneys a cumbersome series of shuttlings.

Pretrial hearings started on February 2, 1970. The trial ended on May 13, 1971. It cost the state more than $2 million and became the lengthiest trial in New York history. The evidence, however, was flimsy.

Almost all of it rested on the testimony of police spies. Gene Roberts showed the court a road map on which one Panther allegedly marked the railroad targets to be bombed—but the map had no railroad lines on it. Carlos Ashwood, another police spy, admitted he had never heard the defendants agree to bomb department stores, subway stations, railroads, or police stations. The "hardest" evidence came from the forced entries into Panther homes without search warrants. Three pieces of pipe and a small amount of gunpowder in Robert Collier's bathroom turned out to be the total Panther assets for bombing five department stores the next day. A defense witness said the pipes were discarded pieces of plumbing Collier had collected to install a shower.[11]

One jury member, Edwin Kennebeck, later wrote in *Juror Number Four,* "We had heard no proof at all that they had done any of the things that the grand juries had accused them of."

Only three Panthers were actually caught at the scene of a potential crime—an automobile parked on Manhattan's East River Drive across the river from a police station. The district attorney said they intended to fire at this distant target, although the only rifle in the car lacked a telescope sight. "I began to realize that the only hard evidence of a shoot-out was police photographs of the red car, with bullet holes in the door—made by the cops' guns," Kennebeck concluded. "If I'm ever accused of shooting someone, I said to myself, I hope that the evidence against me is no more than bullets from *his* gun."

It took only 90 minutes for the jury to acquit all defendants not previously severed from the trial on all counts. The case had almost turned to farce; perhaps its most significant result was the party held a year later for the jury and defendants. "If I was going to indict anybody," said a black juryman, a retired longshoreman, "I would have indicted the D.A. and the judge for a conspiracy to break up the Panther party."[12]

The indictment of 11 more Panthers in Connecticut in August 1969 raised the question of whether the party was an authentic vanguard of black revolt, or nothing more than a street gang dressed up in Marxist rhetoric, as some critics claimed. The case went beyond previous police confrontations and oppression. One Panther had been murdered and other Panthers implicated in his death. Although defense counsel claimed that the leading suspect was not actually a Panther but a police informer, the claim, even if proved, could not diminish the evidence that the Connecticut chapter had been involved in torture and brutality.

The two most prominent defendants were chairman Bobby Seale and Ericka Huggins, the widow of John Huggins. (Huggins had been killed in the Panthers' clash with Karenga's competing US organization in Los Angeles.) Huggins's father was manager of Yale's exclusive Fence Club, where he had worked for 40 years; his mother was on the staff of Yale's Sterling library. A third defendant, Warren Kimbro, was an air force veteran with a successful dry cleaning business. His sister was married to Yale's director of community affairs; his brother was a Dade County, Florida, police sergeant. In contrast with the "lumpen proletariat" background of Panthers elsewhere, Huggins and Kimbro represented a new breed.

All were charged with the death of Alex Rackley, whose body was found at the edge of a Middlefield swamp on May 21, with bulletholes in head and chest, and extensive burns and bruises. Charles Garry, the Panthers' lawyer, insisted that the murder had been ordered by George Sams, who had a police record dating back to age

15 and had been institutionalized at 21 as a virtual psychotic. Sams also admitted being kicked out of the Panthers on two occasions, and supposedly told the police he had "every intention of destroying the [Black Panther] party." The Panthers called him a "pig agent." Huey Newton theorized the FBI had first used Sams and then dumped him.[13]

It reflected little credit on the Panther chain of command that, despite his shoddy past, Sams should arrive in New Haven from New York and convince the local chapter that Rackley was the police agent and should be tied up in Kimbro's house and tortured for three days in order to extract a confession. The Panthers in this period were obviously in a state of shock from mounting infiltration of their ranks. But this hardly detracts from the grisly evidence that Kimbro, who eventually became a state witness, took a .45-caliber pistol from Sams at the swamp and shot Rackley in the head. Sams then presumably put the gun in the hand of Lonnie McLucas, another indicted Panther, who fired a second shot into Rackley's chest.

The Connecticut state's attorney managed to get Seale indicted— 12 out of 20 on the grand jury were friends of the county sheriff— on the grounds that Seale, in New Haven for 12 hours before the shooting on a speaking engagement, had given the order for Rackley's death. The defense attorneys said that Seale knew nothing about the case and that Huggins was only tangential to it. James Ahern, then New Haven's police chief, wrote later there was "not sufficient evidence against Seale, and the New Haven police department never requested an indictment against him, nor did we expect that Markle (the state's attorney) would ask for one." Seale had just spent many months in jail during the Chicago conspiracy trial. Now he would be jailed without bail for two more years.[14]

Little bothered by the implications of Rackley's murder, radical students united behind the Panthers. On May 1, 1970, after President Nixon sent American troops into Cambodia, 15,000 students gathered on the New Haven green. Yale declared a general strike. The masters of Yale's residential colleges voted to open their eating and sleeping facilities to the demonstrators. The university president, Kingman Brewster, Jr., convinced his faculty to back the strike, declaring he was "appalled and ashamed that things should have come to such a pass that I am skeptical of the ability of black revolutionaries to achieve a fair trial anywhere in the United States."

The case finally went to the jury on May 19, 1971, and the verdict seemed to exonerate the Panther leadership. Seale was acquitted in less than two hours. After the jury remained deadlocked on Huggins for five days, defense counsel made a motion to dismiss the case. Judge Harold Mulvey agreed. "With the massive publicity attendant on the trial," Mulvey stated, "I find it impossible to believe that an unbiased jury could be selected without superhuman efforts, efforts which this court, the state, and the defendants should not be called upon to make or endure."

Sams received a life sentence but was released in little more than four years, which possibly supports the Panther's charge that he was a government agent. Kimbro served even less time, possibly his reward for cooperating with the state, then became a student at Harvard and eventually an assistant dean at a Connecticut college. McLucas won acquittal on all charges except conspiracy to commit murder and was sentenced to 12 to 15 years in jail. Although Seale and Huggins had been vindicated by the trial, the case demonstrated the disorganization of Panther chapters. It also demonstrated the government's determination to destroy the party quickly.

This intent was corroborated further on December 8, 1969, when the Los Angeles police raided Panther headquarters at 5 A.M. What was probably intended as a replica of the Chicago massacre failed, however, through the alertness of Panther guards. The Panthers fought back in a six-hour gun battle in which three policemen and three Panthers were wounded.

Charles Garry announced there was a "national scheme by various agencies of the government to destroy and commit genocide" upon the party, and offered 19 "documented" cases of "murder" in proof. Analyzing Garry's figures in a *New Yorker* magazine article, Edward J. Epstein could find only five Panthers killed by police in 1968, five in 1969; and at least one of these shootings occurred during an apparent robbery. Garry retorted that much of the documentation had been lost in FBI raids. Besides, Epstein glossed over such intended genocide as Los Angeles.[15]

Even this accounting ignored the deaths of other black militants that could never be attributed specifically to government agents. On March 10, 1970, Rap Brown, the former SNCC chairman, was due to appear in a Bel Air, Maryland, court on his old Cambridge indictment. Ralph Featherstone and William H. Payne, two veteran SNCC officials, were waiting in their car a mile from the courthouse, presumably to pick up Brown, when a bomb tore their car apart and killed them. James Forman claimed the bomb was "almost surely planted by some government agency" and intended for Brown; but the dynamite could have belonged to SNCC.

The New York and Connecticut cases also confirmed the damage done the Panthers by the dissident faction led by Eldridge Cleaver. Huey Newton, who had tried to run the party from jail through Bobby Seale, increasingly disapproved of Cleaver's policy of immediate guerrilla warfare in the ghettos.

The first open announcement of a schism in the party came with the listing of 38 members purged from the Oakland chapter in March 1969. Many were considered allied with the Cleaver "guerrilla" line. The *Black Panther* newspaper claimed only two chapters had been lost by a "simple defection." But the assassination of two New York members, one allied with Cleaver, the other with Newton, may well have been the result of this vendetta. Seale later admitted that a thousand members around the country had been expelled. The Cleaver purge, along with police repression, almost paralyzed the party for the next few years.[16]*

On April 5, 1969, the New Left turned out 150,000 antiwar marchers in Washington and other cities across the country. The White House ignored them. On April 9, 300 members of SDS marched into Harvard's University Hall, ousted the deans, and demanded that the university abolish ROTC and rescind its purchase of nearby working-class houses. Dr. Jack Stauder, an anthropology teacher soon to be fired, stated that "Harvard's expansion is only part of a general plan to convert Cambridge into a center for imperial research. . . ." President Nathan Pusey called in the state police to oust the students with considerable bloodshed and refused to give up on ROTC until a rally of almost 10,000 students and faculty persuaded him.

It was a frustrating process—constant demonstrations and campus takeovers that still failed to stop the war. These frustrations pushed the action factions in SDS and other Left cells toward increasing violence. The home of San Mateo Junior College's dean was wrecked by a bomb. At least 84 attempted and successful bombings and incidents of arson were recorded on campuses in the first six

---

*Cleaver would voluntarily return from France to the United States and jail in 1975 and announce his conversion to "born-again" Christianity. Half his $100,000 bail was supplied by an evangelical-Christian businessman. After making TV spots for Texas fundamentalists and signing a contract for a new book, Cleaver bought a house in Los Altos, California, where similar homes cost at least $100,000. Some radicals in 1976 called him the "Bicentennial's House Nigger."

months of 1969. Radicals bombed eight Manhattan buildings, including the Armed Forces Induction Center, Chase Manhattan Bank, General Motors, and other war-related corporations. They called it "bringing the war home."[17]

On November 12, 1969, the FBI arrested two members of a revolutionary cell for these New York bombings—22-year-old Jane Alpert, an honors graduate of Swarthmore College and an editor of the "underground" newspaper *Rat;* and Sam Melville, with whom she had been living. Melville and George Demmerle (who turned out to be an FBI informer) were caught in the act of placing their bombs in army trucks at Manhattan's Sixtieth Regiment armory. The FBI was still seeking Patricia Swinton.

Alpert, a shy, slight, bookish woman who had given up graduate studies in Greek at Columbia University after she joined Melville, later claimed her mission in the "bombing collective" was to control targets and possible injury to innocent bystanders. Although the collective carefully sent warnings beforehand, she became disturbed when a bank bombing at midnight injured a dozen clerks, none seriously, because a security guard ignored the warning phone call. "I believed we were acting morally; that if anyone was doing anything concrete to stop the war it was us," she said afterward.

Melville was convicted and confined at Attica State Prison. Alpert, out on bail, fled New York and went underground in May 1970. In October 1971, she heard on the radio of a prisoners' uprising at Attica. Melville, seemingly the only white among the leaders, was killed when state troopers and prison guards stormed the compound in what an investigating commission called the "bloodiest one-day encounter between Americans since the Civil War."

Melville's death at 37 among mainly black and Puerto Rican revolutionaries soon made him something of a legend among the white Left. One thesis, which remains unsubstantiated, is that prison guards considered him a special target—the "Mad Bomber," some papers called him—and virtually assassinated him.

Only two years after his death, Alpert announced her conversion to feminism, and her disenchantment with both Melville and the political Left, in a defiant article. Published by *Ms.* magazine in August 1973 and addressed to "Dear Sisters in the Weather Underground," her article insisted that the "politico-feminist split is a real one" and contained a detailed denunciation of the "sexual oppression of the Left." Alpert pleaded with her sisters in the Weather underground to cast off male domination; refuse to "allow men to rule on your politics. . . . Let your own self-interest be your highest priority."

Alpert turned herself over to the authorities in November 1974, immediately stirring charges on the Left that she had given information to the FBI about underground colleagues. Her defenders— Gloria Steinem of *Ms.* magazine and Karen DeCrow of NOW, among others—stated in a petition that she had "severed her slight contact with the underground. . . ." None of the Left's charges has ever been substantiated.

Alpert served 20 months in jail, and an additional 4 months for contempt of court for refusing to testify at Swinton's trial after the latter's arrest. Swinton, on the other hand, has never been convicted. Robin Morgan, a leader of the "antipolitico" feminists, insisted that Alpert "did time" for Swinton.[18]

Violence had come to have a metaphysical attraction for the New Left. It filled a vacuum caused by SDS's inability to solve its split with the Progressive Labor faction and to develop a coherent program of revolutionary politics. Progressive Labor rejected every new approach—even the Panthers' survival programs and the Women's Liberation movement. It clung dogmatically to the classic Marxist interpretation of the proletariat as the one vehicle of revolution.

The bitter split inside SDS made violent solutions more acceptable to the National Office and its Revolutionary Youth Movement allies. A resolution passed at the national council meeting at Austin, Texas, in late March 1969 committed SDS irrevocably to "the need for armed struggle as the only road to revolution."

This resolution was amplified by a 16,000-word paper called, "You Don't Need a Weatherman to Know Which Way the Wind Blows."* Written by a group of 11 New York and midwestern extremists, including Bill Ayers, Bernadine Dohrn, Jim Mellen, Terry Robbins, and Mark Rudd, it represented an ambitious reformulation of SDS policy. The Weather program made SDS part of a world-wide revolution, essentially an appendage of the black revolution. Weather called for "the destruction of U.S. imperialism and the achievement of a classless world: world communism." Specifically, it would turn SDS from a mass-based organization into a network of highly organized, independent cadres or communes. They would become the "red armies" of the revolution, an elite fighting force separated from most campus membership. Their role in "the heartland of a world-wide monster" was to harry the enemy from the rear

---

*The paper's title came from Bob Dylan's song, "Subterranean Homesick Blues."

with violence while ghetto blacks and African and Third World movements overseas carried out the revolution.[19]

The split between RYM and its Weather collectives and PL had already cut off SDS from liberals in the antiwar movement, and even from the Southern Student Organizing Committee, which failed to make the transistion from liberal populism to Marxism and was dropped in February. The stage was set for a final showdown at the annual convention on June 18 amid the bare cement walls and rusted pipes of Chicago's dank and ancient Coliseum.

PL controlled about a third of the 1,500 delegates, RYM anywhere from 700 to 1,000, depending on the issue. The bitterness between factions had already become so intense that convention marshals at the door frisked every delegate for guns as well as drugs. Much of the debate was carried on in pseudoscientific jumble of Marxist-Leninist rhetoric. Much of it was simply guerrilla theater: delegations standing on their chairs to wave their Little Red Books, chanting such slogans as "Dare to Struggle, Dare to Win."

Klonsky, the outgoing chairman, pleaded in his rasping voice for a coalition between RYM, the Black Panthers, and Women's Liberation. Klonsky's strategy was to throw the Panthers' prestige behind RYM. On June 19, the Panther spokesman started the assault— "Those PLs do more damage to the revolution than the pigs do." Representatives of the Young Lords and the Brown Berets continued the attacks on PL's "racism." Then in an incredibly inept discussion of Women's Liberation, a Panther spokesman extolled the party's support of "pussy power." The delegates sat stunned. Such phrases had supposedly disappeared from the radical vocabulary. The hall suddenly rang with cries of "Fight male chauvinism, FIGHT MALE CHAUVINISM."

The next night the Panthers tried to undo the damage, reading a statement approved by the Young Lords and Brown Berets as well as the Panthers: "If the Progressive Labor Party continues its egocentric policies and revisionist behavior, they will be considered as counter-revolutionary traitors and will be dealt with as such."

But this counterattack only aggravated the previous blunder. PL delegates screamed, "Smash red-baiting, smash red-baiting." Mark Rudd, his hulking shoulders set almost in a boxer's crouch, tried to recess the meeting to stall for time. But Dohrn marched to the rostrum. Some thought her commanding, elegant rather than beautiful; others considered her an opportunistic in-fighter. Now she demanded that every delegate who supported RYM principles follow her to a small arena off the main hall. PL shouted, "No split!" But everyone knew it was the beginning of the breakup.

The RYM caucus debated three hours that night and started again the next morning. Most of the Weather and RYM leadership (now called RYM II because it opposed Weather's call for guerrilla violence) gradually swung toward expulsion of PL. Around 11 P.M., the RYM caucus marched back into the main hall. Dohrn announced that PL was being ousted from SDS.[20]

The Weathermen (they would eventually change their name to Weather people after feminist criticism) now prepared to build "red armies" for guerrilla war through a network of collectives in Seattle, Chicago, Detroit, New York, and a dozen other cities. The collective was a bizarre training ground aiming not only at instruction in military techniques but at reshaping the whole personality of its members toward fanatic dedication.

There were endless lessons in karate, street fighting, and bomb-making. There was a constant round of group therapy sessions, relentless criticism that tore each member apart in order to strip away all remnants of bourgeois culture and leave nothing but instinctive obedience and revolutionary passion. Even sex became part of this process. The Weathermen considered the nuclear family an obstruction to communal organization. "Smash monogamy" became the rule. Everyone had to change bed partners each night, sleeping with the same sex in the process of rotation, so that all individual attachments were wiped out and only commitment to the group remained. Couples who insisted on keeping prior relationships were expelled (although enforcement remained haphazard in some collectives).

The collectives worked frenziedly to create machinelike revolutionaries in less than six months. They went for weeks on a few hours sleep a night. There was never enough food. The living quarters were filthy. "We were bombarded with unreality—it was crazy," Andrea Eagan recalled. "Everyone was terrified of everyone else," said Jonah Raskin. "I always had a feeling of claustrophobia in a Weatherman collective, always felt isolated, felt hate, felt as if we were doomed and suicidal."[21]

To prepare for the climactic guerrilla action in Chicago that fall, the Weathermen planned a series of summer attacks on high schools and colleges—"jailbreaks" they were called. All took place in working-class districts. The Weathermen theory was that these students would be impressed by violence, that a demonstration of Weather courage and bloodletting would inspire students to break out of their schoolroom "jails" and join the Weather revolution in the streets.

At a Detroit working-class beach, the Weathermen handed out leaflets in mid-July, announcing, "The war's on and everybody's got to take sides." The bathers responded by taking the wrong side and trying to beat up the Weathermen. At Macomb County Community College in a working-class Detroit suburb in late July, 10 Weather women invaded a classroom during a final examination, lectured the startled students on imperialism and racism, but failed to make their getaway before police arrived.

Women were pushed to the forefront of these "jailbreaks." Seventy-five women invaded South Hills High School in a working-class district of Pittsburgh on September 4, one group holding a rally at the entrance to recruit allies for the upcoming Chicago action. When the police arrived, the women fought back savagely, and it took eight squad cars of reinforcements to arrest 26. The others escaped.

Again on September 30, women attacked the University of Seattle's Air Force ROTC building, virtually demolishing the office.

By the time the Weathermen staged their stellar attraction in Chicago on October 8, 1969, known as the "Days of Rage," they had already lost the support of RYM II and the Panthers. Klonsky had criticized them at a Cleveland meeting in late August for "fighting the people" instead of serving them. RYM II groups like the Revolutionary League and Revolutionary Union, joined by the Lords and Patriots, held their own demonstrations in Chicago, the largest at the International Harvester plant. Most RYM II people had already pulled out of the Weather collectives.

A few hours before "Rage" began, Fred Hampton demanded that Mark Rudd abandon it. "The Weathermen should have spent their time organizing the white working and lumpen class instead of prematurely engaging in combat with the trigger-happy pigs," a Panther lieutenant insisted. When Rudd impugned the Panthers' revolutionary zeal, Hampton floored him with a blow.[22]

The Weathermen refused to abandon Chicago. Glorifying violence, cutting themselves off from their campus base, they were substituting themselves—in effect, a personal psychodrama—for a mass movement. There were also elements of arrogance, guilt, and the "spoiled brat" syndrome. A good many Weather leaders came from comfortable, if not wealthy, backgrounds. Rudd's father, a lieutenant colonel in the army reserve, was a successful real estate operator in New Jersey. Ted Gold's father was a New York doctor, his mother a college professor. Bill Ayers's father was president of the Commonwealth Edison Company—the Illinois Electric utility monopoly—and one of the most powerful civic leaders in Chicago. Bill had lived for the last few years with Diana Oughton, a member of an equally aristocratic family in Dwight, Illinois, where their Tudor mansion was surrounded by a swimming pool and deer park.

The Weathermen came to Chicago in their leather boots, jackets, and helmets, carrying gas masks and National Liberation Front banners. But instead of the army of 25,000 that the leadership (now called the Weather Bureau) had originally promised, there were only 600, perhaps only half of whom were Weathermen. On October 6, they dynamited the statue in Haymarket Square that memorialized seven policemen killed by a bomb in 1886. On October 8, they rushed through the streets toward the "Gold Coast" and Drake Hotel, the residence of Judge Julius Hoffman, then presiding over the conspiracy trial of the eight arrested during the convention riots in 1968. With rocks and bricks, they smashed apartment and hotel windows, at first eluding 2,000 waiting police, then charging the police head-on. At least six Weathermen were shot and 68 arrested. Twenty-eight police were injured.

The "women's militia" marched the next morning with only 70 women. They startled the police by charging their lines, fighting and screaming before they were pinned to the ground and hauled off to jail.

All that was left of the battered army, perhaps 200, marched through the crowded downtown streets on Saturday, suddenly broke from police lines, and smashed at store windows and parked cars with chains and pipes. They were subdued in less than half an hour. The four "Days of Rage" produced little more than 200 injured Weathermen and a similar number of arrests and cost $2.3 million worth of bailbonds, about a tenth in cash, which was mainly supplied by their families.

There was one last "war council" on December 27, 1969, at Flint, Michigan—400 delegates sitting under a huge cardboard cutout of a machine gun, the speeches and debates swinging wildly between cogency and hysteria. The principal decision was to break the collectives into smaller cells of perhaps four or five members. Early in January 1970, all records were removed from the Chicago headquarters, and the Weathermen—no more than 300 strong—went underground.[23]

Seemingly at the peak of its influence in 1968 and early 1969, SDS had disintegrated with astonishing speed. Yet the symptoms—the rage and futility—had long been present. The New Left had failed to grow up. It wanted too much too fast. Its failure to stop the Vietnam war—and the heightened repression after Nixon's election —created a mood of desperation, a crisis psychology that demanded instant results and instant revolution. The turn to violence and Weather's guerrilla army was one obvious result. Violence became a substitute for theory and organization. The turn to military models and prepackaged Marxist ideology followed naturally. It was easier to adopt the models of Lenin or Mao, easier to fall back on the rhetoric of other revolutions, than to develop a program that specifically fitted the American situation in 1969.

Once SDS had traded in the spontaneity and anarchistic experimentation of its early years for prepackaged ideology, it embarked on an endless quest for revolutionary purity. Decisions were made by waving the Little Red Book. Revolutionary purity demanded a constant raising of expectations that could only lead to self-destruction. Columbia SDS promised "two, three, many Columbias" in 1968, but it could not even hold a few buildings the following year.

SDS's early quest for self-liberation and fulfillment—its struggle against alienation and a bureaucratic system that petrified the human spirit—had been replaced by a cynical brand of Marxism-Leninism. At first SDS had grown by its appeal to needs that all students shared in common—a tradition adopted successfully by women's liberation. Now SDS identified with the Third World revolution; it had become a surrogate for others. The trend toward centralization and manipulation, starting with the National Office faction, had produced the dictatorship of the Weather bureau, with all orders flowing from the top. Ironically, the New Left, which started as a complete rejection of the Old Left, eventually assimilated its worst features.

At the same time, SDS failed to learn from the Old Left that any socialist movement must be part of a continuing historical process. This did not necessarily mean the development of a political party. But it did mean a structure and a stable leadership constantly replenished.

The Old Left offered noteworthy precedents that SDS ignored— the building of radical cells in every local of CIO Left unions, the development of a block-by-block structure by Vito Marcantonio's American Labor party. The Panthers, too, eventually came to the same conclusion, finding community organizing a more productive path to socialism than guerrilla confrontation.

Yet SDS foolishly abandoned the campus base from which it had sprung. This was the seat of its power, not the streets of Chicago. This is where it drew its continuity, where new leaders and organizers should have been recruited. By 1969, Columbia SDS had organizers on every floor of every dormitory, with movies and meetings twice a week. The same level of organization had been reached at Princeton, Cornell, and other universities. Instead of turning to revolution in the streets, SDS should have expanded this type of structure to hundreds of campuses, and produced a growing core of organizers through professional training schools.

Moreover, the growth of a permanent campus structure would have enabled SDS to build a chain of "radical territories" despite the fluctuations of student opinion on campus. A start had been made in such places as Berkeley and Madison, Wisconsin. They provided a need always lacking in SDS—interaction with veterans of the New Left and with radical faculty and remnants of the Old Left who could have added the experience and continuity that SDS sorely missed.

The New Left, unfortunately, could never solve the ambivalence of its academic relationship. It despised most university administrations as corporate "machines" and as handmaidens of the Pentagon in developing new weapons and research for Vietnam. Still, the university remained the best sanctuary available, the best route to self-fulfillment. The closing down of any campus, therefore, was a form of self-destruction.

There was guilt for many in the New Left in the draft protection offered by the academic world. Thousands of radicals went to jail for burning their draft cards or refusing induction. Thousands more evaded the draft in Canada and other havens (a decision generally condemned but also defended strongly as a principled protest against an illegal war). Still, a large proportion of the New Left was able to stay at home and practice its politics because of deferments.

By contrast, the children of the working class rarely had this educational protection. In 1966, in fact, only 2 percent of all draftees were college graduates.[24]

This fact may partly explain the guilt and frequent hostility that SDS held toward working people in its last period. It makes even more ludicrous the Weather invasions of working-class areas. Weather, in effect, was urging labor's children to give up everything their families had earned—the car, the semidetached house—for the Third World. The Weathermen, a self-appointed vanguard, intended to set the terms of revolution for a class it never understood.

Internal dissension and mangled strategy were not the only reasons for the collapse of the New Left, however. Official repression became an increasing factor under President Nixon. The FBI already had more than 2,000 full-time agents and thousands of paid informers assigned to the New Left when Nixon authorized 1,200 more agents in 1970. The FBI was just one of 20 agencies infiltrating the radical movements. As late as 1973, the Internal Revenue Service had a "special services" staff searching the returns of radicals like Julian Bond.[25]

In its frenzy to destroy the New Left, the FBI conducted "hundreds of warrantless, surreptitious entries," according to a report by a United States Senate Select Committee in 1976. When the Socialist Workers party sued for $40 million in damages in 1978, demanding the files of 1,300 informants the FBI used in 35 years of spying and illegal break-ins, a federal judge in New York produced a unique collision between executive and judicial branches by ordering U.S. Attorney General Griffin Bell to turn over the files.

Similarly, a federal jury in 1978 indicted L. Patrick Gray, III, former acting director of the FBI, for ordering break-ins without warrants, mainly directed against the Weather underground. It was the first time the head of the FBI had ever been charged with a criminal act.[26]

To stifle campus protest, Congress passed 10 federal acts by 1970, aimed at intimidating radicals by barring them from federal grants and other monies. Nixon appropriated $20 million in 1970 for special riot training for National Guard units called to the campuses.

The National Lawyers Guild, the subject of illegal wiretaps going back to 1946, was still being penetrated by the FBI in 1975. When the Senate Select Committee revealed that the CIA had opened more than 215,000 letters between 1953 and 1973, Corliss Lamont, chairman of the National Emergency Civil Liberties Committee, found that two letters to his wife were among them and successfully sued the government for $2,000 in damages. Perhaps the pinnacle of the FBI's frenzy came in 1971 when J. Edgar Hoover accused the Catholic priests Daniel and Philip Berrigan of an "incipient plot" to blow up the underground heating system of government buildings in Washington and kidnap Secretary of State Henry Kissinger. The plot turned out to be fantasy.[27]

Still, SDS could have survived government repression if it had taken the leadership of the antiwar movement, kept its base on the campus, and increased its ties to the liberal forces opposing Vietnam. In its quest for instant revolution, it abandoned the one issue through which it could reach a mass constituency.

The most convincing proof of SDS's failure came with the antiwar demonstrations of October 15 and November 15, 1969, called by the Moratorium and the New Mobilization Committee. With former supporters of Eugene McCarthy and Robert Kennedy in charge, the Moratorium drew hundreds of thousands across the country—100,-000 in the Boston area alone. The Mobe brought 250,000 demonstrators to Washington, according to police. Some reporters said 400,-000; the Mobe said 800,000. In any event, it was the largest demonstration Washington had ever seen.

The Mobe, a coalition of 84 organizations ranging from the American Friends Service Committee to the Communist and Socialist Workers parties, even had union officials from the Teamsters and Amalgamated Meatcutters and Butchers. A few Weathermen supposedly visited the Mobe office and suggested that their cadres would leave town in exchange for $25,000 that Weather needed for legal fees. They were turned down.

Nixon had ostentatiously moved 9,000 federal troops into the city, and Deputy Attorney General Richard Kleindienst announced, "We just can't wait to beat up those motherfucking kids." But the demonstration started peacefully enough. Forty thousand marchers passed the White House on their way to Arlington cemetery, each with a card naming an American who had died in Vietnam or a Vietnamese village destroyed by war.

Then about 5,000 Weathermen, and street fighters from other collectives like New York's "Mad Dogs," stormed the South Vietnamese embassy, trashing stores and banks along the way. The next night, carrying National Liberation Front flags and screaming, "Free Bobby Seale," they marched on the Justice Department. Attorney General Mitchell watched from his office window as the police clubbed and gassed them. Later he concluded the scene "looked like the Russian Revolution." The Mobe was a convincing argument—if any was still needed—that Weather had sealed its destruction by cutting itself off from the mainstream.[28]

The trial of the "Chicago Eight" on conspiracy charges, resulting from the Democratic convention demonstrations the year before, indicated again that the Nixon administration would go to any lengths to crush the New Left. The defendants, who included David Dellinger, Tom Hayden, and Abbie Hoffman, among others (with Bobby Seale of the Panthers tossed in for good measure), were indicted under a rider to the 1968 Civil Rights Act. They had, according to the charge, entered Illinois with *intent* to start a riot—not rioting, or even inciting to riot. The government admitted the eight had never met as a single group; Seale said he had never met the others previously.

Specifically, John Froines, an assistant chemistry professor at the University of Oregon, and Lee Weiner, who taught sociology at Northwestern University, were accused of a conspiracy to burn down a fireproof garage under Grant Park. Yet the incident never took place, and the prosecution never produced any bomb parts or materials that could have been used in it.

Ramsey Clark, the United States attorney general at the time of the convention, stated publicly that he saw no evidence for indictment, and that the statute itself was unconstitutional. He felt that the New Left groups involved had made a determined effort to secure permits for their marches, and he himself had called Mayor Daley and requested Soldier's Field as a site for rallies.

On the other hand, Clark found ample evidence to convict a number of policemen—one film, for example, showing police knocking a demonstrator off his bicycle with no provocation and then beating the youth severely. Yet no policeman was ever found guilty.

The trial started on September 25, 1969, before U.S. District Court Judge Julius Hoffman, a cranky, wrinkled, diminutive 74-year-old. He mispronounced names, substituting "Weinsten, Feinstein, and Weinrub" so frequently for Leonard Weinglass, a defense attorney, that it hardly seemed accidental. Abbie Hoffman whimsically insisted he was the judge's illegitimate son.

The inclusion of Seale among the defendants seemed ludicrous enough. He had been completely uninvolved with convention planning; substituted for another speaker only at the last moment; took part in no marches; and gave only two speeches. The best the prosecution could dig up against him was the usual Panther anti-police rhetoric—urging the audience to "barbecue some pork" and send the cops to the "morgue slab."[29]

Yet Judge Hoffman immediately made Seale the focus of prejudice and scorn. Seale's lawyer, Charles Garry, had been ordered to the hospital for an emergency gall bladder operation and begged the judge for a brief postponement. Hoffman not only refused but insisted that William Kunstler, another defense attorney, could represent Seale as well, although Seale submitted a motion specifically rejecting him. This was an obvious denial of the deeply grounded legal principle that a defendant may choose his own counsel.

Each time Seale's name came up in the trial, he demanded personal legal representation. The judge constantly silenced him. "And just be railroaded?" Seale asked. Eventually, Hoffman threatened punishment if he persisted. "What can you do to me that hasn't been done to black people for 300 years?" Seale retorted, finally labeling Hoffman "a racist and a fascist and a pig."

The judge retaliated on October 29 by ordering Seale chained hand and foot to a metal chair with a gag of muslin in his mouth. Seale still interrupted by banging his chains against the metal. Hoffman then ordered a wooden chair, and a larger gag taped over his mouth. On the third day of gagging, Seale choked as he tried to breathe. When Dellinger, Hoffman, and Jerry Rubin tried to protect Seale from the court marshals, who were elbowing him in the face and punching him in the groin, the judge gave them contempt sentences of one to four months in jail. Hayden got three months for saying, "Bobby should not be put in a position of slavery." Of 175 contempt sentences to be served after the trial, about one-third occurred in the three days Seale was gagged.[30]

The judge finally ordered a mistrial for Seale on November 5, severed him from the case, and sent him to jail on 16 separate contempt charges for four years. It was a handy way of eliminating a Panther leader without the necessity of a jury deciding his guilt.

Hoffman continually ruled out evidence crucial to the defense. He refused a statement by Hayden and Rennie Davis at a preliminary meeting in March 1968 that "the campaign should not plan violence and disruption against the Democratic convention." A black Chicago policeman, chairman of the Afro-American Patrolman's League, was not allowed to testify that at preconvention drills the police were taught to scream "Kill, kill, kill." The Reverend Ralph Abernathy, successor to Martin Luther King as head of SCLC, was not allowed to testify because he arrived in court 16 minutes late.

Perhaps the most damaging blow to the defense was that Hoffman barred the testimony of Ramsey Clark. "What I had said and done before the convention, and during it, was most relevant to the trial," Clark concluded. The New York *Times* called it "the ultimate outrage in a trial that has become the shame of American justice."[31]

Judge Hoffman displayed his hostility in many ways. He gave

Abbie Hoffman 14 days in jail for applauding at one point, another 15 days for laughing. Dellinger, a Christian socialist who had preached nonviolence most of his life, got six months in jail for contempt for once calling the judge "Mr. Hoffman" instead of "Your Honor."

Rarely in judicial history had contempt sentences been used so vengefully. The two lawyers, Kunstler and Weinglass, got four years and 13 days, and one year and eight months in jail respectively. Rennie Davis and Jerry Rubin both got two and a half years. The other defendants received lesser terms.

After nearly five months of testimony, the jury acquitted seven defendants on the conspiracy charge and acquitted Froines and Weiner on all counts. The five others were found guilty of intent to riot, which carried a five-year jail term and $10,000 fine.

The jury panel consisted mainly of suburban housewives and widows, inclined to conservative opinions. After the verdict, one juror told the Chicago *Sun-Times* that two jurors "expressed the view that the young people who demonstrated during the convention should have been shot down by the police." Still, the defendants almost came off with a hung jury. John Schultz in his book, *Motion Will Be Denied,* stated that after the trial a reporter was told that four women jurors believed, and still believed, that the seven were innocent on all counts.

One juror later boasted she had manipulated the "compromise" verdict that saved the government from a hung jury and probably dismissal of all charges. She was the fiancée of a Cook County official, part of Mayor Daley's machine—a fact she concealed until after the verdict.

The five convictions for intent to riot, however, were overturned by the U.S. Court of Appeals, Seventh Circuit, on November 21, 1972. The court cited Judge Hoffman's legal errors and found his "deprecatory and often antagonistic attitude towards the defense is evident in the record from the very beginning." After a new trial, all contempt and conspiracy charges against Seale were dropped and the original 175 contempt charges against the others reduced to a handful. Even these were still being challenged in 1978 when defense attorneys claimed that papers released under the Freedom of Information Act revealed improper collusion between Judge Hoffman and the prosecution to provoke incidents that led to contempt.[32]

The conspiracy trial was a flamboyant example of government repression. It served Nixon's purpose in many ways, exhausting New

Left leadership, legal counsel, and funds, as well as adding to the mood of futility infecting the radical movement. Still, by exploiting the hollowness of the case, and, in effect, putting the government on trial, the defendants and their attorneys made the public aware of official duplicity and manipulation that would emerge further in the Pentagon Papers and Watergate investigations. The government's attempt to use the courts for repression proved a disaster not only in Chicago but in New York, Oakland, Seattle, and other cases. Its credibility was becoming increasingly strained.

· 19 ·

The Women's Movement: Personal Becomes Political

Dara Abubakari, a black woman in the separatist movement, saw "only two kinds of oppressed people in this country, and that is black people and women." Thousands of other women, white and black, had come to the same conclusion by 1969. The mounting recognition of women's oppression had produced a new movement, generally given the generic name of Women's Liberation—a sprawling, volcanic movement completely independent of SDS and other organizations of the Left. In many ways, in fact, it arose in revulsion to the Left and the "macho" politics that had dominated the Left. Although its roots were in southern radicalism, particularly the "Mississippi Summer" of 1964, and it drew on SDS's early, free-wheeling quest for self-liberation and self-fulfillment, the women's movement built on the very strengths that the New Left had lost.

It was a movement that came from inner needs and inner pain, not stamped from the outside by Marxist or other ideologies. It was based on needs that all women shared. The central thesis of the movement was that no other problem—economic, or racist, or whatever—could take precedence over women's oppression. "If all women share the same problem, how can it be personal?" demanded Redstockings, a radical women's group. "Women's pain is not personal, it's political."[1]

It was not till the southern revolt against black oppression, specifically in 1964, that the anarchistic style of SNCC and CORE gave black and white women the chance to examine their own plight. There was obviously something unbalanced in a black liberation movement that restricted black women to typing and clerical work. White women from the North rarely got beyond library or teaching assignments. Stokeley Carmichael at one meeting supposedly announced that the "only position for women in SNCC is prone." He was no more sexist than any other male in the movement. His women friends insist the remark was an in joke that no one took seriously. Still, it reflects the prevailing attitudes of the most radical organization in the country in 1964.

A muted rebellion broke out that year among clerks and typists at the Atlanta office, led by Ruby Doris Robinson, one of the few SNCC women to reach executive status. (Fannie Lou Hamer, the impassioned Mississippi organizer, was another exception). Robinson and a group that included Sandra Cason Hayden (she was married to Tom Hayden) and Mary King put their protests into a position paper. Both Hayden and King were white. "Casey" Hayden had come into the movement through the University of Texas and the civil rights movement of the YWCA; King, the daughter of a southern Methodist minister, through the YWCA at Ohio Wesleyan. In 1966, Hayden and King formalized their protest in an article published by *Liberation* magazine. It described the "caste system" that "uses and exploits women" and compared the treatment of women with that of blacks. Although mild in tone, the article stirred a flood of supporting mail from women. At an SDS convention in Illinois shortly after, women staged an angry walkout when men refused to debate the article's thesis.

Not all black women, however, went along with this analysis of oppression. Gloria Richardson, who headed SNCC in Cambridge, Maryland, site of the most violent confrontations of that period, had a majority of women on her executive board and "never felt any anti-women feeling in SNCC."

Further, the caste system in SNCC was complicated by the special black-white pressures of the South. As Angela Davis pointed out, many black men viewed black women "as a threat for their attainment of manhood—especially those black women who take initiative and work hard to become leaders in their own right." The specter of death intensified the "macho" behavior of black males. And the very presence of white women working with blacks in southern towns increased the possibilities of racist violence.

To complicate the situation further, black males often considered "sexual intimacy with the white girls as a weapon of revenge against white society," Dr. Alvin Pouissant, the black psychiatrist, concluded. Black women became "jealous of their boyfriends' attention to white girls."[2]

The tensions of the caste system waned in SNCC by 1966 with the rise of Black Power and the ouster of whites from the staff. But they became increasingly jarring in SDS. At its June 1965 convention, an observer noted that women only "made peanut butter, waited on tables, cleaned up, got laid. That was their role." Marilyn Katz of Chicago JOIN considered "machismo rampant in SDS. If you didn't have a man, you couldn't even speak at a JOIN meeting."

Sharon Krebs labeled the Columbia SDS chapter during the 1968 uprising "completely sexist"—Mark Rudd had issued a notorious order, "Get me a chick to do some typing." As late as 1969, Tom Hayden admitted that the male defendants and staff at the Chicago conspiracy trial were "particularly oppressive" to women. Even at an antiwar rally that January, men in the audience interrupted a feminist speaker with shouts of "Take her off the stage and fuck her."

While women secured a fourth of the SDS executive committee seats in 1963, their representation dropped to 6 percent in 1964, according to Kirkpatrick Sale. No woman held a key national office until 1966, and then only as assistant national secretary.[3]

Perhaps the only area where women held power was in the "free universities," an experimental offshoot of academia that offered intensive courses in Marxism, Black Power, China, and other radical subjects. Carolyn Craven of Berkeley SDS organized a New School there in 1965, the prototype of hundreds of others. By 1968, the San Francisco State Experimental College had grown to 2,000 students. But SDS's enthusiasm diminished as its militants were siphoned off from street actions, and it gradually dropped it sponsorship.

The first strong call for Women's Liberation in SDS was Jane Adams's article in *New Left Notes* of January 20, 1967. At the June convention that year, women insisted on their own workshop, but when a feminist resolution reached the floor, debate was interrupted by heckling and catcalls. The women's caucus at the National Conference on New Politics in August 1967 tried to bring its platform to the floor. But the caucus was placed at the end of the agenda, and then brushed off for lack of time.

Frustrated and angered, the early feminists not only tried to shake up SDS but also to develop a new movement completely outside the framework of Left politics. They forced through a stinging resolution at SDS's national council in December 1968 branding the emerging Marxist-Leninist line as meaningless for women since "a socialist revolution could take place which maintains the secondary position of women in society." Women began to operate on their own. Women's caucuses split off from SDS in Florida and Seattle in 1968 and organized the Women's Radical Action Project at the University of Chicago to defend Marlene Dixon, an ousted sociology professor and feminist.[4]

The pivotal point in the development of an independent women's movement was the founding of the National Organization for Women in 1966, with Betty Friedan as first president. It was essentially a professional and middle-class group, concentrating on equality in jobs and salaries. Friedan's book, *The Feminine Mystique,* in 1963, and Simone de Beauvoir's classic, *The Second Sex,* among other feminist best sellers, were quickly absorbed into the thinking of the average woman, a new form of organizing that influenced an audience in remote corners of the country never touched by more radical sects. When Kate Millett's *Sexual Politics* appeared in 1970, *Time* magazine thought that feminist literature rated a cover story.

In 1967, NOW took a step of considerable radical implications. It came out for complete abolition of all laws restricting a woman's right to abortion. Two men had pushed this demand first in books and articles, but it was NOW's organized support that gave abortion rights momentum. The widespread adoption of the birth-control pill in the early 1960s intensified the recognition that all other feminist rights depended on a woman's control over her body.

The feminists were ready for a complete break with the past: a revolution on the basis of sex, not class. "We had arrived at the point where women's issues had to come before leftist issues," Susan Brownmiller, a pioneer radical feminist, observed. Men, not the economic system in Marxist terms, became the chief oppressor. "Our oppression is total, affecting every facet of our lives," the Redstockings manifesto announced. "We will not ask what is 'revolutionary' or 'reformist,' only what is good for women."

A landmark in this approach was the founding of New York Radical Women in October 1967 by Pam Allen, Shulamith Firestone, and other converts from antiwar and Left groups. Radical feminism saw "feminist issues not only as women's first priority," Firestone proclaimed in her book, *The Dialectic of Sex,* "but as central to any larger revolutionary analysis."[5]

Its overwhelming need was to develop the consciousness of women around this platform. Its method, derived from the "revival meeting" style of SNCC, was for groups of 10 or 15 to meet regularly each week, with every woman in the circle speaking frankly about any problems on her mind. These ranged from the burden of housework and the restrictions of the nuclear family to problems of frigidity. After four or five hours, the "testimony" was analyzed by the group. Women who had never spoken before, or even probed their feelings, developed an awareness of their links to other women and of the necessity for group action.

"Consciousness-raising," as this method was termed, became the most powerful organizing force of the movement. It virtually eliminated the need for the traveling organizers so common in the New Left. Dozens of "C-R" groups in New York, and eventually hundreds throughout the country, arose spontaneously after C-R was featured at the First National Women's Liberation Conference in Chicago in November 1968. "The necessity of squeezing the slave out of oneself drop by drop was, for me, *the* central insight," concluded Vivian Gornick.

The radical feminists became highly sophisticated at confrontations that reached other women through the media. At least 200 New York Radical Women invaded Atlantic City, New Jersey, for the Miss America pageant on September 7, 1968. Their purpose was to spotlight the exploitation of women's bodies by commercial interests, the selling of products through male-oriented sexual titillation. They crowned a live sheep as Miss America to symbolize the brainless subjugation of feminine flesh. The picket line taunted the contestants in song: "Ain't she sweet/Making profit off her meat." At night they infiltrated the convention hall, hanging a "Freedom for Women" banner from the balcony, releasing a few stink bombs, and purportedly discarding some undergarments in an ashcan outside as a rebellion against the stereotyped female figure. The press labeled them "bra-burners," which may have been inaccurate reporting but put this guerrilla theater on many front pages.[6]

Radicals soon split into new groups in an endless process of theoretical and tactical development. WITCH (Women's International Terrorist Conspiracy from Hell) had a Marxist analysis of society's insanity toward women and satirized the heartland of capitalism with a fully costumed witches' dance on Wall Street on Halloween, 1968.

Redstockings considered itself a political striking force. Its name synthesized two traditions—red for revolution, combined with the "blue stocking" label disparagingly pinned on nineteenth-century feminists. When the New York State Legislature held abortion hearings on February 13, 1969, with a panel of eight experts, all men, Redstockings infiltrated the hearing room. Kathie Amatniek, often credited with developing the consciousness-raising technique, suddenly shouted: "All right, now let's hear from some real experts— the women." The women made such a din that the chairman had to adjourn the hearing to another room from which policemen barred the public. The Redstockings sat outside the door for seven hours until a few were allowed to testify.

The campaign for legalized abortion became a turning point in consciousness-raising when hundreds of women met at New York's Washington Square Methodist Church a few weeks later. One by one, they stood up to tell how illegal abortions had scarred their lives —the degradation of their search for help, the filthy back-street abortion mills, the surgical bungling, the physical and emotional damage. The all-day testimony united women in their campaign. Carried by television and radio nationwide, it had the further effect of sharing this agony with the public. "When I decided to tell about my abortion openly, it became the most mature decision of my life," Constance Billé concluded.[7]

Consciousness-raising, too, brought a special emphasis on erotic fulfillment, a debate set off by Anne Koedt's much-publicized article, "The Myth of the Vaginal Orgasm." Koedt theorized that women have always been "defined sexually in terms of what pleases men," and that from the time of Sigmund Freud's insistence on the superiority of the vaginal orgasm, men have classified frigidity as "the failure of women to have vaginal orgasms." Koedt claimed the clitoris was actually the "center of sexual sensitivity" and that "men in fact fear the clitoris as a threat to their masculinity." Koedt's thesis gained a fair amount of acceptance in the movement, and Freud henceforth became anathema to feminists.[8]

The emergence of the Weathermen in 1969 crystallized the antagonism between radical feminism and the political Left. Weather opposed a separate women's movement, insisting that men and women should struggle together against their chauvinism. By destroying monogomous relationships, Weather thought it could develop more self-reliant and independent women for the revolution.

Most radical feminists, on the other hand, saw the Weather collectives as a self-destructive system of sexist polygamy. "Smashing monogomy simply smashed people," Sharon Krebs observed. Male members used the system as a convenient way to sleep with woman after woman. "It was almost as if he *expected* every woman in the world to want to fuck him," Susan Stern wrote about a leading Weatherman. "It was common among SDS men, especially regional and national travellers."

Attacking the "destructive consequences" of smashing monogomy, Bread and Roses, a Boston women's collective, concluded: "Such a denial of love and personal involvement may produce effectiveness and homogeneity and loyalty—but it doesn't produce freedom."

Smashing monogomy, in effect, simply remade women in the image of a macho hero rather than liberating them. It required women to become revolutionaries in terms defined by men, to prove themselves as street fighters of equal or better toughness than men. Fanshen, a women's collective in Seattle, complained that women were "used as cannon fodder for the revolution."[9]

In a biting article, "Goodbye to All That," which summed up the bitterness of many feminists against Weather and the political Left in general, Robin Morgan concluded: "Goodbye to the Weather-Vain, with the Stanley Kowalski image and theory of free sexuality but practice of sex on demand for males . . . goodbye to the dream that being in the leadership collective will get you anything but gonorrhea."

Radical feminists were pulling out of the political Left in considerable numbers by 1970. Marlene Dixon complained that "not one male-dominated organization from the left-liberal New University Conference to the radical youth movement . . . has been willing to place top priority upon the women's struggle."[10]

While pulling out of the Left, radical feminists brought the women's movement important techniques from the Left. They introduced confrontation politics—hundreds of radicals, for example, forced the male editor of the *Ladies Home Journal* to give more space to feminist issues by staging a successful sit-down strike in his office in 1970. The strike had the additional effect of pushing many women editors and writers across the county toward feminism and making them apostles for the movement in their own journals.

Eventually, Gloria Steinem founded *Ms.* magazine in 1972. It was the first exclusive vehicle for feminism, although some radicals considered it tepid.

Still, a characteristic of the movement was that radicals and mainstream women frequently converged on central issues. Most attacked the exploitation of housework. "We are exploited as sex objects, breeders, domestic servants, and cheap labor," Redstockings stated. "We are considered as inferior beings whose only purpose is to enhance men's lives."[11]

Feminists wanted to fulfill their lives with careers outside the house. This required contraceptive and abortion services so that every woman could space her children or remain childless. It also meant that the women's movement would have to build its own alternative institutions—women's health centers and day-care centers for children—when the government failed to provide them. Beyond that, it meant an intensive struggle against the discriminatory policy of higher male salaries in the same job category. In 1965, the median income for white men with four years of high school was $5,976; for white women, only $2,425. For white men with some college education, the median income was $7,257; for white women, $2,999. Black women made less in all categories.

Even the United Electrical Workers, a radical union noted for its feminist positions, had failed to gain parity for women by 1968 in its contract with the General Electric company—women's hourly earnings averaging $2.54 against $3.34 for men.[12]

Some radical feminists carried their attack against the male-dominated nuclear family further. They wanted it abolished, or at least restricted. They not only considered the nuclear family historically linked to private property, and thus the foundation of the capitalist system; they also considered it the structure that maintained the oppression of women and virtual "ownership" of children. Sexual dominion—a hierarchy that ran from man to woman to child—thus became the male's primary route to power. "The nuclear family is a microcosm of the fascist state," concluded one workshop at the Revolutionary People's Constitutional Convention in 1970, "where the woman and children are owned by, and their fates determined by, the needs of men, in a man's world."[13]

The nuclear family has certainly undergone drastic changes in recent years. This process may well be the single most important result of the women's movement, although it stems also from the birth-control and abortion movements, and indeed the whole cultural revolution. "We have redefined the family," Robin Morgan pointed out. A spectrum of new forms has emerged—the communal family, the couple remaining childless by choice, and the female head of household are among the most prominent. But the homosexual household, the breadwinner-wife with husband-housekeeper, and the extended family have become increasingly common.

These drastic changes have already been confirmed by 1977 statistics. As of 1977, only 15.9 percent of all households followed the traditional family pattern—father as sole wage earner, mother as full-time homemaker, and at least one child. In 18.5 percent of all households, by contrast, with one or more children at home, both father and mother were wage earners. More than 50 percent of women with school-age children and no preschoolers had entered the labor force.

The increasing independence of women by 1977 is shown in the statistic that 23 percent of women had never married. A further confirmation of the dwindling nuclear family is that 20.6 percent of all households consisted of a single person, and 19 percent of all women were divorced, separated, or widowed.[14]

By 1970, the mainstream of the movement could be defined as "reformist feminism," centering on the National Organization for Women and concentration on legislation, jobs, and status issues. Still, the August 26 strike that year, largely organized by NOW, drew many radical factions into its coalition. When 25,000 women marched down New York's Fifth Avenue to mark the fiftieth anniversary of women's suffrage (with thousands more marching in other cities), the movement came of age. The strike gave NOW an enormous boost, increasing its chapters to 700, its membership to 40,000, and its budget to $430,000 by 1974 (with an additional $175,000 for special projects).[15]

What NOW contributed to the movement, above all, was a "reformist image" appealing to women in the professions, and in smaller cities and towns, never reached by radicals. NOW's court actions to force equal pay and opportunity for women at the National Broadcasting Company and the New York *Times,* for example, politicized new groups.

Similarly, the abortion-rights campaign increasingly involved women of every income bracket and political affiliation. Radicals like Patricia Maginnis and Lana Phelan in California laid the groundwork of confrontation by referring women for abortion long before the procedure had been legalized. But once abortion rights moved to the stage of new legislation, particularly the campaign for New York's landmark law in 1970, moderates in NOW, Planned Parenthood, the religious denominations, and Democratic and Republican clubs became the backbone of political lobbying.

The radical wing of the movement was always more chaotic, factionalized, and difficult to define. It could generally be grouped under two headings—"radical feminists" and "abstract socialists" (or for simplicity, "politicos.") The politicos wanted to use Marxism, and sometimes a combination of Marx and Freud, "as a method of analyzing the specific nature of our oppression and hence our revolutionary role," according to Juliet Mitchell.

Whereas the radical feminists considered men the main oppressor and all existing societies male-dominated, including those termed communist and socialist, the politicos saw capitalism as the prime evil and believed the system, not men, was the source of women's oppression. The radical feminists claimed that socialism had nothing to offer them—"Marx and Engels didn't deal with half the human species," Robin Morgan insisted. The politicos claimed that oppression started with private property, and that the revolutionary struggle for men as well as women—not an isolated women's movement —was the only approach. "We are socialist feminists because sexism and capitalism form one integrated system," stated the Berkeley-Oakland Women's Union. [6]

If the radical feminists and politicos reflected one split in the movement, the lesbian issue brought out even more tensions. The Daughters of Bilitis, perhaps the first organized lesbian group, had been founded in 1955, but it was only with the growth of the women's movement that radical lesbians protested openly against the second-class citizenship and underground roles society forced on them. Robin Morgan announced her "lesbian identification" in 1968—she was then a mother and living with a man. Kate Millett, who already had stated her bisexuality, urged feminist support of lesbians at the August 26, 1970, strike rally. Some groups, like The Feminists in New York, attacked all relationships with men. They even argued, "You can't be a real radical if you don't sleep with women."

These "separatist" trends affected the abortion campaign—a Fifth Avenue parade in 1971 for abortion rights, for example, was suddenly turned into a lesbian demonstration when many women put on lavender armbands as they marched and shouted lesbian slogans through their bullhorns. A woman's caucus in Los Angeles formed the Lesbian Feminists, pushing the "lesbian line" through its new affiliation with the Women's Liberation Center.

Such aggressive takeovers, duplicated in other cities, appalled many mainstream feminists, particularly in NOW. Betty Friedan, fearful that the lesbian issue would deflect the movement from its main concerns, began a purge of lesbians in the organization in 1970. The issue almost tore the New York chapter apart during the next year. At the Second Congress to Unite Women in May 1970, one delegation appeared in T-shirts with "lavender menace" stenciled on them. "When a woman stood up at a feminist meeting and announced that she was a Lesbian, many women avoided her," reported Martha Shelley.

There were radicals as well who feared the lesbian issue would cripple the movement. Redstockings claimed that lesbians infiltrated and tried to seize almost every independent women's center and publication between 1969 and 1973.[17]

In the end, however, the increasing cohesion and radicalization of the women's movement overcame the "gay/straight" split. The younger members of NOW took the lead—they had swelled its ranks after the strike march. NOW's 1971 convention passed a resolution defining the "oppression of lesbians as a legitimate concern of feminism." At its 1973 convention, NOW established a Task Force on Sexuality and Lesbianism and came out for "civil rights legislation to end discrimination based on sexual orientation. . . ."

By the time of the National Women's Conference at Houston, Texas, in 1977, the lesbian issue provoked few women except the right-wing "Pro-Family" coalition, which brought newspaper ads with a child asking in headline type: "Mommy, when I grow up, can I be a lesbian?" The old tensions were erased when Betty Friedan reversed her antilesbian position and made an impassioned speech for unity. The Sexual Preference resolution—the civil rights for lesbians plank—passed overwhelmingly. "The rafters of the meeting hall," Lindsy Van Gelder wrote, "were suddenly transformed into a pastel sky of hundreds of helium balloons, each emblazoned with the message, 'We Are Everywhere': a visual metaphor for the sisterhood that thousands of women experienced at Houston."

Perhaps the most significant statistic from the Houston convention was that white women made up only 64.5 percent of the 2,000 elected delegates as compared with 84.4 percent of the general female population. In effect, blacks, Chicanas, and other minorities were overrepresented. This was a new development in the movement. Except for a handful of lawyers and other professionals in NOW, black participation had previously been slim. "Black women in the main consider the women's liberation movement a *white middle-class* thing," Congresswoman Shirley Chisholm observed. Angela Davis of the Communist party claimed that "the middle-class, white Women's Liberation Movement has really obscured the whole nature of women's oppression. . . ."[18]

The ghetto black woman, in particular, had been too involved with the struggle for food, clothing, and survival to worry about the theoretical aspects of oppression. She belonged to a group that had never asserted its identity. She was "still waiting to be discovered by the black man," as the *Black Panther* put it, still being stereotyped, mainly by white scholars, as an "aggressive, matriarchal . . . castrator."

It was the Panthers who first came under the influence of the women's movement and demanded a radical new approach to ghetto women. "I was appalled when I first joined the Oakland chapter— it was all male control, just 'beat her ass' in their attitude to women," Elaine Brown recalled. By 1969, however, the Panthers insisted "that male chauvinism must be stamped out because we have come to realize that it is bourgeois." They called women's liberation "one of the most important issues facing the world today."

When Huey Newton got out of jail in 1970, he put three women, including Brown and Ericka Huggins, on the central committee. At first the Panthers clung to the early nationalist thesis that birth control and abortion were white racist plots to diminish the black population. But Panther women forced the acceptance of a woman's right to limit her childbearing. By 1976, women made up half the central committee. When Newton was indicted again and fled the country, and Seale resigned from the party, Brown and Huggins became the first women to be elected to the two top leadership positions.[19]

The women's movement, above all others, has demonstrated that the most effective path to radical change is to build a new system coexistent with the old. When the medical establishment failed to adapt itself to feminist demands, women set up a network of health centers across the country. They provided abortion services in areas where municipal agencies lacked them. They offered alternative approaches to childbirth such as midwifery and at-home deliveries. These self-supporting, almost socialist communes, were also political instruments, campaigning for a national health plan and preaching a Marxist approach to medicine.

The women's movement created a whole range of new issues and new institutions that had never been considered before—the problems of rape, pornography, and battered women in particular. Susan Brownmiller's *Against Our Will* in 1975 focused national attention on rape and speeded up the incipient drive to establish nationwide rape-counseling centers. Battered-women centers sprung up soon after, not only offering immediate professional help but serving as pressure groups to make the police and city administrations deal with male violence against women.

Radical feminists have developed the sophistication to work within the system as well—a prime example being the Coalition of Labor Union Women founded in 1974. The AFL-CIO, unfortunately, remains a bastion of sex discrimination. Although women constitute more than 20 percent of its membership, not one woman sits on its 35-member policy-making executive council. All top positions in its departments, regional offices, and other agencies are held by men.

The feminists have survived and flourished as a national force, possibly because they have taken advantage of a whole spectrum of choices, refusing to be bound by rigid dogmas. The feminist movement, in fact, remains unstructured and obstreperous. New groups form constantly, most of them linked only by exchanging publications and personal correspondence. *Women Today,* a national newsletter, counted several thousand groups in 1973. But even structured organizations like NOW have become more radical as younger members replace professional and business women in the leadership.[20]

The dominant characteristic of the women's movement is that it has kept its unity—feminist issues have always come before all other issues. Although some radicals considered the National Women's Conference in 1977 an instrument of government cooptation, they showed up in force and kept the conference's unity. Whatever the choices women have taken—whether forcing their way into West Point or a Little League baseball team; living in communes and shifting from partner to partner; marrying late or not marrying at all —the personal actions of each woman has advanced the movement.

The struggle for the Equal Rights Amendment assumed a symbolic status in feminist unity. Passed by Congress in 1972, the amendment still lacked the approval of three state legislatures in 1979 to complete the ratification process. ERA will probably have little impact on women's rights, at best clearing up some legal impediments that could have been eliminated by local legislatures and courts. But ERA's psychological influence is profound. It not only signifies that the nation has accepted equality by law; it draws the line between the past and the future, pulling together every faction of the women's movement from mainstream to ultraradicals.

·20·

The Aftermath of Violence

"We've got to turn New York into Saigon," proclaimed Ted Gold, a shy, almost professorial veteran of the Columbia strike of 1968, who had just gone underground with the Weather cadres. In February 1970, Gold's cadre set off three fire bombs at the home of Justice John M. Murtagh, then presiding at the trial of the New York Panthers. The Panthers, logically enough, considered it detrimental to their chances of acquittal. In fact the Weathermen themselves would be the only victims of New Left bombings except for one tragedy in Wisconsin.

The "New Year's Gang," not officially members of Weather but asserting kinship, set off a truckload of explosives one summer night in 1970 against the University of Wisconsin's Mathematics Research Center, which did counterguerrilla and weapons studies for the government, according to the campus newspaper. The blast killed Robert Fassnacht, a 33-year-old research assistant working late in his laboratory. When two brothers, Karleton and Dwight Armstrong, were brought to trial, their defense attorney pleaded, "People must act to stop a government when it runs wild. . . ." But even if American killings in Vietnam had reached the point of "hysteria and paranoia," as historian Henry Steele Commager said, the court found no equation between the war at home and overseas, and the brothers were sent to jail for long terms.[1]

On March 6, 1970, the elegant Federal homes on 11th Street off New York's Fifth Avenue were rocked by a shattering explosion. It virtually demolished a 125-year-old townhouse owned by James Platt Wilkerson, a radio station owner vacationing in the Caribbean, punched huge holes in adjoining houses, and smashed windows throughout the block. At least three members of a Weather cell, who were never identified, escaped out the back garden. Two women, probably Cathlyn Wilkerson, the owner's daughter and a 1966 graduate of Swarthmore College, and Kathy Boudin, daughter of the radical lawyer Leonard Boudin and a graduate of Bryn Mawr in 1965, escaped out the front. None was ever seen in public again.

Three bodies were found in the rubble. Ted Gold had been crushed by beams. Diana Oughton's body was so mutilated it could only be identified from a print of a severed finger. The body of Terry Robbins, who had organized the most militant SDS chapters in the Midwest in previous years, defied identification; his presence was only confirmed by messages from friends. The Weathermen had turned the townhouse, stocked with dynamite and blasting caps, into a bomb factory. They had probably been assembling a bomb when a misconnected wire detonated the explosives.

A few days later, three corporate offices in New York were bombed, presumably by another Weather cell. In early June, the Weathermen struck at what they called the very heartland of oppression—New York City police headquarters—where bombs seriously damaged the second floor. Other explosions were set off at the Hall of Justice in Marin County, California, and at the Long Island City courthouse in New York. Seemingly to prove that no escapade was beyond their reach in 1970, the Weathermen plotted the escape of Dr. Timothy Leary, high priest of the drug culture, from a minimum-security California prison where he was serving a 10-year sentence on a marijuana charge. After boosting him over the prison wall, they managed to provide a forged passport and get him safely on a plane to Algeria, which provided sanctuary.

The Weather communiqués stressed that their attacks were only a miniscule reflection of the government's havoc in Vietnam—they telephoned a warning before each bombing and the few injuries that occurred were minor. The Nixon administration had suddenly stepped up the tempo of the war when the President announced to a startled nation on April 30, 1970, that he had opened a new military theater by ordering American troops into Cambodia. The invasion seemed an outrageous reversal of Nixon's pledge to reduce American forces, and he had presumably honored the neutrality of Cambodia until then. The anger at this news was aggravated by the further revelation that Nixon's second war had actually begun secretly 14 months before with 3,630 unannounced B-52 air strikes against Communist hideouts in Cambodia.

The Cambodian invasion provoked a furious reaction. The United States Senate, which had allowed its constitutional power to declare war to be usurped in the case of Vietnam, now demanded the removal of troops from Cambodia and an end to air support by July. The campuses erupted in a series of strikes that closed down 536 colleges and universities, some for weeks, some for the entire year. It was the first general student strike in the country's history. It affected the most conservative institutions—half the Catholic colleges were shut down. At the very moment of SDS's disintegration, Cambodia fused the remnants of the Left with student liberals and the mainstream of the antiwar movement.

In a quickly organized march, 100,000 demonstrators converged on Washington on May 9. Draft resistance stiffened appreciably—more than half of those ordered to report never showed up at induction centers that month. At Santa Barbara, California, students had just burned a Bank of America branch, and during the rioting, the police killed Kevin Moran, a senior at the university, and wounded four others. After Cambodia, student rioting broke out again, and the National Guard armory was destroyed by fire. In the post-Cambodia rioting in Buffalo, New York, 12 students were shot in a clash with police. In Seattle, students trashed the downtown streets and set fire to the Air Force ROTC.[2]

In May 1970 alone, Kirkpatrick Sale estimated 169 incidents of bombing arson. The *Black Panther* newspaper listed 423 attacks on police stations and 101 on military installations during the year.

Antiwar demonstrations had been minimal at black campuses until rioting broke out at North Carolina Agricultural and Technical State University in May 1969, and a black student, Willie Ernest Grimes, was killed in a clash with police and guardsmen. The science building was burned down at Lane College, Tennessee. Following the Cambodian invasion, state troopers and police opened fire on black student demonstrators at Jackson State College, Mississippi, killing Phillip Gibbs and James Earl Green and injuring 12 others. Two more black student demonstrators were killed by National Guardsmen and police at Southern University in Louisiana in May 1972.[3]

The most violent aftermath of the Cambodian invasion, however, broke out at an unlikely campus in Ohio. Kent State University had always been considered one of the Midwest's conservative institutions, jokingly nicknamed "Apathy U." Still, SDS and the Black

United Students had built strong chapters there. When SDS demon-strated against ROTC in 1969, the university banned SDS from the campus.

Vice President Spiro Agnew had been appointed the White House's blunderbuss against student dissent. "The next time a mob of students, waving their non-negotiable demands, starts pitching rocks at the student union," Agnew told Florida Republicans shortly before the Cambodian invasion, "just imagine they are wearing brown shirts or white shirts and act accordingly." After demonstra-tors filled Kent's main street on the nights of May 1 and May 2, 1970, Ohio's Governor James A. Rhodes inflamed the mood by calling them "worse than the Brown shirts and communist element and also the nightriders and the vigilantes."[4]

The anti-Cambodia demonstrations in town were followed by the burning of the ROTC building on May 2. Mayor Le Roy Satrom declared a state of emergency and asked the governor to call out the National Guard.

On Monday, May 4, at noon, students rang the "victory bell" for a rally set days before and supported by many faculty members. Campus police with bullhorns and the campus radio had just an-nounced the meeting had been banned by General Robert H. Can-terbury of the guard. But most students were in class and unaware of the ban. James Michener in his book *Kent State* records that Canterbury told a bystander, probably a faculty member: "These students are going to have to find out what law and order is all about."

With anywhere from 500 to 1,000 students gathered near the victory bell, the guard was ordered to load and lock their rifles. Few people on campus believed the troops carried bullets; most state guards had restricted them following the 1967 debacle in Detroit when jittery and undisciplined guardsmen fired at anything that moved. The guard now used tear gas against the rock-throwing demonstrators, but a unit of about 113 men was gradually forced by students toward the athletic field's chain-link fence.

This unit then began to march up Blanket Hill. Only small groups of students were taunting them, mainly on the soldiers' right flank, at least 70 to 100 yards away. "Far from being sur-rounded, the Guard had empty space on all sides," Michener noted. "At 12:24, with the escape route back to ROTC completely unimpeded and with alternate ones available either to the left flank or to the rear, some Guardsmen on the trailing right flank suddenly stopped, wheeled 135 degrees to the right—that is they turned almost completely around—faced the students who had collected on the south side of Taylor Hall, and dropped their rifles to ready position."

Suddenly a shot rang out, perhaps two, although none of the three top officers seemed to have given any order. Michener found testimony, never contained in any public record, that as the troops marched up Blanket Hill, one said, "If they charge us, shoot them." A university electrician, standing closest to the guard, was asked, "Did you hear an officer say, 'Turn around and fire three rounds?' " The electrician replied "Well, I heard . . . well, yes I heard it." Peter Davies, Jr., an investigator for the United Methodist Church, also reported that some guardsmen had agreed beforehand to "punish" the students.[5]

About two seconds after the first shot (all recorded on tape by journalism students), there was a heavy barrage for eight seconds, another pause, then a last few shots. Twenty-eight guardsmen had fired, although some had pointed their weapons into the air.

Four students lay dead—the closest 265 feet away, the farthest 390 feet. Nine students were seriously wounded, including one paralyzed for life. No evidence was produced that any of the four killed had made any overt action or threat against the guard.

Although a special Ohio grand jury, presumably partial to the guard, concluded that the soldiers thought they would be in imminent danger if they hadn't fired, former Governor William Scranton of Pennsylvania, heading the President's Commission on Campus Unrest, called the shots "unnecessary, unwarranted, and inexcusable." Nixon repudiated the commission's report.

At a federal trial for civil damages brought by parents of dead and injured students, Canterbury admitted he was "horrified" when his troops started firing and said they were not "surrounded at that precise, that instant." Captain Ronald Snyder also admitted he had lied about finding a gun on one of the dead students, possibly to build up the self-defense thesis. A voluminous FBI report, never made public, showed that none of the guardsmen had been in danger or needed weapons for self-protection; that no sniper had fired at any soldier; and that no guardsman had been hurt by a rock or missile. In fact, all but 4 of 13 students struck by bullets were hit in the back or side, indicating they could not have been threatening the troops.

No guardsman had been punished by 1978.* "Have we come to such a state in this country," asked Arthur S. Krause, a dead student's father, "that a young girl has to be shot because she disagrees deeply with the actions of her Government?"[6]

The violent campus demonstrations after Cambodia contrasted sharply with the Panthers' concentration on "survival programs" in the ghettos. Most black radicals had abandoned instant revolution for new approaches like James Forman's Black Manifesto. Approved by the Black Economic Development Conference in Detroit in April 1969, with the support of Julian Bond, Fannie Lou Hamer, and other SNCC veterans, the manifesto demanded $500 million from the "racist white" churches and synagogues of the country as moral reparations, not unlike West Germany's payments to Israel, for 300 years of black oppression. It was only "$15 per nigger," as Forman put it.

The money would go for the purchase of land for black farmers in the South, for a skills-training center, for a black labor strike and defense fund, and for publishing and printing centers, among other projects.

Unannounced, Forman invaded the Sunday morning service of New York City's Riverside Church on May 4, 1969, to make his demands. Dr. Ernest Campbell, a white minister, cut him off, arguing that even if the demands were justified, Forman should not interrupt the service. When Forman persisted, the minister, choir, and majority of worshippers left the church.

Forman got virtually nowhere with other denominations. The newly elected black president of the American Baptist Convention supported the manifesto but raised no money. Bishop John E. Hines of the Episcopal Church called the manifesto "calculatedly revolutionary Marxist." Still, at a stormy meeting in Pittsburgh in September, the Episcopal House of Deputies granted $200,000. By the summer of 1970, Forman's Development Conference had raised only $300,000.[7]

If there was any commitment to moral reparations, the money would certainly not be going for schemes that smacked of black separatism and even rural communism. President Nixon's solution,

---

*Governor James A. Rhodes and 27 National Guardsmen, defendants in a civil suit, signed a statement of regret for the shooting on January 4, 1979. Ohio's State Controlling Board approved payments of $675,000 to the victims and families of victims.

backed by miniscule government money, was "black capitalism." The guilt or commitment that America's religious denominations had brought to the southern campaigns of the early 1960s had been depleted by 1970, or swallowed up by Nixonian conformity.

The desertion of white liberals at this point was particularly harmful because an innovative attack against racism had just been started by the League of Revolutionary Black Workers in Detroit. At least 40 percent of 350,000 members of the United Automobile Workers in the area were black. But the union had maintained its racist policy of white leadership as fiercely as the auto manufacturers had kept blacks from supervisory positions.

At Chrysler's Hamtramck plant, 60 percent of Local 3 members were black, but all union officers were white. At Dodge plants in the area, 99 percent of general foremen and 95 percent of plant foremen were white. Not a single black sat on UAW's national board. Increasingly, the UAW had assumed management's responsibility for worker discipline. The union leadership in the process stifled wildcat strikes and other opposition to the segrationist status quo.

The League of Revolutionary Black Workers was organized by a disparate coalition of Panthers, black unionists, SNCC veterans like James Forman, and white Marxists from Progressive Labor and the Revolutionary Union. They had finally agreed on one objective, that the "basic power of the black people lies at the point of production." They also agreed, in the words of the Chrysler Revolutionary Union Movement (known as CRUM, while Dodge and Ford chapters were obviously DRUM and FRUM), that the "UAW bureaucracy is just as guilty, and its hands are just as bloody, as the white racist management of the Chrysler corporation."

The League focused its struggle on management's speed-up of the assembly line. Chrysler Local 7, for example, had raised auto production 63 percent from the late 1950s to the late 1960s, although its membership was cut more than half. The league claimed this heightened productivity came from black sweat—"Nigger-mation," the league called it.

At Chrysler's Eldon Avenue plant, a woman with 26 years on the line was ordered home by her doctor for high blood pressure but returned to work after management warned she would lose her salary benefits. A week later she fainted on the job and died soon after. A Vietnam veteran was killed when a defective jitney overturned—

Chrysler later admitted 167 safety violations. By 1971, the Michigan Department of Labor found most of them still uncorrected.

The league called a series of wildcat strikes in 1970, and management fired most of the organizers. Still, a black member running for president of Chrysler Local 961, barely defeated in his first try by a white shop steward, won the post in 1973 by a two to one margin. Another black was elected president of Ford Local 900; five black officers were elected at Chrysler Local 1258 despite a predominantly white membership.[8]

The shift from instant revolution to long-range organizing was also reflected in the recruitment of radicals in the nation's jails. With a high proportion of black and minority inmates, they were a fertile source of Panther organizing, particularly in California and New York. Many blacks had been shut away for years on minor offenses that whites with adequate legal counsel would probably have escaped. The racist attitudes of corrections officers added to routine brutality. The Panthers had formed sizable cadres at San Quentin and Soledad prisons in California by 1970, when Cleaver's dissident factions challenged Huey Newton's authority.

The most skilled and impassioned organizer at Soledad prison was 27-year-old George Jackson, serving a sentence of one year to life for an $18 robbery in which he may have been an innocent accomplice. He had already been jailed for nine years by 1970 when his book, *Soledad Brother,* would make him the most noted convict in the country.

Jackson's organizing skills had also made him a field marshal in the Panthers. He apparently remained loyal to Newton after the Cleaver defections. Yet there is some evidence that Jackson's supporters outside of prison were linked to a purged Panther guerrilla underground led by Elmer "Geronimo" Pratt, a former paratrooper and a member of the Green Berets. There is also evidence that the white, ultraleft "Venceremos" wing of the Revolutionary Union, which split off in 1970, trained at guerrilla tactics with Pratt in a remote area of the Santa Cruz mountains.

George's 17-year-old brother, Jonathan, would lead a bloody guerrilla raid on August 7, 1970. James McClain, a San Quentin inmate, was on trial at the Marin County Courthouse on a charge of stabbing a prison guard. Ruchell Magee and William Christmas, two other inmates, were in court to testify in his defense. McClain had recently been held in the same cell block as George Jackson, which indicates some link between the inside and outside groups.

At 11 A.M., Jonathan walked into the courtroom, obviously unsearched, and pointed a .38-caliber revolver at Superior Court Judge Harold Haley's head. He gave two other weapons to McClain and Magee. Taking the judge, Assistant District Attorney Gary Thomas, and three women as hostages, Jonathan and the three prisoners fled to a waiting van. There were at least 100 law officers in the parking lot area, and San Quentin guards fired on the van, killing Jonathan. Thomas managed to grab Jonathan's pistol and started shooting, later claiming, "I got three of them." The judge, Christmas, and McClain were killed; Magee, Thomas, and one woman were wounded.[9]

A week later, Angela Davis, already a national figure as a result of Governor Reagan's attempt to oust her from her teaching position, was charged as an accomplice in the raid. The government claimed that three guns used by Jonathan belonged to Davis. She fled Los Angeles and hid at a friend's apartment in Chicago. Both eventually came to New York, where they were arrested on October 13, 1970.

After Davis's extradition to California, the government fought off the defense's request for bail for eight months, despite protests from the YWCA, NAACP, and other organizations. Bail was finally set at $102,500 (and put up by a white farmer in Fresno) only after the California supreme court abolished the death penalty and its no bail for a capital crime provision.

Davis went on trial in 1971 for murder, kidnapping, and conspiracy. At the age of 26, her beauty, poise, and intelligence—she had studied at Brandeis and Frankfurt Universities and the Sorbonne and received her degree in philosophy under Herbert Marcuse—added more luster to the sensationalism of the courthouse raid. Her radical affiliations were equally newsworthy. She had moved from SNCC to the Black Panthers to the Communist party and had campaigned avidly for George Jackson and the "Soledad Brothers," accused of killing a white guard in Soledad Prison that January.

Although Davis had met George Jackson only once at Marin County jail on July 8, 1971, they had fallen in love through their letters. The prosecution would stress this attachment as the cause of her presumed involvement in the raid. "I'm totally intoxicated, overflowing with you, wanting you more than ever before," Jackson had written in his diary.

Her trial became an international theatrical event. Posters of her chiseled profile hung in left-wing homes throughout Europe. The prosecution hammered away at her passion for George. But while witnesses testified she had been seen with Jonathan a few days before the raid, the connection between Angela and the three guns proved elusive.

The defense showed that no Davis fingerprint had been found on the van or any guns or ammunition. Davis had purchased the .38-caliber automatic pistol and the .30-caliber carbine from a Los Angeles sporting goods store in 1968 and 1969. She had bought the 12-gauge shotgun at a San Francisco pawn shop in 1970, joking with the owner who recognized her and asked for her autograph. There had been no secrecy in any purchase. All guns were registered.

The guns had been kept in an unlocked closet of an apartment and used for target practice at a public range by members of the Che-Lumumba Club. Davis left them there when she moved out of the apartment in July, but she and some friends noticed they were gone when they visited in August.

The defense counsel stressed the absurdity of a brilliant scholar handing over guns that were registered in her name to a 17-year-old guerrilla. Could a woman of her achievements "go out and buy a shotgun to blow a judge's head off and give her own name and sign an autograph? . . ." The jury agreed that the state's evidence was flimsy, and on June 4, 1972, declared her not guilty on all counts.[10]

While the Davis trial was going on, George Jackson was killed at San Quentin on August 21, 1971. Not long before, Jackson had told a reporter from the *Pacific Sun* that they "will never let me out of here alive."

The official version claimed that Stephen Bingham, a young lawyer who had just come to visit Jackson in prison, was the pivot of an escape plot. After the meeting, Jackson was being searched in the Adjustment Center, when he supposedly pulled a pistol from his Afro-style hair and began the shootout in which three guards and two prisoners were killed. Jackson then forced the guards to open the cell door; ran to the prison yard with another inmate, John Spain, a Panther captain; and was shot down trying to reach the prison wall. This official version, however, changed frequently in the next few weeks.

Spain's lawyer, Charles Garry, claimed that Jackson had not been seriously injured in the prison yard by bullets from the tower guards. Yet a short time later he was dead. "In all likelihood, George Jackson was murdered," Garry insisted.

The mystery of Bingham's involvement has never been solved, nor has he been seen since he left San Quentin. The grandson of Hiram Bingham III, a governor and U.S. senator from Connecticut, and nephew of U.S. Representative Jonathan B. Bingham of New York, young Bingham worked with SNCC in Mississippi, with the Peace Corps in Africa, and as an organizer for Cesar Chavez in the grape fields before practicing law in California.

The official version held that Bingham had hidden a gun for Jackson in his briefcase or tape recorder (which was actually loaned him on the spot by another visitor with Panther connections). Yet a veteran guard testified he had inspected the briefcase and tape recorder. The guards first stated they had put Jackson through a skin search when they noticed a gun in his hair; in court they said he was fully clothed when searched.

Garry's theory in court was that the police had plotted to kill Jackson and had smuggled a .38-caliber revolver into San Quentin in a paper bag. Louis Tackwood, probably a double agent then working for the Los Angeles police, concluded that the police wanted to "destroy the Panthers."

At the trial, Tackwood became Garry's witness. He testified that the smuggled police revolver was intentionally inoperable, and that the guards planned to have it passed to Jackson and then kill him on August 23. Instead, Jackson was killed on the wrong date two days ahead. John Spain was eventually found guilty of the murder of the guards, but Jackson's death remains a riddle despite Garry's insistence that the police-conspiracy theory has "not been challenged seriously."[11]

The black and minority prisoner had become the symbol for the Left of racist oppression in America. The uprising and carnage at Attica prison in upstate New York on September 9, 1971, was therefore interpreted by many radicals as a calculated political act to stop the growth of revolutionary organization in the prisons.

In rebellion against their treatment, the Attica prisoners had seized the jail and taken 40 hostages as security. "Man, we ain't shit in here, white or black, don't make no fuckin' difference," a white inmate from the South told Tom Wicker of the New York *Times,* an observer on the scene. "We gone stick together, we gone get what we want, or we gone die together."

On the morning of September 13, state troopers and corrections officers moved in to retake the prison. Twenty-nine inmates were killed as well as 10 hostages (all by official bullets, not by prisoners' knives or weapons, as government sources first reported.) No real consideration had been given to retaking the jail blocks with tear gas or other nonlethal weapons. Three years afterward, during hearings on his confirmation to be Vice-President of the United States, Nelson Rockefeller, governor of New York during the uprising, finally admitted "that if this would happen again I would think that . . . the proper way to proceed" would be "to go ahead . . . without weapons."[12]

The violence at Attica reflected a rage with deep historical roots. The Panthers had claimed from the start that most black inmates were essentially "political prisoners," that the "sanctioned" violence of the state—in particular, relentless oppression by white police forces—channeled the rage and frustration of the ghettos into crime. The Panthers wanted only black police in the ghettos, and trials by black juries. The logic of the Panther position lay in statistics—the inordinately high percentage of blacks filling the jails.

In effect, the violence at Attica, whether by guards against inmates or inmates against guards, or by Rockefeller himself, was rooted in the past. Rockefeller's decision to attack with guns might well have been different had the majority of the inmates been white. His reaction conformed to established patterns. We had condoned the forceful and bloody expulsion of the Indian and Spanish-speaking Americans from their land because the building of the white man's empire took precedence. We had developed the stereotype of the "savage Indian" in order to sanctify a far greater savagery, and the public, in large part, came to accept the thesis that the only good Indian was a dead one.

Above all, southern whites (with the complicity of most northerners until the abolition movement) had incorporated violence into their state laws both before and after the Civil War in order to keep black labor tied helplessly to the exploitation of the economic system. Violence by those in power served the system as a means of extracting economic surplus at the most favorable terms. Slavery was simply more blatant than contemporary techniques. Police violence in the ghettos in recent years provided a subtler version of maintaining the system. Now, economic surplus depended on exorbitant rents and overpriced merchandise, mainly for the benefit of absentee landlords and storeowners.

The violence of the past was destined to be re-created by its victims. The young Mexican-Americans in East Los Angeles (known as Chicanos) organized themselves on the Panther model, wearing brown berets instead of black. Seven Chicano youths were roughed up by police in 1969 during a burglary investigation in San Francisco, and a plainclothes policeman was killed in the struggle. La Confederación de la Raza Unida, a coalition of 70 Chicano groups, defended their case, and all seven were acquitted. When Los Angeles police broke up a La Raza rally against the Vietnam war in 1970, one Chicano was killed and hundreds injured. Twenty percent of the casualties in Vietnam were Chicano, contrasted with 7 percent for the population as a whole. Chicanos saw this as one more form of oppression. Thus their links to the black ghettos were intensified, and they were drawn into the defense committee during Angela Davis's trial.

The violence of the past against Spanish-speaking people sought its retribution in New Mexico through Reies Lopez Tijerina, son of a poor sharecropper, and his "Alianza" movement. The Alianza, with about 14,000 members, wanted to recover millions of acres from private and federal ownership that they claimed had been deeded their ancestors through Spanish and Mexican land grants. Much of it was communal property, awarded these settlers by Mexico in 1806. The Alianza said it had been taken away in the decades after the Mexican War in 1848 despite the treaty of Guadalupe Hidalgo, which ostensibly guarded existing holdings.

When the Alianza failed to recover their lands in court, 20 members, armed with rifles and pistols, descended on the county courthouse at Tierra Amarilla in June 1967 to make a citizens' arrest of District Attorney Alfonso Sanchez. After an exchange of gunfire in which two lawmen were injured, the Alianza fled to the mountains, taking two hostages. The D.A. called the Alianza movement "communism." The Albuquerque *Tribune* concluded: "There is just one word for the outbreak of violence at Tierra Amarillo yesterday—revolution."

Pursued by National Guard tanks and helicopters, Tijerina and his men were finally arrested. The judge interpreted broadly their use of the citizens' arrest provision, and they were acquitted. In 1969, Tijerina led another raid on federal property claimed by the Alianza and was convicted of assaulting two forest rangers. This time Tijerina went to jail.

"The land is our mother," said Elizabeth Martinez, descendant of Jose Martinez family groups which had an 1832 grant. "It cannot be bought or sold. Without it, we perish."[13]

The Chicano movement contained small but vigorous Marxist-Leninist elements from the Socialist Workers party and from a group known as the Center for Autonomous Social Action (CASA), with roots in the Communist party. But the largest socialist following came from Raza Unida. Tijerina had cut most of his ties to it by 1972. Cesar Chavez, who had organized the Chicano lettuce pickers in California, drifted from Raza Unida toward the Democratic party and eventually merged his union into the AFL-CIO. The leadership of Raza Unida, therefore swayed back and forth between Jose Angel Gutierrez, who grafted his vehement nationalism onto a Marxist framework, and "Corky" Gonzales, a pragmatic liberal. By 1977, Gonzales had won out.

Thus, the Chicano movement went from nationalism in the 1960s to a multiplicity of socialisms in the 1970s and ended up in pragmatism.

The socialist development of another oppressed minority, the Puerto Ricans, was essentially concentrated on one objective in the 1970s—independence for Puerto Rico. The movement drew on older radicals from the American Labor party of the 1940s and recent converts like the Young Lords. Its base was the Puerto Rican Socialist party, which considered United States policy on the island a prime example of colonialism. Both Democratic and Republican administrations had offered mainland industry heavy tax rebates and cheap labor for settling on the island and had raised the specter that an independent Puerto Rico would be a captive of Cuba or Moscow.

These fears were accentuated by linking the Socialists to a rash of bombings, presumably by the Armed Forces of National Liberation of Puerto Rico (FALN)—at least 65 bombings were attributed to it between 1974 and 1978, including one explosion at a Manhattan restaurant in 1975 that killed four people. Actually, the FBI had never really penetrated FALN. It claimed to have identified one member, who worked for the Hispanic Affairs department of the Episcopal Church and whose Chicago apartment contained a supply of dynamite and arms. But while the FALN took credit for most of the bombings, there was no proof of FALN's connection to the Socialists.

Socialist politics were further confused by the split between those voters in Puerto Rico who wanted to keep the present commonwealth status, and those who wanted the island to become the fifty-first state. At the 1976 elections, the Socialists and other radicals polled only about 6 percent of the vote—the sentiment for independence at best running 10 percent. The reliance of Socialist politics on the independence movement, therefore, limited its growth as long as the Socialist party seemed to represent Castro's Cuba.[14]

The first protests of American Indians in the 1970s concentrated on specific rights. There was virtually no Marxist influence in the rigid, traditional tribal structures of the Indian reservations. But a growing militancy, centered around the American Indian Movement (AIM) and stirred by 150 years of oppression, moved many of the poorer Indians to the Left.

The original plans for an Indian march on Washington in November 1972 were entirely peaceful. But when the government broke its promise to provide adequate meeting halls and housed the delegations in rat-infested quarters, militants occupied the Bureau of Indian Affairs, taking 11 hostages. The Nixon administration turned down all 20 points in their demands. The Indians then burned a courthouse in Custer, South Dakota, and kidnapped the mayor of Gallup, New Mexico. The climactic confrontation in 1973 was the 71-day seige of Wounded Knee, South Dakota—an armed takeover that resulted in the prosecution of Russell C. Means, Dennis J. Banks, and other AIM leaders. Pedro Bissonette of AIM, sought on a fugitive warrant charge, was shot and killed by police a few months later.

At the same reservation in 1975, there was more bloodshed as tensions mounted between AIM, representing the poorest, full-blooded Indians, and the tribal puppet governments they called "Uncle Tomahawks." After the FBI claimed that four Indians had kidnapped two whites, releasing them a few hours later, the FBI arrested one of the presumed kidnappers. Indians then opened fire on an FBI car. In the shootout, two FBI agents and one Indian were killed.

The demands of 850,000 Indians varied greatly among reservations isolated by geography and cultural differences, and among radical and conservative factions. Increasingly their protests became more sophisticated, involving a coal company's attempt to strip mine Indian property, and the government's attempt to divert the Truckee

River in Nevada, which would dry up an Indian lake and diminish tribal income. Radical white lawyers like William Kunstler took on AIM's cases, and the Indian movement became a prominent cause for the white Left.

The most direct confrontations were legal suits to reclaim some of the millions of acres of land ostensibly taken from the tribes by broken treaties and subterfuge. In Rhode Island, the Narragansett tribe sued for 3,200 acres; other tribes in Maine sued for 12.5 million acres (a claim that Congress will probably settle for $37 million.) The Mashpee Indians on Cape Cod, Massachusetts, went to court for 11,000 acres, valued at $30 million, now in the hands of realtors and a large development corporation. But an all-white federal jury turned them down, agreeing with the defendants' claim that the Mashpees lacked the autonomy and sovereignty to be a tribe.[15]

It might be postulated from America's record of sanctioned violence that the violence of white men is often good; that our attitudes toward it are generally shaped by those in power; and that when violence becomes part of the natural order, such as the westward expanding empire that swallowed up the lands of the Indians and Spanish-speaking peoples, it is no longer even seen as violence. On the other hand, the violence of blacks and other minorities has always been considered criminal.

The violence of the New Left became a terrible shock for most Americans. It originated with whites, and even worse, whites mainly from the middle class. It was, moreover, the most lengthy and widespread violence the country had ever known—previous outbursts such as the New York draft riots of 1863 or John Brown's raids were local or involved few participants.

Violence, after all, has always played a role in social and political change—even in the origins of the American Revolution. More recently, the creation of the states of Eire and Israel must be attributed in part to the use of violence. Thus, violence has proved to be constructive as well as destructive. The problem with New Left violence, specifically that of the Weathermen and other bombing groups, was its pointless strategy, the failure to link it to a meaningful program.

By failing to take the leadership of the antiwar movement, the New Left isolated itself from the mainstream. This isolation became acute with the presidential campaigns of Eugene McCarthy and Robert Kennedy in 1968, which attracted a liberal, and often radical, constituency against Vietnam that should have been sought by the Left. The fury on almost every campus against Cambodia in 1970 was the last chance to unify a broadly based movement.

Isolated, and desperate to find one, true revolutionary mechanism, the New Left fell back on a politics of despair. Its simplistic Marxism offered martyrdom rather than coherent strategy. By 1970, Weather was cut off not only from the mainstream but from its campus base. Its concept of itself as a guerrilla Fifth Column to sabotage the American imperialist machine at home turned it into a terrorist splinter group divorced from reality.

If violence is to be used constructively in effecting social and political change, it must rise from two essential sources. It must have moral justification and what might be called "historical necessity." Admittedly, necessity is a difficult standard. It assumes that the direction and flow of social progress can be interpreted correctly. It also assumes that this interpretation has been accepted by a movement of sufficient size and commitment to give it a chance of success.

Violence may overturn social structures, and even governments, but it cannot replace them unless it is rooted in mass support. Hannah Arendt concludes, "Out of a barrel of a gun grows violence, and immediate obedience, which then immediately ceases when the gun is removed. This is not power."[16]

We have, then, seen the development of two historical traditions: constructive violence and sheer terrorism. The terrorist group—whether Symbionese Liberation Army in California or Baader-Meinhof group in West Germany—exists in a vacuum of purposeless bloodshed. It may clutch at moral justification—the SLA squeezed $2 million out of Patricia Hearst's father for food for the poor, which was hardly the beginning of an ideology. Ulrike Meinhof's funeral may have drawn a few thousand people to the cemetery, mainly curiosity seekers. But neither Baader-Meinhof, nor the Red Brigades in Italy, have yet proved to have enough of a following on the Left to give them a place in the developing process of revolt.

By contrast, the abolitionists before the Civil War employed constructive violence. When they used it to block the return of fugitive slaves to the South, their justification was the total moral evil of slavery. Even though they were breaking the law of man, they appealed to a "higher law" of God. Their moral fervor was bolstered by the inexorable movement in other countries against slavery, which supported their claim to historical necessity.

Obviously, the legitimization of violence depends on who eventually sets the standards. Like the abolitionists, the founders of Israel combined enough moral justification and historical necessity to convert outcast terrorists into national heroes almost overnight. The Jewish settlers, struggling to oust the British from their World War I mandate over Palestine, had behind them two thousand years of religious yearnings to reclaim their homeland, the political justification of Britain's Balfour Declaration, and the overwhelming urgency of a sanctuary for survivors of the Nazi holocaust.

These premises for the founding of Israel were bolstered by international reality. Both the United States and Soviet Union wanted a state of Israel for their own complex motives.

Guerrilla warfare undoubtedly contributed to Israel's achievement of statehood, or speeded up a process that would have been stalled by the British government for years. Violence in Israel, in addition, has been legitimized by history. One final proof, and final irony, is that Menachem Begin, leader of an early anti-British guerrilla organization, became prime minister of Israel three decades later, and sits at conferences with British officials who had once hunted him as a criminal.[17]

The Weathermen failed to achieve any legitimacy in 1970 because their program represented only symbolic self-indulgence. Like the Narodniki youth of pre-1900 Russia, Weather created violence accomplishing nothing but giving a brief, existential "meaning" to their lives. Like the shooting of steel magnate Henry Clay Frick by the anarchist Alexander Berkman, Weather violence had no possibility of changing the system.

The Weathermen's purpose was to "bring the war home." Yet a few hundred guerrillas rampaging through Chicago in the Days of Rage and breaking a few Rolls Royce windows neither affected the war nor gave anyone added insight into the meaning of capitalist oppression. The Weathermen claimed credit for exploding a pipe bomb at the entrance of the Bank of America in New York's financial district. Yet the bombing of banks, corporate headquarters, courthouses, or Judge Murtagh's home, had no direct relationship to the war, as far as most people were concerned, and had equally small impact on the government's prosecution of the war.

The absurdity of the Weather program was that it was no longer concerned with the oppression of its immediate constituency, mainly the campuses, but sought to become a surrogate for blacks and Third World revolutionaries, who neither requested nor wanted its help. In effect, the violent arm of the New Left had gone askew.

·21·

The American Left Today

What had it all come to by the 1970s, these violent years of the American Left? The dreams of cataclysmic revolution had faded. There were still bombings, of course; 160 were recorded in 1974. But the Left had generally agreed that decisive change—even change along socialist lines—would have to come in other ways. Huey Newton of the Black Panthers stated bluntly: "It is not impossible for a form of socialism to be voted in peacefully in the United States at a later time."

The Left groped its way toward change, searching for systems of mass participation on a local level. The previous decade, climaxed by the disintegration of SDS, had led most radicals to conclude that the Leninist concept of one, dominant vanguard party was no longer a useful American form. The Left would now seek power through local coalitions. In Berkeley in 1971, the "April coalition," a mix of the New Left, Panthers, and peace movement, elected two radical black men and a radical white woman to the city council, as well as the city's first black mayor. Although the coalition failed to pass an amendment for community control of the police, it gave Berkeley the first semiradical administration in any city in recent years.[1]

Local coalitions sometimes had hidden socialist objectives. Tom Hayden, formerly of SDS, called his platform a "Campaign for Economic Democracy" and amassed 1 million votes (40 percent of the total cast) for the Democratic nomination for the United States Senate in California in 1976. Ken Cockrel, on the other hand, a black with an avowedly Marxist platform, was the only candidate without Democratic and Auto Workers union backing elected to the Detroit city council in 1977.

The first hardline advocate of Gay Rights, and an equally hardline feminist (who happened to be an unwed mother), were elected to the ruling body of San Francisco, the Board of Supervisors, in 1977.

Harvey Milk walked to City Hall with a parade of supporters and announced, "I want to introduce my lover." Carol Silver brought her male housemate and children. Milk and Silver headed a coalition of radicals, feminists, homosexuals, and ethnic minorities that defeated the traditional power centers of business and finance.[2]*

The trend toward coalition had started in late April and early May 1971, when hundreds of thousands of demonstrators against the Vietnam war poured into the streets of Washington, D.C., and other cities. Attorney General Mitchell ordered the police and National Guard in Washington to arrest them at random. Thirteen thousand were jammed into prisons and open-air pens with virtually no legal charges against them. The revulsion against Vietnam, it turned out, had fused the remnants of the Left with liberal Democrats and peace groups in an effective stand against the war.

The immediate result of this fusion was the presidential candidacy of United States Senator George McGovern of South Dakota. He was essentially a creation of the anti-Vietnam movement, offering the hope that left-liberal demands could be achieved within the Democratic platform. His campaign pushed the party leftward, as the makeup of the national convention indicated. Thirty-six percent of the delegates were women; 15 percent were black. Issues were debated at the convention—women's rights, abortion rights, for example—that had never been raised before. Yet McGovern proved a weak candidate, vacillating on his pledge to pull out of Vietnam, stymying the abortion plank, and watering down his tax plan to woo corporation support. McGovern's attempt to move Left, often with rash programs, at the same time as he appealed to party moderates, lost him votes from both liberals and conservative labor and produced an apathy evident at the polls. Only 55 percent of the eligible electorate bothered to vote.

Nixon's depressing pretenses at ending the Vietnam war contributed to this apathy. He was selling the voters "Vietnamization" —the policy of making the South Vietnam government so strong militarily and economically that it could survive on its own. He shrewdly cut American troops in Vietnam to 158,000 by December 1971. At the same time, Nixon's brutal Christmas bombing of North Vietnam—2,000 air strikes in 11 days—aimed at hammering Hanoi into acceptance of his peace terms.

This hard line against Communism overseas and rebellious stu-

---

*Milk and Mayor George Moscone were shot to death on November 27, 1978, by a recently resigned member of the Board of Supervisors.

dents and blacks at home helped produce Nixon's impressive plurality of 60.7 percent of the vote in the 1972 elections, compared with 37.5 percent for McGovern, and 1.8 percent for splinter parties. Actually McGovern's share of the total vote was only slightly less than Humphrey's in 1968. The difference was that Nixon had picked up the extreme right-wing votes of Governor George Wallace, who had been forced to drop out of the race when critically wounded in an attempted assassination.[3]

The Watergate revelations at that point were too skimpy to affect the elections. The "Pentagon Papers," a secret collection of Vietnam documents, were "leaked" to the press, presumably by Daniel Ellsberg, in June 1971. But the New Left received no credit for these events, although they stemmed from its perceptions and teachings for almost a decade.

Both the Pentagon Papers and Watergate dealt with one central theme—the excesses of presidential power, particularly as they affected America's imperialist strategy. Radicals had warned about intervention in Greece, Guatemala, the Bay of Pigs, Chile—warnings that had started with Henry Wallace and the Progressive party in 1948. The New Left had interpreted the American attempt to dominate Southeast Asia as the final catastrophe in a policy of cold war exploitation—President Johnson's manipulations in drafting the Tonkin Gulf resolution months before the alleged event took place were now exposed in the Pentagon Papers. Watergate, on the surface, showed Nixon ruthlessly determined to crush all opposition, all dissent, even by illegal means. But the scandal went deeper into the illness of the country as the New Left analyzed it.

Watergate revealed the accumulation of power approaching dictatorial dimensions. It showed corporate ambitions and Nixon's hunger to dominate history teamed together: Lockheed Aircraft bribing its way into foreign markets, ITT maneuvering with the CIA to overthrow the democratically elected socialist government of Chile. Nixon needed corporate riches for his campaign chest. The Associated Milk Producers gave him $187,000 to influence the price levels of milk; ITT gave $400,000 to grease the way for an insurance company merger; the president of Phillips Petroleum said he "personally" gave Nixon $50,000. Millions of dollars were "laundered" secretly into his campaigns. When it all came out at the congressional hearings, the result was Nixon's resignation, the imprisonment of Attorney General Mitchell and many of their associates, and, in sum, one of our greatest internal crises since the Civil War.[4]

Despite the Left's contributions to Watergate, there was no radical organization strong enough on the campuses to call for a nationwide strike that might have brought down Nixon sooner. As a result, the liberal establishment finally drove Nixon from office, joined by Republican moderates who saw the Constitution endangered.

The process of investigation and impeachment—the process that really made the American people understand Watergate—was led by a combination of liberal newspapers like the Washington *Post* and strict constitutionalists in Congress like U.S. Senator Sam Ervin of North Carolina. What remained of the Left was so cut off from reality as to make it almost an anachronism.

In its customarily flamboyant style, the Weather underground announced in 1974: "Our intention is to disrupt the empire." To this end, it claimed 25 guerrilla bombings over the past five years. (The FBI shortly afterward credited them with 19 bombings.) Weather had managed to plant its bombs at such sensitive targets as the Pentagon computer room, the Senate wing of the Capitol building, and the State Department building in Washington. But despite this impressive list, the so-called disruption of an empire accomplished little more than inconveniencing a few officials for a few hours.

The purpose of bombing groups like Weather was to attack institutions of such importance that the stability of the state would be damaged, bringing popular insurrections and a "revolutionary situation." This rationale, of course, overemphasized the vulnerability of the modern state and failed to grasp its extensive powers for repression. The rationale also ignored the fact that bombing could alienate the Left's own constituency. In reality, Weather largely paralyzed the Left and hindered the emergence of new movements.

Weather bombings, and other bombing groups' actions at this time, were purely symbolic—the bombings of San Francisco's Sheraton-Palace hotel by the Red Guerrilla Family in October 1974, for example.[5] Yet the rate of bombings continued to be high—the George Jackson Brigade set off 11 explosions in Oregon and Washington state before its last known members were convicted in 1978; the New World Liberation Front boasted of an average of two bombings a month around San Francisco in 1974 and 1975.

Although some analysts claimed symbolic bombing was essential to hold remnants of the movement together, the Weather underground and similar groups were displaced persons, cut off from tumultuous changes in the country: the dethronement of a President, the defeat of American forces by a tiny Southeast Asian nation—in effect, the death of the Communist-containment policy. Since the Left had no organized structure large enough to influence these events, a few radicals sought to express themselves and live out their fantasies through violence.

The Symbionese Liberation Army (SLA) had been founded by an escaped black prisoner, who called himself General Field Marshal Cinque. His recruits, however, were almost all from white, middle-class, even conservative families. Although a few came from the Maoist-oriented Venceremos Brigade, SLA itself had no ties to any political organizing in California, in fact, no coherent politics except the metaphysical slogans that Cinque fed them.

SLA would have been quickly forgotten except for two startling events: its cold-blooded murder of Marcus A. Foster, a black super-intendent of schools in Oakland, California, on November 6, 1973, and its kidnapping of Patricia Hearst, the 19-year-old daughter of Randolph Hearst, the multimillionaire newspaper publisher, on February 4, 1974. The gunning down of Foster as he entered his car set SLA apart from Weather and other bomb groups, which had scrupulously avoided injuring anyone, the Wisconsin accident notwithstanding.

The kidnapping of Patty Hearst would make her part of American mythology. She was remolded into "Tania," the revolutionary desperado and pleader for the SLA cause; she participated in a bank robbery, photographed, without any attempt at disguise, carrying an automatic rifle.

Patty Hearst missed being trapped by the police at a Los Angeles hideout when Cinque and five others were killed in the ensuing gunfight or burned to death in the ruins of the building in May 1974. She escaped capture until September 1975. Then she challenged the mental agility of a world-wide audience, which tried to keep up with the twists and turns of her confessions, culminating in her eventual insistence that the SLA had tortured and brainwashed her into compliance. She was convicted and given a 35-year-sentence but later released after 22 months in jail.[6]

The "Wilmington Ten" were among those falsely charged with violence in the 1970s as a result of other reckless bombings in this period. They were, in fact, considered "prisoners of conscience" by Amnesty International, recipient of the 1977 Nobel Peace Prize. A black community group was trying to integrate the local schools of

Wilmington, North Carolina, in 1971. There were constant clashes between blacks and whites. A grocery store was bombed on February 6. A black divinity student, Ben Chavis of the United Church of Christ's Commission for Racial Justice, and eight other blacks and one white, were indicted, convicted, and sentenced to jail for a total of 282 years for arson and conspiring to shoot at the police. Yet the evidence was slim. Two witnesses, for example, placed Chavis and four other defendants far from the scene of the bombing. Three witnesses for the prosecution admitted lying. The key witness, an unstable 18-year-old, recanted his testimony, then recanted the recantation.

The case became particularly embarrassing to President Jimmy Carter when he started his campaign for human rights, aimed primarily at Soviet bloc countries, only to be confronted with the same problem at home. The resulting pressure forced parole and reduced sentences for nine of the ten. But by 1978, Chavis was still in jail, and the Justice Department filed a court brief supporting the defense contention of a denial of due process and fair trial.[7]

The Marxist-Leninist parties failed to develop new forms of organizing applicable to the 1970s. The Communist party, with a membership of only 10,000 or less, seemed no more than a sectarian group, advocating reformist legislation. It had abandoned violence—it would only be a last resort in the future if social change could not be secured in other ways, the leadership announced in 1973. It ran its own candidates in some elections and backed mainstream liberals in others, either openly or behind the scenes. It had only one stellar attraction, Angela Davis, who was mainly responsible for new recruits on the campuses, where the party made more inroads than it had in 20 years.

Its main burden, as always, was its unwavering fealty to the Soviet Union. Although the vast majority of those Americans who considered themselves socialists now repudiated the Moscow brand of Communist bureaucracy and totalitarian oppression of human rights, the CP's rigidity had long extended to "Eurocommunism." When Santiago Carrillo, chairman of the Spanish Communist party and a prominent advocate of Eurocommunism, came to lecture at Yale University in November 1977, the CP's *Daily World* assailed him as "revisionist" and "anti-Soviet."

All the Marxist-Leninist parties together had no more than 25,000 members now. The Socialist Workers (Trotskyists), with about 2,000 members, followed a policy of coalition with mass movements, at-tempting to control them through front groups. They were promi-nent in the Washington and San Francisco demonstrations of 1971. Their youth cadres, particularly the women, organized around femi-nist issues. But their most productive action was their lawsuit against the FBI's program of disruption. The party forced the FBI to open hundreds of pages of its files and thus made the public aware of the government's illegal searches and harassment in the 1960s.[8]

The Marxist-Leninist parties split into an increasing number of factions, each vulnerable to the shifts in the international Communist lineup. The Progressive Labor party, fervent Maoists between 1961 and 1971, denounced the Chinese leadership after the Nixon détente for selling out to capitalism and soon faded into obscurity. The October League, also devout Maoists, had some success organizing black workers at the General Motors plant in Fremont, California, in 1973. The Revolutionary Communist Party, an offshoot of San Francisco's Revolutionary Union, organized effectively at the Farah garment strike in Texas from 1972 to 1974. But by 1978, this splinter party claimed that the present Chinese government was the product of an anti-Maoist, right-wing coup selling out Chairman Mao's revo-lutionary line.[9]

All domestic Marxist-Leninist parties clung to the orthodox con-cept of a vanguard party, each insisting it had to have dominant hegemony over the Left, each insisting it held the only true and effective line. Such inflexibility was clearly meaningless in the 1970s. The time of the vanguard party had passed. The movement toward socialism would have to be organized independently, and national organizations would have to interlock with local groups as a sustain-ing, not dominating force.

This was the basis for two new national groups. The first was the Democratic Socialist Organizing Committee (DSOC), headed by Michael Harrington. Founded in 1973, DSOC consisted mainly of socialists working primarily within the Democratic party, seeking to propogandize for socialism and to move the party leftward. It also sought an opening to remnants of the New Left, with Harrington admitting his error in breaking with young radicals in the early 1960s. DSOC wanted a "nondoctrinaire" movement with room for diversity on issues that previously divided socialists. Thus, it sup-ported the Socialist-Communist joint ticket at the 1978 French elec-tions, opposed intervention in Angola, and backed independence for Puerto Rico.

DSOC claimed almost 3,000 members. Many of its leaders were

once vehement anti-Communists and advocates of the cold war who had turned against the Vietnam War and America's containment policy. For Harrington, the issue of Communism was "not central anymore"—he backed the strategy of Eurocommunism, particularly in the Italian party.

While DSOC often seemed more left-Democratic than "left social-ist," it aimed for mass organizing around specific issues. In 1977, it brought together 1,200 delegates for three days on the unemploy-ment crisis. They included not only the classic elements of earlier coalitions—labor, liberals, and blacks—but delegates from the Na-tional Organization for Women and radicals of the 1960s.

A second important organization was the New America Move-ment. Its membership was about 1,000, with its strongest chapters in Los Angeles, Chicago, Detroit, and Boston. Most members had belonged to the Old and New Left. But they had broken with the concept of a vanguard party, insisting now on "totally democratic socialism." They were critical of the Left's past errors—identifica-tion with the Third World struggle, an impatient hunger for quick, oversimplified social change.

NAM's chapters worked mainly with community coalitions like Massachusetts "Fair Share," which wanted to reduce taxes for small homeowners and close tax loopholes for industry. The Midwest Academy in Chicago trained local organizers for these campaigns. Its Detroit chapter helped in the election of Ken Cockrel to the city council. Yet NAM never established close links with the women's movement or the black movement. Its theories were often hard to differentiate from those of DSOC.[10]

The search for new coalitions seized on the nation's two-hun-dredth birthday in 1976, with Left parties, black militants, Puerto Rican nationalists, feminists, and homosexuals rallying 30,000 peo-ple in Philadelphia to protest the failures of the Bicentennial dream. The Puerto Rican Socialist party, demanding Puerto Rican indepen-dence from the United States, made its theme "a Bicentennial with-out colonies."

With the decline of the vanguard party, new structures had to be developed. The commune—many coming out of the New Left—proved both innovative and durable. The Translove commune near the University of Michigan campus at Ann Arbor, founded by White Panther members, saw only two reasons for working—"either because it's interesting or because it's essential." The COPS commune, founded by Berkeley radicals, ran a bakery operated three days a week for their own members and the Panthers and loaned out to other communes the rest of the week.

By contrast, the Renaissance Church of Beauty commune at Turners Falls, Massachusetts, followed conservative economics and ran businesses, including a health food restaurant, pizza house, grocery store, and transport company, that brought in more than $1 million a year.

At best, the commune could develop a new dimension in personal liberation that the radicals of the 1960s saw as an essential step toward economic liberation. The counterculture of the previous decade, and the development of at least 2,000 rural communes and perhaps 3,000 urban communes by 1970, expressed "the need of the young for unrestricted joy," as Theodore Roszak put it.

The communes also served as the core of a new class. Workers making their living from such items as leather goods and jewelry, cut themselves off from the factory system. They were generally producing for subsistence, not for profit. And if there were profits, they were put back into the commune—the Renaissance Church was building a model village for its members on an 80-acre plot.[11]

His pleasure in his work put the commune worker in sharp contrast with the assembly-line worker, whose increasing distaste for his job in the 1970s stemmed not just from his wages but from the dreary monotony of performing the same, unvaried task day after day, unable to see his minute function as part of the finished product. Such monotony became a factor in the rising number of workers seeking early retirement. It occasionally caused open rebellion —the General Motors strike in 1972 at Lordstown, Ohio, for example, was led by young workers demanding more control over dehumanizing work assignments, standards of production, and decision making. In Sweden and elsewhere in Europe, some manufacturers had already experimented with rotating workers from one function to another and even with changing the assembly-line system so that a few individuals could work on a product from start to finish.

The commune also began to develop as a political base. On Washington's birthday 1974, Samuel H. Lovejoy severed the supporting cables of a 500-foot tower at Montague, Massachusetts, and toppled this structure around which Northeast Utilities was erecting a $1.3 billion nuclear-power plant. Lovejoy, who immediately turned himself over to the police, was a 27-year-old organic farmer at a commune a few miles away.

Lovejoy's "raid" represented a new phenomenon—the commune as an increasing source of political organizing and protest. Communes along the eastern seaboard have been integral to the mounting antinuclear campaign, particularly the "Clamshell Alliance," which has fought against the proposed nuclear plant at Seabrook, New Hampshire. Clamshell staged a sit-down of 2,000 demonstrators at the nuclear site on April 30, 1977, establishing a tent city and refusing to be budged by the police. Many were arrested, but demonstrators continued to picket the site. In June 1978, the Nuclear Regulatory Commission suspended the construction license of the plant pending an Environmental Protection Agency report.

The antinuclear campaign has become crucial for people of all classes who see their homes and safety endangered by the possibility of nuclear fallout, the lack of safeguards against emergency failures, and the hazards of waste disposal. It has proved the most effective issue around which to organize popular support—antinuclear alliances springing up in Colorado, New York, Washington, and many states. "People feel trapped by technology and they have had no way of expressing resistance to it until now," the West German leader of the antinuclear campaign explained after his supporters battled 4,000 police at the Frohnde nuclear site.

The commune has asserted itself in ecology politics. Ecology gives the Left the chance of "attacking the 'living space' of capitalism," as Herbert Marcuse put it. It allows an attack on corporate greed and exploitation that damages individual lives—the dumping of chemical waste near Niagara Falls, New York, by Hooker Chemical Co., for example, which turned out to be so dangerous for pregnant women and newborn infants that they had to be evacuated.[12]

Finally, the commune represents a rural form of "liberated territory," a concept developed further by the Left through radicalized city governments in Berkeley; Austin, Texas; and Madison, Wisconsin, a city of 175,000 strongly influenced by the university community. Paul R. Soglin, who helped organize the Dow Chemical demonstrations in the late 1960s, had the backing of the Left in his election as mayor of Madison in 1973 and his re-elections in 1975 and 1977, although his programs turned out more liberal than radical.

Berkeley, Austin, and Madison guarantee radicals a territory in which they can pursue their own "life-style." They also provide a training ground for community organizing projects, for struggles in which class-consciousness is strengthened and self-confidence tested. Berkeley radicals lost one of their three city council seats at the 1977 elections but won four out of five vacant council seats in an upset in 1979. The liberal-radical coalition in Austin, which had taken control of the city government from the real-estate and "big-growth" interests, was eventually defeated and had to start its struggle anew. Yet the liberated territory has proved of particular value to oppressed groups—in San Francisco, for example, it enabled the gay rights movement to develop a political base in a few years.[13]

The homosexual was always isolated in the 1960s, even among radicals. Allen Young, an analyst of the homosexual role in SDS from 1967 to 1969, felt "totally alone as a homosexual" at its meetings. He concluded: "The traditional Left, both Old Left and New Left, has been as oppressive to homosexuals as has been establishment America."

While lesbian militancy emerged from, and, despite temporary harassment, was finally integrated into the feminist movement, male homosexuals had to carve out their liberated territories by violent clashes. The decisive step was the police raid of June 27, 1969, on the Stonewall Inn, the most popular gay bar in New York's Greenwich Village. The police had long made a policy of harassing and arresting homosexuals, who accepted their beatings and jailings stoically. At Stonewall, however, they fought back for the first time, holding the raiding force inside the bar for 45 minutes while reinforcements outside tried to batter down hastily erected barricades. After a rally in Washington Square a month later, with signs proclaiming "Homosexual Revolution," the first militants organized themselves into the Gay Liberation Front (GLF).

Gay rights was the first target, but many members considered themselves political radicals as well. GLF delegations in San Francisco and other cities marched in the New Mobe demonstrations on November 15, 1969, carrying "Homosexuals against War" banners, and chanting, "Say it clear, Say it loud, We're gay and we're proud." Another police raid in New York in March 1970 produced important political support for the movement. Congressman (later Mayor) Ed Koch wrote the Police Commissioner that "it is not a violation of the law to be either homosexual or heterosexual, and the law should never be used to harass either."

Militants invaded the convention of the American Psychiatric Association in San Francisco in May 1970, grabbing the microphones to announce, "We're fed up being told we're sick" and denouncing many doctors as "the pigs who make it possible for the cops to beat homosexuals." Gay Pride Week started on June 22, with 10,000 people marching in New York from Greenwich Village to Central Park. Similar parades were held the next year in Los Angeles and other cities. The motto "Out of the Closets and into the Streets" emphasized the radical nature of the movement. GLF's first national conference in San Francisco in August 1970 showed the extent of grass-roots support.

Still, the gay movement developed parallel tensions to the women's movement. "Perhaps we are all working towards a socialist society," Sandy Bixton observed. "But it seems that as long as gay liberation is a male-dominated movement, we will not be able to win the battle of sexism." As a result, women formed their own organization within Gay Activists Alliance, which was organized in December 1969. Similarily, GLF women broke off to form the Radical Lesbians the following spring.[14]

In the last decade, Gay Liberation has considerably altered the way an estimated 13 million male and 9 million female homosexuals live. In New York and other homosexual centers, police oppression has diminished. The homosexual's access to jobs, to apartments, and even to suburban housing has been bolstered both by law and social acceptance. Above all, many homosexuals have proudly proclaimed their identity.

No city better exemplifies the importance of a liberated territory than San Francisco, where gays constitute 100,000 to 200,000 out of a total population of 750,000. This voting bloc was crucial in the election of a radically oriented board of supervisors in 1977. One reporter counted more than 30 gay organizations locally, even Gay Asians and Gay American Indians. Richard Hongisto, a former county sheriff, actively recruited gay personnel for his staff. The police cemented their relationship by playing an annual softball game against a leading gay team. While ordinances guaranteeing equal rights to homosexuals in jobs, housing, and other areas have been defeated by referendum in Dade County, Florida, and elsewhere in recent years, the liberated-territory concept has proved strong in San Francisco, New York, Boston, and New Orleans, where the size of the gay electorate can make itself felt at the polls.

The Black Panthers had been trying to build a radical coalition in Oakland, California, since 1968, but their gains had been uneven.

They elected a member to the county school board and four members to the Berkeley community development council. Although Bobby Seale polled more than 35 percent of the vote in the runoff election for mayor of Oakland in 1973, the Panthers remained at the fringes of power. They would help elect an Alameda County supervisor and the first black mayor of Oakland in 1977, which was undoubtedly a factor in Governor Jerry Brown's appointment of blacks to important judicial posts and the new money he poured into Oakland for ghetto revitalization. Still, the Panther blueprint for community control, particularly of the police and the Port of Oakland commission, was not realized.

The Panthers, in fact, were plagued by internal problems. Seale had purportedly resigned—"I want to build a house, grow a garden . . ."—but he was probably purged. When Huey Newton returned from three years of exile in Cuba after jumping bail in 1974, Elaine Brown resigned as well. She had been co-leader of the party in his absence and had almost won a city council seat in 1977.

Newton claimed he had fled because he couldn't receive a fair trial in the alleged shooting of a young prostitute—a claim that gained some credence when the FBI admitted it had tapped his phone illegally. The case against Newton ended in a mistrial in March 1979, with the jury divided 10 to 2 for acquittal.[16]

If the Panthers' insistence that they could adopt socialist principles to their local conditions seemed shaky, the prospects for the black movement as a whole became equally uncertain. Blacks had reached high office, of course, in the South as well as North—as mayors of Atlanta and New Orleans, to cite two examples. "I grew up in a South that was an armed camp, ruled by force," recalled Frank Smith, a former SNCC organizer. "Today, my sister is No. 2 in her class at the only high school in Newman, Georgia. My father's income has gone from $4,000 to $9,000 in ten years."

Even in Mississippi, Governor Finch, billed as the "workingman's governor," invited blacks to his inaugural ball in 1976 and kissed the wives of black and white politicians with equal aplomb. At the Democratic national convention in 1976, Aaron Henry of the NAACP threw his arms around Ross Barnett, Jr., son of the former governor, a bitter segregationist.

Such progress, however, cloaked far deeper problems. "Its dreams are dead," the Reverend Robert Chapman, the Episcopal archdeacon of New York, said of Harlem in 1978. "Its people are despairing and worse off than they ever were, and all the high hopes of the 1960s are gone." A quarter of the population of Central Harlem lived on welfare. The infant mortality rate, a key health index, had jumped from 37 deaths to almost 43 per thousand in a few years before 1976.[17]

Not just in Harlem, but in every ghetto, the official rate of teen-age unemployment was 40 percent in 1978, but many experts placed it at 60 percent. Black unemployment as a whole had doubled in the previous decade, and tripled for teen-agers. Thirty-one percent of all blacks lived below the official poverty line in 1976; 45 percent lived in poverty areas. The richest one-fifth of southern families received more than 40 percent of the region's income in 1978, while the bottom fifth received only 5 percent, according to the Institute for Southern Studies. This gap had hardly changed in 25 years, despite the blacks' supposed gains—and it was virtually the same in the Northeast as in the South. The black underclass, in sum, remained in "a hopeless state of economic stagnation, falling further and further behind the rest of society," according to William J. Wilson, a University of Chicago sociologist. Supreme Court Justice Thurgood Marshall called "the position of the Negro today in America . . . a tragedy."

The real rewards from the struggles of the 1960s had gone to a limited group of educated, middle-class blacks. Thirty percent of all black families had incomes of $15,000 or more by 1976. These blacks at the top made up about 11 percent of total college enrollment; blacks at the bottom largely accounted for the 42 percent of black 17-year-olds who were functionally illiterate.[18]

But even with these middle-class gains, the median income of black families in the South was only 59 percent of that of white families in 1975 (62 percent in the country as a whole). While black women were achieving parity with whites at lower-paying jobs, they were still far behind at the top levels. Not one of 1,400 city jobs in Atlanta paying $13,000 and up was held by a black woman in 1975.

Despite their election to political offices, blacks rarely achieved power that gave them community control, particularly in the South. In Mississippi, blacks made up only 2.6 percent of the legislature compared with 37 percent of the population. Yet the legislature in 1978 was still avoiding federal court orders to redraw its districts so that black voters would get equal representation. In Georgia, the black vote was often diluted by electing local officials on a county-wide basis. As a result, neither Terrell nor Sumter counties, whose black electorate made up 67 and 40 percent of the population, had elected a black official by 1978.[19]

The United States Supreme Court's *Bakke* decision in 1978 apparently signaled the end of an era of progress. Despite vagueness in the court's language, the decision largely inhibited colleges and universities from redressing the racial injusticies of hundreds of years by setting favorable admission quotas for blacks and other minorities. There were further signposts that low-income blacks were being ignored—California's Proposition 13, in particular, which promised property-tax relief by slashing welfare and other social services for the poor.

Some erstwhile liberals had become neoconservatives, urging the rollback of welfare programs, denouncing quotas as un-American and affirmative action programs as reverse discrimination, evoking statistical magic to prove that busing could not help black pupils. Nathan Glazer, the Harvard sociologist, often the voice of neoconservative academics, denied the very existence of the problem: "Racial discrimination is not a major factor affecting blacks in education or in jobs."[20]

If one follows the Marxist analysis that capitalism inevitably breeds its own crises by failing to solve contradictions in the system, the ghetto may prove the most hazardous contradiction of this decade. Society seems intent on excluding the ghetto black from employment. More and more teen-agers drift into maturity without ever finding a steady job. Many will become permanently superfluous. Automation has continually eliminated unskilled labor—even messenger boys are being eliminated by the development of an electronically operated mail-delivery cart. Semiskilled workers as well are threatened by the movement of factories to the South and Southwest; and in the ultimate contradiction of the system, American corporations, now manufacturing in Taiwan and South Korea to exploit the low wage-scales, have already abandoned the ghetto as a source of employment.

If the system finally relegates the ghetto worker to permanent unemployment, cutting welfare, health care, and other services to a minimum, we may soon have walled-in enclaves of desperation in the core cities.

The rage that ripped through the ghettos in the late 1960s has been kept reasonably bottled up in the last decade. There have been exceptions, principally the Black Liberation Army, possibly an offshoot of

Eldridge Cleaver's guerrilla faction. "All we do is stop the police from killing us," Clark E. Squire announced after he was sentenced to life imprisonment for killing a state trooper in a New Jersey shootout in 1973, along with Joanne Chesimard. Two other policemen were allegedly murdered by the BLA in Manhattan, and the New York police claimed to have shot seven BLA members to death.

An even more extensive wave of violence—the murder of 14 whites by the "Zebra" gang—swept San Francisco in early 1974. The motivation seemed more religious than political. After the arrest of seven black members of a fanatical sect of the Nation of Islam, purportedly dedicated to the murder of whites, the random shootings stopped as suddenly as they had begun.

The lack of politically inspired upheavals in the ghettos may be attributed partly to a stepped-up policy of repression under President Nixon, including extensive penetration of radical groups by the FBI and other agencies, partly to a revulsion among black leaders against the mounting deaths of blacks in confrontations with the police. "We have to start talking about how to win, not how to get killed," the *Black Panther* newspaper announced in 1972.[21]

The government has also demonstrated a remarkable ability to stabilize economic crises and to pacify potential rebellion among workers. During the recession of 1974–75, Detroit would have been the logical candidate to repeat its explosive riots of 1967. The auto industry, by far the largest employer in the area, had laid off 275,000 workers, about half of them black. As unemployment benefits ran out after six months, rumors of revolt were common until Congress extended the benefits for another 39 weeks, the first such renewal ever made. By October 1975, the economy had been bolstered through federal intervention. Auto sales were up 23 percent. The auto plants had rehired most of their workers.

Such intervention has become an increasingly important instrument for regulating contradictions in the system under both Republican and Democratic administrations. It has been used to rescue tottering industries as well as depressed areas of employment. Capital and union labor are indeed a partnership in the corporate, liberal state, dedicated both to the stifling of radical turmoil and the preservation of jobs and corporate prosperity. In a society paying patriotic lip service to the myths of free enterprise, the government, ironically, extended huge loans to keep Lockheed aircraft alive in the 1970s.

The system has been equally adept at absorbing the Left. Many organizers from SNCC have moved into prestigious and high-paying positions. There are a few exceptions: Stokeley Carmichael has stayed in the ghettos, recruiting for the All-Africa People's Revolutionary Party; Charles Sherrod remained with a farmers' cooperative in Georgia. A few have rebeled permanently against the competitive job market—"My years with SNCC was the only time I ever felt clean," one veteran explained. But on the whole, former radicals have successfully entered the government or academia. Marion Barry, long a city councilman in the District of Columbia, was elected mayor in 1978. Julian Bond has been a Georgia state representative and senator for a decade. John Lewis holds a prominent post in the Carter administration. At least a dozen former SNCC organizers got their Ph.D. degrees and secured professorial appointments.[22]

There is no reason to assume that black radicals should have remained as organizers in the ghettos. Still, their success-oriented careers raise serious questions about the ability of the Left to develop new forms of mass organizing. Can a political office contribute significantly to black liberation? Kenneth Gibson, as mayor of Newark, New Jersey, for example, has certainly advanced blacks in jobs and housing. But neither he, nor any black mayor, has developed a structure of community power in the schools, health services, unions, and other bases in which people can participate to take control gradually into their hands.

An underlying problem is that the ghetto struggle is being ignored by the increasingly prosperous black middle class, and even by the lower middle class. Black professionals particularly have often moved to the suburbs like their white counterparts. In the South and other rural areas, black farmers with 25 acres or so have reached modest affluence by a combination of subsistence farming and commuting to jobs at nearby factories.

A further problem is the ideological split between the black nationalists and "scientific socialists," who stress the necessity of destroying capitalism in order to destroy racism. This split, of course, has diminished as the Panthers turned against violence and the nationalist guerrilla wing disintegrated. Many socialists have finally realized that racism predates class exploitation and exists even in countries with Marxist governments.

The central problem of the black Left is its failure to come up with a workable strategy to reinvigorate Marxism in new, humanitarian forms. The special requirements of the Panther structure, particularly its dependence on a black and minority-group population of at least 50 percent, confine its applicability to a few cities. Panther organizing becomes almost meaningless in a ghetto like Harlem, whose complex political life remains locked into the standard Democratic-Republican alignments of the white world.

Thus, the immediate prospects of the black Left are limited by a failure of innovative programs and new leadership to develop them. The furious energy unleashed in the 1960s will probably not emerge again until the ghettos approach desperation.

While the 1970s were obviously a fallow period for the Left, its achievements in the previous decade cannot be underestimated. It had shaken and shaped the decisions and direction of the country as few other forces in American history since abolitionism. It had opposed our neoimperialist foreign policy relentlessly and helped to end the most reckless manifestation of that policy, the Vietnam war. The Left's confrontation with neoimperialism had followed a consistent line since the Progressive campaign in 1948. Once Henry Wallace had set forth his vision of coexistence—"friendly peaceful competition" that would make the United States and Soviet Union "gradually become more alike"—the Left's assault on cold war stereotypes had helped create a core around which ever larger coalitions could join in pushing the government toward stabilized relations with China and Russia.[23]

It would be foolish to assume that imperialist adventures have been permanently blocked; that an imperialist presidency, reaching its apogee with Johnson and Nixon, could not be resurrected; that the powers of the FBI and other agencies to crush domestic dissent, and of the CIA to manipulate the affairs of foreign countries, could not be unleashed again.

Yet by the late 1970s, the country had become so united against foreign interventions that Congress would prohibit by law President Carter's attempt to aid anti-Communist groups in Angola. And much as the administration might have wanted to hold the shah of Iran on his throne, as it had done 25 years earlier, both domestic and international pressures stopped the White House from covert or open interference in the Iranian revolution.[24]

If the Left could be credited with even a few of these achievements, they would seem to make the radical tumult of recent years worthwhile. The remaining question, however, was whether the black or white Left or the women's movement had done more than shake the nation, whether they had developed the coherence and power to organize large groups of people into radical structures. There was, in fact, little indication of what structures might be developed in the next decade. Since the collapse of SNCC and CORE, the main residue of Black Power was the memory of ghetto riots and the possibility that a future explosion could be incomparably more damaging.

Huey Newton's prediction that socialism might eventually be achieved through the ballot box seemed to rule out violence for the moment. But the semisocialist structures the Panthers developed would only satisfy ghetto anger temporarily. Unless black community control could expand quickly alongside bourgeois capitalism, the ghettos were likely to become the starting point of another uprising.

While the white Left had proved its organizing abilities on the campuses and in the streets during the 1960s, it was mainly the Vietnam war, and a larger confrontation with neoimperialism, that gave unity to its diverse factions. By the 1970s, there was no overwhelming "revolutionary situation" to knit together all elements of the oppressed.

This may explain why the Left was drifting through a transitional stage in the 1970s, why the violence and revolutionary drive of the previous decade had been channeled into reformism. In itself, reformism did not mean retreat. Rather, it marked a period of consolidation and regrouping while prior gains were being fused into the mainstream.

No single structure dominated the Left at this time as the Communist party dominated in the 1930s, and SDS in the 1960s. Instead, the Left contained a multiplicity of agencies—liberated territories like San Francisco, community-control struggles in the ghettos, communes organizing around ecological issues. Not all agencies of the Left even considered themselves Marxist.

The crucial problem of this transitional stage was that the Left generally had found orthodox Marxism-Leninism inapplicable to immediate American needs. Except for the Communist party, most American socialists had rejected the Soviet model. The replacement of Mao's policy of continuous revolution by an all-out economic buildup in 1979 diminished China's luster for the ultra-Left. American problems were simply a small reflection of the problems of

Eurocommunism. Even the powerful Italian Communists were uncertain in 1979 whether their party could gain more inside or outside the government.

The American Left, in fact, will not recover the momentum of the 1960s until economic pressures produce a new crisis. Its most apparent symptom was rampant inflation, approaching European levels and eroding American affluence. Gas threatened to reach one dollar a gallon. The United States showed a continued foreign trade deficit; the dollar faltered overseas. The flood of foreign goods into the country and the movement of American manufacturing plants to low-wage areas of the Far East intensified unemployment problems.

All these pressures, ironically enough, first brought a reaction in the middle class, which found its instrument of rebellion in California's tax-limitation law, Proposition 13. But even the highest-paid levels of union labor, whose income had generally kept up with inflation, were finding the pressures severe. Once rising interest rates made it impossible for union members to borrow money for their homes and cars, or keep up the payments on their furniture, workers would find that their plight was not too different from other oppressed groups. Economic pressures were likely to produce what the Vietnam war had never created—an alliance between many unions and the Left.

The disenchantment of these groups with the political process had already been reflected in their abstention from the polls. Only about 38 percent of the eligible electorate voted in the November 1978 elections.[25]

If economic needs and class interest provide the surest unifying structure against oppression, the women's movement in particular has combined them to reach and hold a larger constituency than any other group on the Left. It has always placed women first. The structures around which it organizes, whether health clinics or child-care centers, are concerned principally with feminist demands. Any experiments in socialism or semisocialism flow naturally from this emphasis. Of all the movements that have come out of the 1960s, therefore, radical feminism most truly represents an evolutionary process with many agencies of change, each searching for its own mode of collective power.

The prevailing lesson from the past failures of the Left is that public ownership of the means of production in itself cannot guarantee individual happiness. Collective power must not be strengthened at the expense of individual rights. Collective needs must be balanced with individual needs.

What the American Left must guarantee is a fusion of personal liberation and socialist economics. The feminists grasped this goal from the start, stressing that socialism in its present forms would not necessarily eliminate male chauvinism, male domination, or self-perpetuating, essentially male bureaucracies.

This vision of "socialist humanism" or "democratic socialism" offers a pragmatic basis for Marx's concept of humanity seeking progressively higher stages of development. The prospects for the Left hinge on this attempt to fuse democratic values and a socialist vision of society into a uniquely American unity.

Acknowledgments

My largest debt, as always, is to my wife, Joan Summers Lader. Her patience and loyalty eased the strain of more than five years of work. But beyond that, she was an invaluable associate in research and checking. Her criticism and editorial comment improved every page. This book owes her more than I can possibly detail.

My editor at W.W. Norton, Jim Mairs, provided astute literary judgment and forced me to seek more objective perspectives. He has also been a devoted friend and adviser. Similarly, my agent, Roberta Pryor of International Creative Management, has always sustained me with her vigor and cheerfulness. The fact that she and ICM's predecessor agencies have represented me for 30 years testifies to a treasured relationship.

Although I alone must be held accountable for the views expressed here, I owe a particular debt to friends and associates who read sections of the book related to their expertise. Susan Brownmiller gave her tested experience to the women's movement chapter. Professor Stephen H. Cohen of Princeton University sharpened my Marxist analysis. Max Gordon, a former *Daily Worker* editor, was endlessly helpful in reviewing chapters on the Communist party. William Reuben, long known for his research and writing on the cases of the Rosenbergs and Alger Hiss, was invaluable in these and many other areas.

Much of the research for the book was done in the New York Public Library's Frederick Lewis Allen Memorial Room. I have always been grateful for the privilege of using it on this and other books, and particularly grateful to Joseph Mask, Faye Simkin, and Walter Zervas of the administrative staff; and to Paul Schmidt of the library's Jefferson Market branch for his research help.

I am indebted also to the New York Public Library for access to the Vito Marcantonio and Norman Thomas papers; to the Public Library's Schomburg Center for Research in Black Culture for the use both of its research files and printed materials; and to the Tamiment Collection at New York University's Bobst Library, which made available the Nelson Frank and George Vickers papers, as well as its extensive files of the *Black Panther* newspaper, *New Left Notes,* and other Left periodicals.

Columbia University's Oral History Collection kindly gave me the use of its interviews with Julius Emspak, Lee Pressman, and Henry Wallace; and Catholic University's John Mullen Memorial Library allowed access to its Philip Murray papers.

Sara M. Evans of the University of Minnesota graciously allowed me to draw on her Ph.D. dissertation, "Personal Politics: The Roots of Women's Liberation in the Civil Rights Movement and the New Left." Alice Lake supplied her excellent research file and reporter's notes from "Mississippi Summer" of 1964. Margot Adler allowed me the use of her papers and diaries from Mississippi and Berkeley; and Gloria Richardson kindly opened her personal files on the organizing of Cambridge, Maryland.

Albert J. Zack of the AFL-CIO supplied me with the proceedings against those CIO unions charged with being Communist-dominated. The United Electrical Workers Union permitted me to use its research files. I am also indebted to Lucy Komisar for her materials on Eurocommunism; to Luke Wilson for his papers on the American Labor party; to Professor Henry J. Silverman of Michigan State University for his unpublished paper, "Youth Movements in the 20th Century"; and to Edith Tiger of National Emergency Civil Liberties Committee for her help in arranging interviews.

Acronyms

ACCF	American Committee for Cultural Freedom
ACLU	American Civil Liberties Union
ACTU	Association of Catholic Trade Unions
ADA	Americans for Democratic Action
AEC	Atomic Energy Commission
AFL	American Federation of Labor
AIM	American Indian Movement
ALP	American Labor party
COFO	Council of Federated Organizations
CIO	Congress of Industrial Organizations
CIO PAC	CIO Political Action Committee
CP	Communist party
CORE	Congress for Racial Equality
CRC	Civil Rights Congress
DSOC	Democratic Socialist Organizing Committee
ERAP	Economic Research and Action Project
FALN	Armed Forces of National Liberation of Puerto Rico
FEPC	Fair Employment Practices Commission
FSM	Free Speech Movement
GAA	Gay Activists Alliance
GLF	Gay Liberation Front
HUAC	House Un-American Activities Committee
IDA	Institute for Defense Analysis
IUE	International Union of Electrical, Radio, and Machine Workers
IWW	International Workers of the World (Wobblies)
JOIN	Jobs or Income Now
KKK	Ku Klux Klan
MFDP	Mississippi Freedom Democratic party
MIA	Montgomery Improvement Association
MOBE	National (later New) Mobilization Committee to End the War in Vietnam
M2M	May 2 Movement
NAACP	National Association for the Advancement of Colored People
NAM	New America Movement
NATO	North Atlantic Treaty Organization
NCC	National Coordinating Committee to End the War in Vietnam

NLG	National Lawyers Guild
NMU	National Maritime Union
NSA	National Student Association
OPA	Office of Price Administration
PCA	Progressive Citizens of America
PL	Progressive Labor
RAM	Revolutionary Action Movement
ROTC	Reserve Officers Training Corps
RYM	Revolutionary Youth Movement
SANE	Committee for a Sane Nuclear Policy
SCLC	Southern Christian Leadership Conference
SLA	Symbionese Liberation Army
SLID	Student League for Industrial Democracy
SNCC	Student Nonviolent (later National) Coordinating Committee
SNYC	Southern Negro Youth Congress
SPU	Student Peace Union
SWP	Socialist Workers party
UAW	United Automobile Workers of America
UE	United Electrical, Radio and Machine Workers of America
UEMDA	UE Members for Democratic Action
UN	United Nations
VDC	Vietnam Day Committee
VEP	Voter Education Project
WSA	Worker-Student Alliance
YPSL	Young People's Socialist League

Notes and Sources

To keep the notes manageable, I have followed the practice of frequently grouping the sources for two or more paragraphs under one footnote number. Titles in full are given only when first cited in each chapter.

Manuscripts, diaries, and other unpublished sources are listed individually in the footnotes. Many are credited in the Acknowledgments section.

The most commonly used magazine and newspaper sources—*Black Panther, Studies on the Left,* New York *Times,* for example—are cited in the footnotes. Seventeen magazines for the period covered by this book were read in full. Sectarian publications include *New Left Notes, Political Affairs, Radical America, Socialist Revolution.* More popular journals include *Dissent, Liberation, Nation, New York Review of Books, Partisan Review.*

This book depends heavily for interpretation and analysis on interviews with those involved in Left movements after 1946. Each person interviewed gave generous amounts of time; many agreed to a second and third interview. I am much indebted to all of the following individuals:

John Abt	Jeremy Brecher
Margot Adler	Grace Breslauer
Kathie Amatniek	Elaine Brown
James Aronson	Susan Brownmiller
C. B. Baldwin	Joseph Cadden
Marion Barry, Jr.	Stokeley Carmichael
Benjamin Bedell	George Blake Charney
Madelon Bedell	Lucinda Cisler
Geraldine Bender	Ramsey Clark
Robert Bendiner	Lewis Cole
Jane Benedict	Courtland Cox
Louise Berman	Ivanhoe Donaldson
Julian Bond	Frank Donner
Hyman Bookbinder	Virginia F. Durr
Nancy Borman	Andrea Eagan
Ed Bradley	Deirdre English

Stephen Fischer
Robert Fitch
Albert Fitzgerald
Harry Fleischman
James Forman
Charles R. Garry
John Gates
John Gerassi
Simon W. Gerson
Emily Gibson
Elinor Gimbel
Todd Gitlin
Arthur J. Goldberg
Max Gordon
Marian Gruber
Lawrence Guyot
Wallace Hamilton
William Hansen
Helen Harrington
Casey Hayden
Tom Hayden
Dorothy Healey
James Herndon
David Horowitz
Ericka Huggins
Esther Jackson
Paul Jacobs
Matthew Jones
John Judis
Tom Kahn
Marilyn Katz
Mary King
Herbert Kohl
Paul Krassner
Sharon Krebs
Joyce Ladner
Robert Lewis
Allard Lowenstein
Joseph Lyford
Conrad Lynn
James J. Matles
Donald McMillan

Daniel Millstone
Jessica Mitford
Frank Morelli
E. D. Nixon
Earl Ofari
Constance Webb Pearlstien
James Peck
Lana C. Phelan
Alvin F. Pouissant
Cordell Reagon
Alan Reitman
Charles O. Rice
Gloria Richardson
Howard Rodman
Helen Rosen
Samuel Rosen
Annette T. Rubinstein
Robert Rusch
Kirkpatrick Sale
Junius Scales
Cleveland Sellers
Ralph Shikes
Frank Smith
Nat Spero
Walter Stafford
Nancy Stearns
Russell Stetler
Walter Tillow
Alvin Udell
Edward Wallerstein
Pat Watters
Palmer Webber
James Weinstein
Jean Wiley
Doxey Wilkerson
Luke Wilson
Henry Wittner
Miriam Wittner
Morton Yarmon
Howard Zinn

Prologue

1. Interview with Elaine Brown.

2. Duane Elgin, Arnold Mitchell, "Voluntary Simplicity (3)," *CoEvolution Quarterly* (Summer 1977): 10, an updated version of Stanford Research Institute Business Intelligence report in *Voluntary Simplicity,* June 1976.

3. Robert C. Tucker, *The Marxian Revolutionary Idea* (New York, 1970), p. 180.

4. Catherine Drinker Bowen, *Yankee from Olympus* (Boston, 1944), p. xii.

Chapter 1   The Campaign against Labor and the Left, 1946

1. New York *Times,* May 25, 1946.

2. *Time,* June 3, 1946, p. 20. *NYT,* May 25, 1946.

3. Harry S. Truman, *Memoirs* (Garden City, N.Y., 1955), 1: 495. *NYT,* May 28, 1946; June 4, 1946.

4. This and preceding paragraph: *NYT,* March 6, 1946; June 3, 1946. Crawford from *In Fact,* April 29, 1946, p. 1. Sabath memorandum of March 7, 1946, from Marcantonio papers, New York Public Library, box 18.

5. *Congressional Record,* 79th Cong., 2d sess., 92, pt. 5: 5942.

6. This and preceding paragraph: *United States News,* June 14, 1946, p. 32. *Congressional Record,* p. 5941. Hook from *In Fact,* April 29, 1946, p. 1.

7. Cabell Phillips, *The Truman Presidency* (New York, 1966), p. 121. *Congressional Record,* p. 5933. John W. Scoville, *Labor Monopolies—Or Freedom* (Committee for Constitutional Government, New York, 1946).

8. U.S. Senate Committee on Small Business, *Report of Smaller War Plants Corporation,* 79th Cong., 2d sess., Document 206, p. 49.

9. *United States News,* May 24, 1946, p. 43. Frank Cormier and William J. Eaton, *Reuther* (Englewood Cliffs, N.J., 1970), p. 219. *United Electrical Workers Fight for a Better America* (New York, 1946).

10. *Time,* May 27, 1946, p. 18.

11. This and preceding paragraph: *United Electrical.* Cormier and Eaton, *Reuther,* pp. 221, 224, 226, 232.

12. Tom Clark from Merle Miller, *Plain Speaking* (New York, 1973), p. 225. Snyder from John Morton Blum ed., *The Price of Vision: The Diary of Henry A. Wallace, 1942–1946* (Boston, 1973), p. 540.

13. This and preceding paragraph: Truman, *Memoirs,* 1: 502. *NYT,* May 26, 1946. *Congressional Record,* pp. 5741–50. The change involved rule XXVII, clause 1.

14. *Congressional Record,* pp. 5741–50, 5755–58.

15. *NYT,* May 27, 1946; May 28.

16. *United States News,* May 31, 1946, p. 34. *NYT,* May 25, 1946; May 30. Helen Fuller, "Has Truman Lost Labor?" *Nation,* June 10, 1946, p. 826.

17. *NYT,* May 26, 1946; May 28. Annette T. Rubinstein, ed., *I Vote My Conscience, Debates, Speeches and Writings of Vito Marcantonio* (New York, 1956), pp. 217–18. *Congressional Record,* pp. 5926–45.

18.   This and two preceding paragraphs: Truman, *Memoirs,* 1: 502. *NYT,* May 30, 1946; June 4, June 6; June 12. The Case bill also allowed a court injunction to break a strike in case of "obstructional" picketing; any worker who disregarded a presidential return-to-work order would lose all rights under the National Labor Relations Board.

Chapter 2   Vito Marcantonio and the Congressional Battleground

1.   *New York World-Telegram,* November 13, 1946.

2.   Ibid., November 13, 1946. Interviews with Frank Morelli, Luke Wilson.

3.   Marcantonio speeches of August 31, 1942, and February 26, 1943, in Annette T. Rubinstein, ed., *I Vote My Conscience* (New York, 1956), pp. 167, 172, 174.

4.   Rubinstein, ibid., pp. 406–9.

5.   Marcantonio papers, New York Public Library, box 6 (Letter of June 25, 1945).

6.   Interview with Robert Rusch. Marcantonio's techniques of organizing from interviews with Jane Benedict, Helen Harrington, Ed Wallerstein.

7.   Salvatore La Gumina, *Vito Marcantonio, The People's Politician* (Dubuque, Iowa, 1969), p. 42.

8.   Alan Schaffer, *Vito Marcantonio, Radical in Congress* (Syracuse, N.Y., 1966), p. 97. Stephen B. Sarasohn, "Struggle for Control of the ALP" (Master's thesis, Columbia University, 1948), pp. 100–155.

9.   Marcantonio summed up his foreign-policy views in a letter to the *New York Times,* October 30, 1948.

10.   This and preceding paragraph: interview with Ed Wallerstein. Rubinstein, *I Vote,* pp. 139–45.

11.   This and preceding paragraph: Rubinstein, *I Vote,* p. 220 on British loan. George Charney, *A Long Journey* (Chicago, 1968), p. 110 on Korean war. Marcantonio papers, box 49 on fur union.

12.   Charney, *A Long Journey,* p. 110.

13.   *NYT,* February 3, 1939. La Gumina, *Marcantonio,* p. 125.

14.   Rubinstein, *I Vote,* p. 49.

15.   Interviews with Miriam and Henry Wittner, and others requesting anonymity.

Chapter 3   The Left's Challenge to Truman, 1946–47

1.   Harry S. Truman, *Memoirs* (Garden City, N.Y., 1955), 1: 556. John Morton Blum, ed., *The Price of Vision: The Diary of Henry A. Wallace, 1942–1946* (Boston, 1973), pp. 591–601.

2.   This and two preceding paragraphs: Curtis D. MacDougall, *Gideon's Army* (New York, 1965), 1: 64–70. Truman, *Memoirs,* 1: 557. Blum, *Price,* p. 612. Cabell Phillips, *The Truman Presidency* (New York, 1966), p. 130.

3.   James F. Byrnes, *Speaking Frankly* (New York, 1947), p. 240. David E. Lilienthal, *Journals of David E. Lilienthal* (New York, 1964), 2: 169–70. Truman, *Memoirs,* 1: 560.

4. CIO, *Eighth Constitutional Convention, Final Proceedings* (Washington, D.C., 1946), pp. 111, 165.

5. This and preceding paragraph: Byrnes, *Speaking,* p. 45. Truman, *Memoirs,* 1: 82. Walter Millis, ed., *The Forrestal Diaries* (New York, 1951), pp. 39–41. Interview with C. B. Baldwin.

6. *Life,* February 17, 1941, p. 61. Mr. X, "The Sources of Soviet Conduct," *Foreign Affairs,* July 1947, pp. 566–82.

7. Harry Schwartz, *Russia's Postwar Economy* (Syracuse, N.Y., 1947), p. 12. Truman quotation from *NYT,* June 24, 1941.

8. Gabriel Kolko, *The Politics of War* (New York, 1968), pp. 442, 584. Arthur M. Schlesinger, Jr., "Origins of the Cold War," *Foreign Affairs,* October 1967, pp. 22–50.

9. Schlesinger, "Origins," p. 45.

10. This and preceding paragraph: Truman, *Memoirs,* 1: 87, 422, 530. Kolko, *Politics,* p. 592. Gar Alperowitz, *Atomic Diplomacy: Hiroshima and Potsdam* (New York, 1967), pp. 227, 237–38. William Appleman Williams, *The Tragedy of American Diplomacy* (New York, 1959), p. 169. Blum, *Price,* p. 497. Eisenhower quotation from *Newsweek,* November 11, 1963, p. 107.

11. This and two preceding paragraphs: Fuller quotation from *Daily Worker,* March 5, 1944. *United Electrical Workers News,* December 14, 1946. Earle quotation from CIO, *Ninth Constitutional Convention, Final Proceedings* (Washington, D.C., 1947), p. 278.

12. This and preceding paragraph: Len De Caux, *Labor Radical* (Boston, 1970), p. 462. *Steel Labor,* June 1946. CIO, *Eighth Convention,* p. 114. Max M. Kampelman, *The Communist Party vs. the CIO* (New York, 1957), p. 48.

13. Ronald L. Filippelli, "United Electrical, Radio and Machine Workers of America, 1933–1949" (Ph.d diss., Pennsylvania State University, 1970), p. 149. Murray quotation from labor official requesting anonymity.

14. Kampelman, *Communist Party,* p. 75.

15. Lee Pressman interview, Columbia University Oral History Project, p. 390. Filippelli, "United Electrical," pp. 141, 167. Interview with Charles O. Rice. Michael Harrington, "Catholics in the Labor Movement: A Case History," *Labor History,* Fall 1960, pp. 231–63.

16. United Electrical Workers, *Eleventh Convention Proceedings* (New York, 1946), pp. 59, 153. *UE News,* September 14, 1946.

17. Interview with C. B. Baldwin.

18. *New Republic,* November 18, 1946, p. 644.

19. Truman, *Memoirs,* 2: 105–6.

20. Millis, *Forrestal,* p. 263.

21. This and preceding paragraph: MacDougall, *Gideon's Army,* pp. 100, 114, 134, 174. Edward L. and Frederick H. Schapsmeier, *Prophet in Politics: Henry A. Wallace and the War Years, 1940–1965* (Iowa City, 1970), p. 152. Norman D. Markowitz, *The Rise and Fall of the People's Century: Henry A. Wallace and American Liberalism, 1941–1948* (New York, 1973), p. 220.

22. Truman, *Memoirs,* 2: 115.

23. This and preceding paragraph: CIO, *Ninth Convention,* p. 275, 287.

24. Ibid., p. 187. Interview with James Matles.

25. This and three preceding paragraphs: CIO, *Ninth Convention,* p. 203. Filippelli, "United Electrical," p. 175. Saul D. Alinsky, *John L. Lewis* (New York, 1970), pp. 337–38.

26. This and preceding paragraph: Eugene Dennis, *What America Faces* (New York, 1946), pp. 37–38. Joseph Starobin, *American Communism in Crisis, 1943–1957* (Cambridge, Mass., 1972), p. 161. *Washington Post,* May 2, 1948. David A. Shannon, *The Decline of American Communism* (New York, 1959), p. 139. Interview with James Matles. MacDougall, *Gideon's Army,* pp. 260, 262. Richard J. Walton, *Henry Wallace, Harry Truman and the Cold War* (New York, 1976), p. 260.

27. This and preceding paragraph: Interviews with C. B. Baldwin, James Matles, Ralph Shikes.

Chapter 4   The Wrath of the Prophets: Henry Wallace and the Progressive Party, 1948

1. This and two preceding paragraphs: biblical quotation from *NYT,* March 19, 1948. Hyde Park quotation from *Philadelphia Inquirer,* July 25, 1948. *Chicago Daily News,* May 28, 1947. Interview with Palmer Webber.

2. Field quotation from Curtis D. MacDougall, *Gideon's Army* (New York, 1965), 2: 345. Interview with Albert Fitzgerald. Farley from Gardner Jackson, "Henry Wallace: A Divided Mind," *Atlantic Monthly,* August 1948, pp. 27–33.

3. Merle Miller, *Plain Speaking* (New York, 1973), p. 176. Interview with C. B. Baldwin.

4. This and preceding paragraph: Interviews with C. B. Baldwin, Ralph Shikes, and Progressive party officials requesting anonymity. *Time,* March 8, 1948.

5. Ilo Wallace quotation, and "guru" material in previous paragraphs, are from Progressive officials requesting anonymity.

6. Henry A. Wallace, *Century of the Common Man* (New York, 1943), p. 22.

7. Wallace relationship with Truman from interviews with C. B. Baldwin, Elinor Gimbel, Ralph Shikes, and other Progressive officials requesting anonymity.

8. This and preceding paragraph: *Life,* March 1, 1948, pp. 23–25. *NYT,* February 19, 1948. Money sources from MacDougall, *Gideon's Army,* 1: 21, 296; and interview with Gimbel.

9. This and two preceding paragraphs: Norman D. Markowitz, *The Rise and Fall of the People's Century* (New York, 1973), p. 257. Interviews with Albert Fitzgerald and James Matles.

10. This and preceding paragraph: Irwin Ross, *The Loneliest Campaign* (New York, 1968), pp. 113, 126.

11. This and preceding paragraph: Communist quotation from MacDougall, *Gideon's Army,* 2: 337, 341. Clark quotation from Miller, *Plain Speaking,* p. 225. *NYT,* July 21, July 22, 1948.

12. This and preceding paragraph: MacDougall, *Gideon's Army,* 2: 698, 789. Karl M. Schmidt, *Henry A. Wallace: Quixotic Crusade, 1948* (Syracuse, N.Y., 1960), pp. 86–87, 259.

13. This and two preceding paragraphs: MacDougall, *Gideon's Army,* 2: 633. Henry A. Wallace, *Towards World Peace* (New York, 1948), pp. 63–64, 87, 93, 96, 114. Jackson, "Wallace."

14. This and preceding paragraph: *Nation,* July 24, 1948, pp. 87–88. Wallace, *Towards World Peace,* p. 33. Dickson Hartwell, "The Abundant Mr. Wallace," *Collier's,* September 20, 1947, pp. 24–25. Jackson, "Wallace."

15. This and preceding paragraph: *NYT,* February 22, 24, 26; March 14, 15, 1948.

16. *NYT,* May 12, 18, 1948.

17. This and two preceding paragraphs: *NYT,* February 21, March 31, 1948. Wallace, *Towards World Peace,* pp. 115, 117. Harry S. Truman, *Memoirs* (Garden City, N.Y., 1955), 2: 124.

18. This and two preceding paragraphs: *NYT,* July 23, 25, 1948. *Philadelphia Inquirer,* July 25, 1948.

19. This and preceding paragraph: Rabbit quotation from Schmidt, *Wallace,* p. 56. Democratic party quotation from CBS News, February 23, 1948.

20. Alistair Coleman, "Why I'll Vote for Thomas," *Nation,* October 2, 1948, pp. 368–70. MacDougall, *Gideon's Army,* 2: 549, 846.

21. Interviews with C. B. Baldwin, Albert Fitzgerald.

22. This and preceding paragraphs: Interviews with John Abt, C. B. Baldwin, Grace Breslauer, Frank Donner.

23. Southern campaign mainly from interviews with Virginia Durr, Junius Scales, Palmer Webber. Birmingham, Durham, Savannah, and Memphis from MacDougall, *Gideon's Army,* 2: 390, 677, 709, 728. Wallace at Charlotte from *Time,* September 6, 1948, p. 19. New York rallies from *Time,* September 20, 1948, p. 27. Virginia Durr, "Remembering Clark Foreman," *Bill of Rights Journal,* December 1977, pp. 1–3.

24. This and preceding paragraph: *NYT,* September 29, 1948. Truman, *Memoirs,* 2: 213–16. Ross, *Loneliest Campaign,* pp. 212–14.

25. This and three preceding paragraphs: MacDougall, *Gideon's Army,* 2: 797, 857. Schmidt, *Wallace,* p. 236.

26. This and preceding paragraph: Interviews with Palmer Webber, C. B. Baldwin. Murray S., Jr., and Susan Stedman, *Discontent at the Polls* (New York, 1950), p. 122. Samuel Lubell, *The Future of American Politics* (New York, 1952), pp. 210–13. B. J. Widdick, *Labor Today* (Boston, 1964), p. 127. Milton Edelman, "Labor Vote in '48," *Nation,* October 23, 1948, pp. 461–65.

27. MacDougall, *Gideon's Army,* 2: 884.

Chapter 5   The Purge of the CIO Left, 1948–50

1. This and two preceding paragraphs: CIO, *Proceedings, Tenth Constitutional Convention* (Washington, D.C., 1948), pp. 170, 252, 255 283, 300. Interview with Albert Fitzgerald.

2. CIO, *Proceedings,* p. 282. *Oregon Journal,* November 24, 1948.

3. Samuel Lubell, *The Future of American Politics* (New York, 1952), p. 180.

4. This and three preceding paragraphs: Interviews with Albert Fitzgerald, Max Gordon, James Matles. George Charney, *A Long Journey* (Chicago, 1968), p. 184. Charles P. Larrowe, *Harry Bridges: Rise and Fall of Radical Labor in the United States* (New York, 1972), p. 256, 295.

5. This and three preceeding paragraphs: James Matles and James Higgins, *Them and Us* (Englewood Cliffs, N.J., 1974), pp. 174–86. Philip Murray papers, Catholic University, box A 4–44. *Labor Leader,* January 17, 1949.

6. This and preceding paragraph: Interview with Charles O. Rice. Ronald L. Filippelli, "United Electrical, Radio and Machine Workers of America, 1933–1949" (Ph.D. diss., Pennsylvania State University, 1970), p. 198. Matles and Higgins, *Them and Us,* p. 203. Louis Koenig, *The Truman Administration: Its Principles and Practices* (New York, 1956), p. 48.

7. Lee Pressman interview, Columbia University Oral History collection, p. 184. Interview with James Matles.

8. This and three preceding paragraphs: Interview with Frank Donner. Pressman, Columbia Oral, p. 184. John Chamberlain, "Phil Murray," *Life,* February 11, 1946, p. 79. Charles A. Madison, *American Labor Leaders* (New York, 1950), p. 317. Thomas R. Brooks, *Toil and Trouble: A History of American Labor* (New York, 1964), p. 200.

9. This and preceding four paragraphs: Julius Emspak interview, Columbia University Oral History Collection, pp. 27–224. Interviews with Albert Fitzgerald, James Matles. Larrowe, *Bridges,* pp. 246, 321.

10. This and preceding paragraph: Nelson Frank papers, Tamiment Collection, New York University Library (uncatalogued at time of use). *New York World-Telegram,* October 29, 1946; August 20, November 21, December 21, 1947. *NYT,* February 28, 1947; March 27, 1957; August 8, 1958. Filippelli, "United Electrical" pp. 160–61. F. S. O'Brien, "The 'Communist-Dominated' Unions in the United States Since 1950," *Labor History,* Spring 1968, pp. 184–209.

11. This and three preceding paragraphs: United Electrical Workers, *Fourteenth Convention Proceedings* (New York, 1949), pp. 143, 200, 245, 261, 266, 325. Filippelli, "United Electrical," pp. 214–26. Matles and Higgins, *Them and Us,* p. 194.

12. Victor Riesel column in *New York Post,* October 13, 1949.

13. This and three preceding paragraphs: Matles and Higgins, *Them and Us,* p. 201. *New York World-Telegram,* March 5–7, 1946. *NYT,* October 12, 1947. Murray Kempton, *Part of Our Time* (New York, 1955), p. 95.

14. This and three preceding paragraphs: A. H. Raskin, "Presenting the Phenomenon Called Quill," *NYT Magazine,* March 5, 1950, p. 11. Interview with George Charney.

15. This and preceding paragraph: James R. Prickett, "Some Aspects of the Communist Controversy in the CIO," *Science and Society,* Summer-Fall 1969, pp. 301–2. Paul Jacobs, *The State of the Unions* (New York, 1963), p. 90. David J. Saposs, *Communism in American Unions* (New York, 1959), p. 211. CIO, *Official Reports on the Expulsion of Communist Dominated Organizations From the CIO* (Washington, D.C., 1954).

16. This and two preceding paragraphs: interview with Charles O. Rice. Philip Taft, "The Association of Catholic Trade Unionists," *Industrial and Labor Relations Review,* January 1949, pp. 210–18. Philip S. Foner, *The Fur and Leather Workers Union* (Newark, N.J., 1950), p. 660. Max M. Kampelman, *The Communist Party vs. the CIO* (New York, 1957), p. 254.

17. This and preceding paragraph: Al Richmond, *A Long View from the Left* (Boston, 1973), p. 284. United Electrical Workers, *Proceedings,* in 1946, p. 65; in 1947, p. 27; in 1948, p. 58. Larrowe, *Bridges,* p. 258.

18. C. Wright Mills, "The Labor Leaders and the Power Elite," in Arthur Kornhauser, Robert Dubin, Arthur M. Ross, eds., *Industrial Conflict* (New York, 1954), pp. 144, 146. Raskin in *NYT,* April 24, 1960.

19.   This and preceding paragraph: Ronald Radosh, *American Labor and United States Foreign Policy* (New York, 1969), pp. 323, 325, 438. *New York Herald Tribune,* January 29, 1950.

20.   This and two preceding paragraphs: Harry Conn, "The CIO—Is It Growing Old?" *New Republic,* November 26, 1951, p. 16. Mary Heaton Vorse, "State of Unions," *Nation,* December 5, 1953, pp. 467–68. James Higgins, "Still Poison," *Nation,* May 22, 1954, pp. 443–44. Frank Donner, "Decline of the AFL-CIO" (address at United Electrical Workers 27th International Convention, August 30, 1962). *New York Post,* September 9, 1955.

21.   This and preceding paragraph: Raskin in *NYT,* April 24, 1960. Larrowe, *Bridges,* p. 290. *New York Post,* December 9, 1955. Donner, "Decline." Kermit Eby, *Protests of an Ex-Organization Man* (Boston, 1961), p. 44.

Chapter 6   Destroying the Communist Party: The 1949 Trial

This chapter is largely based on interviews. Since individual interviews frequently pertain to many parts of the chapter, specific citations have been omitted. Interviews relating to the Communist party include George Charney, John Gates, Simon Gerson, Max Gordon, Dorothy Healey, Donald McMillan, Junius Scales, and Doxey Wilkerson. Interviews relating to the relationship of the Communist party with the labor movement, American Labor party and other groups include John Abt, Frank Donner, Robert Fitch, Albert Fitzgerald, Robert Lewis, James Matles, Charles O. Rice, Robert Rusch, Alvin Udell, and Ed Wallerstein. Interviews with William Reuben were particularly important for the sections on Alger Hiss and related material.

1.   This and six preceding paragraphs: American Civil Liberties Union, *Peekskill* (New York, 1950), appendix I in particular. *Christian Science Monitor,* September 6, 1949. *New York Sun,* August 29, 1949. *Nation,* September 10, 1949, p. 213. Howard Fast, *Peekskill: USA* (New York, 1951), pp. 7–86, 109, in particular. Interviews with Miriam and Henry Wittner.

2.   This and four preceding paragraphs: *NYT,* October 15, 1949. *Newsweek,* October 24, 1949, p. 24. *Time,* April 11, 1949, p. 23.

3.   This and three preceding paragraphs: Dennis v. United States, 341 U.S. 494 (1951). *NYT,* February 5, October 15, 1949. Simon Gerson, "Jury System and Democratic Rights," *Political Affairs,* July 1952, pp. 35–44. Janney from *Time,* September 5, 1949, p. 15; *Newsweek,* September 5, 1949, p. 21; *Nation,* September 3, 1949, p. 215.

4.   This and preceding paragraph: *NYT* editorial, June 5, 1951. *Nation,* July 1, 1950, p. 4. A. L. Wirin and Sam Rosenwein, "Smith Act Prosecutions," *Nation,* December 12, 1953, pp. 485–90.

5.   Alan Barth, *Prophets with Honor* (New York, 1974), p. 175. Dennis v. U.S., *NYT,* June 5, 1951.

6.   Wirin and Rosenwein, "Smith Act."

7.   This and preceding paragraph: Herbert L. Packer, *Ex-Communist Witnesses* (Palo Alto, Calif., 1962), p. 203. Frank J. Donner, "The Informer," *Nation,* April 10, 1954, pp. 298–309. Harvey Matusow, *False Witness* (New York, 1955), pp. 131–32, 192, 237–43.

8. This and preceding paragraph: *Nation,* November 10, 1951, pp. 397–98; September 15, 1951, p. 203; July 18, 1953, p. 52.

9. Dennis v. U.S.

10. This and preceding paragraph: Wirin and Rosenwein, "Smith Act." Dennis v. U.S.

11. This and three preceding paragraphs: *New Republic,* January 22, 1951, p. 6; May 14, 1951, p. 6. Cabell Phillips, *The Truman Presidency* (New York, 1966), pp. 351, 364. *Nation,* October 4, 1952, p. 286.

12. This and preceding paragraph from *coram nobis* petition filed by National Emergency Civil Liberties Foundation in federal district court, Southern District of New York, July 27, 1978. Earl Latham, *The Communist Controversy in Washington* (Cambridge, Mass., 1966), pp. 186–94.

13. This and preceding paragraph: *New Republic,* June 18, 1951, pp. 3–4; Arnold J. Heidenheimer, "Techniques of Intimidation," October 29, 1951, pp. 14–15. *NYT,* December 2, 1976, p. 47.

14. This and three preceding paragraphs: *NYT,* September 30, 1950. Carey McWilliams, *Witch Hunt* (Boston, 1950), pp. 109, 120, 324. Alonzo L. Hamby, *Beyond the New Deal: Harry S. Truman and American Liberalism* (New York, London, 1973), p. 400. Goodwin Watson, "Battle for Free Schools," *Nation,* November 3, 1951, pp. 371–73.

15. This and two preceding paragraphs: Joseph Starobin, *American Communism in Crisis, 1943–1957* (Cambridge, Mass., 1972), pp. 57, 89. John Gates, *The Story of an American Communist* (New York, 1958), p. 186.

16. This and preceding paragraph: Starobin, *American Communism,* p. 198. Nathan Glazer, *The Social Basis of American Communism* (New York, 1961), p. 128. George Charney, *A Long Journey* (Chicago, 1968), p. 230. Gates, *Story,* p. 142.

17. *New Masses,* February 12, April 9, 1946.

18. This and preceding paragraph: Richard Crossman, ed., *The God That Failed* (New York, 1949), p. 34. Clinton Rossiter, *Marxism: The View from America* (New York, 1960), p. 151. Glazer, *Social Basis,* pp. 178, 219.

19. This and preceding paragraph: Robert Thompson, "Strengthen the Struggle against White Chauvinism," *Political Affairs,* June 1949, pp. 14–27. Harold Cruse, *Crisis of the Negro Intellectual* (New York, 1967), p. 147. Henry Haywood, "Further on Race, Nation," *Political Affairs,* October 1952, pp. 47–59. Glazer, *Social Basis,* pp. 175, 179.

20. This and two preceding paragraphs: *New York Daily Mirror,* August 4, 1946; October 19, 1948. *New York Daily News,* November 1, 1946. *New York Journal-American,* October 3, 1949. *NYT,* November 8, 1950.

21. This and two preceding paragraphs: *Political Affairs,* December 1952, pp. 4–13. Marcantonio Papers, New York Public Library, box 49. *NYT,* November 5, 1953.

22. This and preceding paragraph: Al Richmond, *A Long View from the Left* (Boston, 1973), pp. 316, 351–53. Wirin and Rosenwein, "Smith Act." Claude Lightfoot, "Struggle to End the Cold War at Home," *Political Affairs,* September 1955, pp. 28–47.

23. Yates v. United States, 354 U.S. 298 (1957).

Chapter 7 "A Cowed and Frightened People"—The Agony of Radicalism, 1950–55

1. This and preceding paragraph: Harry Fleischman, *Norman Thomas* (New York, 1964), p. 268. *Nation,* December 10, 1955, p. 501. Murray Kempton, "The Progressives' Long Winter," *Nation,* March 11, 1950, pp. 219–21.

2. This and two preceding paragraphs: interview with C. B. Baldwin. David A. Shannon, *The Decline of American Communism* (New York, 1959), p. 98. David J. Saposs, *Communism in American Politics* (Washington, D.C., 1960), p. 185. Pettis Perry, "Perspectives in the 1952 Elections," *Political Affairs,* September 1952, pp. 6–20.

3. This and two preceding paragraphs: *NYT,* June 28, 1950. I. F. Stone, *The Hidden History of the Korean War* (New York, 1969), pp. 16, 45, 71. Strobe Talbott, ed., *Khrushchev Remembers* (Boston, 1970), pp. 367–68.

4. This and preceding paragraph: Arthur M. Schlesinger, Jr., *The Imperial Presidency* (Boston, 1973), pp. 131, 135. *New York Herald Tribune,* January 4, 1951. Francis Williams, *A Prime Minister Remembers, Earl Attlee's Memoirs* (London, 1962), p. 235.

5. This and preceding paragraph: Harry S. Truman, *Memoirs* (Garden City, N.Y., 1956), 2: 435–50. Willard Shelton, "Inevitable Showdown," *Nation,* April 21, 1951, pp. 362–63.

6. This and preceding paragraph: Arnold Rogow, "Defense or Depression," *Nation,* May 30, 1953, pp. 455–56. *U.S. News & World Report,* May 14, 1950. *NYT,* August 25, 26, 1950. *Nation,* September 9, 1950, p. 221.

7. This and four preceding paragraphs: Much of the material on the Rosenbergs is drawn from interviews with William Reuben and his study of government documents released under the Freedom of Information Act. Kaufman quotation from Eric Bentley, ed., *Thirty Years of Treason* (New York, 1971), p. 939.

8. This and two preceding paragraphs: William A. Reuben, *The Atom Spy Hoax* (New York, 1954), pp. 341, 373, 396, 422–23, 433. The Rosenbergs' sons, who took their name from their foster parents, suggest in their book that their mother and father were probably Communists: Robert and Michael Meeropol, *We Are Your Sons, The Legacy of Ethel and Julius Rosenberg* (Boston, 1975), p. 352. But they offer no concrete evidence to support this information. The U.S. Supreme Court had already adjourned for its summer recess. Convening the Court at the government's request to override Justice Douglas's stay was unprecedented. The American Civil Liberties Union in 1977 (*NYT,* March 18) passed a resolution asking House and Senate Judiciary Committees to investigate "ex parte" relations—private communications—between federal judges and prosecutors and other law enforcement officials. The resolution came after FBI documents revealed that Judge Kaufman—now chief judge, Second Circuit Court of Appeals in New York—had conferred with others before imposing sentence on the Rosenbergs, raising the possibility of an improper "ex parte" relationship.

9. This and preceding paragraph: McCarthy quotation from Richard H. Rovere, *Senator Joe McCarthy* (New York, 1959), p. 15. *Nation,* January 10, 1953, pp. 31–32; November 13, 1954, p. 415; July 16, 1955, p. 47.

10. This and two preceding paragraphs: *NYT,* June 6, July 1, November 11, 1954. Lawrence S. Wittner, *Rebels against War* (New York, 1969), p. 200. Carey

McWilliams, "Oppenheimer Case," *Nation,* May 1, 1954, pp. 373–79. Carey McWilliams, "Gray Report," *Nation,* June 12, 1954, pp. 493–95.

11.   This and four preceding paragraphs: *Nation,* August 5, 1950, p. 119; August 11, 1951, p. 101. Bentley, *Thirty Years,* p. 340. Cedric Belfrage, *The Frightened Giant* (London, 1957), pp. 149, 157. Lillian Hellman, *Scoundrel Time* (Boston, 1976), pp. 92–94.

12.   This and preceding paragraph: *Nation,* August 21, 1954, p. 145. Carey McWilliams, "Can of Worms," *Nation,* August 28, 1954, pp. 163–64.

13.   This and preceding paragraph: *NYT,* August 28, 29; December 21, 24, 26, 1952. *NYT,* August 20, 25, 1954. "Barred Visitors: McCarran Act," *Scientific American,* March 1952, p. 35. "Many Top Chemists Barred from World Chemical Conclave," *Science News Letter,* September 15, 1951, p. 160.

14.   This and three preceding paragraphs: Sidney Hook and H. Stuart Hughes, "Western Values and Total War," *Commentary,* October 1961, pp. 277–304. Sidney Hook, *Heresy, Yes, Conspiracy, No* (New York, 1953), pp. 18, 20, 106, 117, 183, 277.

15.   This and preceding paragraph: Bentley, *Thirty Years,* p. 621. Alan Reitman, ed., *The Pulse of Freedom* (New York, 1975), pp. 192–93. FBI documents, secured through the Freedom of Information Act in 1977, revealed that the lawyer Morris Ernst, an influential ACLU board member, had been passing information on that organization to his friend J. Edgar Hoover since 1942. The same documents showed that a few ACLU officials had given the FBI information between 1953 and 1959 (*NYT,* August 5, 1977).

16.   This and preceding paragraph: Michael Harrington, "American Committee for Cultural Freedom," *Dissent,* Spring 1955, pp. 113–22. Christopher Lasch, *The Agony of the American Left* (New York, 1969), pp. 92, 101–2, 104. *NYT,* April 27, May 8, May 9, 1966; May 9, October 3, 1967. Jason Epstein, "The CIA and the Intellectuals," *New York Review of Books,* April 20, 1967, pp. 16–21. Sol Stern et al., "National Student Association and the CIA," *Ramparts,* March 1967, pp. 29–39. Sidney Hook, "Neither Blind Obedience Nor Uncivil Disobedience", *NYT Magazine,* June 5, 1966, pp. 52–53.

17.   This and preceding paragraph: Fleischman, *Thomas,* p. 257. Bernard K. Johnpoll, *Pacifist's Progress, Norman Thomas and the Decline of American Socialism* (Chicago, 1970), pp. 265, 267, 279, 281–82. *NYT,* March 27, September 10, 1964.

18.   This and preceding four paragraphs: William D. Miller, *A Harsh and Dreadful Love, Dorothy Day and the Catholic Worker Movement* (Garden City, N.Y., 1974), pp. 225, 276–78, 282, 285–88, 290, 310. Dwight Macdonald, "Dorothy Day," *New Yorker,* October 4, pp. 37–40; October 11, pp. 37–42, 1952. "Violations of New York State Defense Emergency Act," *Commonweal,* July 15, 1955, pp. 363–64.

19.   This and two preceding paragraphs: Bernard Nossiter, "Labor and McCarthy," *Nation,* July 24, 1954, pp. 70–72. Sidney Lens, "Labor at the Altar," *Nation,* December 17, 1955, pp. 522–23.

20.   Ronald Radosh, *American Labor and United States Foreign Policy* (New York, 1969), pp. 24, 323, 347. Bernard Nossiter, "Butler Bill," *Nation,* September 4, 1954, pp. 192–93.

21.   This and preceding paragraph: Interview with James Matles. "The Program, National Committee, Communist Party, USA," *Political Affairs,* May 1956, p. 28.

22. This and preceding paragraph: Interviews with C. B. Baldwin, Ralph Shikes. *Life*, May 14, 1956, p. 174.

23. This and preceding paragraph: Annette Rubinstein, ed., *I Vote My Conscience* (New York, 1956), pp. 441, 446. William L. Patterson, *The Man Who Cried Genocide* (New York, 1971), p. 156.

24. This and three preceding paragraphs: Interviews with Louise Berman, Frank Morelli, Helen Harrington, Miriam and Henry Wittner. *Catholic Worker,* September 1954. *Congressional Record,* 83rd Cong., 2d sess., (100): 3175–76. The American Labor party, which Marcantonio had already left, dissolved on October 8, 1956.

25. *Liberator,* January 1, 1831.

Chapter 8   The Montgomery Bus Boycott, 1955

1. This and three preceding paragraphs: Interview and author's correspondence with E. D. Nixon. Interview with Virginia F. Durr. Martin Luther King, Jr., *Stride towards Freedom* (New York, 1958), pp. 41–43. Lerone Bennett, Jr., *What Manner of Man, A Biography of Martin Luther King, Jr.* (Chicago, 1964), p. 59.

2. This and three preceding paragraphs: Charles V. Hamilton, *The Black Experience in American Politics* (New York, 1973), p. 180. Henry Lee Moon, "Negro Vote in the South: 1952," *Nation,* September 27, 1952, pp. 245–48; also pp. 251, 257. *Nation,* January 5, p. 3; February 9, 1952, p. 124; September 17, 1955, p. 234. Dan Wakefield, "Justice in Sumner," *Nation,* October 1, 1955, pp. 284–85. Julius Lester, ed., *The Seventh Son: The Thought and Writing of W. E. B. Du Bois* (New York, 1971), 2: 646.

3. This and three preceding paragraphs: Alan Reitman, ed., *The Pulse of Freedom* (New York, 1975), pp. 180–82. Numan V. Bartley, *The Rise of Massive Resistance, Race and Politics in the South during the 1950's* (Baton Rouge, La., 1969), pp. 30, 82. Louis E. Lomax, *The Negro Revolt* (New York, 1962), p. 75. Dan Wakefield, "Respectable Racism," *Nation,* October 22, 1955, pp. 399–400. Henry Lee Moon, "Score on Integration," *Nation,* December 17, 1955, pp. 526–29.

4. This and two preceding paragraphs: Wilson Record, *Race and Radicalism, The NAACP and the Communist Party in Conflict* (Ithaca, N.Y., 1964), p. 162. Kenneth B. Clark, "Civil Rights Movement," in James A. Geschwender, ed., *The Black Revolt* (Englewood Cliffs, N.J., 1971), p. 62. Stetson Kennedy, "Bombs Bring Us Together," *Nation,* February 2, 1952, pp.105–7. Interviews with Esther Jackson, Palmer Webber. Sharecropper organizing in the 1930s is described in Theodore Rosengarten, ed., *All God's Dangers* (New York, 1974). See also Mark Naison, "Historical Notes on Blacks and American Communism," *Science & Society,* Fall 1978, pp. 324–43.

5. This and preceding paragraph: Interviews with Esther Jackson, Junius Scales, and black movement worker requesting anonymity.

6. This and two preceding paragraphs: *Daily Worker,* December 21, 1947. Record, *Race,* p. 152. William A. Nolan, *Communism versus the Negro* (Chicago, 1951), p. 113. William L. Patterson, *The Man Who Cried Genocide* (New York, 1971), pp. 11, 157, 161, 167, 199.

7. Interview with Doxey Wilkerson. Doxey Wilkerson, "The Negro and the American Nation," *Political Affairs,* July 1946, pp.652–58. James Allen,

"Negro Question," *Political Affairs,* November 1946, pp. 1046–56. William Z. Foster, "On the Question of Negro Self-Determination," *Political Affairs,* January 1947, pp. 54–56.

8. The Communist party's new black policy is described in the following articles in its journal, *Political Affairs:* Frederick C. Hastings, "For a Mass Policy," March 1955, pp. 5–29; John Swift, "Independent Political Action," April 1955, pp. 4–18; Max Weiss, "Geneva and 1956," January 1956, pp. 1–18.

9. This and preceding seven paragraphs: Interview with Junius Scales.

10. This and preceding four paragraphs: Harold Cruse, *The Crisis of the Negro Intellectual* (New York, 1967), p. 243. *New Africa,* May 1949, p. 3. William E. B. Du Bois, *Autobiography* (New York, 1968), pp. 362, 383, 394, 396. William E. B. Du Bois, "I Won't Vote," *Nation,* October 20, 1956, pp. 324–25. Elliott M. Rudwick, *William E. B. DuBois, A Study in Minority Group Leadership* (Philadelphia, 1960), pp. 285–89.

11. This and three preceding paragraphs: Paul Robeson, *Here I Stand* (London, 1958), pp. 9–44. Paul Robeson, Jr., "Paul Robeson: Black Warrior," *Freedomways* 2 (1971): 22–27. Shirley Graham, *Paul Robeson: Citizen of the World* (New York, 1946), pp. 23, 139, 167, 193, 207–34. Marie Seton, *Paul Robeson* (London, 1958), pp. 20, 46, 77.

12. This and preceding four paragraphs: Interview with William Reuben, Palmer Webber. Author's correspondence with Lloyd L. Brown, Clark Foreman. Robeson, *Here I Stand,* pp. 46–48. *NYT,* April 21, 1949.

13. This and four preceding paragraphs: Eugene H. Robinson, "A Distant Image," *Freedomways* 2 (1971): 69. Cruse, *Crisis,* pp. 228, 291, 295, 297. Interview with Junius Scales.

14. This and two preceding paragraphs: Interviews with E. D. Nixon, Virginia F. Durr. Howell Raines, *My Soul Is Rested* (New York, 1977), pp. 34, 44, 50.

15. This and five preceding paragraphs: M. L. King, Jr., *Stride,* pp. 20, 53, 61, 97, 102. *NYT,* March 20, 1956. Bennett, *What Manner,* p. 50.

16. This and five preceding paragraphs: M. L. King, Jr., *Stride,* pp. 134, 137–38. Interview with Virginia F. Durr. Gayle v. Browder, 142 F. Supp. 707 (M.D. Ala 1956) affirmed, 352 U.S. 903 (1956).

17. M. L. King, Jr., *Stride,* p. 195.

Chapter 9   The Soviet Dream Disowned, 1956–58

1. Lewis Feuer, ed., *Marx & Engels* (Garden City, N.Y., 1959), p. x. Lewis Feuer, *The Conflict of Generations* (New York, 1969), p. 374. *Nation,* May 3, 1958, pp. 383–84.

2. This and preceding paragraph: David Egger, Ellen Maytag, "Class of 1958 Speaks Up," *Nation,* May 17, 1958, pp. 432–39. Dick Bruner, "Negroes Bid for Union Power," *Nation,* March 5, 1960, pp. 207–9.

3. This and preceding paragraph: *Daily Worker,* February 16, April 2, April 19, May 7, May 15, September 21, 1956. Townsend Hoopes, *The Devil and John Foster Dulles* (Boston, 1973), pp. 283–85.

4. Alan Reitman, ed., *The Pulse of Freedom* (New York, 1975), p. 205. C. Hermann Pritchett, "Warren Court," *Nation,* July 14, 1956, pp. 31–33;

Ephraim London, "Watkins Decision," *Nation,* June 29, 1957, pp. 558–89; Laurent B. Frantz, "Bankrupt Inquisition," *Nation,* July 20, 1957, pp. 26–29.

5.   This and many following sections of the chapter are based on interviews with John Gates, George Charney, Max Gordon, Dorothy Healey, Donald McMillan, Junius Scales, Doxey Wilkerson, and present and former members of the Communist party requesting anonymity.

6.   This and two preceding paragraphs: *Daily Worker,* March 16, April 2, June 12, 1956. *NYT,* June 5, 1956.

7.   This and two preceding paragraphs: Nikita Khrushchev, "Report to the 20th Congress, Communist Party Soviet Union," *Political Affairs,* July, pp. 51–64; Pietro Nenni (abstract of article published in Rome), July, pp. 40–45; John Gates, "Time for a Change," November 1956, pp. 43–56.

8.   Joshua Kunitz, "Khrushchev and the Jews," *Monthly Review,* July–August 1956, pp. 92–99. *Daily Worker,* June 13, 1957. National Committee, Communist Party USA, "Statement," *Political Affairs,* July 1956, pp. 34–36. John Gates, *The Story of an American Communist* (New York, 1958), p. 163.

9.   This and preceding four paragraphs: *Daily Worker,* October 22, 25, 29; November 26, 29, 1956. Hoopes, *Dulles,* p. 373. John O'Kearny, "Hungary: Myth and Reality," *Nation,* February 2, 1957, pp. 91–94. Herbert Aptheker, "Ideas in Our Time," *Political Affairs,* October 1957, pp. 19–30. Frederic W. Collins, "Liberation," *Nation,* March 30, 1957, pp. 272–75.

10.   This and preceding paragraph: *Daily Worker,* November 4 editorial, 5, 20, 23, 1956. Hyman Lumer, "Truth about Hungary," *Political Affairs,* July 1957, pp. 21–30. Gates, *Story,* p. 178. "Assessing the Damage," *Monthly Review,* December 1956, pp. 257–72.

11.   This and two preceding paragraphs: *Daily Worker,* October 3, 1956; February 9, 13, December 31, 1957; January 9, 1958. Jack Goldring, "American Road to Socialism," *Political Affairs,* August 1956, pp. 50–53; William Z. Foster, "On the Party Situation," October 1956, pp. 15–45; Foster, "Marxism-Leninism and American Prosperity," February 1957, pp. 39–48; Foster, "Party Crisis and the Way Out," December 1957, pp. 46–61; National Committee, Communist Party USA, "Report," March 1958, pp. 1–6. David A. Shannon, *The Decline of American Communism* (New York, 1959), p. 328.

12.   Murray Kempton, *Part of Our Time* (New York, 1955).

13.   Vivian Gornick, *The Romance of American Communism* (New York, 1977), p. 100.

14.   Howard Fast, *The Naked God* (London, 1958), p. 154.

15.   George Charney, *A Long Journey* (Chicago, 1968), p. 323.

Chapter 10   The Black Rebellion Begins, 1960–62

1.   This and preceding paragraph: August Meier and Elliott Rudwick, *CORE, A Study in The Civil Rights Movement* (Chicago, 1975), p. 102. Southern Regional Council, "The Student Protest Movement, 1960" (Report, February 25, 1960, and succeeding reports at Schomburg Center for Research in Black Culture). Louis E. Lomax, *The Negro Revolt* (New York, 1962), p. 124.

2.   This and three preceding paragraphs: Interviews with Julian Bond, Esther Jackson, James Peck. Lewis quotation from Helen Fuller, "We the People of Alabama," *New Republic,* June 5, 1961, pp. 21–23. James Peck, *Freedom*

Ride (New York, 1962), pp. 119, 122. *NYT,* March 26, 31, April 17, 26, 1960. *New York Post,* March 2, April 3, 1960.

3.   This and preceding paragraph: *Nation,* November 8, 1959, p. 390; Wilma Dykeman and James Stokeley, "Courage in Action," December 22, 1956, pp. 531–33. William Manchester, *The Glory and the Dream* (Boston, 1973), p. 809. *U.S. News & World Report,* June 20, 1960, p. 116.

4.   This and two preceding paragraphs: Interview with Howard Zinn. *Florida Flambeau* (Florida State University), March 15, 1960. *NYT,* March 31, 1960. *New York Post,* March 2, 1960; February 21, 1961. Jack Greenberg, "Case against Jim Crow Seating," *New Leader,* March 14, 1960, pp. 7–9.

5.   This and two preceding paragraphs: Interview with Casey Hayden. Helen Fuller, "Southern Students Take Over," *New Republic,* May 2, 1960, pp. 14–16. Lerone Bennett, Jr., *What Manner of Man* (Chicago, 1964), pp. 117–18. Truman from WICB-TV, Ithaca, N.Y., broadcast in *New York Post,* April 20, 1960; *Newsweek,* March 28, 1960, pp. 25–27. *Birmingham News,* October 6–11, 1957. C. Eric Linden, "Strategy of a Sit-In," *Reporter,* January 5, 1961, pp. 20–23. Peck, *Freedom Ride,* p. 127.

6.   This and three preceding paragraphs: Charles V. Hamilton, *The Black Experience in American Politics* (New York, 1973), p. 193. Lomax, *Negro Revolt,* p. 127. Meier and Rudwick, *CORE,* pp. 102, 110, 126. "The Student Protest Movement: A Recapitulation," Southern Regional Council, September 29, 1961.

7.   This and two preceding paragraphs: *Nation,* March 12, 1960, p. 218. Fuller, "Students." Lomax, *Negro Revolt,* p. 129. "Negro Progress in 1961," *Ebony,* January 1962, p. 21. *Wall Street Journal,* February 23, 1960.

8.   This and two preceding paragraphs: Interview with James Peck. Meier and Rudwick, *CORE,* pp. 33–38, 135–37. Lomax, *Negro Revolt,* p. 136. CORE, "Sit-Ins—The Students Report," May 1960; "Jailed In," April 1961 (pamphlets at Schomburg Center). *New York Post,* May 15, 1961.

9.   This and two preceding paragraphs: Interview with James Peck. *NYT,* May 17, 1961. Meier and Rudwick, *CORE,* p. 138. Howard Zinn, *SNCC, The New Abolitionists* (Boston, 1964), p. 42. *Newsweek,* May 29, 1961, pp. 21–22.

10.   This and two preceding paragraphs: Interview with Cordell Reagon. Zinn, *SNCC,* pp. 51–54. *Life,* May 26, pp. 22–24; June 2, 1961, pp. 46–55. *NYT,* September 16, 1961. Robert Martinson, "Private Notes of a Freedom Rider," *Nation,* January 6, 1962, pp. 4–6.

11.   This and two preceding paragraphs: Inge Powell Bell, *CORE and the Strategy of Nonviolence* (New York, 1968), p. 10. Major Johns, Ronnie Moore, "It Happened at Baton Rouge," April 1962 (CORE pamphlet). *NYT,* June 2, 1961. Meier and Rudwick, *CORE,* pp. 138–52. Lomax, *Negro Revolt,* pp. 96–99.

12.   This and two preceding paragraphs: Interviews with Conrad Lynn and John Gerassi bear on the whole Williams section. "John Schultz Interviews Williams," *Studies on the Left* 2 (1962). Robert F. Williams, *Negroes with Guns* (New York, 1962), pp. 58, 68. Williams, "Can Negroes Afford to Be Pacifists?" *Liberation,* September 1959, pp. 4–7. Julian Mayfield, "Challenge to Negro Leadership," *Commentary,* April 1961, pp. 297–305.

13.   This and two preceding paragraphs: George L. Weissman, "Kissing Case," *Nation,* January 17, 1959, pp. 46–49. Williams, *Negroes,* pp. 58–59, 62–66, 68, 77–80. NAACP statement, *Liberation,* October 1959, pp. 7–8.

14. This and two preceding paragraphs: *The Militant,* September 4–11, p. 3. Meier and Rudwick, *CORE,* pp. 202–3. Harold Cruse, *The Crisis of the Negro Intellectual* (New York, 1967), p. 368.

15. This and three preceding paragraphs: *NYT,* November 14, December 7, 1966; January 17, 1976. *New York Post,* August 23, 1967. Georgie Anne Geyer, "Odyssey of Robert Williams," *New Republic,* March 20, 1971, pp. 15–17. "Williams on Revolution," *National Guardian,* January 6, 1968. Williams, "Minority Revolution," in John Gerassi, ed., *The Coming of the New International* (New York, 1971) pp. 568–86.

Chapter 11   Building a Black Base, 1961–63

1. Tom Hayden, "Revolution in Mississippi" (SDS pamphlet, January 1962), pp. 11–12.

2. This and two preceding paragraphs: Interview with Cordell Reagon. Hayden, "Revolution," p. 10. Janet Feagans, "Voting Violence and Walkout in McComb," *New South,* October 1961, pp. 3–4. Howard Zinn, *SNCC, The New Abolitionists* (Boston, 1964), p. 83. Alice Lake, notebooks and memoranda for article for *Redbook,* August 1964.

3. Gregory from Jack Newfield, *A Prophetic Minority* (New York, 1966), p. 74. James Forman, *The Making of Black Revolutionaries* (New York, 1972), p. 286. Interviews with Joyce Ladner, Walter Stafford.

4. This and two preceding paragraphs: Pat Watters, Reese Cleghorn, *Climbing Jacob's Ladder, The Arrival of Negroes in Southern Politics* (New York, 1967), pp. 156, 162. Sally Belfrage, *Freedom Summer* (New York, 1965), p. 131. *NYT,* August 23, 24, 1964. Anne Moody, *Coming of Age in Mississippi* (New York, 1968), pp. 284, 295.

5. This and two preceding paragraphs: Hayden, "Revolution," p. 16. Staughton Lynd, ed., *Nonviolence in America* (Indianapolis/New York, 1966), pp. 428–34. Newfield, *Prophetic,* pp. 79–81.

6. This and preceding paragraph: Margaret Long, "They Know They're Niggers," *New South,* October 1962, pp. 3–8. Zinn, *SNCC,* p. 9. Len Holt, *The Summer That Didn't End* (New York, 1965), p. 32. Moody, *Coming,* p. 247.

7. This and four preceding paragraphs: August Meier and Elliott Rudwick, *CORE* (Chicago, 1975), pp. 175–79. *National Guardian,* June 27, 1964. Evans, Novak in Andrew Kopkind, "New Radicals in Dixie," *New Republic,* April 10, 1965, pp. 13–16. Interview with Cordell Reagon.

8. This and three preceding paragraphs: Watters, Cleghorn, *Climbing,* pp. 55–63, 213–16. Fred Powledge, *Black Power, White Resistance* (Cleveland/New York, 1967), pp. 65, 71.

9. This and two preceding paragraphs: Inge Powell Bell, *CORE and the Strategy of Nonviolence* (New York, 1968), p. 164. Forman, *Making,* 375. Moody, *Coming,* 253–66. *National Guardian,* August 20, 1965. James Farmer, *Freedom—When?* (New York, 1965), p. 98. Hamilton Bims, "Deacons for Defense," *Ebony,* September 1965, pp. 25–30.

10. *Nashville Banner,* February 17, 1964.

11. This and three preceding paragraphs: Interviews with Stokeley Carmichael, Gloria Richardson. Lynd, *Nonviolence,* p. 41. "Gloria Richardson: Lady General of Civil Rights," *Ebony,* July 1964, pp. 23–31. Howard Zinn, "Battle-Scarred Youngsters," *Nation,* October 5, 1963, pp. 193–97.

12. This and two preceding paragraphs: Newfield, *Prophetic,* p. 77. Forman, *Making,* p. 232. Holt, *Summer,* p. 133.

13. This and three preceding paragraphs: Interviews with Tom Hayden, Daniel Millstone. Zinn, *SNCC,* pp. 74–77. Meier and Rudwick, *CORE,* pp. 168–71, 218. Farmer, *Freedom,* pp. 4–17.

14. This and three preceding paragraphs: Interview with Cordell Reagon. "Agony of Albany," *New South,* October–November 1963, pp. 12–16. Howard Zinn, *Albany: A Study in National Responsibility* (Southern Regional Council, Atlanta, 1962). Zinn, *Southern Mystique* (New York, 1964), pp. 161–211. Zinn, *SNCC,* pp. 124–36. Lerone Bennett, Jr., *What Manner of Man* (Chicago, 1964), p. 185. William R. Miller, *Martin Luther King, Jr.* (New York, 1968), pp. 113–28.

15. This and three preceding paragraphs: *NYT,* May 3, 7, 8, 9, 21, 1963. Lerone Bennett, Jr., "Mood of the Negro," *Ebony,* July 1963, pp. 27–38. Miller, *King,* pp. 131–50. Bennett, *What Manner,* pp. 131–53.

16. This and preceding paragraph: "Birmingham and Beyond," *New South,* October–November 1963, pp. 17–23. Forman, *Making,* pp. 312–27. Meier and Rudwick, *CORE,* p. 219. *National Guardian,* May 16, 1963. Powledge, *Black Power,* pp. 78–79.

17. This and four preceding paragraphs: Interview with Gloria Richardson. Meyer from *Nation,* July 27, 1963, pp. 41–42. Forman from *Making,* p. 335. Lewis from Margaret Long, "March on Washington," *New South,* September 1963, pp. 3–19; and Massimo Teodori, ed., *The New Left: A Documentary History* (New York, 1969), p. 101.

18. This and preceding paragraph: Lewis from Watters, Cleghorn, *Climbing,* p. xv. Long, "March." "Biggest Protest March," *Ebony,* November 1963, p. 29.

19. This and preceding paragraph: Moody, *Coming,* p. 275, 285. Julius Lester, *Look Out, Whitey!* (New York, 1968), p. 104. Malcolm X (with Alex Haley), *Autobiography* (New York, 1966), pp. 278–81. *NYT,* September 16, 1963, November 19, 1977.

Chapter 12   1964: Summer of Decision

1. This and previous paragraph: Alice Lake, notebooks and memoranda for article for *Redbook,* August 1964. Doar from Len Holt, *The Summer That Didn't End* (New York, 1965), pp. 49–50. Hoover on King from Edward Peeks, *The Long Struggle for Black Power* (New York, 1971), p. 4. Hoover from *Newsweek,* July 13, 1964.

2. This and four preceding paragraphs: Alice Lake, notebooks. Andrew Kopkind, "New Radicals in Dixie," *New Republic,* April 10, 1965, pp. 13–16. Interview with Walter Stafford.

3. This and five preceding paragraphs: Moses from Lake notebooks. Elizabeth Sutherland, ed., *Letters from Mississippi* (New York, 1965), pp. 142–44. Holt, *Summer,* pp. 44–91. *NYT,* June 26, August 5, 1964. *National Guardian,* July 4, 1964. Dr. Spain from Cleveland Sellers (with Robert Terrell), *The River of No Return* (New York, 1973), p. 107. Interviews with Margot Adler, Cleveland Sellers.

4. This and preceding paragraph: William Bradford Huie, *Three Lives for Mississippi* (New York, 1965), pp. 186–91, 240–44. Louis E. Lomax, "Mississippi Eyewitness," *Ramparts,* December 1964, pp. 8–23.

5. This and preceding paragraph: August Meier and Elliott Rudwick, *CORE, A Study in the Civil Rights Movement* (Chicago, 1975), p. 277. *NYT,* October 21, 27; December 30, 1967.

6. This and two preceding paragraphs: Robinson from Sally Belfrage, *Freedom Summer* (New York, 1965), pp. 149, 170–75, 222–25. Sutherland, *Letters,* p. 88. Tompkins from Lake, notebooks. Pat Watters and Reese Cleghorn, *Climbing Jacob's Ladder* (New York, 1967), p. 139.

7. This and preceding paragraph: Payne from Mitchell Cohen and Dennis Hale, *The New Student Left* (Boston, 1966), pp. 50–58. Sutherland, *Letters,* pp. 48, 60, 105. Susskind from *National Guardian,* July 4, 1964.

8. This and two preceding paragraphs: Interview with Stokeley Carmichael. Margot Adler diaries. Lake notebooks.

9. This and preceding paragraph: Adler diaries. Lake notebooks.

10. This and preceding paragraph: Meier and Rudwick, *CORE,* pp. 205–7. Howard Zinn, *SNCC, The New Abolitionists* (Boston, 1964), pp. 171, 174, 182–83.

11. This and four preceding paragraphs: Sellers, *River,* p. 130. Holt, *Summer,* pp. 161, 163–66. Sutherland, *Letters,* p. 211. *NYT,* January 9, May 23, 1964. Alex Poinsett, "Poverty amidst Plenty," *Ebony,* August 1965, pp. 104–14.

12. This and five preceding paragraphs: *NYT,* April 11–14, July 3, 1964. Prendergast from James Farmer, *Freedom—When?* (New York, 1965), pp. 27–31. Harlem riot, Gray, Rustin from Fred Ferretti, *New York Herald Tribune,* July 20, 1964. Epton from Kirkpatrick Sale, *SDS* (New York, 1974), pp. 135–36.

13. This and two preceding paragraphs: *New York Daily News,* July 22, 1964. Eastland from *National Guardian,* August 1, 1964. Truman Nelson, *Torture of Mothers* (Newburyport, Mass., 1965), p. 89. Farmer, *Freedom,* p. 31.

14. This and preceding paragraph: Interview with Russell Stetler. Press release, July 20, 1964, in Doris Kearns, *Lyndon Johnson and the American Dream* (New York, 1976), p. 192.

15. This and two preceding paragraphs: Interview with Gloria Richardson.

16. This and preceding paragraph: *Baltimore Afro-American,* July 12, 13, 16, 1963.

17. This and preceding paragraph: Interviews with Stokeley Carmichael, Gloria Richardson. *Salisbury Times* (Md.), June 8, 1964. Sellers, *River,* p. 76.

18. This and preceding paragraph: Robert L. Scott, Wayne Brockriede, *The Rhetoric of Black Power* (New York, 1969), p. 132. Malcolm X (with Alex Haley), *Autobiography* (New York, 1966), pp. 361, 367.

19. This and preceding paragraph: Malcolm X, *Autobiography,* pp. 367, 423. Julius Lester, *Look Out, Whitey!* (New York, 1968), p. 91.

20. This and preceding paragraph: Hans J. Massaquoi, "Mystery of Malcolm X," *Ebony,* September 1964, pp. 38–46. Malcolm X, *Autobiography,* pp. 334, 362, 424, 459.

21. This and preceding paragraph: *Ebony,* September 1964. Malcolm X, *Autobiography,* pp. 35, 437, 439, 446–47. On life sentences being served for Malcolm X murder, see *NYT,* July 27, 1978.

22. This and two preceding paragraphs: *NYT,* August 22–August 27, 1964. Richard Rovere, "Letter from Washington," *New Yorker,* October 16, 1965, pp. 233–44. Holt, *Summer,* pp. 161–81. Rauh from Jack Newfield, *A Prophetic Minority* (New York, 1966), pp. 187–89.

23. This and two preceding paragraphs: Interview with Stokeley Carmichael. James Forman, *The Making of Black Revolutionaries* (New York, 1972), pp. 389, 395 (Hamer quotation).

24. This and two preceding paragraphs: Rovere, "Letter." Jerry De Muth, "Tired of Being Sick and Tired," *Nation,* June 1, 1964, pp. 548–51. Only 5.7 percent of eligible blacks were registered in Mississippi in 1964; only two blacks registered in Panola County in 50 years: *Nation,* January 4, p. 3; May 17, pp. 526–29, 1965.

Chapter 13   The New Left and the Berkeley Uprising, 1960–64

1. This and preceding paragraph: Interview with David Horowitz. D. Horowitz, *Student* (New York, 1962), pp. 83, 104.

2. This and preceding seven paragraphs: Interviews with Dorothy Healey, David Horowitz, Tom Hayden. Michael Rossman, *The Wedding within the War* (New York, 1971), pp. 68, 79–80, 198. Horowitz, *Student,* p. 21.

3. This and preceding four paragraphs: Horowitz, *Student,* pp. 21, 39, 115. Senate Internal Security Subcommittee of the Commitee on the Judiciary, *Report on the Hearings of Dr. Linus Pauling,* 87th Cong., 1st sess., 1961. Lawrence Wittner, *Rebels against War* (New York, 1969), pp. 244, 258–61.

4. This and two preceding paragraphs: Wittner, *Rebels,* pp. 247–49, 262–67. Michael Ferber, Staughton Lynd, *The Resistance* (Boston, 1971), pp. 12, 21.

5. This and two preceding paragraphs: Hans V. Tofte, head of the CIA's covert activities during the cold war, claimed in a letter to the *New York Times* (December 20, 1978) that the CIA "denied Iranian oil to Soviet Russia" and that Kermit Roosevelt "reflected his grandfather's admonition about speaking softly and walking with a big stick." Norman Gall, "Anatomy of a Coup," *Nation,* October 26, 1963, pp. 253–56. "How the U.S. Blocked Guiana's Independence," *Liberation,* April 1964, pp. 7–8. Leslie Dewart, "Cuban Crisis Revisted," *Studies on the Left,* pp. 15–40.

6. This and two preceding paragraphs: *Berkeley Gazette,* April 23, 1961. *Nation,* March 10, 1962, p. 205. Dan Kurzman, "Lovestone's Cold War," *Nation,* June 25, 1966, pp. 17–22.

7. This and six preceding paragraphs: Interviews with Tom Hayden, Tom Kahn. Hayden memo from Kirkpatrick Sale, *SDS* (New York, 1974), p. 43; also pp. 21, 52.

8. This and preceding paragraph: Interview with Todd Gitlin. Lewis Feuer, *The Conflict of Generations* (New York, 1969), pp. 407–12.

9. This and preceding paragraph: Interview with Russell Stetler. Sale, *SDS,* pp. 58, 65–67.

10. This and preceding paragraph: Irving Howe, "New Styles In 'Leftism,' " *Dissent,* Summer 1965, pp. 295–323. Michael Harrington, "Is There a New Radicalism?" *Partisan Review,* Spring 1965, pp. 194–205.

11. This and preceding paragraph: Interviews with Marilyn Katz, Russell Stetler. Jack Newfield, *A Prophetic Minority* (New York, 1966), p. 140.

12. This and five preceding paragraphs: Interviews with Todd Gitlin, Russell Stetler. Sale, *SDS,* pp. 121–22, 161. Jerome from Newfield, *Prophetic,* p. 159.

Philip A. Luce, "Why I Quit the Extreme Left," *Saturday Evening Post,* May 8, 1965, pp. 32–33.

13. This and three preceding paragraphs: Interviews with Lewis Cole, Dorothy Healey, James Weinstein.

14. Feuer, *Conflict,* pp. 11–12.

15. This and preceding paragraph: Richard Flacks, "Who Protests: The Social Bases of the Student Movement," in Julian Foster, Durward Long, *Protest! Student Activism in America* (New York, 1970), pp. 134–57. Flacks, "The Liberated Generation: Exploration of the Roots of Student Protest," *Journal of Social Issues,* July 1967, p. 67. See also Flacks, *Youth and Social Change* (Boston, 1971). Kenneth Keniston, *Youth and Dissent* (New York, 1971), pp. 155, 274–78, 307. Leonard L. Baird, "Who Protests: A Study of Student Activists" in Foster and Long, *Protest!,* pp. 123–33. Seymour L. Halleck, "Hypotheses of Student Unrest," in Foster and Long, *Protest!* pp. 105–22. William Watts and David Whittaker, "Free Speech Advocates at Berkeley," *Journal of Applied Behavioral Science,* January 1966, p. 53, conclude that protesters largely came from homes where both mother and father had academic degrees. David L. Westby, *The Clouded Vision, The Student Movement in the United States in the 1960's* (Lewisburg, Pa., 1976), p. 45, found in a study with Richard E. Braungart that "the solid majority of the parents of Left-wing students were politically to the Left. . . ." S. M. Lipset, "The Activists: A Profile," in Daniel Bell and Irving Kristol, *Confrontation: The Student Rebellion and the Universities* (New York, 1969), pp. 51–52, concluded: "The activists are more radical than their parents; but both parents and children are located on the same side of the spectrum."

16. This and two preceding paragraphs: Martin Duberman, "Arguments: Anarchism Left and Right," *Partisan Review,* Fall 1966, pp. 610–15. Greg Calvert and Carol Neiman, *A Disrupted History, The New Left and the New Capitalism* (New York, 1971), pp. 14, 117. Rossman, *The Wedding,* p. 15.

17. This and three preceding paragraphs: *NYT,* December 9, 1964. Mario Savio, "An End to History," pp. 216–19 in Seymour M. Lipset and Sheldon Wolin, *The Berkeley Student Revolt* (Garden City, N.Y., 1965). Cleveland from Massimo Teodori, ed., *The New Left: A Documentary History* (New York, 1969), pp. 150–51.

18. This and preceding paragraph: Rossman, *The Wedding,* p. 123. Berkeley Division, Academic Senate, "Report of Ad Hoc Committee on Student Conduct" (November 12, 1964), in Margot Adler papers.

19. This and two preceding paragraphs: ACLU, "The Campus and the Constitution" (undated), in Adler papers. Savio from Feuer, *Conflict,* p. 444, n. 21.

20. This and preceding paragraph: Kerr from *San Francisco Examiner,* October 3, 1964; repeated in Ed Montgomery column, November 25. Colin Miller, "Press and Student Revolt" in Michael V. Miller, Susan Gilmore, eds., *Revolution at Berkeley* (New York, 1965), p. 324.

21. This and two preceding paragraphs: Savio from Hal Draper, *Berkeley: The New Student Revolt* (New York, 1965), p. 98. *San Francisco Chronicle,* December 3, 4, 6, 9, 1964. Miller and Gilmore, *Revolution,* p. 332. Interview with Margot Adler.

22. This and two preceding paragraphs: Feuer from *San Francisco Chronicle,* December 9, 1964. *Berkeley Daily Gazette,* December 9, 1964. *Daily Californian,* December 9, 1964. Kerr from A. H. Raskin, "The Berkeley Affair," *NYT Magazine,* February 14, 1965, pp. 24–25.

23.   This and two preceding paragraphs: Newfield, *Prophetic,* pp. 183–84. Sheldon
S. Wolin and John H. Schaar, "Berkeley and the Fate of the Multiversity,"
New York Review of Books, March 11, 1965, pp. 15–18. Richard H. Somers,
"The Berkeley Campus in the Twilight of the FSM: Hope or Futility?" pp.
419–40 in James McEvoy, Abraham Miller, eds., *Black Power and Student
Rebellion* (Belmont, Calif., 1969), Philip Meyer and Michael Maidenberg,
"The Berkeley Rebels Five Years Later" (*Detroit Free Press* and Knight
newspapers, 1969). Henry C. Finney, "Political Libertarianism at Berkeley,"
Journal Of Social Issues, 27 (1971): 35–61.

Chapter 14   From Civil Liberties to Ghetto Riots, 1965

1.   Interview with Stokeley Carmichael. Henry from Pat Watters, *Down to Now*
(New York, 1971), p. 304.

2.   This and two preceding paragraphs: Interviews with Cleveland Sellers, Cordell Reagon. Pat Watters and Reese Cleghorn, *Climbing Jacob's Ladder, The
Arrival of Negroes in Southern Politics* (New York, 1967), p. 245; Ouletta from
pp. 274–75. Benjamin Muse, *The American Negro Revolution, 1963–1967*
(Bloomington, Ind., 1968), p. 163–64.

3.   This and three preceding paragraphs: Andrew Kopkind, "Selma," *New Republic,* March 20, 1965, pp. 7–9; Kopkind, "A Walk in Alabama," April 3,
1965, pp. 7–8. *NYT,* August 21, 1965. Elizabeth Heard, "A Murder Trial,"
New South, October 1965, pp. 2–7. Cleveland Sellers (with Robert Terrell),
The River of No Return (New York, 1973), p. 128. Stanley Plastrik, "Marching on Montgomery," *Dissent,* Spring 1965, pp. 145–47.

4.   This and three preceding paragraphs: Interview with Tom Kahn. Bayard
Rustin, "From Protest to Politics," *Commentary,* February 1965, pp. 25–31.
Staughton Lynd, "Coalition Politics or Nonviolent Revolution?" *Liberation,*
June/July 1965, pp. 18–21. Greg Calvert and Carol Neiman, *A Disrupted
History* (New York, 1971), p. 133.

5.   This and preceding paragraph: Interview with Lawrence Guyot. Sellers,
River, p. 133. Andrew Kopkind, "New Radicals in Dixie," *New Republic,*
April 10, 1965, pp. 13–16.

6.   This and three preceeding paragraphs: Interviews with Joyce Ladner, Alvin
Pouissant, Walter Stafford, Jean Wylie. Lerone Bennett, Jr., "Rebel with a
Cause," *Ebony,* July 1965, pp. 146–53.

7.   This and two preceding paragraphs: Interviews with Courtland Cox, Casey
Hayden, Howard Zinn. Sellers, *River,* p. 130.

8.   This and three preceding paragraphs: *NYT,* June 5, 1965. Watters and Cleghorn, *Climbing,* pp. 261, 266. William Brink and Louis Harris, *Black and
White* (New York, 1966), pp. 86–87. Alex Poinsett, "Why Blacks Don't
Vote," *Ebony,* March 1976, p. 33. William A. Price, "Economics of the Negro
Ghetto," *National Guardian,* September 3, 1966. Christopher Jencks, "Ac-
commodating Whites," *New Republic,* April 16, 1966, pp. 19–22. "Old militants" from interview with Emily Gibson.

9.   This and preceding four paragraphs: "State of the Southern States," *New
South,* Spring 1966, pp. 80–96; Vern Rony, "Swan Song in Black and White,"
Summer 1967, pp. 2–39. John Hulett, *The Black Panther Party* (New York,
1966), pp. 7–15.

10. This and three preeding paragraphs: Interviews with Courtland Cox, Stokeley Carmichael, Cleveland Sellers. Jack Newfield, *A Prophetic Minority* (New York, 1966), pp. 108–9. Lerone Bennett, Jr., "Stokeley Carmichael," *Ebony*, September 1966, pp. 25–32. Robert Lewis Shayon, "Real Stokeley Carmichael," *Saturday Review*, July 9, 1966, p. 42.

11. This and four preceding paragraphs: Newfield, *Prophetic*, p. 111. Interviews with Carmichael, Cox, Sellers. Martin Duberman, "Black Power in America," *Partisan Review*, Winter 1968, pp. 34–38. *NYT*, November 9, 1966.

12. This and preceding paragraph: Interview with Lawrence Guyot. *NYT*, November 9, 1966.

13. This and three preceeding paragraphs: *Guardian*, April 24, 1965. David Dellinger, "March on Washington and Its Critics," *Liberation*, May 1965, pp. 6–7. *New Republic*, August 7, 1965, p. 5. Jonathan Mirsky, "The War Is Over," *Ramparts*, December 1967, pp. 36–42.

14. This and three preceding paragraphs: Louis Menashe and Ronald Radosh, *Teach-Ins: USA* (New York/Washington, 1967), pp. 31, 44, 149, 278.

15. This and preceding paragraph: Dellinger, *Liberation*, May 1965. Dellinger, *More Power than We Know* (Garden City, N.Y., 1975), pp. 11–12. Kirkpatrick Sale, *SDS* (New York, 1974), pp. 177–81, 189. Lynd from *Liberation*, June/July, 1965, p.1.

16. This and three preceding paragraphs: Nathan Glazer, *Remembering the Answers* (New York, 1970), p. 227. Sale, *SDS*, pp. 186–87, 209–10, 221, 234, 250.

17. This and preceding paragraph: Interviews with Tom Hayden, Marilyn Katz. Paul Jacobs, Saul Landau, *The New Radicals, A Report with Documents* (New York, 1966), pp. 252–57.

18. This and four preceding paragraphs: Thomas Powers, *The War at Home* (New York, 1973), pp. 82–92. Carl Oglesby, "Notes on a Decade Ready for the Dustbin," *Liberation*, August/September, 1969, pp. 5–19.

19. This and three preceding paragraphs: Interviews with Stokeley Carmichael, Cleveland Sellers. Jacobs and Landau, *New Radicals*, pp. 249–52. "State of the Southern States," *New South*, Fall 1967, pp. 81–110. James Forman, *Sammy Younge, Jr.* (New York, 1968), p. 223. Reese Cleghorn, "No Seat for the Negro Who Won," *New Republic*, January 29, 1966, pp. 11–12.

20. This and two preceding paragraphs: August Meier and Elliott Rudwick, *CORE, A Study in the Civil Rights Movement* (Chicago, 1975), p. 415. King to Chicago from interview with Tom Kahn. Also, William R. Miller, *Martin Luther King, Jr.* (New York, 1968), p. 236; Margaret Long, "The Movement," *New South*, Winter 1966, p. 1.

21. This and four preceding paragraphs: Interviews with Emily Gibson, Dorothy Healey, Earl Ofari. Jerry Cohen, William S. Murphy, *Burn, Baby, Burn!* (New York, 1966), pp. 317–18; Parker from p. 278; p. 206. Muse, *American Negro*, p. 206. Anthony Oberschall, "The Los Angeles Riot of August, 1965," in James A. Geschwender, ed., *The Black Revolt* (Englewood Cliffs, N.J., 1971), pp. 5–7.

22. This and two preceding paragraphs: James A. Geschwender, "Civil Rights Protests and Riots," in Geschwender, *Black Revolt*, pp. 300–311. H. Edward Ransford, "Isolation, Powerlessness, and Violence" in ibid., pp. 389–401. David O. Sears, T. M. Tomlinson, "Riot Ideology in Los Angeles," in ibid., pp. 375–88.

23. *NYT*, August 5, 1966.

Chapter 15   Into the Streets: Black Power and Antiwar Resistance, 1966

1. This and preceding paragraph: Interviews with Matthew Jones, Cordell Reagon. *NYT,* August 5, 1966. Carl T. Rowan, "Crisis in Civil Rights Leadership," *Ebony,* November 1966, pp. 27–38.

2. This and four preceding paragraphs: Interviews with Stokeley Carmichael, Ivanhoe Donaldson, Dorothy Healey, Tom Kahn. Pat Watters, *Down to Now* (New York, 1971), pp. 349–50.

3. This and preceding paragraph: James Forman, *Sammy Younge, Jr.* (New York, 1968), pp. 4–42, 191–93, 225, 234. Alvin F. Pouissant, "A Psychiatrist Looks at Black Power," *Ebony,* March 1969, pp. 142–52.

4. This and two preceding paragraphs: Irving Howe, "New Styles in Leftism," *Dissent,* Summer 1965, pp. 295–323. David Closens, "Ameer Baraka," *Ebony,* August 1969, pp. 75–83. Interview with Paul Jacobs.

5. This and four preceding paragraphs: Interviews with Stokeley Carmichael, Lawrence Guyot, Cordell Reagon. *NYT,* June 8, 1966. Martin Luther King, Jr., *Where Do We Go from Here: Chaos or Community?* (New York, 1967), p. 33. Bradford Chambers, *Chronicles of Black Protest* (New York, 1969), p. 216. Michele Wallace, *Black Macho and the Myth of the Superwoman* (New York, 1979), p. 38.

6. This and five preceding paragraphs: Interviews with Carmichael, Alvin F. Pouissant. Chambers, *Chronicles,* p. 270. King, *Where,* p. 30. Andrew Kopkind, "The Birth of Black Power," *Ramparts,* October 1966, pp. 4–8.

7. This and preceding paragraph: King, *Where,* pp. 25–65, 48. *Time,* July 1, 1966, pp. 11–17. Robert L. Scott and Wayne Brockriede, *The Rhetoric of Black Power* (New York, 1969), pp. 81–82.

8. Stokeley Carmichael, "What We Want," *New York Review of Books,* September 22, 1966, pp. 5–8. Stokeley Carmichael and Charles V. Hamilton, *The Politics of Liberation in America* (New York, 1967), p. 47.

9. This and two preceding paragraphs: Smith from *NYT,* July 6, 1966. Inge Powell Bell, *CORE and the Strategy of Nonviolence* (New York, 1968), pp. 187–89. August Meier and Elliott Rudwick, *CORE, A Study in the Civil Rights Movement* (Chicago, 1975), pp. 400, 416–19.

10. This and two preceding paragraphs: William Brink and Louis Harris, *Black and White* (New York, 1966), p. 67. Rizzo from Nora Sayre, *Sixties Going on Seventies* (New York, 1973), p. 67; also pp. 125–26. *Philadelphia Inquirer,* August 12, 1966. *Philadelphia News,* August 16, 1966. James Forman, *The Making of Black Revolutionaries* (New York, 1972), pp. 460–70. *National Guardian,* August 27, 1966.

11. This and four preceding paragraphs: Interviews with Carmichael, Sellers, Pouissant. Brink and Harris, *Black and White,* p. 61. Forman, *Making,* pp. 471–74. "State of the Southern States," *New South,* Fall 1966, pp. 96–114. *New Republic,* September 24, 1966, p. 8.

12. This and five preceding paragraphs: Interview with James Weinstein. James Peck, "Thirty Years on the Picket Line," *Liberation,* March 1966, pp. 37–39. *New Left Notes,* April 1, 1966. *New Republic,* March 26, 1966, p. 9. Kirkpatrick Sale, *SDS* (New York, 1974), pp. 254–55, 303–4 (for McNamara), 312.

13. This and five preceding paragraphs: Interview with Paul Jacobs. *New Left Notes,* March 11, August 5, 1966. Jerry Rubin, *Growing (Up) at 37* (New

York, 1976), p. 79. Serge Lang, *The Scheer Campaign* (New York, 1967). Buddy Stein and David Wellman, "The Scheer Campaign," *Studies on the Left*, January–February 1967, pp. 62–77.

14. This and three preceding paragraphs: Carl Davidson, "National Vice President's Report," *New Left Notes*, February 3, 1967, pp. 4–5. Sale, *SDS*, pp. 277, 306–7.

15. This and three preceding paragraphs: Interview with John Judis, Todd Gitlin. Carl Davidson, "Towards A Student Syndicalist Movement, or University Reform Revisited"; and "The Praxis of Student Power" in Immanuel Wallerstein and Paul Starr, eds., *The University Crisis Reader* (New York, 1971), 2:99–106, 109–11. *Studies on the Left*, January–February, 1967, pp. 3–21. "Genovese Looks at the American Left, New and Old," *National Guardian*, February 19, 1966, pp. 6–7. Michael Harrington, "Is There a New Radicalism?" *Partisan Review*, Spring 1965, pp. 194–205.

16. This and two preceding paragraphs: Sidney Lens, "Ideology of Profits," *Liberation*, October, 1966, pp. 23–25; Lens, "Road to Power and Beyond," November 1968, pp. 8–15. Interview with Lewis Cole.

17. This and seven preceding paragraphs: Herbert Marcuse, *One Dimensional Man* (Boston, 1964), particularly pp. 9, 32; Marcuse, "Repressive Tolerance," particularly pp. 81, 109–16, in Marcuse, Robert Paul Wolff, Barrington Moore, Jr., *A Critique of Pure Tolerance* (Boston, 1969). "A liberal wants to free . . ." from Ronald Aronson, "Dear Herbert," *Radical America*, April 1970, p. 9. "I cannot imagine . . ." from Robert W. Marks, *The Meaning of Marcuse* (New York, 1970), p. 92; also particularly pp. 11, 29, 68, 74, 89, 128. Herbert Marcuse, *Counter Revolution and Revolt* (Boston, 1972), particularly pp. 36, 77, 131. Sol Stern, "On Herbert Marcuse," *Ramparts*, June 29, 1968, pp. 55–58.

18. This and three preceding paragraphs: Interviews with Stokeley Carmichael, William Hansen, Alvin F. Pouissant. Pouissant, "How the White Problem Spawned Black Power," *Ebony*, August 1967, pp. 88–94.

19. This and four preceding paragraphs: Huey P. Newton (with J. Herman Blake), *Revolutionary Suicide* (New York, 1974), pp. 9, 14. Bobby Seale, "Selections from the Biography of Huey P. Newton," *Ramparts*, October 26, 1968, pp. 21–34.

20. This and six preceding paragraphs: Newton, *Revolutionary*, pp. 137–38. "Panther Power" from *Black Panther*, September 14, 1968. "Enclave-like" and "reactionary and insane" from Theodore Draper, "The Black Panthers" in Irving Howe, ed., *Beyond The New Left* (New York, 1970), pp. 221–38. "The white girl's . . ." from *Ramparts*, October 26.

21. This and two preceding paragraphs: *Black Panther*, September 14, 1968. "10 Points" from Newton, *Revolutionary*, pp. 129–31.

Chapter 16   Guerrilla Warfare, 1967

1.   This and eight preceding paragraphs: Interviews with Julian Bond, Stokeley Carmichael, Tom Hayden, Alvin F. Pouissant, Gloria Richardson, Jean Wiley. James Forman, *The Political Thought of James Forman* (Detroit, 1970), p. 139. Ivanhoe Donaldson from Howell Raines, *My Soul Is Rested* (New York, 1977), p. 259.

2. This and two preceding paragraphs: *NYT,* August 11, 1967. Huey P. Newton, *Revolutionary Suicide* (New York, 1974), pp. 168–69. Cleaver quotation from Andrew Kopkind, "To Off a Panther," pp. 56–68 in Kopkind and James Ridgeway, *Decade of Crisis: America in the 1960s* (New York, 1972). Lee Lockwood, *Conversation with Eldridge Cleaver* (New York, 1970), pp. 11–16. Kathleen Cleaver, "On Eldridge Cleaver," *Ramparts,* June 1969, pp. 4–11. Gene Marine, *The Black Panthers* (New York, 1969), pp. 48–53.

3. This and preceding paragraph: Interview with Paul Jacobs. Cleaver letter from Don A. Schanche, *The Panther Paradox: A Liberal's Dilemma* (New York, 1970), p. 6.

4. Newton, *Revolutionary,* pp. 150–52.

5. This and preceding paragraph: James Forman, *The Making of Black Revolutionaries* (New York, 1972), pp. 519–20. Interview with Stokeley Carmichael.

6. This and preceding paragraph: Cleveland Sellers, *The River of No Return* (New York, 1973), p. 190. H. Rap Brown, *Die, Nigger, Die!* (New York, 1969), quotation from p. 73; also pp. 21, 44, 47, 58–59, 85, 91.

7. This and preceding paragraph: *NYT,* March 29, 1967. Forman, *Political,* pp. 94, 117. Brown, *Die,* p. 85. *New Left Notes,* July 10, 1967.

8. This and preceding paragraph: Interviews with Stokeley Carmichael, Gloria Richardson. *NYT,* July 25, 26, 1967. Forman, *Making,* pp. 504–5.

9. This and three preceding paragraphs: Police chief and Carmichael quotations from *Newsweek,* August 7, 1967, pp. 28, 32. *New Left Notes,* August 7, 1967; March 11, 1968. Brown, *Die,* p. 101.

10. This and two preceding paragraphs: Russell Sackett, "In a Grim City," *Life,* July 28, 1967, pp. 27–28. Tom Hayden, *Rebellion in Newark* (New York, 1967), pp. 29, 45, 53, 75–76. Louis G. Goldberg, "Ghetto Riots and Others," in James A. Geschwender, ed., *The Black Revolt* (Englewood Cliffs, N.J., 1971), pp. 414–31.

11. This and two preceding paragraphs: Bob Clark, "Nightmare Journey," *Ebony,* October 1967, pp. 120–30. *NYT,* July 25, 1967. *New Left Notes,* August 21, 1967. Harris from Benjamin Muse, *The American Negro Revolt* (Bloomington, Ind., 1968), p. 309. Forman, *Political,* p. 164.

12. This and preceding paragraph: Dotson Rader, *I Ain't Marchin' Anymore!* (New York, 1969), pp. 16–18, 30–33. *New Left Notes,* January 13, 1967. Kirkpatrick Sale, *SDS* (New York, 1974), pp. 344–45.

13. This and two preceding paragraphs: Interview with Todd Gitlin. *New Left Notes,* March 20, October 23, November 5, 1967. Michael Ferber, Staughton Lynd, *The Resistance* (Boston, 1971), pp. 140–45.

14. This and three preceding paragraphs: Davidson from *New Left Notes,* November 13, 1967. *National Guardian,* March 25, 1967. Todd Gitlin, "The Dynamics of the New Left," *Motive,* October 1970, pp. 48–60. Sale, *SDS,* pp. 398–402.

15. This and two preceding paragraphs: Milton Mankoff and Richard Flacks, "The Changing Social Base of the American Student Movement," in Philip G. Altbach and Robert S. Laufer, eds., *The New Pilgrims* (New York, 1972), pp. 46–62. Yankelovich Survey, "What They Believe," *Fortune,* January 1969, pp. 68–70. Sol Stern et al., "National Student Association and the CIA," *Ramparts,* March 1967, pp. 29–39. Andrew Kopkind, "The Big Fix," *New York Review of Books,* March 23, 1967, pp. 4–5.

16. This and four preceding paragraphs: *East Village Other,* November 1–15, 1967. Interview with Paul Krassner. Abbie Hoffman, *Revolution for the Hell of It* (New York, 1968), pp. 32–33, 211. Jerry Rubin, *DO IT* (New York, 1970), pp. 202–4, 116. *New Republic,* August 27, 1966, p. 4.

17. This and three preceding paragraphs: Interview with Ivanhoe Donaldson. Renata Adler, "Letter from the Palmer House," *New Yorker,* September 23, 1967, pp. 56–88. Kopkind and Ridgeway, *Decade,* pp. 11–21. Dwight Macdonald, "Politics," *Esquire,* December 1967, p. 18. Forman from Andrew Kopkind, "They'd Rather Be Left," *New York Review of Books,* September 28, 1967, pp. 3–5. Forman, *Making,* pp. 493–98. Michigan delegate from Richard Blumenthal, "New Politics at Chicago," *Nation,* September 25, 1967, p. 274. Todd Gitlin, "Chicago's Black Caucus," *Ramparts,* November 1967, pp. 99–114.

18. This and three preceding paragraphs: Davidson from Norman Mailer, *The Armies of the Night* (New York, 1968), p. 250; also 72–79, 100–102, 228, 245. Interview with Cordell Reagon. John Wilson, "Blacks and the Anti-War Movement," *Liberation,* November 1967, pp. 29–31. Allen Woode, "The March on the Pentagon," *Ramparts,* February 1968, pp. 46–51.

19. This and two preceding paragraphs: Goldfield from *New Left Notes,* October 30, 1967. Mailer, *Armies,* pp. 125, 249, 253, 261 (for Calvert). Thomas Powers, *The War at Home* (New York, 1973), pp. 239–41. Martin Jezer, "Pentagon Confrontation," *Liberation,* November 1967, pp. 8–11. David Dellinger, *More Power Than We Know* (Garden City, N.Y., 1975), pp. 53–55.

20. This and two preceding paragraphs: Ferber and Lynd, *Resistance,* pp. 201–2, 209. Marjorie and Thomas Melville, *Whose Heaven, Whose Earth* (New York, 1971), p. 298.

21. This and previous paragraph: SDS staff from *New Left Notes,* August 7, 1967. William T. Divele (with James Joseph), *I Lived inside the Campus Revolution* (New York, 1970), pp. vii, ix. King from Robert L. Allen, *Black Awakening in Capitalist America* (Garden City, N.Y., 1969), p. 170; also pp. 166, 169. Julian Bond, *A Time to Speak, A Time to Act* (New York, 1972), p. 47.

22. This and six preceding paragraphs: Eldridge Cleaver, "My Father and Stokeley Carmichael," *Ramparts,* April 1967, pp. 10–14. Interview with Paul Jacobs. Newton, *Revolutionary,* pp. 192–204, 209–15. Marine, *Black Panthers,* pp. 76–81, 83–91. Charles Garry (with Art Goldberg), *Street Fighter in the Courtroom* (New York, 1977), pp. 100–130.

23. This and two preceding paragraphs: Groppi from David Llorens, "Miracle in Milwaukee," *Ebony,* November, 1967, pp. 29–37. King from *NYT,* April 5, 1967; and *Liberation,* April 1968, pp. 3–8. Eldridge Cleaver, "The Land Question," *Ramparts,* May 1968, pp. 51–53.

24. This and preceding paragraph: Interview with Lawrence Guyot. Phyl Garland, "Taste of Triumph for Black Mississippi," *Ebony,* February 1968, pp. 25–32.

Chapter 17   The Violent Year, 1968

1. This and two preceding paragraphs: Huey P. Newton, "We Are Nationalists and Internationalists," in John Gerassi, ed., *The Coming of the New International* (New York, 1971), pp. 563–68. Interview with Cleveland Sellers. *New Left Notes,* February 26, 1968. Pat Watters and Weldon Rougeau, "Events

at Orangeburg" (Report of Southern Regional Council, Atlanta, February 25, 1968). Cleveland Sellers, *The River of No Return* (New York, 1973), p. 223. "State of the Southern States," *New South,* Winter 1968, pp. 120–47.

2.   This and three preceding paragraphs: Interviews with Stokeley Carmichael, Gloria Richardson, Cleveland Sellers. Huey P. Newton, *Revolutionary Suicide* (New York, 1974), pp. 171–72. James Forman, *The Making of Black Revolutionaries* (New York, 1972), pp. 521, 531, 534–39. Julius Lester, *Revolutionary Notes* (New York, 1969), pp. 144, 148. Sellers, *River,* pp. 247–49. *NYT,* October 7, 1968.

3.   This and four preceding paragraphs: Peter Bailey, "Nikki Giovanni," *Ebony,* February 1972, pp. 49–56. Interview with Courtland Cox. Don A. Schanche, *The Panther Paradox* (New York, 1970), pp. 46, 54. *NYT,* November 18, 1975; April 29, 1976; November 17, 1976.

4.   This and preceding paragraph: *NYT,* January 17, February 5, 1975; April 1, April 2, April 29, May 21, 1976; November 30, 1977.

5.   This and preceding four paragraphs: Gene Marine, "Persecution and Assassination of the Black Panthers," *Ramparts,* June 29, 1968, pp. 37–46. Schanche, *Panther,* pp. 55–60. Interview with Paul Jacobs. Gene Marine, *The Black Panthers* (New York, 1969), pp. 95–104, 159–64. Schanche, "Panthers against the Wall," *Atlantic,* May 1970, pp. 55–61. Interview with Eldridge Cleaver, *Playboy,* December 1968, p. 89. Charles Garry, *Street Fighter in the Courtroom* (New York, 1977), pp. 138–52.

6.   This and four preceding paragraphs: Interviews with Dorothy Healey, Paul Jacobs, and two others requesting anonymity. Marine, *Black Panthers,* p. 183. Mary Ellen Leary, "Uproar over Cleaver," *New Republic,* November 30, 1968, pp. 21–24.

7.   This and four preceding paragraphs: Jessica Mitford, *The Trial of Dr. Spock* (New York, 1969), pp. 5, 65. Noam Chomsky, Paul Lauter, Florence Howe, "Reflections on a Political Trial," *New York Review of Books,* August 21, 1968, pp. 23–30. Interview with William P. Homans, Jr.

8.   This and three preceding paragraphs: Kirk Sale, *SDS* (New York, 1974), pp. 427–29. Sperling from David Dellinger, "Lessons from Chicago," *Liberation,* October 1968, pp. 3–11. *New Left Notes,* February 12, March 4, 1968. *NYT,* November 10, 1968.

9.   This and three preceding paragraphs: Johnson from Jon Bradshaw, "Richard Goodwin," *New York,* August 18, 1975, pp. 29–32. Oglesby from Massimo Teodori, ed., *The New Left: A Documentary History* (New York, 1969), pp. 445–50.

10.   *New Left Notes,* March 25, 1968.

11.   This and four preceding paragraphs: Interviews with Lewis Cole, Andrea Eagan. Sale, *SDS,* pp. 410–11, 418, 423, 441 *n.* Rudd from Immanuel Wallerstein and Paul Starr, eds., *The University Crisis Reader* (New York, 1971), 2: 178–79; also 1: 24. James S. Kunen, *Strawberry Statement—Notes of a College Revolutionary* (New York, 1969), p. 120. Jerry L. Avorn, *Up against the Ivy Wall* (New York, 1968), pp. 3–10, introduction. "The Siege of Columbia," *Ramparts,* June 15, 1968, pp. 26–39. Barbara and John Ehrenreich, *Long March, Short Spring* (New York, 1969), p. 97. Stephen Donado, "Columbia: Seven Interviews," *Partisan Review,* Summer 1968, pp. 354–92.

12.   This and four preceding paragraphs: Interviews with Sharon Krebs, Howard Rodman. Ellen Kay Trimberger, "Why a Rebellion at Columbia Was Inevitable," *Trans-Action,* September 1968, pp. 28–38. Brown from Avorn, *Up*

against, p. 19, 55. Dotson Rader, *I Ain't Marchin' Anymore!* (New York, 1969), p. 141.

13. This and three preceding paragraphs: *L'Express* correspondents, "One Week in Paris," *Ramparts,* June 29, 1968, pp. 2–3. Daniel and Gabriel Cohn-Bendit, *Obsolete Communism, The Left-wing Alternative* (New York, 1968), pp. 11, 199. Peter Caws, "What Happened in Paris," *Partisan Review,* Fall 1968, pp. 519–25; also "Rapport Interdisciplinaire Nanterre, 11 Juin 1968," pp. 536–41; Peter Brooks, "The Fourth World, Part III: Paris," Winter 1969, pp. 11–35.

14. This and three preceding paragraphs: Cohn-Bendits, *Obsolete,* pp. 64, 148, 199. Cohn-Bendit, "The Battle of the Streets," in Carl Oglesby, ed., *The New Left Reader* (New York, 1969), pp. 255–66. Ehrenreichs, *Long March,* pp. 73–97. Jean-Paul Sartre, "The Risk of Spontaneity and the Logic of the Institution," in Arthur Lothstein, ed., *"All We Are Saying . . ."* (New York, 1970), pp. 284–302.

15. This and four preceding paragraphs: Truman from Trimberger, "Rebellion." Diana Trilling, "On the Steps of Low Library," *Commentary,* November 1968, pp. 29–55. Avorn, *Up against,* pp. 179–81.

16. This and two preceding paragraphs: *Fortune* editorial, June 1968. Tom Hayden, "Two, Three, Many Columbias," *Ramparts,* June 15, 1968, p. 40. Daniel Yankelovich poll for *Fortune* in *The Changing Values on Campus* (New York, 1972), p. 64.

17. This and two preceding paragraphs: Dohrn and Bell from Sale, *SDS,* pp. 451, 466, 469. "The Movement: A New Beginning," *Liberation,* March/April 1969, pp. 6–20.

18. This and preceding paragraph: Daley, Dunn from *NYT,* April 16, 1968. *Chicago Daily News,* August 25, 1968. Kunstler from Judy Clavir and John Spitzer, eds., *The Conspiracy Trial* (New York, 1970), p. 14. David Dellinger, "Lessons from Chicago"; Walter Schneier, "Chicago: Terror on Display"; David Stein, "Notes on a Police State," *Liberation,* October 1968, pp. 3–11, 12–13, 17.

19. This and three preceding paragraphs: Interview with Ramsey Clark. Clavir and Spitzer, *Conspiracy,* p. 46. Michael Rossman, *The Wedding within the War* (New York, 1971), pp. 274–75. Theodore H. White, *The Making of the President* (New York, 1969), pp. 288, 294. Leo Whelan, "U.S. Postage Paid from Chicago," *Partisan Review,* Fall, 1968, pp. 525–29. David Dellinger, *More Power than We Know* (Garden City, N.Y., 1975), p. 123.

20. This and four preceding paragraphs: Dellinger, *More Power,* p. 185. White, *Making,* p. 301. Editors' report, "Decline and Fall of the Democratic Party," *Ramparts,* September 28, 1968, pp. 20–42. *Liberation,* October 1968, pp. 3–11. Tom Hayden, *Rebellion and Repression* (New York, 1969), p. 79.

21. This and two preceding paragraphs: *NYT,* July 24, 25, 28, 1968.

22. This and four preceding paragraphs: Sale, *SDS,* pp. 503, 540. Paul, Jon and Charlotte, eds., *Fire! Reports from the Underground Press* (New York, 1970), p. 116. Loren Baritz, ed., *The American Left, Radical Political Thought in the Twentieth Century* (New York, 1971), pp. 448–54. Lerone Bennett, Jr., "Confrontation on the Campus," *Ebony,* May 1968, pp. 27–34.

23. This and three preceding paragraphs: Interviews with James Herndon, David Horowitz, Paul Jacobs. Richard M. Scammon, ed., "America Votes, No. 8," *Congressional Quarterly* (Washington, D.C., 1970). Kathleen Cleaver, "On Eldridge Cleaver," *Ramparts,* June 1969, pp. 4–11.

24. This and three preceding paragraphs: *New Left Notes,* December 4, 11, 23, 1968; January 8, 15, 1969. Interview with Lewis Cole. Princeton from Sale, *SDS,* p. 479. Edward J. Bacciocco, Jr., *The New Left in America, Reform to Revolution,* 1956–1970 (Stanford, Calif., 1974), pp. 215–20.

25. This and preceding paragraph: Alan Adelson, *Students for a Democratic Society* (New York, 1972), pp. 229–31. James Weinstein, "The Left, Old and New," *Socialist Revolution,* July/August 1972, pp. 22–33; Max Gordon, "Communists of the 1930s and the New Left," January/March 1976, pp. 11–66 (with Weinstein response).

26. Interview with Jeremy Brecher.

Chapter 18   The Limits of Radicalism, 1969

1. This and two preceding paragraphs: Julian Foster and Durward Long, "Dynamics of Institutional Response," in *Protest! Student Activism in America* (New York, 1970), pp. 417–46. Michael W. Miles, *The Radical Probe, The Logic of Student Rebellion* (New York, 1971), pp. 11, 259. Howard Schuman, "Two Sources of Anti-War Sentiment in America," *American Journal of Sociology,* November 1972, pp. 513–36.

2. This and preceding paragraph: FBI from U.S., Senate, Select Committee to Study Governmental Operations with Respect to Intelligence Activities, Final Report, *Supplementary Detailed Staff Reports On Intelligence Activities and the Rights of Americans,* Book III, 94th Cong., 2d sess., 1976, p. 510. Daniel Yankelovich, *The Changing Values on Campus* (New York, 1972). Gallup Poll, Fall 1970.

3. This and two preceding paragraphs: *The Black Panther,* May 31, 1969. Levertov, pamphlet from Immanuel Wallerstein and Paul Starr, eds., *The University Crisis Reader* (New York, 1971), 1: 176, 169. *New Left Notes,* May 30, 1969.

4. This and four preceding paragraphs: Dugald Stermer, "Who Owns the Park?" and Robert Scheer, "Who Ripped Off the Park?" *Ramparts,* August 1969, pp. 8–10, 42–49. Todd Gitlin, "Meaning of People's Park," *Liberation,* July 1969, pp. 17–21. Yankelowich Survey, *Fortune,* January 1969, pp. 68–70.

5. This and preceding paragraph: Interviews with Elaine Brown, Ericka Huggins. *Black Panther,* March 31, April 21, July 12, September 6, November 1, November 22, 1969; January 3, September 26, 1970. Huey P. Newton, *To Die for the People* (New York, 1972), p. 25.

6. This and preceding paragraph: *Black Panther,* February 19, 1972. Newton, *Die,* pp. 47, 74, 197.

7. This and four preceding paragraphs: Interview with Panther associate requesting anonymity. *Black Panther,* April 2, July 12, 19, September 27, 1969. *New Left Notes,* May 13, 1969. Bobby Seale, *A Lonely Rage* (New York, 1978), p. 176. Hampton from Michael J. Arlen, *An American Verdict* (Garden City, N.Y., 1973), p. 100. Frank Browning, "The Young Lords," *Ramparts,* October 1970, pp. 19–25. Lincoln Hospital from *NYT,* November 29, 1978.

8. This and preceding paragraph: Theodore Draper, "Case for Black Studies," *Antioch Review,* Summer 1969, p. 157. *Black Panther,* May 11, 1969. Michael Thelwell, "From San Francisco and Cornell," *Ramparts,* July 1969, pp.

47–52. Dean Theodore L. Gross in *NYT,* May 6, 1978 (quoting *Saturday Review,* February 4, 1978).

9.   This and preceding paragraph: Hoover from Arlen, *American,* p. 93. Leonard from Christopher Chandler, "Black Killings in Chicago," *New Republic,* January 10, 1970, pp. 21–24. *NYT,* February 13, 1974; May 7, 1976. *Los Angeles Times,* April 14, 1975. Edward J. Epstein, "The Panthers and the Police: A Pattern of Genocide," *New Yorker,* February 13, 1971, pp. 45–77.

10.   This and preceding paragraph: *NYT,* February 13, 1974. Chandler, "Killings." Hanrahan from Arlen, *American,* pp. 19–21; grand jury from pp. 58–59; also p. 60. Epstein, "Panthers."

11.   This and two preceding paragraphs: *Black Panther,* April 20, 1969. Murray Kempton, *The Briar Patch* (New York, 1973), pp. 14, 28–29, 31–32, 37, 41, 161, 200–203. Edwin Kennebeck, *Juror Number Four* (New York, 1973), pp. 179, 184, 188. Robert Lefcourt, ed., *Law against the People* (New York, 1971), pp. 3, 21, 197, 200, 203.

12.   This and two preceding paragraphs: Kennebeck, *Juror,* pp. 143, 200. Catherine Breslin, "One Year Later: The Radicalization of the Panther 13 Jury," *New York,* May 29, 1972, pp. 53–63.

13.   This and two preceding paragraphs: Interviews with Charles Garry, Ericka Huggins. *Black Panther,* March 28, August 8, 1970. Gail Sheehy, *Panthermania* (New York, 1971), pp. 12, 43–55, 69. Charles Garry, *Street Fighter in the Courtroom* (New York, 1977), pp. 183, 187, 204, 206. Newton, *Die,* p. 224.

14.   This and preceding paragraph: Sheehy, *Panthermania,* pp.65–69. Garry, *Street,* pp. 183, 187, 213. James Ahern, *Police in Trouble* (New York, 1972), p. 34.

15.   This and five preceding paragraphs: Brewster from Francine du Plessix Gray, "Panthers at Yale," *New York Review of Books,* June 4, 1970, pp. 29–36. Sheehy, *Panthermania,* p. 96. Mulvey from Garry, *Street,* pp. 215–16; also p. 196. Epstein, "Panthers." *Black Panther,* December 13, 1969. Angela Davis, *An Autobiography* (New York, 1974), pp. 226–31.

16.   This and two preceding paragraphs: Cleveland Sellers, *The River of No Return* (New York, 1973), p. 263. James Forman, *The Making of Black Revolutionaries* (New York, 1972), p. 542. Interviews with Paul Jacobs, Robert Fitch. *NYT,* March 10, April 18, 1971. *Black Panther,* March 29, 1969; November 29, 1971. Cleaver's return from *NYT,* November 18, 1975; November 20, 1975; January 10, April 2, 1977; also Philip Bronstein, "Eldridge Cleaver—Reborn," *Midstream,* January 1977, pp. 57–63.

17.   This and preceding paragraph: Stauder from Wallerstein and Starr, *University,* 1:462–68. *New Left Notes,* April 17, 1969. Robert Lekachman, "Harvard—Feints at Revolution," *Dissent,* July–August 1969, pp. 321–25. Kirkpatrick Sale, *SDS* (New York, 1974), pp. 512–13. *NYT,* November 11, 1969.

18.   This and six preceding paragraphs: *NYT,* November 12, 13, 14, 16, 19, 1969; Alpert quotation from January 14, 1975. Edward Grossman, "Jane and Sam: A Requiem for Two Bombers," *Midstream,* March 1974, pp. 26–42. Jane Alpert, "Mother Right: A New Feminist Theory," *Ms.,* August 1973, pp. 52–55, 88–94. Judith Coburn, "The Issue That's Splitting Feminists," *Voice,* April 7, 1975, p. 8. For Swinton, *NYT,* April 9, 1975; October 7, 1977. Interviews with Nancy Borman, Susan Brownmiller, Andrea Eagan, Robin Morgan.

19.   This and two preceding paragraphs: *New Left Notes,* April 4, June 18, 1969.

20. This and five preceding paragraphs: Harlan E. Joyce, "Dixie's New Left," *Trans-action*, September 1970, pp. 50–56. Harold Jacobs, ed., *Weatherman* (Palo Alto, Cal., 1970), p. 5. Andrew Kopkind, "The Real SDS Stands Up," in Jacobs, *Weatherman*, pp. 15–28; also p. 5. Susan Stern, *With the Weathermen* (Garden City, N.Y., 1975), pp. 16, 39. Panther quotation from Alan Adelson, *Students for a Democratic Society* (New York, 1972), p. 237. Young Lords from Sale, *SDS*, p. 569.

21. This and two preceding paragraphs: Interviews with Andrea Eagan, David Horowitz, Sharon Krebs. Stern, *Weathermen*, p. 114. Jonah Raskin, *Out of the Whale* (New York, 1974), p. 127.

22. This and three preceding paragraphs: Thomas Powers, *Diana: The Making of a Terrorist* (Boston, 1971), p. 133, 167. *New Left Notes*, September 12, 1969 (dated August 29 on cover). Klonsky from Sale, *SDS*, p. 595; also pp. 588–89. *Black Panther*, October 18, 1969. Interview with Marilyn Katz.

23. This and four preceding paragraphs: Interviews with John Judis, James Weinstein. Sale, *SDS*, pp. 603–9, 613. Powers, *Diana*, pp. 172–73.

24. This and six preceding paragraphs: Interviews with Lewis Cole, Robert Fitch, Todd Gitlin. Draftees from Lawrence M. Baskir, William A. Strauss, *Chance and Circumstance* (New York, 1978). Richard Flacks, "New Left and American Politics after Ten Years," *Journal of Social Issues*, 27 (1971): 21–34.

25. David Dellinger, *More Power than We Know* (Garden City, N.Y., 1975), p. 65. Jason Berry, *NYT*, December 1, 1976.

26. This and preceding paragraph: FBI from U.S. Senate, Select Commitee, "Staff Reports," pp. 355, 361. *NYT*, June 20; also April 11, November 24, 1978.

27. This and preceding paragraph: Sale, *SDS*, pp. 643–45. Bob Bailey, "FBI's War on the Guild," *Rights*, September/October 1977, pp. 3–6. *NYT*, February 19, November 24, 1978. Francine du Plessix Gray, "Politics of Salvation II," *New York Review Of Books*, June 15, 1972, pp.14–21.

28. This and four preceding paragraphs: *NYT*, October 16, November 13, 1969. Jeremy Larner, "The Moratorium—A View from the Inside," *Life*, November 28, 1969, pp. 53–60. Kleindienst from Andrew Kopkind, "To the Comfort Station," in Kopkind and James Ridgeway, eds., *Decade of Crisis* (New York, 1972), pp. 11–21. Powers, *Diana*, p. 161. Murray Kempton, "Washington after Dark," *New York Review Of Books*, December 18, 1969, pp. 10–15. Mitchell from *NYT*, November 22, 1969. Armand L. Mauss, "The Lost Promise of Reconciliation," *Journal of Social Issues*, 27 (1971): 1–20.

29. This and five preceding paragraphs: Interview with Ramsey Clark. J. Anthony Lukas, *The Barnyard Epithet and Other Obscenities* (New York, 1970), pp. 7, 23, 42. Bobby Seale, *Seize the Time* (New York, 1970), p. 352. Dellinger, *More*, pp. 228–29, 235. "Barbecue," etc. from Jason Epstein, "Trial of Bobby Seale," *New York Review of Books*, December 4, 1969, pp. 35–50. Paul Glusman, "Behind the Chicago Conspiracy Trial," *Ramparts*, January 1970, pp. 39–47.

30. This and two preceding paragraphs: *Black Panther*, November 15, 1969. Epstein, "Seale." Dellinger, *More*, pp. 241, 245. Tom Hayden, *Trial* (New York, 1970), p. 64.

31. This and two preceding paragraphs: Lukas, *Barnyard*, pp. 37, 73. Hayden, *Trial*, pp. 62, 74. Lefcourt, *Law*, p. 289, citing *NYT* editorial. Interview with Ramsey Clark.

32.   This and five preceding paragraphs: Lukas, *Barnyard,* pp. 26, 93, 98. Hayden, *Trial,* pp. 64, 82. Schultz from Dellinger, *More,* p. 205; also pp. 207–9 (on juror). *NYT,* October 29, November 6, 1973; May 8, 1978.

Chapter 19   The Women's Movement: Personal Becomes Political

1.   This and preceding paragraph: Abubakari from Gerda Lerner, ed., *Black Women in America* (New York, 1972), pp. 585–87. Redstockings, *Feminist Revolution* (New Paltz, N.Y., 1975), p. 21.

2.   This and four preceding paragraphs: Interviews with Casey Hayden, Mary King, Gloria Richardson. Sara M. Evans, "Personal Politics: The Roots of Women's Liberation in the Civil Rights Movement and the New Left" (Ph.D. diss., University of North Carolina, 1976), pp. 59, 107. I am indebted to the author for permission to use this perceptive study. Casey Hayden and Mary King, "Sex and Caste," *Liberation,* April 1966, pp. 35–36 (original draft given me by the authors). Sara Evans, "Women's Consciousness and the Southern Black Movement," *Southern Exposure,* Winter 1977, pp. 10–18. Cynthia Washington, "We Started from Different Ends of the Spectrum," *Southern Exposure,* Winter 1977, pp. 14–15. Angela Davis, *Autobiography* (New York, 1974), p. 161. Alvin F. Pouissant, "Stresses of the White Female Workers in the Civil Rights Movement in the South," *American Journal of Psychiatry,* October 1966, pp. 401–7.

3.   This and two preceding paragraphs: Interviews with Marilyn Katz, Sharon Krebs. "Peanut butter" from Evans, *Personal,* pp. 146, 199. Rudd from Peter Babcox, "Meet the Women of the Revolution," *NYT Magazine,* February 9, 1969, p. 34. Tom Hayden, *Trial* (New York, 1970), p. 107. "Take her" from Judith Hole and Ellen Levine, *Rebirth of Feminism* (New York, 1971), pp. 133–34.

4.   This and two preceding paragraphs: Paul Lauter and Florence Howe, *The Conspiracy of the Young* (New York, 1970), pp. 90–94. *New Left Notes,* January 20, November 13, 1967; January 8, 1969. Evans, *Personal,* pp. 233, 249, 252. Hole, Levine, *Rebirth,* p. 120.

5.   This and three preceding paragraphs: Interviews with Jean Faust, Susan Brownmiller. The first published demands for repeal of restrictive abortion laws came from Dr. Garrett Hardin (lecture of April 29, 1964, University of California, Berkeley), and Lawrence Lader, *Abortion* (New York, 1966). Redstockings from Susan Brownmiller, "Sisterhood Is Powerful," *NYT Magazine,* March 15, 1970, pp.26–27. Shulamith Firestone, *The Dialectic of Sex* (New York, 1970), p. 72.

6.   This and preceding paragraph: Vivian Gornick, *The Romance of American Communism* (New York, 1977), p. 258. Redstockings, *Feminist,* p. 135. Robin Morgan, *Going Too Far* (New York, 1977), p. 101; Morgan, *Sisterhood Is Powerful* (New York, 1970), pp. 62–65.

7.   This and two preceding paragraphs: Interviews with Kathie Amatniek, Constance Billé, Lucinda Cisler. *NYT,* February 14, 1969.

8.   Koedt from Shulamith Firestone and Anne P. Koedt, eds., *Notes from the Second Year: Women's Liberation* (New York, 1970), pp. 37–41.

9.   This and three preceding paragraphs: Interview with Sharon Krebs. Weathermen, "Honky Tonk Women," in Harold Jacobs, ed., *Weatherman* (Palo Alto,

Cal., 1970), pp. 313–20. Bread and Roses Collective, "Weatherman Politics and the Women's Movement," in Jacobs, *Weatherman,* pp. 327–36. Susan Stern, *With the Weathermen* (Garden City, N.Y., 1975), p. 70. "Letters to the Movement (No. 1 from Fanshen Collective)," *Liberation,* Autumn 1970, pp. 75–83.

10. This and preceding paragraph: "Goodbye" from Morgan, *Going* pp. 123–24. Marlene Dixon, "On Women's Liberation," *Radical America,* February 1970, pp. 26–34.

11. Redstockings from Brownmiller, "Sisterhood."

12. This and previous paragraph: Morgan, *Sisterhood,* p. 461. "EEOC and UE vs. GE" (United Electrical Workers), 2: 1357.

13. Redstockings, *Feminist,* p. 106. Margie Stamberg, "Marry or Die," in Mitchell Goodman, ed., *The Movement towards a New America* (Philadelphia/New York, 1970), pp. 48–49. "Nuclear family" from Donn Teal, *The Gay Militants* (New York, 1971), p. 176.

14. This and two preceding paragraphs: Interview with Robin Morgan. Morgan, "Who Is the Real Family," *Ms.,* August 1978, pp. 43–46. *NYT,* May 7, 1978.

15. Jo Freeman, *The Politics of Women's Liberation* (New York, 1975), pp. 84–91.

16. This and previous paragraph: Juliet Mitchell, "Out from Under," *Liberation,* December 1971, pp. 7–13. Interview with Deirdre English, Robin Morgan. Berkeley-Oakland Women's Union Speech, National Conference on Socialist Feminism, *Socialist Revolution,* October/December 1975, pp. 93–100.

17. This and three preceding paragraphs: Morgan, *Going,* p. 175. Teal, *Gay,* p. 192. Redstockings, *Feminist,* p. 106. Freeman, *Politics,* p. 138. Maren Lockwood Carden, *The New Feminist Movement* (New York, 1974), p. 68. Hole and Levine, *Rebirth,* pp. 3, 94. Martha Shelley, "Notes of a Radical Lesbian," in Morgan, *Sisterhood,* p. 306. Interview with Kathie Amatniek.

18. This and two preceding paragraphs: Interview with Lana C. Phelan. Lindsy Van Gelder, "Four Days That Changed the World," *Ms.,* March 1978, pp. 52–54, 86. Chisholm from Helen H. King, "Black Woman and Women's Liberation," *Ebony,* March 1971, pp. 68–76. Davis from *Black Panther,* March 11, 1972.

19. This and two preceding paragraphs: Interviews with Elaine Brown, Ericka Huggins. Robert Chrisman and Nathan Hare, eds.; *Contemporary Black Thought* (Indianapolis/New York, 1973) pp. 138–57. *Black Panther,* July 5, September 13, 1969.

20. This and preceding paragraph: Annemarie Troger, "Coalition of Labor Union Women," *Radical America,* November/December 1975, pp. 85–114. Harry Kelber, Letter, *NYT,* November 29, 1978. Freeman, *Politics,* p. 147.

Chapter 20   The Aftermath of Violence

1. This and preceding paragraph: Gold from Kirkpatrick Sale, "Ted Gold: Education for Violence," *Nation,* April 13, 1970. *NYT,* August 25, 1970; November 2, 1972; October 23, 1973; April 11, 1977. Henry Steele Commager, "Defeat of America," *New York Review Of Books,* October 5, 1972, p. 7.

2. This and five preceding paragraphs: Weather Underground, *Prairie Fire, The Politics of Revolutionary Anti-Imperialism* (Brooklyn, N.Y./San Francisco,

1974), p. 4. David Dellinger, *More Power than We Know* (Garden City, N.Y., 1975), pp. 141–54. Ralph W. Conant, *The Prospects for Revolution* (New York, 1971), pp. 58–59. "Letters to the Movement (Seattle Liberation Front)," *Liberation,* Autumn 1970, pp.75–83.

3. This and preceding paragraph: Kirkpatrick Sale, *SDS* (New York, 1974), pp. 617, 638, 641. *Black Panther,* December 19, 1970; November 23, 1972.

4. This and preceding paragraph: *New Left Notes,* April 24, 1969. Agnew from *NYT,* May 4, 1977. Rhodes from James Michener, *Kent State* (New York, 1971), pp. 77, 251.

5. This and three preceding paragraphs: Michener, *Kent,* pp. 331, 340, 361, 364, 372, 425. Electrician from Peter Davies, Jr., *NYT,* May 4, 1976; also April 30, July 23, 1972.

6. This and four preceding paragraphs: Michener, *Kent,* pp. 104–5, 287, 340. Canterbury from *NYT,* July 29, 1975; also May 7, 1978. Snyder from Davies, *NYT,* ibid. Krause letter from *NYT,* May 7, 1978. Civil suit from *NYT,* January 5, 1979.

7. This and three preceding paragraphs: Arnold Schuchter, *Reparations* (New York, 1970), pp. 4, 7–10, 14, 195–96. James Forman, *The Making of Black Revolutionaries* (New York, 1972), p. 548. *Ebony,* January 1970, p. 103.

8. This and five preceding paragraphs: Interview with Jeremy Brecher. "Dodge Rebellion," *Ramparts,* November 17, 1968, p. 12. Thomas R. Brooks, "DRUM Beats in Detroit," *Dissent,* January/February 1970, pp. 16–25. Eric Perkins,"LeagueofRevolutionaryBlackWorkers,"*Radical America,* March/April 1971, pp. 51–62. Dan Georgakas and Marvin Surkin, "Niggermation in Auto," *Radical America,* January/February 1975, pp. 31–56. *Black Panther,* April 6, 1969.

9. This and four preceding paragraphs: Angela Davis, *Autobiography* (New York, 1974), pp. 252–54, 277. Davis, *If They Come in the Morning* (New York, 1971), pp. 16, 121. George L. Jackson, *Blood in My Eye* (New York, 1972), p. 30. Jo Durden-Smith, *Who Killed George Jackson?* (New York, 1976), pp. 104, 112, 204.

10. This and seven preceding paragraphs: Davis, *Autobiography,* pp. 12, 308, 335. Davis, *If They,* 25, 35, 51, 199, 224, 251–52, 261, 273.

11. This and seven preceding paragraphs: *Pacific Sun,* April 16–22, 1976. Charles Garry, *Street Fighter in the Courtroom,* (New York, 1977), pp. 243, 250–53, 265–66. Durden-Smith, *Who Killed,* pp. xxi–ii, 43, 48, 73–74, 136. *NYT,* September 22, 1974; August 26, 1976. *Black Panther,* August 28, 1971.

12. This and preceding paragraph: Tom Wicker, *A Time To Die* (New York, 1975), pp. 247, 310. *Black Panther,* September 18, 1971. Interview with Elaine Brown.

13. This and three preceding paragraphs: Peter Nabokov, *Tijerina and the Courthouse Raid* (Albuquerque, 1969), pp. 99, 126, 254. *NYT,* August 30, 31, 1970. Elizabeth Martinez, Letter, *New York Review of Books,* February 12, 1970, pp. 37–38. Sandra Levinson and Carol Brightman, *Venceremos Brigade* (New York, 1971), p. 233.

14. This and five preceding paragraphs: Richard A. Garcia, "The Chicano Movement and the Mexican-American Community, 1972–1978"; Tomás Almaguer, "Chicano Politics in the Present Period," *Socialist Review,* July/October 1978, pp.117–41. *NYT,* May 25, October 1, 27, 28, 1974. Arthur Liebman, "Student Left in Puerto Rico", *Journal of Social Issues,* 27(1971): 167–81.

15. This and four preceding paragraphs: Alvin Josephy, "Wounded Knee and All That," *NYT Magazine,* March 18, 1973. *NYT,* March 3, 1974; November 6, 1978. *Guardian,* January 18, 1978. "Indians for Sovereignty," *Nation,* February 25, 1978, p. 204; "Skyhorse and Mohawk," December 24, 1977, p. 682. E. L. Meyer, "Bury My Heart on the Potomac," *Ramparts,* January 1973, pp. 10–12.

16. Arendt in Alexander Klein, ed., *Dissent, Power and Confrontation* (New York, 1971), p. 211. Hannah Arendt, *On Revolution* (New York, 1963), p. 47.

17. This and two preceding paragraphs: Barrington Moore, Jr., "Thoughts on Violence and Democracy," in Robert H. Connery, ed., "Urban Riots, Violence and Social Change," *Proceedings of the Academy of Political Science* (Vol. 29, No. 1, New York, 1968). *NYT,* December 2, 1977. Henry Silverman, "Youth Movements in the Twentieth Century," (Paper delivered before American Historical Association, December 28, 1973.)

Chapter 21   The American Left Today

1. This and preceding paragraph: Newton from *NYT,* July 17, 1977. *U.S. News & World Report,* July 21, 1975, pp. 23–26. Interview with Dorothy Healey.

2. This and preceding paragraph: *In These Times,* January 4/10, 1978, p. 5. For Harvey Milk, *NYT,* January 12, 1978.

3. This and three preceding paragraphs: James O'Brien, "The Anti-War Movement and the War," *Radical America,* May/June 1974, pp. 53–86. *NYT,* August 28, 1968; December 28, 1971; November 8, 1972; June 6, 1974.

4. *NYT,* September 29, 1973; February 21, 1976.

5. This and two preceding paragraphs: Weather from *Prairie Fire* (Brooklyn, N.Y., 1974), p. 1. *NYT,* March 3, 20, 28, 1975; July 16, 1976; July 13, 16, 1978.

6. This and three preceding paragraphs: Vin McLellan and Paul Avery, *The Voices of Guns* (New York, 1977), pp. 34, 174–77. *Newsday,* October 4, 1978.

7. This and preceding paragraph: *National Catholic Reporter,* March 24, 1978, p. 17. Peter Biskind, "USA: Political Prisoners by Any Other Name," *Seven Days,* May 23, 1977, pp. 23–25. *Guardian,* January 18, 1978, p. 3. *NYT,* January 24, November 23, 1978.

8. This and three preceding paragraphs: Interviews with Dorothy Healey, Max Gordon. John Judis, "From the New Left to a New Socialist Party," *Socialist Revolution,* November/December 1973, pp. 55–81. *Viewpoint,* November/December 1977, p. 4. *NYT,* January 11, 1974; March 30, 1976.

9. This and preceding paragraph: James O'Brien, "American Leninism in the 1970s," *Radical America,* November 1977/February 1978, pp. 27–62. *NYT,* February 25, 1974. *Voice,* September 18, 1978, p. 35.

10. This and four preceding paragraphs: Ronald Radosh, "The Democratic Socialist Organizing Committee," *Socialist Revolution,* July/August 1973, pp. 75–87; "New America Movement," January/February 1971, pp. 31–67. Harrington from *In These Times,* March 2/8, 1977, p. 7. *Viewpoint,* May/June 1977, p. 7; November/December 1977, p. 1. Interviews with Max Gordon, Marilyn Katz.

11. This and four preceding paragraphs: Bicentennial from *NYT,* July 5, 1976. Richard Fairchild, ed., *Utopia USA* (San Francisco, 1972), pp. 9, 158–63, 172–76. Theodore Roszak, "Youth and the Great Refusal," in Michael Brown, ed., *The Politics and Anti-Politics of the Young* (Beverly Hills, 1969), pp. 3–21. *NYT,* May 18, 1977.

12. This and three preceding paragraphs: Grohnde from *NYT,* March 30, 1977; also March 2, 1974; May 8, 1977. Herbert Marcuse, "Ecology and Revolution: A Symposium," *Liberation,* September 1972, pp. 3–12; Murray Bookchin, "On Spontaneity and Organization," March 1972, pp. 5–17.

13. This and preceding paragraph: Interviews with Nancy Borman, Paul Jacobs. *NYT,* February 15, April 21, 1977. Terri Schultz, "How Madison's Radical Mayor Has Mellowed with Age," *NYT* Magazine, April 17, 1977, pp. 49–56.

14. This and three preceding paragraphs: Interview with Wallace Hamilton. Allen Young, "Out of the Closet," *Ramparts,* November 1971, pp. 52–54. Donn Teal, *The Gay Militants* (New York, 1971), pp. 36, 38, 99, 123, 127, 143–45, 149. Karla Kay and Allen Young, eds., *Out of the Closets: Voices Of Gay Liberation* (New York, 1972), pp. 143–44, 327, 352.

15. This and preceding paragraph: Herbert Gold, "A Walk on San Francisco's Gay Side," *NYT* Magazine, November 6, 1977, pp. 67–14. *NYT,* October 3, 1973; July 26, 1978. Kay and Young, *Out,* p. 355.

16. This and two preceding paragraphs: Interviews with Ericka Huggins, Herbert Kohl. *NYT,* October 26, November 22, December 14, 1977; March 20, 1978; March 25, 1979. Bobby Seale, *Seize the Time* (New York, 1970), pp. 233–34.

17. This and two preceding paragraphs: Interviews with Stokeley Carmichael, Frank Smith. *NYT,* January 21, July 16, 1976; March 1, 1978.

18. This and previous paragraph: Wilson from *NYT,* February 28, 1978. Marshall from *NYT,* July 2, 1978. *NYT,* December 23, 1977; November 7, 12, 1978.

19. This and preceding paragraph: Lerone Bennett, Jr., "The Black Worker," *Ebony,* December 1972, pp. 73–82. *NYT,* October 20, December 18, 29, 1977; February 28, April 2, May 18, 1978.

20. Glazer from *NYT,* December 23, 1977.

21. This and two preceding paragraphs: Squire from *NYT,* March 16, 1974; also November 15, 1973; January 29, April 19, May 2, 1974; March 30, 1975; March 16, 1976; March 27 Review of Week, October 26, 1977. *Black Panther,* November 1972.

22. This and two preceding paragraphs: Interviews with Marion Barry, Jr., Matthew Jones. *NYT,* January 4, February 28, April 5, 1975. *Voice,* September 18, 1978.

23. Wallace from Curtis D. MacDougall, *Gideon's Army* (New York, 1965), 1: 64–70.

24. *NYT,* May 26, 1978.

25. *NYT,* March 8, 1979.

A Bibliographical Note

The literature about the Left, the black movements, and the women's movement since 1946 is obviously so vast that a separate study would be needed to encompass it even partially. There are good bibliographies in two books: Edward J. Bacciocco, Jr., *The New Left in America, Reform to Revolution, 1956–1970* (Stanford, Calif., 1974), and Massimo Teodori, ed., *The New Left: A Documentary History* (Indianapolis, 1969). Although covering international movements as well, the bibliography in Klaus Mehnert, *Twilight of the Young, The Radical Movements of the 1960s and Their Legacy* (New York, 1977), is worth attention.

The books that I have found most valuable are generally listed in the footnotes of each chapter. On Henry Wallace and the Progressive party, Curtis D. MacDougall, *Gideon's Army* (New York, 1965, 2 vols.), and John Morton Blum, ed., *The Price of Vision: The Diary of Henry A. Wallace* (Boston, 1973), are essential reading. Norman D. Markowitz, *The Rise and Fall of the People's Century: Henry A. Wallace and American Liberalism, 1941–1948* (New York, 1973) is the best academic study.

None of the academic works on Vito Marcantonio and the American Labor party has the necessary analytic depth. But Annette T. Rubinstein, ed., *I Vote My Conscience, Debates, Speeches, and Writings of Vito Marcantonio* (New York, 1956) is a fine compendium of his thinking.

On the Communist party, Joseph Starobin, *American Communism in Crisis, 1943–1957* (Cambridge, Mass., 1972) is a scholarly study by a former party functionary. Important personal memoirs by former Communists include: George Charney, *A Long Journey* (Chicago, 1968), and John Gates, *The Story of an American Communist* (New York, 1968).

On the CIO Left unions, Philip S. Foner, *The Fur and Leather Workers Union* (Newark, N.J., 1950), is a masterful but partial study. James J. Matles and James Higgins, *Them and Us* (Englewood Cliffs, N.J., 1974), an engrossing account of the United Electrical Workers struggle for survival is strangely flawed in glossing over the Communist party's role in deserting the union. Len De Caux, *Labor Radical* (Boston, 1970), is a vivid, personal memoir of the Left's ouster by a former CIO official. David J.

Saposs represents the anti-Communist position in *Communism in American Unions* (New York, 1959). The transformation of big labor into an arm of the government is acutely analyzed in Ronald Radosh, *American Labor and United States Foreign Policy* (New York, 1969).

Among the mass of works on the cold war and McCarthyism, I found the following most valuable: William Appleman Williams, *The Tragedy of American Diplomacy* (Cleveland/New York, 1959); Gar Alperowitz, *Atomic Diplomacy: Hiroshima and Potsdam* (New York, 1967); Gabriel Kolko, *The Politics of War* (New York, 1968); Alonzo L. Hamby, *Beyond the New Deal: Harry S. Truman and American Liberalism* (New York/-London, 1973); Townsend Hoopes, *The Devil and John Foster Dulles* (Boston, 1973); Carl Solberg, *Riding High, America in the Cold War* (New York, 1973); Alan Barth, *Prophets with Honor* (New York, 1974); Carey McWilliams, *Witch Hunt* (Boston, 1950); and Mary Sperling McAuliffe, *Crisis on the Left: Cold War Politics and American Liberals* (Amherst, Mass., 1978).

No superior, comprehensive work has yet appeared on the black liberation movements. The most ambitious approach, although troubled by thereotical vagaries, is Harold Cruse, *Crisis of the Negro Intellectual* (New York, 1967). Other worthwhile overall surveys include Charles V. Hamilton, *The Black Experience in American Politics* (New York, 1973); James A. Geschwender, ed., *The Black Revolt* (Englewood Cliffs, N.J., 1971); and Pat Watters and Reese Cleghorn, *Climbing Jacob's Ladder, The Arrival of Negroes in Southern Politics* (New York, 1967). The personal memoirs of two towering figures are essential: William E. B. Du Bois, *Autobiography* (New York, 1968) and Malcolm X (with Alex Haley), *Autobiography* (New York, 1966).

Black organizing in the South in the 1960s, particularly by CORE and SNCC, is excellently detailed by James Forman, *The Making of Black Revolutionaries* (New York, 1972); Cleveland Sellers (with Robert Terrell), *The River of No Return* (New York, 1973); Howard Zinn, *SNCC, The New Abolitionists* (Boston, 1964); and August Meier and Elliott Rudwick, *CORE, A Study in the Civil Rights Movement* (Chicago, 1975). Howell Raines provides a fine collection of taped reminiscences in *My Soul Is Rested, Movement Days in the Deep South Remembered* (New York, 1977).

The most important personal insights into the black revolt are in Huey P. Newton (with J. Herman Blake), *Revolutionary Suicide* (New York, 1974); Angela Davis, *Autobiography* (New York, 1974); George L. Jackson, *Blood in My Eye* (New York, 1972). Charles Garry (with Art Goldberg) presents a somewhat dry but essential summary of Panther court cases in *Street Fighter in the Courtroom* (New York, 1977).

The best general analysis of the New Left can be found in Immanuel Wallerstein and Paul Starr, eds., *The University Crisis Reader* (New York, 1971); Julian Foster and Durward Long, *Protest! Student Activism in Amer-*

ica (New York, 1970); Kenneth Keniston, *Youth and Dissent* (New York, 1971); Philip G. Altbach and Robert S. Laufer, eds., *The New Pilgrims* (New York, 1972); Carl Oglesby, ed., *The New Left Reader* (New York, 1969); and Andrew Kopkind and James Ridgeway, *Decade of Crisis: America in the 1960s* (New York, 1972). For Berkeley specifically: Seymour M. Lipset and Sheldon Wolin, *The Berkeley Student Revolt* (Garden City, N.Y., 1965). For the antiwar movement: Michael Ferber and Staughton Lynd, *The Resistance* (Boston, 1971).

The only superior and comprehensive treatment of the New Left's central organization is Kirkpatrick Sale, *SDS* (New York, 1974). Harold Jacobs, ed., *Weatherman* (Palo Alto, Calif., 1970), provides a fine collection of papers. There are fascinating insights in Thomas Powers, *Diana: The Making of a Terrorist* (Boston, 1971), and Susan Stern, *With the Weathermen* (Garden City, N.Y., 1975), but many of Stern's highly emotional conclusions must be discounted.

The women's movement still lacks an exhaustive study. The most balanced accounts are Judith Hole and Ellen Levine, *Rebirth of Feminism* (New York, 1971); Jo Freeman, *The Politics of Women's Liberation* (New York, 1975); and Maren Lockwood Carden, *The New Feminist Movement* (New York, 1974).

Supplementary Bibliography

This is a limited list of books and articles that have proved valuable. It does *not* include those already in the footnotes and in the Bibliographical Note except in a few cases.

Albert, Michael. *What Is to Be Undone.* Boston, 1974.

Anthony, Earl. *Picking Up the Gun, A Report on the Black Panthers.* New York, 1970.

Aya, Roderick, and Miller, Norman, eds., *The New American Revolution.* New York, 1971.

Barbour, Floyd, ed. *Black Power Revolt.* Boston, 1968.

Bell, Daniel. *The End of Ideology.* New York, 1966.

Boggs, James. *The American Revolution, Pages from a Negro Worker's Notebook.* New York, 1963.

Brisbane, Robert H. *Black Activism, Racial Revolution in the United States, 1954–1970.* Valley Forge, Pa., 1974.

Brooks, Thomas R. *Toil and Trouble, A History of American Labor.* New York, 1964.

Carmichael, Stokeley. *Testimony of Stokeley Carmichael.* Committee on The Judiciary, U.S. Senate Subcommittee to Investigate the Administration of the Internal Security Act. Washington, D.C., 1970.

Chrisman, Robert, and Hare, Nathan, eds. *Contemporary Black Thought.* New York, 1973.

Conant, Ralph W. *The Prospects for Revolution.* New York, 1971.

Coser, Lewis, and Howe, Irving. "Authoritarians of the Left," *Dissent,* Winter 1955, pp. 40–50.

Cranston, Maurice, ed. *The New Left.* New York, 1971.

Dickstein, Morris. *Gates of Eden, American Culture in the Sixties.* New York, 1977.

Draper, Theodore. *The Rediscovery of Black Nationalism.* New York, 1970.

Ericson, Edward E., Jr. *Radicals in the University.* Stanford, Calif., 1975.

Franklin, Bruce. *From the Movement.* New York, 1971.

Freeland, Richard M. *The Truman Doctrine and the Origins of McCarthyism.* New York, 1972.

Freeman, James Morton. *No Friend of Labor.* New York, 1948.

Galenson, Walter. *The CIO Challenge to the AFL, A History of the American Labor Movement, 1935–1941.* Cambridge, Mass., 1960.

Glazer, Nathan. *The Social Basis of American Communism.* New York, 1961.

Goodman, Paul, ed. *Seeds of Liberation.* New York, 1964.

Grant, Joanne, ed. *Black Protest, History, Documents and Analysis, 1619 to the Present.* New York, 1968.

Herring, George C., Jr. "Lend-Lease to Russia and the Origins of the Cold War, 1944–1945," *Journal of American History,* June 1969, pp. 93–114.

Howe, Irving, ed. *The Radical Papers.* Garden City, N.Y., 1966.

Jackson, Gardner. "Henry Wallace: A Divided Mind." *Atlantic Monthly,* August 1948, pp. 27–33.

Kennan, George F. *Democracy and the Student Left.* Boston, 1968.

Keniston, Kenneth. *The Uncommitted, Alien Youth in American Society.* New York, 1965.

Lasch, Christopher. *The Agony of the American Left.* New York, 1969.
_____. *The New Radicalism in America.* New York, 1966.

Langer, Elinor. "The Oakland 7." *Atlantic Monthly,* October 1969, pp. 77–82.

Lens, Sidney. *Radicalism in America.* New York, 1969.

Levitan, Sar A.; Johnston, William B.; Taggart, Robert. *Still A Dream, The Changing Status of Blacks Since 1960.* Cambridge, Mass., 1975.

Liebert, Robert. *Radical and Militant Youth, A Psychoanalytic Inquiry.* New York, 1971.

Lipset, Seymour Martin, and Schaflander, Gerald M. *Passion and Politics: Student Activism in America.* Boston, 1971.

Lubell, Samuel. *The Future of American Politics.* New York, 1952.

May, Henry F. "The End of American Radicalism." *American Quarterly,* Winter 1950, pp. 291–302.

Meier, August. "Successful Sit-Ins in a Border City." *Journal of Intergroup Relations,* Summer 1961, pp. 230–37.

McEvoy, James, and Miller, Abraham, eds. *Black Power and Student Rebellion.* Belmont, Calif., 1969.

Miller, Michael V., and Gilmore, Susan, eds. *Revolution at Berkeley* New York, 1965.

Mortimer, Wyndham. *Organize!* Edited by Leo Fenster. (Boston, 1971).

Peterson, F.Ross. *Prophet without Honor: Glen Taylor and the Fight for American Liberalism.* (Lexington, Ky., 1974).

Paterson, Thomas G. "The Abortive American Loan to Russia and the Origins of the Cold War, 1943–1946." *American Journal of History,* June 1969, pp. 70–92.

Peirce, Neal R. *The Deep South States of America.* New York, 1974.

Peeks, Edward. *The Long Struggle for Black Power.* New York, 1971.

Powledge, Fred. *Black Power, White Resistance, Notes on the New Civil War.* New York, 1967.

Rogin, Michael Paul. *The Intellectuals and McCarthy.* Cambridge, Mass., 1967.

Rubenstein, Richard E. *Rebels in Eden, Mass Political Violence in the United States.* Boston, 1970.

Southern Regional Council. "The Student Protest Movement, 1960." Atlanta, 1960.

Spender, Stephen. *The Year of the Young Rebels.* London, 1969.

Theoharis, Athan. "The Truman Administration and the Decline of Civil Liberties."

Alice Walker. "The Civil Rights Movement: What Good Was It?" *American Scholar,* Autumn 1967, pp. 550–54.

Warren, Frank A. III. *Liberals and Communism.* Bloomington, Ind., 1966.

Waskow, Arthur I. *From Race Riot to Sit-In, 1919 and the 1960s. Garden City, N.Y., 1966.*

Wechsler, James A. The Age of Suspicion. New York, 1953.

Westby, David L. *The Student Movement in the United States in the 1960s.* Lewisburg, Pa., 1976.

Index

The Author

Lawrence Lader has written eight books. *The Bold Brahmins* was praised as a definitive study of the New England antislavery movement. His biography of Margaret Sanger in 1955 made him an early spokesman for planned parenthood and population control. His book *Abortion* in 1966 opened a national debate on one of the most controversial subjects of our time. Subsequently he became a cofounder and chairman for six years of the National Abortion Rights Action League. Working closely with radical feminists, he helped organize the campaigns that produced the New York State law of 1970 and the Supreme Court decision of 1973 establishing abortion rights.

A graduate of Harvard and founder of the radio station there, Lader's career as a magazine writer, editor, and foreign correspondent started during World War II—in which he served as a lieutenant in the army—with his "Letter" from the South Pacific for the *New Yorker*. He has written more than 400 articles for *American Heritage*, the *New Republic*, the *New York Times Magazine*, *Reader's Digest*, and other national magazines.

Power on the Left, which took more than five years to write, is the result of Lader's own involvement in radical politics. From 1946 to 1951, he was a district leader and public relations adviser to Congressman Vito Marcantonio of New York, perhaps the most flamboyant radical ever to sit in the House of Representatives. Lader himself ran for the New York State Assembly on Henry Wallace's Progresive party ticket in 1948.

A former adjunct associate professor in New York University's department of journalism and former president of the American Society of Journalists and Authors, Lader is married to Joan Summers, the opera singer. They live in Manhattan with their 15-year-old daughter.